LYMAN BOSTOCK

LYMAN BOSTOCK

The Inspiring Life and Tragic Death of a Ballplayer

K. Adam Powell

ROWMAN & LITTLEFIELD
Lanham • Boulder • New York • London

Published by Rowman & Littlefield
A wholly owned subsidiary of The Rowman & Littlefield Publishing Group, Inc.
4501 Forbes Boulevard, Suite 200, Lanham, Maryland 20706
www.rowman.com

Unit A, Whitacre Mews, 26-34 Stannary Street, London SE11 4AB

Copyright © 2017 by Rowman & Littlefield

All rights reserved. No part of this book may be reproduced in any form or by any electronic or mechanical means, including information storage and retrieval systems, without written permission from the publisher, except by a reviewer who may quote passages in a review.

British Library Cataloguing in Publication Information Available

Library of Congress Cataloging-in-Publication Data Available

Name: Powell, K. Adam, 1979–, author.
Title: Lyman Bostock : the inspiring life and tragic death of a ballplayer / K. Adam Powell.
Description: Lanham : Rowman & Littlefield, [2016] | Includes bibliographical references and index.
Identifiers: LCCN 2016025176 (print) | LCCN 2016051406 (ebook) | ISBN 9781442252059 (hardcover : alk. paper) | ISBN 9781442252066 (electronic)
Subjects: LCSH: Bostock, Lyman, 1950–1978. | Baseball players—United States—Biography. | African American baseball players—Biography.
Classification: LCC GV865.B677 P68 2016 (print) | LCC GV865.B677 (ebook) | DDC 796.357092 [B]—dc23
LC record available at https://lccn.loc.gov/2016025176

∞ ™ The paper used in this publication meets the minimum requirements of American National Standard for Information Sciences Permanence of Paper for Printed Library Materials, ANSI/NISO Z39.48-1992.

Printed in the United States of America

CONTENTS

Preface   vii
Acknowledgments   xi

1 California Dreaming (1950–1968)   1
2 Coming of Age in Times of Confusion (1968–1970)   19
3 New Decisions, New Opportunities (1971–1972)   33
4 The Path to the Big Leagues (1972–1974)   53
5 A Rookie's Journey (1975)   69
6 The Great Breakout (1976)   87
7 Something to Prove (1977)   115
8 Settling into Stardom (1977)   139
9 A Life-Changing Negotiation (1977 Off-Season)   159
10 The Big Slump (1978)   179
11 Redemption and Happiness (1978)   199
12 Another Day in Comiskey and Gary (September 23, 1978)   221
13 Passing into Legend   235
14 Saying Goodbye (September 24–28, 1978)   247
15 The Trials of Leonard Smith (1979)   269
16 Moving On (1979–1980s)   279
17 Lyman Bostock's Legacy   287

Notes   299

Bibliography	311
Index	319
About the Author	335

PREFACE

Writing this book has been both a joy and a tremendous emotional challenge. It took me six years to determine that this book needed to be written—that a brilliant, talented man's legacy was being largely forgotten through the simple passage of time. At the end of the day, when weighing whether or not to take on this project, one prevailing idea continued to bubble to the surface of my thoughts: a belief that Lyman Bostock's story—a classic American tale of rising from urban poverty to success, wealth, and fame under unique and challenging circumstances—hadn't gotten its just recognition in baseball history.

On the evening of September 23, 1978, Lyman Bostock was a young man living the quintessential American dream. He was an approachable, attractive, young black male who had risen from poverty and obscurity to fame and fortune in Major League Baseball, one of the most popular spectator sports in the United States. Lyman personified what so many young people all over America strive to become, both now and back then. From his trips to elementary schools in Gary, Indiana, where he hung out with local youths, to the baseball clinics he held in Southern California during the off-season, he insisted on giving back to children, many of whom dreamed of someday charting their own paths toward becoming a Lyman Bostock.

A textbook example of being in the right place at the right time, Lyman caught lightning in a bottle in the fall of 1977 when he and his agent, Abdul-Jalil Al-Hakim, parlayed a tremendous two-season run with the Minnesota Twins into a contract with the California Angels that made him one of America's highest-paid athletes. He was getting to play the sport he loved in Los Angeles, the place he'd called home for most of his life. He was in the fifth year of a happy marriage to his college sweetheart, and he was in a financial position to take care of his mother, who had raised him largely by herself. He had countless friends all over the country as a result of his two-decades-long baseball odyssey. He was in peak physical health.

Through it all, he had kept his humility, his sense of humor, and his sense of family. Lyman knew who he was and what he was all about. And as he'd promised publicly and privately, both to those who knew him well and to those who had never met him, Lyman hadn't let the money go to his head. People were still talking about his magnanimous gesture of donating his April salary to charity during the horrific slump with the Angels the previous spring. They would still be talking about it for decades to come.

By dawn the morning of September 24, 1978, Lyman Bostock was dead—victim of a single shotgun blast fired from the gun of a stranger. A career of tremendous promise, a life of direction and purpose, was gone in the blink of an eye.

Extensive research into Lyman Bostock's career has brought me to a few conclusions. Had he managed to stay healthy, not only could he have won multiple batting titles in the 1980s—perhaps even challenging Wade Boggs's claim to superiority as the American League's top hitter of the decade—but he could also have put together a career worthy of the Hall of Fame. And considering that his California Angels would make three American League Championship Series appearances from 1979 to 1986, it's certainly possible that, had he lived, he could have helped them win a World Series. Fate simply didn't provide him the opportunity.

The more I researched Lyman Bostock, read what he had said to various reporters over the years, and spoke to those who knew him, the more I realized that there was much more to learn about this man than simply his deeds on the baseball diamond. And there was much to learn *from* him. Much to learn about his spirit of generosity. Much to learn about his friendly, gregarious nature. The more I got to know Lyman Bostock through extensively researching his life, the more I wanted to be like him and the more I tried to inject his spirit into my own day-to-day activities. In that regard, Lyman Bostock continues to live on in those who find inspiration in his life story and in those who attempt to honor his memory and legacy. My hope is that anyone who picks up this book will find similar inspiration from the remarkable life and times of Lyman Bostock.

ACKNOWLEDGMENTS

A great number of people made the production of this book possible. The first person is Lyman Bostock himself, whose remarkable rise to become one of the American League's top players of the 1970s created a fascinating storyline.

I must thank Bob Hiegert, Lyman Bostock's college coach, for the time he spent talking with me about Lyman and bringing his early life into focus. Perhaps more so than any other single individual with exceptions of Lyman's mother, the late Annie Pearl Bostock, and his wife, Yuovene, Hiegert played the most essential role in Lyman's rise from an impressionable kid from inner-city Los Angeles in the late 1960s to a star with the Minnesota Twins and California Angels in the mid- to late 1970s. Coach Hiegert took me back to his outstanding teams of the early 1970s at San Fernando Valley State College in Northridge, California, that Lyman played with. He also provided compelling insight into the process of Lyman's signing with the Minnesota Twins. Coach Hiegert's crisp and accurate recollections of names, games, and other occurrences from nearly a half century ago were essential in telling the story of Lyman's life. In addition to Coach Hiegert, I'd like to thank Amy Millstone and Nick Bocanegra at the Cal State Northridge athletic communications office for their assistance.

I would also like to thank Dick Enberg for taking the time to respond to my inquiry for his recollections covering Lyman with the California Angels in 1978. Mr. Enberg took the time to get back to me during the middle of baseball season, just a couple of weeks before earning the Ford

C. Frick Award for a career of excellence in his profession. I'm grateful for his assistance on this book and wish him a long and happy retirement. I would also like to express appreciation to Paul Hutchins, who was willing to provide firsthand recollections of an unforgettable night in the intensive care unit of St. Mary's Mercy Hospital in Gary, Indiana.

Multiple outstanding sportswriters around the country took the time to get to know Lyman Bostock and to acquire the direct quotes attributed to him during his playing career. The results are spread throughout this book, and they all deserve credit for their fine work. This book is a tribute to their outstanding contributions to sports journalism as much as it is a tribute to the memory of Lyman Bostock.

Among the sportswriters whose work I reference are Bob Fowler and Dick Miller of *Sporting News*; Dave Anderson, Murray Chass, and Joseph Russo of the *New York Times*; Steve Jacobson of *Newsday*; Milton Richman of United Press International; William R. Barnard, Bob Greene, Brent Kallestad, Gene LaHammer, John Nadel, Howard Ulman, and Barry Wilner of the Associated Press; Skip Bayless, Mike DiGiovanna, Larry Green, Earl Gustkey, Don Merry, Jim Murray, Scott Ostler, Ross Newhan, Mike Penner / Christine Daniels, Rich Roberts, Bob Secter, and John Weyler of the *Los Angeles Times*; Jill Painter of the *Los Angeles Daily News*; Tom Briere, Dick Cullum, Sid Hartman, Gary Libman, Patrick Reusse, and Joe Soucheray of the *Minneapolis Tribune*; Richard Dozer, David Israel, K. C. Johnson, and Dave Nightingale of the *Chicago Tribune*; Bill Gleason and Brian Hewitt of the *Chicago Sun-Times*; Brian Bragg, Jim Hawkins, Jack Saylor, and Charlie Vincent of the *Detroit Free Press*; Thomas Boswell of the *Washington Post*; Ken Nigro of the *Baltimore Sun*; Tom Weir of the *Oakland Tribune*; Claire Smith of the *Hartford Courant*; Ray Kennedy of *Sports Illustrated*; Frank Mazzeo, Brad Ritter, and Paul Wertz of *Valley News*; Steve Dilbeck of the *San Bernardino Sun-Telegram*; Tracy Ringolsby and Loel Schrader of the *Long Beach Independent-Press-Telegram*; Terry Galvin of *Florida Today*; Neal Russo of the *St. Louis Post-Dispatch*; Sam Weisburg of the *Lowell Sun*; Cliff Morlan of the *Bemidji Pioneer*; syndicated national columnists Dick Young and Murray Olderman; Dave Kellogg of the *Tucson Daily Citizen*; Earl Gault of the *Spartanburg Herald-Journal*; Tim Connaughton of the Society of American Baseball Research; Mike Damergis, who conducted an in-depth interview with former California Angel Carney Lansford on Lyman Bostock; and Tom Singer of MLB.com.

ACKNOWLEDGMENTS

In addition, this book references authors of other sports books, including Malcolm Allen, Mark Armour, and Rob Goldman, who spoke with Don Baylor about the last day of Lyman Bostock's life for their respective works on the 1970 Baltimore Orioles and the history of the California Angels; Brent Kelley, who conducted an extensive interview with Lyman Bostock Sr. for his oral history project on the Negro Leagues; and Wil A. Linkugel, Edward Pappas, and Dan Gutman, who produced interesting segments on Lyman Bostock for their books *They Tasted Glory: Among the Missing at the Baseball Hall of Fame* and *Baseball Babylon: From the Black Sox to Pete Rose, the Real Stories behind the Scandals that Rocked the Game.*

Lyman Bostock's uncle, Thomas Turner, is one of the individuals I would have most liked to have spoken with, but, sadly, he passed away a couple of years before I took on this project. But thanks to ESPN's Jeff Pearlman, as well as Tom Rinaldi and the production crew of ESPN's *Outside the Lines*, multiple interviews with Mr. Turner live on for posterity. Jeff Pearlman wrote the definitive story on Lyman's Bostock death in his 2008 feature for ESPN.com, "Fifth and Jackson," which is cited at different points in this book. Pearlman's article was an inspiration for me in taking on this project.

A special thanks also goes out to the good people at the Davis Library at the University of North Carolina at Chapel Hill, who were tremendously helpful during my research. There I was able to exhaustively search the archives of the *Minneapolis Tribune* and *Los Angeles Times*, flagship newspapers of the two big league cities in which Lyman Bostock played. I also want to thank Lyman's high school alma mater, Manual Arts High School in Vermont Square, Los Angeles—and especially principal Erica M. Thomas-Minor and business manager Oswaldo Bonilla—for providing me the rights to use images from the 1968 edition of the school's yearbook, *The Artisan*.

Thanks also to Clyde Doepner and Mike Kennedy of the Minnesota Twins, as well as Brian Coombes of the Tacoma Rainiers, for their assistance with photographs. Mike McCormick and Jeff Petty granted permission to publish photographs of Lyman Bostock from his days with the Minnesota Twins from their personal collections, which added significantly to this book. I appreciate their willingness to participate. The Associated Press and Corbis/Bettman also provided usage rights for certain images. Special thanks to Christen Karniski of Rowman & Littlefield, who saw this project through with me from proposal to final product. Thanks for everything you did to make this book a reality.

Finally, I thank my beautiful wife, Julie, for putting up with me and my work and give all my love to my two children, Colt and Jenna. May you learn from the example of Lyman Bostock. Do not be afraid to chase your dreams, and may you find within yourself a grateful heart and charitable spirit when good things come your way.

I

CALIFORNIA DREAMING (1950–1968)

Go West, young man, and grow up with the country.—Horace Greeley, *New York Tribune*, July 13, 1865[1]

In the spring and summer of 1941, in the months leading up to the Japanese invasion of Pearl Harbor—a moment that forever changed the lives and paths of countless young men of his generation—Lyman Wesley Bostock was a local kid made good. The pride of Birmingham, Alabama. Born in Jefferson County on March 11, 1918, during the climactic final months of what would later come to be known as the Great War, Lyman Bostock had risen from the sandlots of Birmingham, and the pipeworks and ironworks teams of his early adulthood, to find a prominent role on one of the best black ball clubs in the American South, the Birmingham Black Barons. A smooth-fielding first baseman able to hit to all fields, he earned a place that summer in the East-West All-Star Game, where he stood alongside Negro League greats such as Satchel Paige and played in front of an estimated fifty thousand fans jammed into Chicago's Comiskey Park.

In modern times, a strong, power-hitting first baseman with a reputation for solid defensive skills like Lyman Bostock Sr. may very well have gotten a chance to play in the Major Leagues. But the onset of World War II—and the times—wouldn't allow him to play at that level. Like many of his contemporaries of all races, he would lose four of his prime seasons doing his part to help the United States prevail in World War II. He would return stateside and find more glory on the diamond in the late 1940s, just as America's most popular spectator sport of the era was

Lyman Bostock Sr. emerged from the sandlots of Birmingham to find a place on one of the top Negro League ball clubs of his era, the Birmingham Black Barons, prior to the United States' involvement in World War II. (Photo used with permission of Steve Petrucco.)

changing its attitude about racial integration. But opportunity to follow Jackie Robinson and other men of his race into the formerly all-white American and National Leagues would forever elude him.

"Lyman Bostock Sr. was one of the better baseball players of the 1940s, but few people realized it," wrote Tracy Ringolsby of the *Long Beach Independent-Press-Telegram* in 1977. "The elder Bostock was hidden from the general public in the Negro Leagues, forced to perform in second-rate parks for second-rate salaries because of the color of his skin."

Lyman Bostock Sr. was part of a dying breed—men who had played well in the Negro Leagues when it was still a viable and profitable entity in the early 1940s but were past their prime after World War II, when the big leagues started accepting top African American players in higher numbers. By the early 1950s, he had been forced to find playing opportunities in Canada, where he began to be estranged from his namesake, Lyman Wesley Bostock Jr., born on November 22, 1950—an estrangement that never had a chance to come full circle.

Lyman Jr., known by most who knew him as "Lyman" and by some family members as "Wesley," would himself rise to prominence as a baseball player in the coming decades. But for the most part, the two Lyman Bostocks weren't in each other's lives. Separated from his father by his parents' divorce and then his mother's relocation to the West Coast, Lyman Bostock Jr. grew up knowing little about his father as a person, though he was superficially aware of his exploits on the baseball diamond.

"Some ballplayers are born to play the game. And I think it was a tradition in my family for ballplayers I'm just carrying out right now," Lyman Jr. once said.[2]

While things were undeniably strained between father and son as a result of their lack of proximity to each other, there is no denying that Lyman Jr. was a beneficiary of genetics. He inherited much more than his father's name. He acquired his father's athleticism, his quickness, his hand-eye coordination. He inherited his father's baseball instincts—that unwritten, unspoken ability to play a difficult game with grace and seeming ease.

Though they didn't know each other well, they shared unmistakable characteristics. There were physical similarities. Both finished their growth at over six feet tall. They were both left-handed hitters and right-handed throwers. Both were handsome men with prominent, chiseled features. They also shared similar characteristics at the plate. Good bat quickness, an easy, fluid swing. A consistent ability to hit line drives to all fields. An occasional tendency to be free-swinging. They shared strong-willed personalities as well as a determination to receive what they felt was fair compensation for their talents. Both would make financial demands of management that their bosses weren't prepared to accept, resulting in their moves to other ball clubs.

However, unlike his father, who was hit by a historic double whammy of war and prejudice, the younger Lyman Bostock benefited from his times. Among the first wave of players to test the waters of an open market as free agency emerged in professional baseball in the 1970s, Lyman Bostock Jr. had half the teams in major league baseball bidding for his services during the fall of 1977. The most Lyman Bostock Sr. ever made in a season was around $5,000 in the 1940s. By the time Lyman Bostock Jr. reached his heights in baseball, he was making that much per game.

More than thirty years after his father had broken into the Negro Leagues, the son was asked whether his father was disappointed that the major league train had passed him by. "He doesn't think of himself that way," Lyman Bostock Jr. said. "He looks at me as being very lucky. And I look at myself as being very lucky. I was born at the right time."[3]

Like his father, Lyman Jr. eventually returned home. But unlike his father, who was Alabama born and bred, the son called Los Angeles home. It was where he and his mother had established roots twenty years earlier. Where Annie Pearl Bostock started a new chapter in her life with her young son when he was seven years old.

Despite being estranged from his father, Lyman Bostock Jr. inherited a baseball legacy that would see him reach the height of his profession. A legacy that touched the lives of numerous people throughout the country, from Southern California to Minnesota, from Florida to the Pacific Northwest, and throughout the American League. A legacy that would come to a violent and utterly senseless end at a Midwestern city intersection on a Saturday night.

* * *

From his earliest days, a bat and a ball were in Lyman Wesley Bostock Jr.'s hands. He would later recall playing all day long, from sunrise to darkness, in Birmingham and in Gary, Indiana—where he lived off and on from the time he was three until he was nearly eight. Though the equipment had improved from the days his father used to swing metal pipes and tree limbs, young Lyman's baseball roots were established on the same parched sandlots that his father had frequented three decades earlier in Birmingham and at Roosevelt Park in Gary, as well as on the corner of Harrison Street and Twenty-First Avenue.

Annie Pearl Bostock, Lyman's mother, had married his father and namesake in 1949 after a brief courtship. But with Lyman Sr. living mostly in Canada, playing out the final years of his professional baseball career, they were largely apart for their brief marriage, as Annie was left at home in Birmingham to care for the baby.

"She told me how he used to go away on the train or bus for weeks at a time," Bostock would recall in 1977.[4]

A couple years after Annie and Lyman Sr. divorced in the winter of 1952, she moved with her young son to Gary, where a couple of her brothers found work in the area's booming steel mills. Lyman would return to Birmingham regularly in those early years, as Annie often came back during the summer to see her parents and other relatives. But the trips to Alabama would decrease as the years passed. A small, talkative boy, little Lyman caught the eye of his mother's brothers with his relentless desire to play baseball. You could say it was in his blood.

"Even when he wasn't great I told everyone I had a nephew that was going to play major league ball," said one of Lyman's numerous uncles, Herman Turner. "The guy loved to play so much he would take a whipping to be out playing ball. He'd just slip out the back [door]. He was a tough, rough kid, but he was also a sweet kid. He let others use his things all the time. There wasn't a whole lot, but he shared it. He loved the game and he loved people."[5]

"We called him 'Red Bone,'" said another uncle, Thomas Turner. "He was a scrawny kid, and he'd get out there in the sun and he'd just turn red. He turned so red, it seemed like he was x-rayed and you could see his bones."[6]

Gary was one of the more appealing destinations in America for blacks migrating from the South in the 1950s, and Annie quickly found work maintaining a supply room at Methodist Hospital. Lyman began kindergarten in Gary in the autumn of 1955 and spent his first few years of elementary school in Gary city schools. Though Gary brought opportunity to Annie that she hadn't found back in Birmingham, she believed there was an even better place in America to live and raise her son. So on a warm morning in 1958, Annie climbed aboard a Greyhound bus in her native Birmingham, young Lyman by her side. They were heading to

California on a three-day, one-way trip to start a brand new life. With just seven dollars in her pocket but boundless optimism for the future, Annie held Lyman's small hand as they boarded the bus. Lyman sat in a window seat on the long westward journey and looked upward, his view an endless sea of sky and clouds.

As the Greyhound hummed its way across Texas, through the vast expanses of New Mexico and Arizona, and finally into California, Lyman continually fixed his gaze toward the sky, watching the trajectory of planes as they raced through the air. Why couldn't he and his mother be on one of those planes, the little boy thought to himself, flying at high speed to the West Coast in a matter of hours instead of on this cramped bus for days on the long journey to California? "When you're that age [and poor], you are in a wanting period," Bostock would say two decades later. "You learn to live with what you have."[7]

"When you're seven, you know you're poor because you know you don't have the things that you want. You know that when you ask for something that you have to wait for it and sometimes never get it. You know that you're going to get only one or two Christmas presents. But those are things you learn to live with."[8]

Despite her lack of financial resources as she headed to California, Annie had big plans for Lyman. She knew the boy wasn't going to get nearly as fair a shake in Alabama, or even in Indiana, as he would in California, where African Americans had long found significantly more tolerance and opportunity than back east.

As it turned out, Annie and Lyman were a tiny part of a gigantic migration of black Americans in the mid-twentieth century that permanently changed the country's demographic footprint. According to statistics calculated through the 1960 census, eighteen million African Americans—approximately one-tenth of the nation's population at that time—had migrated around the country in the preceding decades. In 1910, approximately 90 percent of America's black population lived in southern states that made up the old Confederacy. A half century later, approximately half of America's blacks had moved north and west, mostly to large cities such as New York, Philadelphia, Detroit, Chicago, and Los Angeles.

Many moved to "sun-drenched California—the nation's largest state, pulsing with exuberant growth and vitality," as narrator Martin Gabel described it in the 1966 television documentary *The Making of the Presi-*

dent: 1964. "These newcomers have come to dwell in endless suburbs. Some seeking the good life and new hope. Others in flight from the turmoil and congestion of the east."

Lyman started third grade in California and would spend the next decade in the Los Angeles public school system, working his way toward the high school diploma that was one of his mother's dreams for him. After initially living with one of Annie's twelve brothers, they settled into an apartment at 4609 South Hoover Street, in the Vermont Square section of Los Angeles.

Vermont Square was an area filled with people similar to the Bostocks—minorities, especially Hispanics, African Americans, and Asian Americans. Many of them lived in single-parent homes. The nearby Harbor Freeway was under construction, slowly trudging south from the heart of downtown Los Angeles to link up with nearby communities such as Watts. Living in the shadow of the nearby Los Angeles Memorial Coliseum and the recently completed Los Angeles Memorial Sports Arena, located just a mile away from his front doorstep, Lyman grew up happy and healthy.

Shortly after arriving in the Golden State, Annie bought her son a baseball glove so he could learn how to play properly. From soon after their move to Vermont Square and throughout the early 1960s, Lyman could routinely be found around the corner of Forty-Seventh and Hoover Streets, actively recruiting other local kids for pickup games on nearby vacant lots. One decided that he liked the little boy's new glove the day after he brought it to the field.

"When I was eight years old, my mother bought me my first glove. But someone stole it the next day," Lyman said in *Sporting News* nearly two decades later. "My mother wasn't about to buy me another one. But a friend of hers at work gave her a replacement. Unfortunately, it was a left-hander's model and I'm right-handed."[9]

Playing regularly against older and more physically developed boys not only sharpened young Lyman's baseball skills but required him to adapt in the field. Skinny but coordinated, he showed natural ability from a very young age. He could make contact with the ball even as a small child. He enjoyed the competitive nature of the game. He enjoyed hanging out with neighborhood kids, laughing together and teaming up with them to play. In those early days of sandlot games in Southern California,

Lyman picked up traits he would carry to the baseball diamond throughout his life.

Since he didn't have a strong throwing arm, Lyman played a very shallow outfield. Not only would he learn how to charge after balls hit over his head, often diving recklessly for them, but he would also learn how to make over-the-shoulder catches look somewhat routine. Furthermore, using a left-handed glove forced Lyman to make basket catches like Willie Mays, one of California's baseball heroes of his childhood and his father's former Negro Leagues contemporary.

"I was either a little younger or a little smaller than the boys I played with. I just didn't have the arm to make long throws, so I moved in. That meant that balls hit over my head had to be caught over-the-shoulder."

Many years later, Lyman would still regularly drop his glove down around his waist and haul in routine fly balls basket-style.

"Since it was the only glove I had, I had to use it. It was the only way I could catch the ball. It became a habit," he said.[10]

* * *

While Vermont Square was a far cry from the richest parts of Los Angeles, where the movie stars and studio executives lived and played, Annie Bostock made sure that Lyman had a suitable environment to grow up in.

"It's a tough area," Bob Hiegert, who would later become Lyman's college coach, says of the area where Lyman grew up. "The home that they lived in was a very nice apartment. He had a nice home life, and he had somebody at home for him all the time. That's not the case with a lot of the African American kids down there. He had a support group through his mother and through her friends and relatives down there that helped him."[11]

Annie found another job in a hospital in Los Angeles that supported her and Lyman throughout his childhood. She would still be working that job well into Lyman's adult life. Capable of modestly supporting both herself and Lyman through her employment, Annie toiled diligently as Lyman grew up.

Lyman was Annie's life. Her pride and joy. Unlike many young boys of his race, who had no home structure and ran around America's cities aimlessly, Lyman had attention, support, love, and discipline at home.

"Lyman had a good home," said Hiegert. "She took care of him. And he was very supportive of her all the way through. That part was kind of a special thing you don't see that often with kids of his age and energy."

Although his father wasn't there to provide a consistent male role model, his mother was a rock of stability. She cleaned his clothes, cooked his meals, made sure he was able to get to school, and scolded him when he talked back to her, demonstrated poor manners, or brought home a less-than-stellar report card. All while working full-time, without another adult in the house to assist her.

"His mother was the bellwether for him," said Hiegert. "Very dignified lady. Took no nonsense from him. And kept him on the straight and narrow. And was there. Really a wonderful woman to talk to. She was very good. She really made a lot of sense."

"Everything she did, she did for that boy," added Annie's brother, Thomas Turner. "He was the light of her life."[12]

Annie laid the groundwork for her son's future success by establishing clear guidelines in her house. Clean up after yourself. Make good grades. Don't loiter around street corners at night, hanging around with the wrong crowd. Don't stay out late, period. Lyman didn't like to upset his mother, so he rarely gave her any grief during his childhood.

"The difference with him was that he had a respect at home for his mother, and his family structure, that was important to him," Hiegert added. "He didn't want to let her down, and he made sure he did that. Lyman was grounded at home."

Annie Pearl Bostock, almost entirely by herself, raised a little boy into a confident, easygoing man who would become universally revered by those who crossed his path.

"He was a very well-mannered kid. Had a great sense of humor. A lot of fun," said Hiegert. "But it didn't exert itself. The more you knew him, the more comfortable he was, the more infectious he was as far as getting people to be his friends, and open up a little bit more."

In later years, Lyman would make sure his mother was taken care of. Her strong example and stern leadership paved the way for him to succeed beyond anyone's wildest dreams when the two of them boarded the Greyhound bus for California in 1958.

* * *

Los Angeles was booming, not just as a population center but as an international hub of business, commerce, and tourism in the late 1950s and early 1960s. Disneyland had been completed in Anaheim in 1955 and was drawing huge crowds, bringing in thousands upon thousands of new visitors to the region. The city had been awarded the 1960 Democratic National Convention, where John F. Kennedy passed one significant hurdle on his way to the White House, only to be cut down on November 22, 1963—Lyman's thirteenth birthday.

In 1961, when Lyman was ten years old, the people of Vermont Square and surrounding communities got an exciting new neighbor. The American League was expanding for the first time in its history, and Los Angeles was chosen for its second major league club. Around this time Lyman decided he wanted to be a ballplayer himself someday.

The Dodgers had made their way to Southern California after the 1957 season, abandoning Ebbets Field and the people of Brooklyn to establish the West Coast as a mainstream host in the big leagues. The Dodgers set up shop in the Los Angeles Coliseum while Dodger Stadium was being built in Chavez Ravine, a massive tract of land ideally situated around the city's primary transportation arteries. The Dodgers brought a world championship to Los Angeles in 1959—just their second season in town—and set numerous attendance records at the Coliseum.

The expansion Los Angeles Angels played their first season at Wrigley Field, located just a mile and a half from Lyman and his mother's apartment along South Hoover Street. The ten-year-old made his way to see the Angels at Wrigley Field multiple times in their inaugural season. That September, the Angels called up a nineteen-year-old native Californian who would become one of Lyman's favorite players. Lyman loved the effort and the determination of young Jim Fregosi. Even as an adult, Lyman didn't forget the contributions Fregosi made to those early Angels squads.

"He grew up around Wrigley Field in Los Angeles," recalled Fregosi when he was manager of the Angels. "And he talked to me about when he was a kid and watched me play when I came up with the Angels."[13]

Another one of Lyman's favorite ballplayers growing up was Carl Yastrzemski, the Red Sox legend. Like Lyman, Yastrzemski also batted left-handed. Yaz demonstrated a cool poise and scrappy hustle on the field that Lyman himself would later try to emulate. As a kid, Lyman even had a Carl Yastrzemski model bat and would try to swing like the Red Sox outfielder—raising his arms high and swinging mightily in an impression of the stance that helped make Yaz a superstar.

"I never collected baseball cards or anything like that," Lyman would say years later. "But I always like Yastrzemski's style."[14]

Lyman was a well-mannered kid who, by and large, stayed out of trouble during his youth in Vermont Square, avoiding the more dangerous trappings of black urban life. One of the few times anybody saw him get really upset during his childhood was when a neighborhood friend, Wilmer Aaron, accidentally broke the Yastrzemski bat that Lyman cherished. Wilmer, a cousin of Hank Aaron and a future teammate at Manual Arts High School, went on to become a first-round draft selection of the Baltimore Orioles in 1971, but never managed to get past Double-A.

Entering Manual Arts High School as a freshman in the fall of 1964, Lyman was a small but athletic young man. Manual Arts High had produced Paul Blair, who that September made his big league debut with the Baltimore Orioles. But in those pubescent days, Lyman was a far cry from a big league prospect. He went out for baseball as a freshman at Manual Arts in the spring of 1965 but wasn't close to ready for the varsity team.

"I remember when I went out for my high school team," Lyman would say more than a decade later. "My coach told me I was too small for first base and didn't have a good enough arm for center field. So I tried out for second base and I got cut for the junior varsity team."[15]

Lyman was devastated at the dismissal. For the son of a former pro ballplayer, the rejection was personal. He hadn't been prepared for the possibility of not being selected, and he took the news quite hard.

"I was so upset, I cried like a baby," Lyman said. "I wasn't the same for two days."

One of the advantages of attending a large public high school like Manual Arts was that the school had two other junior varsity baseball squads in addition the main JV team. As a result, Lyman wasn't shut out from playing scholastic baseball, even after he was cut his freshman year.

"Finally, the coach came to me and said the school really had three jayvee teams," Lyman said. "I wound up on the third-string JV team, but I learned how to play."

Called the "Bee" and "Cee" teams, the extra junior varsity units provided Lyman a chance for redemption. But it was a hard road. For three straight late winters and early springs, from 1965 to 1967, Lyman toiled away on the various Manual Arts' JV squads, failing to draw much attention to himself with his play. He finally graduated to the main JV team by his junior year. But an injury, combined with the blow to his pride because he couldn't crack the varsity, wore on the young ballplayer, nearly compelling him to quit the game he loved so much.

"Once I got hurt and almost quit," Lyman recalled. "Another time, I didn't even get to pick out a bat. I had to use the old ones."

As Lyman attended class, studied, and sought respect from his Manual Arts classmates for his baseball abilities, a building tumult was growing in Los Angeles—a tumult that would explode in a series of shocking and unforgettable scenes in the coming months and years.

* * *

In the summer of 1965—just before Lyman was to begin his sophomore year at Manual Arts—the nearby community of Watts erupted with racially motivated aggression. Following the arrest of two African American men during a traffic stop on the evening of August 11, 1965, the residents of Watts poured out of their homes in a unified symbol of urban unrest. For approximately a week, the buildings of Watts burned as black residents, angered at police hostility and a lack of quality jobs in the area, lashed out at everything and everyone. Buildings were set ablaze. Stores were looted and vandalized. Countless arrests were made. More than thirty people would die in one of the worst riots in U.S. history up to that time.

Fortunately, Lyman and his mother weren't affected directly by the Watts riots, which took place less than seven miles from their front doorstep. But it was a mere prelude of what was to come as the turbulent 1960s raged on.

Two years later, as Lyman's senior year of high school began, Manual Arts High School was under siege. As the Vietnam War continued to escalate out of control and untold numbers were dying for a cause that many Americans didn't understand or see as just, a growing number of young people began to break away from the system. It was a period of unprecedented distrust and conflict between the establishment and high school and college youth, who were increasingly angered and jaded by the lack of progress in ending the conflict in Vietnam and the plight of urban blacks. Manual Arts High School became the site of a remarkable series of events in the fall of 1967, as a movement to oust the school's principal, Robert F. Denahy, erupted into a violent conflict that brought considerable media attention to the school. Many parents of Manual Arts students began to speak out against Denahy's leadership, which led to a drama-filled autumn in and around the school's campus.

"The fall semester at Manual Arts was marked by picketing, threats, open violence, and the complete disruption of normal school processes," said a passage in Manual Arts' 1968 student yearbook, *The Artisan*. "What began during the summer as subtle pressure soon became harassment and finally violence, as members of militant groups attempted to remove the Principal, and run the school more to their liking.

"The removal of the Principal was not the main issue, but was set forth as such by the militants to focus attention on Manual. The issue was the running of the central cities' schools and the role of Black Power advocates in determining curricula, faculties, and administration of these schools."

The board of education, refusing to yield to threats of further violence and unrest, wouldn't remove Denahy, which only added fuel to the controversy. The board believed that, contrary to the stance of the militant groups, Denahy alone couldn't take full blame for the problems at Manual Arts. They promised to continue aiding the school in a variety of ways, but that wasn't enough for the impatient protestors.

"Not receiving action upon the issue which they had created, the militants took more direct means," the yearbook continued. "Disruption of classes and administrative functions began. Students were accosted outside the school. Handouts of a provocative nature were often distributed. After the arrest of certain persons for interference in a disciplinary matter in the Boy's Vice-Principal Office, open rioting broke out."

Hundreds upon hundreds of rioters descended on Manual Arts High to express their views, resulting in a demonstration that put countless lives at risk.

"The rioters, reported at nearly 1,000, and composed of a very few Manual students, for two days stormed the campus and disrupted traffic on Vermont Avenue, set fires and threw bricks, beat up passing pedestrians and motorists, and threatened students and faculty. Many policemen were needed to restore order and protect the property, students, and faculty of Manual Arts."

The school's faculty—angry themselves and afraid for their own lives, as well as for the lives of their students—finally went to the board of education to demand action be taken. There was a one-day student-teacher boycott of classes, which drew a different kind of attention to the crisis.

"The faculty took matters into its own hands, and instead of reporting to school on Monday, October 21, went to the school board to demand immediate attention to Manual's problems, and an injunction against those who disrupted school procedure," recalled the school yearbook. "Both were promised by the board, so the faculty returned to school. The injunction was granted by the Los Angeles Superior Court, and a task force was sent to Manual by the board to investigate the problems, of which all had complained. The rioting subsided, and some immediate aid in the form of additional personnel and monies was given to Manual."

In December, Principal Denahy took a leave of absence due to an unexplained illness, claiming doctor's orders. The picketers disappeared, and Manual Arts High School returned to as near as normal as an institution could after such a hostile and threatening set of circumstances. Later it was revealed that Denahy would not return to Manual Arts. In late January, Fred T. Frazer of nearby Maclay Junior High School was named by the board of education as the school's new principal.

* * *

In the winter of 1967 and 1968, just a few weeks removed from the rioting outside Manual Arts High that had created such an anxious and uncertain environment, Lyman played for the school's "Bee" basketball squad. They were a far cry from Manual Arts' varsity, which won the Southern League championship that winter, but they played a competitive brand of basketball against other nearby high schools including Dorsey, Fremont, Chatsworth, and Los Angeles High.

The Toilers' "Bee" basketball squad had a losing record, suffering five losses by three points or less. Lyman was shorter than most of his teammates, but he played hard on the court—perhaps a little too hard. In one particular game, Lyman severely turned his ankle. He was limping around Manual Arts High for much of that winter but showed up for baseball tryouts in February eager to prove himself in his final prep season on the diamond.

Lyman hadn't yet made the varsity in high school, but in the spring of 1968 he came out determined and primed to earn a spot on Manual Arts' top team. Ripping line drives to all fields and digging out grounders, Lyman quickly proved not only that he was the team's best hitter but that he was an improving defensive first baseman.

"He was only 5–8 as a high school senior at Manual Arts," said Fred Scott, Lyman's high school coach. "He didn't even make the varsity until his senior year at Manual. But he had a great, natural swing—the kind you don't teach."[16]

Scott and the other baseball coaches at Manual Arts served as mentors and friends to Lyman, helping him develop the necessary confidence to take his abilities to the next level. In the team's photograph for the 1968 yearbook, Lyman sat to the immediate left of coach Scott, a beaming smile on his face as he rested his right hand in the webbing of his glove.

"Lyman mentioned a couple of times that the coaches at Manual helped him quite a bit," said his future college coach.[17]

Although he was known for being a gregarious cutup off the field, Lyman took practice seriously his senior year, earning the respect of his coach and teammates for coming to practice every day focused and ready to work. "Lyman was a fun-loving guy who had his share of laughs off the field. But at baseball practice, he was all business. I never had to discipline him," said Scott.[18]

Not only did Lyman take himself seriously on the field, but he also took the time to make sure he looked good on the diamond. Like his old man playing in the Negro Leagues two decades earlier, Lyman took pride in his appearance.

"[My mother would] say I was so much like my father," Lyman would recall. "She said I would always have my glove oiled and my shoes polished before a game, and when I was excited, I would pace just like he did."[19]

Lyman enjoyed a stellar senior year at the plate for the Toilers, with his average hovering around or over .400 for much of the spring. He had a shot late in the season of breaking Manual Arts' school record for single-season hitting and was leading the city of Los Angeles in hitting heading into the final game. But he wound up setting a much less dignified record instead.

"I remember I had a chance to set a school batting record in my final year in high school, but I struck out five times [consecutively]. That was a school record," Lyman joked years later.[20]

"He was slowed down all his senior season due to an ankle sprained during basketball season," recalled coach Scott. "Still, he would've won the city batting title if he hadn't gone 0-for-5 the final day."[21]

* * *

1st row-Coach Scott, L. Bostock, D. City, W. Aaron, C. Carter, L. Smith, L. Harris, Mgr. 2nd row-M. Adolph, K. Allen, T. Sanders, W. Showers, M. Miller. 3rd row-C. Dierden, G. Moses, W. Barker, E. Baker, E. Courtney.

Lyman (second from left) poses alongside his high school coach, Fred Scott (far left), who was an influential figure in his early development. An All-City selection at first base his senior year at Manual Arts, Lyman batted .375 for the Toilers that spring. (Photo used with permission of Manual Arts High School.)

1st row-Coach Scott, L. Bostock

Despite his promising senior season at Manual Arts High School, Lyman wasn't selected in the 1968 Major League Baseball amateur draft. The St.

Louis Cardinals, who were one of baseball's powerhouses of the late 1960s, were interested in the young Los Angeles talent, but they didn't feel confident that they were going to sign him. Having experienced the nomadic baseball life firsthand in her younger days and seeing how it had contributed to the breakdown of her relationship with Lyman's father, Annie Bostock didn't want her son going off to play baseball for money until he had a little more education.

Though the powers of the Pacific 8 Conference, such as Southern Cal and Arizona State, never came calling on Lyman, his senior season .375 batting average, which ranked second in the city of Los Angeles, drew the attention of Bob Hiegert, who had built a small college powerhouse baseball program at San Fernando Valley State. Hiegert saw in Lyman a young man with raw talent who he thought might develop into a productive player for the Matadors.

"He was at Manual Arts High School, and I saw him play a game," recalls Hiegert. "The Cardinals' scout called me. He said that they weren't going to sign him. He didn't think he wanted to sign. Annie Bostock wanted her son to go to college."

Although he had shown promise at the plate, Lyman wasn't fully developed physically as a high school senior and therefore didn't demonstrate the prodigious potential that could have gotten him drafted straight out of high school. While Hiegert was impressed with Lyman's hitting and base running, he thought he had a long way to go defensively.

"Lyman was not a super-outstanding athlete in high school," Hiegert remembered. "He was very good. But he wasn't the kind of kid that would get your attention because he didn't do the kinds of things that a major college coach, or a pro scout, looks for unless you watch the kid quite a bit. The Cardinals guy had done that.

"He did not have quick feet for an infielder. He wanted to play second base, and I said, 'No way.'

"He didn't move his feet fast enough to do that, to play pro ball, or play on the college level. But he took good actions on the bases. He was doing the right thing baseball-wise. He made good contact, but he was not a strong kid. His arm strength was down."

Despite Lyman's physical limitations, Hiegert received glowing reports on his approach to the game, as well as the way he received and accepted coaching. "One of the things with him that his high school coach mentioned and the [Cardinals] scout mentioned, he listened. He really wanted to get better. You might hear a coach or a scout say that, but then you work with him. He was one of those guys."

Hiegert began to recruit Lyman, inviting him to campus and offering him a scholarship to attend Valley State. Lyman took up Hiegert's offer of a campus visit and made his way up to Northridge for what would be a fateful meeting.

"He applied to then San Fernando Valley State College. And I had him come for a lunch, showed him around the campus, and offered him," Hiegert replied. "At the time, the only thing we could offer kids was tuition and books. I think it was like a seventy-five-dollar-a-semester scholarship. Which was as much as we were giving any of the kids at the time. Tuition was fifty dollars. And there was a twenty-five-dollar book deal along with it."

After giving it a couple days' thought and consulting with his mother, Lyman accepted Hiegert's offer. When it came time to graduate from Manual Arts High in June 1968, he had a plan for the future. He was heading up to Northridge to play baseball and study for a degree. Shoulders firm, head tilted slightly to the left, Lyman struck a serious pose in his Manual Arts senior yearbook photograph. Sharply dressed, wearing a coat and tie, sporting a fresh haircut and the type of thin mustache long admired by young men finally able to grow facial hair, Lyman stared directly into the camera with focused eyes.

He had flourished both as an athlete and as a young man during his time at Manual Arts. And as he headed off to college, he wouldn't forget those who had helped shape his youth.

2

COMING OF AGE IN TIMES OF CONFUSION (1968–1970)

> We've got some difficult days ahead. But it really doesn't matter with me now, because I've been to the mountaintop. Like anybody, I would like to live a long life; longevity has its place. But I'm not concerned about that now. I just want to do God's will. And He's allowed me to go up to the mountain. And I've looked over. And I've seen the Promised Land. I may not get there with you. But I want you to know tonight, that we, as a people, will get to the Promised Land. So I'm happy tonight. I'm not worried about anything. I'm not fearing any man. Mine eyes have seen the glory of the coming of the Lord!—
> Excerpt from Martin Luther King's last speech, April 3, 1968 [1]

The June 9, 1968, Sunday morning edition of the *Los Angeles Times* was filled with remarkable stories indicative of remarkable times. The day before, Robert F. Kennedy had been laid to rest in Arlington National Cemetery in Washington on a hill adjacent to his brother, the assassinated former president John F. Kennedy. In March—three months prior to his assassination in the kitchen of the Ambassador Hotel, just six miles from Lyman's childhood home—Robert Kennedy and fellow senator Eugene McCarthy, one of his foremost rivals for the Democratic presidential nomination, visited the campus of San Fernando Valley State College. Setting the tone for what was to come once Lyman arrived on campus a few months later, some of the students had demonstrated and burned draft cards while Janis Joplin played her music for the assembled crowd. The same day that Robert Kennedy was buried, James Earl Ray, the prime suspect in the murder of Martin Luther King Jr., was apprehended at Heathrow Airport in London.

That Sunday's *Los Angeles Times* reported that future Hall of Famer Don Drysdale of the Los Angeles Dodgers set a new major league record with fifty-eight and two-thirds consecutive scoreless innings the previous night, while also having his scoreless streak snapped by the Philadelphia Phillies.

Also in the sports pages that Sunday were the Helms Athletic Board's selections for the area's top high school baseball players. Lyman Bostock was named first-team All-Southern League first baseman for his senior season efforts at Manual Arts, though he relinquished player-of-the-year honors to Dorsey High star pitcher and future big leaguer Derrel Thomas. Two more future major leaguers—Doug DeCinces of Monroe High and Gary Matthews of San Bernardino High—also earned All-Mid-Valley League honors that spring.

Lyman would arrive at San Fernando Valley State College a few weeks later as one of the top prep baseball talents from inner-city Los Angeles. But baseball wasn't Lyman's first priority when he got to Northridge. In fact, baseball didn't seem to be much of a priority at all as Lyman began his freshman year of college in the late summer of 1968. When he first arrived at Valley State, Lyman's two primary focuses were girls—one in particular—and the movement to raise awareness about issues important to young black people.

The year before, in 1967, construction was completed on Valley State's first coed dormitory, where Lyman would live his freshman year. Northridge Hall, located along Zelzah Avenue, was a state-of-the-art facility in its time that featured a spacious cafeteria, a convenient pool, and plenty of areas for study and student interaction. It was there that Lyman first laid eyes on Yuovene Brooks, a beautiful freshman coed. Like Lyman, Yuovene had also grown up in South Los Angeles, in Compton. Confident in himself—and unwilling to let this gorgeous young woman walk away from him without making some kind of move—Lyman went over and introduced himself. As they say, the rest is history.

"He was standing a few feet away, holding court, yakking, yakking, yakking away," said Yuovene in Jeff Pearlman's 2008 ESPN article, "Fifth and Jackson." "He followed me across the room, and we were together beginning that day."

"They were absolute opposites. He'd light up a room, raising conversation, laughing, having a good time, and she was quiet," added Lyman's college coach Bob Hiegert.[2]

The fall of Lyman's senior year at Manual Arts High School had been filled with pickets, threats, intimidation, and the disruption of normal school protocol. Lyman had been exposed to the draw of the Black Power movement, and he was sucked into it during his early days on the Valley State campus.

"There was all sorts of campus unrest. Berkeley was having all kinds of student unrest issues," said Hiegert. "We had a pretty active group on campus that Lyman was a part of. It was then called the Black Studies program. And then with a bunch of very aggressive kids, they carried a lot of their social activities out of the classroom."

* * *

Monday, November 4, 1968, began as a typical day on the campus of San Fernando Valley State College. It was the day before the fateful election pitting Republican Richard M. Nixon against Democrat Hubert H. Humphrey and southern demagogue George Wallace. In the prior day's edition of the *Valley News*, there had been a feature on Hiegert's class of thirty-four varsity and freshman newcomers for Valley State's baseball team. Lyman was one of ten All-Conference high school players from around Los Angeles—the only one from Manual Arts High School—that were supposed join the Valley State freshman squad the ensuing spring. But events of the day took precedence for the eighteen-year-old college newcomer.

"I didn't even play ball my first two years [in college]," Lyman said. "I was more interested in having a good time."[3]

For months, if not years, a festering frustration had been growing among African American students on the Valley State campus about the school's small number of black athletes, as well as perceived slights by some of the school's coaches. Although Valley State had an enrollment of approximately 18,500 students, just 200 were African American. Only a handful of black students were represented on the school's athletic teams. There were rumors that a white coach had struck a black student-athlete. Protesting the racist attitudes of university physical education instructors, the Black Student Union decided to hold a provocative demonstration the day before the election by taking control of the school's administration building.

Lyman Bostock

Lyman strikes a serious pose in his senior yearbook photograph at Manual Arts High School. He graduated in the spring of 1968 and matriculated to San Fernando Valley State College in nearby Northridge. (Photo used with permission of Manual Arts High School.)

"Lyman got caught up with some kids that did not have his personal best interests," said Hiegert. "They had a message they were trying to establish, which was called the Black Student Union. They pushed their cause on the campus, as was going on with other groups, like the Students for a Democratic Society. They were involved in a lot of campus unrest activity."

Hanging out in the dorms and off campus, Lyman caught hell from members of the Black Student Union when the subject of baseball was brought up. At a time when antagonism between young blacks—particularly young black men—and the so-called establishment was at its peak, baseball was seen by many of them as yet another glaring example of how their race was being held back. Baseball was the ultimate game of the establishment, they argued. The sport still rigidly enforced a strict reserve clause at the major league level, effectively making the players the property of the managers and owners. There were always more white faces than black faces in the stands at ballgames, Lyman was told. Almost all of the men in control of the sport were white. While blacks had been playing in the big leagues for over twenty years by the late 1960s, they were still subjected to humiliation and unfair treatment in some circles, such as when they traveled throughout the American South. And it was unheard of at that time for a black man to have a prominent role such as field manager or general manager.

Given his personality, it was easy for Lyman to get caught up in the activities of the Black Student Union. They seemed to be his friends—like-minded young men eager for social change. Like Lyman, many of them came from meager backgrounds. A good portion of them came from single-parent homes. Some of them had barely managed the academic record needed to enroll at Valley State.

"I think the kids that Lyman hung around with when he first came in, they were in college based on grade point average and the normal kinds of things," Hiegert said. "But if they were not on the normal scale, they were admitted to an experimental kid program. So there were some things with these kids that were one, not 100 percent pure and true. But as a seventeen-, eighteen-year-old kid, you pretty much believe what you're saying."

Lyman listened to their speeches, believed their rhetoric. He allowed himself to get caught up in something that could have easily derailed his athletic career long before it had a chance to blossom.

"Lyman was the kind of kid that if he said something to somebody, saying, 'Yes, I'll support you,' or 'Yes, I will do that,' he would do that. If he gave his word, he gave everything he had," said Hiegert.

"There was this cause, and he was really into it," said Yuovene.[4]

* * *

Accounts varied on how many members of the Black Student Union streamed into the corridors of Valley State's administration building shortly after noon on November 4, 1968. Reports ranged from forty to sixty. Lyman was among them. Quietly taking position, the demonstrators—many of whom wore Black Student Union sweatshirts—quickly worked their way up to the fifth floor of the building, securing the stairways and entrances as they went. As they swept through the fifth floor, the students pulled administrators and coaches out of their individual offices, herding them into a conference room.

"They ordered most of us, administrators and secretaries, into the presidential conference room and held us there three or four hours," said Dr. Donald Krimel, executive assistant to the president.[5] "There were implied threats of violence."[6]

Athletic Director Glenn Arnett was stunned when a group of the protestors barged into his office. Kicking his chair out from under him, one of the protestors intimidated the school official saying, "Stand on your feet, you pig, when I'm talking to you."[7]

George Holland, associate dean of fine arts, spoke of being hit twice by the demonstrators and having his arm wrenched by the angry mob. The vice president for administrative affairs, Harold Spencer, described being kicked in the chest. Knives were pulled. While most were steak knifes, at least one butcher's knife was reportedly involved. Fire extinguishers were taken off their mounts and sprayed throughout the area. Phones were thrown off desks.

Acting school president Paul M. Blomgren was brought into the conference room where the other instructors, secretaries, and administrative personnel were being held. "Get over there, sit down, and shut up," the throng told him.

At first, the protestors didn't know who he was. For more than thirty minutes, Blomgren quietly remained in the conference room with his colleagues. "Personal safety of the college personnel was definitely in jeopardy," Blomgren said. "From that point on, my first and only concern was the safety of those individuals."[8]

After identifying himself as the school's president, Blomgren was taken downstairs into a first-floor room where Black Student Union leaders had assembled. Calling the administrators "white pigs," the students lashed out at them for their perceived racism.

"They told us black people had been treated like pigs for 400 years, and that now we would just have to get used to it," said Krimel.[9]

In all, approximately three hundred students were involved. While most of the media attention focused on the Black Student Union representatives who took control of the fifth floor, more than three times as many white students, representing groups including Students for a Democratic Society and Students for Education, Action, and Change, took control of three lower floors during the sit-in, which lasted about four hours.

As Krimel and over thirty other school administrators held fast on the fifth floor, Blomgren was presented with a list of demands by the Black Student Union. Blomgren hastily signed the agreement, which included nine requests from the students. One was a promise of amnesty after the sit-in was concluded. As word got around that police were about to retake control of the building and the threat of violence became imminent, the students quietly gave up their positions and abruptly left the area. Lyman joined the large group of protestors who quickly exited the building and returned to Northridge Hall. Around a half-dozen cops entered the building after the students left, restoring order and avoiding what could have been a potentially lethal confrontation comparable to the tragedy that would occur on the campus of Kent State University two years later.

The following day, November 5, Blomgren declared the agreement he had signed with the Black Student Union was null and void, stating that he was under duress when he signed it. "Any document arrived at when people are held hostage, or force is being used, is not a mutual agreement," Blomgren said at a news conference. "It is simply a list of terms dictated by those who have force."

As his nineteenth birthday approached in late November, Lyman was in hot water with the law. Nearly a hundred Los Angeles police officials combed through the Valley State campus the day after the protest, getting information on the various Black Student Union members that could potentially be used in building criminal cases against them. In all, thirty-three students, Lyman included, would be charged for taking thirty-four people hostage for approximately four hours. As part of his involvement in the demonstration on the Northridge campus, Lyman had been charged with multiple felonies, including kidnapping, assault with intent to commit bodily harm, robbery, and conspiracy. He, along with twenty other demonstrators, surrendered to police three days after the sit-in at the Van Nuys Municipal Court and was promptly freed on bail. Lyman and three other BSU leaders (Archie Chatman, Eddie Dancer, and Arthur Jones) were considered by police investigators to have played the most active role in the sit-in and were given the largest bail amounts.

"There were some criminal charges on some of the kids, and Lyman was one of them that was arrested," said Hiegert.

Fearful and unsure of what to do next, Lyman reached out to two of his former high school teachers at Manual Arts High School, Dorothy Millhouse and Levi Dangerfield, for advice and assistance as he awaited his December preliminary hearing. Both Millhouse and Dangerfield had been instrumental in guiding Lyman through the successful completion of his high school studies.

Millhouse would speak out publicly in defense of Lyman, as well as two other young men from Manual Arts involved in the demonstration, Shelton Jones and Arnold Boyd. Millhouse called on Valley State's faculty and the district attorney to come up with a more reasonable solution than criminal prosecution for the individuals involved in the campus sit-in. Calling Lyman and his classmates the "cream of the crop—the very best students we had," Millhouse made an impassioned plea for amnesty for the three young men.

"Our students are not criminals," Millhouse, an English instructor, told the *Valley News*. "We cannot be silent when they are made scapegoats for a long-standing problem in American society."[10]

Three days after the incident, faculty members involved in the sit-in spoke in detail about their ordeal, generating understandable sympathy from other members of the faculty who weren't in the building at the time of the protest. But there was at least one faculty member, Donald Freed, who disapproved of the fact that members of the Black Student Union weren't invited to the closed-door session to defend themselves or to air their grievances as the administrators spoke out against their demonstration.

"One administrator after another told how frightened they were," replied Freed, a white anthropology professor. "In short, they were treated like a nigger for one-half hour and have yet to recover."[11]

* * *

Baseball was an afterthought for Lyman as 1968 moved into 1969. Though he had found genuine love in his first months at Valley State through his blossoming relationship with Yuovene Brooks, his baseball career was going nowhere. Through his activities with the Black Student Union, it looked very much like his standout senior season at Manual Arts High School could very well be his last hurrah on the baseball diamond.

"People were wrong to pressure him not to play baseball," said Yuovene. "If you're meant to do something—and Lyman was factually meant to play baseball—you shouldn't deny yourself. But we were young."[12]

A month and a day after he was involved in the student uprising, Lyman was listed as one of the incoming freshmen for the Valley State baseball squad, despite all the issues of his first few months on campus.

That same day, the *Los Angeles Times* reported that over a hundred major leaguers, including top stars such as Roberto Clemente, Willie Mays, Pete Rose, Carl Yastrzemski, Brooks Robinson, Harmon Killebrew, and Don Drysdale, were refusing to sign contracts for the 1969 season unless the owners negotiated with them on a pension program during the off-season. It was one of the first public battles between the Major League Baseball Players Association, headed by organized labor expert Marvin Miller, and the big league owners—the ramifications of which would have a significant impact on ballplayers in the future.

The 1969 season came and went for Valley State's baseball squad. The Matadors found success but were forced to turn down a postseason bid because of a bevy of late-season injuries. Lyman didn't play that spring, but he managed to focus enough on his studies to stay in school for his sophomore year.

"The 1969 team, we could not go to the Regional playoffs because we had three catchers get hurt in the last game of the year," recalled coach Hiegert. "And at that time, there was a clause that said unless you have a representative team of players at each position, you had to turn the bid down. So we had to turn the bid down."

After missing out on an opportunity to gain critical seasoning at the college level with the Valley State freshman team, Lyman wasn't fully prepared when he arrived for fall practice in 1969, leading up to the 1970 season. He was looking to earn a prominent role on the Matadors' varsity squad, but his time off the diamond had taken its toll.

"I didn't see him the summer, watch him in the summer, and he came out in the fall. He was coming in for the 1970 team," said Hiegert. "Because we had to turn the bid down in 1969, the players came back, as I did, a little more focused, determined to have a great year."

When he first took the field for Valley State, Lyman remained in the infield, as he had during his high school days back at Manual Arts. Since he was right-handed, he could play either of the corner infield spots. But when Lyman showed up for Valley State's workouts in the fall of 1969, he was rusty. He wasn't focused. He goofed off. And despite his natural skill, he simply wasn't as good as several other players at Hiegert's disposal.

"Lyman came in as a first baseman and third baseman. He liked to play third, but he was tall—about six one, I don't think he weighed 150, 155 pounds then—pretty good running speed, no arm strength at all. At our level, first and third basemen had to swing the bat a little bit, with a little more power, and he had neither," remembered Hiegert. "But he covered a lot of ground.

"We had a returning All-American at first base, and we had two kids that were coming in that were third basemen who were much better than he was. So he went to the fall practices, and did all right but not great."

Lyman had gotten onto Hiegert's radar as a potential future contributor, but he wasn't realistically in line to make a major contribution to Valley State's 1970 squad, which had aspirations for a championship after missing out on the West Regionals in 1969. By December—just weeks before in-season workouts began—Lyman began to show signs of discontent. He started showing up late to workouts, or not at all. He continued to hang out with some of the same Black Student Union folks who had contributed to the loss of his first potential season with the Matadors' freshman squad in 1969.

"It was about December when he missed a couple of practices, came out late. And he was being escorted around by older kids that did not have his best interests in mind," Hiegert said. Growing more and more impatient with the gifted but immature sophomore, Hiegert cut his losses, telling Lyman that he wasn't welcome on the team anymore.

"I, in a sense, cut him. I told him he was done," Hiegert said. "I told him he couldn't stay with the team. The fall of '69 is when this happened."

* * *

Although he still had Yuovene, whom he affectionately called by her maiden name of "Brooks," Lyman had little else to show for his first three semesters of college by the time the spring semester of 1970 rolled around, other than having passed some classes and staying academically eligible.

Frustrated by his encounters with Hiegert but unwilling to completely walk away from baseball—which he felt deep down was his destiny—Lyman was a regular at Matador games in the winter and early spring of 1970. Lyman would sit forlornly in the bleachers behind home plate or stand around the protective fence separating him from the field, observing the action with little to say to anyone—a rarity for a young man who loved to talk. Surely Lyman knew he could play baseball well at the collegiate level. But at the same time, he was watching his career—and his window of opportunity—slip by with each passing game.

"He came to some of the games just kind of keeping his head around, seeing what was going on," said Hiegert.

Lyman was a witness to history in the spring of 1970, as Hiegert and the Matadors won the California Collegiate Athletic Association and the NCAA West Regional, moving on to the College Division World Series in Springfield, Missouri. Valley State then went all the way, sweeping Southwest Missouri State and Nicholls State in a pair of elimination games before beating Nicholls State a second time to claim the national championship.

Later, accounts of Lyman's college years in media guides and various press reports would claim in error that he was member of Valley State's 1970 national championship squad. But in reality he was a bystander, forced only to watch Valley State reach its lofty heights.

No longer as inspired by the causes of the Black Student Union, Lyman entered a period of soul-searching in the spring and summer of 1970 during which he realized that baseball was more important to him than any other extracurricular activity.

"In 1970 we won the national championship," recalled Hiegert. "I think it took Lyman about six or seven months to figure it out. And by that time, he already had himself in trouble. He got kicked off the baseball team, in a sense. And his support group that he was hanging around with, I don't think he liked. And he really wanted to get back into a competitive situation."

After watching the Matadors go all the way and bring the national title back to Northridge, Lyman knew what he had to do. He had to go back to Hiegert and attempt to get back in the coach's good graces and on the team. He simply couldn't give up on his dream without at least asking for one more chance to play. During the summer of 1970, a few weeks after he had returned from Missouri with the national championship trophy, Hiegert was sitting in his office when there was a knock on the door.

"That following summer he came into my office," Hiegert recalled. "He came to me. That had to be a hard thing for him to do, because he had a lot of pride."

Understanding the significance of the moment, Lyman didn't waste the coach's time. He knew if he said the wrong thing, he could very well miss out on his last chance to make a career out of baseball. So Lyman said the one thing that couldn't fail him at that moment.

"I'm sorry, coach," Lyman said.

"He came in and I sat him down," Hiegert recalled. "He said that he was sorry. He had gotten into a lot of issues and stuff, but that he really wanted to play baseball."

"Well, let me tell you something. You came out and you embarrassed yourself," Hiegert retorted. "And your teammates. You didn't do what you're supposed to do. You didn't get to practice on time. You were screwing around out there half the time. You're not pulling your weight. Why do you expect a second chance?"

"Because I'd really like to play baseball. And I've made some mistakes," Lyman said meekly.

Coming off the glory of a national championship—and knowing he'd need a solid bat in the Matador lineup the following year—Hiegert was in the mood to give Lyman another opportunity. But the veteran coach made it clear that he was taking a zero-tolerance approach to the brash youngster's antics on the field.

"OK, that's what life's about," Hiegert told Lyman. "You can be a part of that opportunity. But you're on a really, really short leash. If you don't come to practice—if you screw around in practice—you're done. We're not putting up with any more of it. You're going to have to win back the confidence of your teammates, because you kind of screwed them over last year.

"We needed the best twenty-five players we can have. And you probably would have been one of them. But you quit on us."

"It won't happen again," Lyman said simply.

And with that, Lyman Bostock was once again a member of San Fernando Valley State College's baseball team, just as the Matadors made preparations to defend their national championship.

Lyman meant it when he said the issues of his past wouldn't reemerge. When he reported for fall workouts in 1970, he was engaged. He was on time every day. He wasn't distracted. As in his senior year at Manual Arts High, he was all business. No longer was he laughing and cutting up when he should have been focused and paying attention. He was starting to find his groove again at the plate, ripping line drives to all fields.

Once Lyman dedicated himself to baseball and put in the necessary time and effort to refine his natural talents, everything began to take care of itself.

"From that point on, he was a model kid," Hiegert said. "He would have been a model kid to start with, had he not taken some sidesteps, but that's the kind of kid he was. He looked at the whole situation and said, 'What I really want to be doing, I'm not doing. And I've got one chance to change that,' and he did. And he made the most of that opportunity."

3

NEW DECISIONS, NEW OPPORTUNITIES (1971–1972)

We must teach our children to dream with their eyes open.—Harry Edwards, sociologist[1]

Lyman entered the 1971 baseball season in a prime position not only to help a San Fernando Valley State team that was defending a national championship but also to make amends for a less-than-stellar start to his collegiate experience. Valley State's run to the 1970 NCAA title had lit a fire under Lyman. And while he hadn't officially been part of the title run, the Matadors' championship season had provided him a glimpse of what was possible if he trained his energy and focused on becoming the best baseball player he could be.

A few weeks after his summer conversation with Bob Hiegert, in the fall of 1970, Lyman officially returned to the Valley State baseball squad. He would be playing on a largely veteran squad that didn't have time for antics and drama.

"The 1970 team won the national championship," recalled Hiegert. "In '71, a lot of those kids held over from the '70 team. We couldn't spend a lot of time recruiting because we had a lot of kids who were going to play for sure. He came back in the fall and I said, 'Well, we'll start over, Lyman, if you want. But certainly it's up to you. If you don't work hard, if you miss practice, you're done.'"[2]

Hiegert reminded Lyman that talent alone wouldn't get him where he wanted to be in baseball. "You have some talent, but so does everybody else out here, and they follow the rules," Hiegert told him. "He came back, and I never had a bit of trouble out of him at all. He worked his head off, and he got the support of his teammates."

Suddenly, Lyman's immaturity and a lack of focus were no longer concerns for Hiegert. He no longer had to worry about whether Bostock was going to be on time, ready for workouts, and concentrating on getting better. Lyman also repaired the relationships with his teammates that might have been strained by the events of the prior couple of years, before Lyman dedicated himself properly.

"The '71 team was a very difficult team for Lyman, because he was involved with some of those kids in the off-field activities," said Hiegert. "And some of them wanted to back him up, and kind of did. But there was a feeling with some of the kids that he had to earn his way back, which he did with the '71 team."

Already respected by his teammates for his calm, pleasant demeanor, he now earned their respect with the way he conducted himself during workouts.

"For the most part, going back to his days at Northridge, Bostock was easy to get along with," wrote *Valley News* sports reporter Frank Mazzeo in 1977. "He had his share of bumps in the road, but that's not all that unusual for a young man emerging from a background such as Bostock's. Bostock usually was pleasant and personable."

As Lyman's relationship with Yuovene deepened, Hiegert no longer had to worry about the company he was keeping. Lyman, in fact, was starting to become emblematic of the right way to do things, the type of player that Hiegert could hold up as an example to his other players.

"I ran a very disciplined baseball program," said Hiegert. "There were things you had to do, or you couldn't play. We spent a lot of time on the mental errors—finding what the offense could do from the standpoint of leverage, where we were in the count, and taking a lot of the mistakes away from the hitter at the plate. Swings and fake bunts and all kinds of stuff. Lyman listened to all that stuff and put it into play, and got better. He got stronger.

"Lyman was a 100 percent guy. He never did anything 50 percent. He was as intense a competitor as I ever coached."[3]

Along with mental maturity came physical maturity. Lyman had grown a couple of inches since arriving at Valley State as a gangly teenager back in 1968. He had kept himself in good physical condition, adding muscle to his new height. And now that baseball was once again his passion, he was pushing himself to take advantage of the new opportunity.

"I think he grew about three inches in college," Hiegert recalled. "When he came in, I think he was five eleven, five ten maybe. And when he got out of there, he was six one, six two, and had put on about twenty-five pounds of muscle. He grew and matured, I think a lot better as time went on."

Though Lyman was a corner infielder when he first arrived in college, Hiegert saw an opportunity to use his speed and natural athleticism to the club's benefit in the Matadors' outfield. So as Valley State transitioned from the 1970 to the 1971 season during fall workouts, Lyman began his own transition into a left fielder.

"I moved him to the outfield. Put him in left field," said Hiegert. "We had another kid that was playing in center field, Marty Friedman, who was an outstanding player. Between those two kids, I don't think a ball fell in the outfield at all, because they could both run like the devil and catch. Lyman worked pretty hard at his outfielding skills."

Offensively, Lyman wouldn't hesitate to swing—and swing hard—at the first pitch. He often got behind in the count because of his free-swinging nature. Hiegert worked with him on being more patient, on hitting the ball to all fields instead of trying to yank everything to right field. "We had to cut down on a lot of stuff at the plate. He was a real over-swinger. Real aggressive kid at the plate. He had to learn how to take some pitches and learn how to hit the other way," said Hiegert.

Lyman didn't need a ton of help on the bases. He had good instincts about when to take off, when to stay back, and how to create problems for the defense when he was on base. "Very, very good baserunner. Great, natural instincts on the basepaths," Hiegert remembered.

As he prepared to take on a starting role in Valley State's outfield leading up to the 1971 season, Lyman had to learn how to play the left field wall at Northridge, which could cause serious injury if misplayed.

"Defensively, our field, we had a concrete block wall in the outfield with the warning track. You had to learn to play that wall, or you would kill yourself. It was as simple as that," said Hiegert. "We spent hours teaching the kids how to go back on balls and how to use that track coming off the thing. And he figured that out. He became a really good outfielder and learned how to use his arms to his advantage."

***

Lyman started the 1971 season a little lower in the Matadors' lineup than he would have probably preferred. But once he started producing, Hiegert was incentivized to move him up.

"He had to hit sixth when he first came up in '71, but we moved him up farther in the lineup," said Hiegert. "And he learned how to take some pitching, learned how to hit behind people, and how to move the ball around a little bit. He hit second and third for us. At no time did he ever step backwards. That's the difference. He kept getting better."

In his team's opening contest within the California Collegiate Athletic Conference on February 27, 1971—a 5–2 triumph over UC-Riverside—Bostock demonstrated an ability to manufacture a run, beating out an infield hit, reaching second on an error by the shortstop, taking third on a base hit, and scoring on a sacrifice fly. Lyman belted his first home run for the Matadors on March 6, a 5–4 victory on the road against Arizona State in Tempe. His solo blast in the second inning scored the Matadors' first run of the game.

Through early March, Lyman was Valley State's leading hitter with a scorching .436 clip. He was working opposing pitchers, getting ahead in the count, and seeing pitches he could drive to both fields. With his natural swing taking care of the rest, things were really coming together at the plate.

Though Valley State lost five out of six during one tough stretch early on, and were just 13–13–1 through twenty-seven games, they were again proving that they could compete with the best collegiate teams on the West Coast. That included defending major college national champion Southern Cal, who the Matadors pushed to the limit in a mid-March game in Los Angeles. Though Lyman went hitless in four at bats—including a strikeout with the bases loaded and nobody out in the seventh inning—Valley State's hurlers held Southern Cal scoreless until the bottom of the eighth, when a bloop double down the left field line scored Trojans outfield star and future big leaguer Fred Lynn for a 1–0 final score.

Following the loss against Southern Cal, Lyman began a fourteen-game hitting streak. By late April, Valley State was in first place in their league with a 14–3 mark and was coming off a win over UCLA, another Pac-8 school. With twenty hits in his last forty-six plate appearances—good for a .435 average over his fourteen-game hitting streak—Lyman was hitting .360 with forty hits, second-most on the Matadors' squad.

"Lyman is doing a good job defensively as well as with his hitting, and is getting closer and closer to becoming the complete ball player," Hiegert told the *Valley News*.

The Matadors finished the regular season with a 20–3 mark in conference play. Hiegert was named coach of the year, while Lyman earned a place on the CCCA's second-team all-conference squad. Heading into the postseason, Lyman had 41 hits in 119 at bats, good for a .345 average. He had three home runs, eight doubles, and three triples, along with four stolen bases. He wasn't a huge RBI man for the Matadors that season, with just twelve runs batted in, but he scored twenty-four runs.

* * *

As the Matadors prepared for their Western Regional showdown—hopeful to make a return to the College Division World Series—Lyman finally had to pay society for his involvement in the Valley State administration building sit-in during the fall of his freshman year. Although legal maneuvering and political wrangling had held up their cases for several months, Lyman finally reported to the Los Angeles County Jail in the spring of 1971.

"He had played the baseball season, but his court date came up," Hiegert recalled. "He spent a couple weeks in the county jail, and was released."

On a late May morning, Hiegert headed into Los Angeles and picked up Lyman from jail.

"I know it was towards the end of May. We were hosting the [West] Regional in 1971," he said. "I went down to get Lyman. I visited him before in jail, and he didn't know when he was going to be released. I found out when he was getting out, so I went down to L.A. and picked him up."

The time in jail had been harrowing for Lyman, as he saw firsthand the consequences of his actions by spending several days with hardened criminals. He knew he didn't want to go back. Though his experience with the Black Student Union had given Lyman a new perspective on race relations in the United States, it had also come very close to shattering a promising future on the baseball diamond.

On the way back to Northridge, coach and player stopped for a quick bite to eat. "We stopped on the way back. He was pretty shaken up. We stopped at a Denny's, and we had breakfast. He ate a lot," Hiegert remembered.

Lyman's brush with the law—and jail time—had scared him straight. Never again would he face legal trouble.

"He was scared to death," Hiegert told Jill Painter of the *Los Angeles Daily News* in 2008. "Three weeks in jail really woke him up and scared him. He was squared away before that, but he had a lot of time to think about things. He really wanted to concentrate on baseball and get himself through school. He was finally settled in. He was a sociology major. He met his wife in school then. They were dating. He put 100 percent of his energies to baseball and campus life. He was one of the true leaders on the team."

After a few days in the batting cage to get his timing back and in the outfield running down fly balls to work out the kinks and get his legs back under him, Lyman was ready for the West Regional.

"We came back to school and got him set up—he worked out with us for a couple of days—and then he was eligible for the Regional. And he came back and played the Regional," said Hiegert.

Valley State got a rude awakening on their home field in the opening game of the West Regional on May 21, as the University of San Diego showed up and shocked ace pitcher Bob LoPresti and the defending national champions, 2–1. The loss forced Valley State into the loser's bracket and a matchup with UC-Irvine, which the Matadors won the following day, 10–5. Lyman contributed an RBI single to the win.

After defeating Puget Sound in another elimination contest, Valley State readied for a rematch with San Diego. Lyman got a key hit in the first inning of the all-important regional showdown, knocking a seeing-eye ground ball single into right field to give Valley State a 3–2 advantage after San Diego opened the scoring with two first-inning runs. But Valley State's pitching couldn't handle San Diego's bats, as the Toreros slammed out fourteen hits, including three homers, in a 10–4 blowout that ended the Matadors' season two victories short of another World Series trip.

"We didn't play as well as we should have, and, of course, we didn't get back to the World Series. We placed second to San Diego," said Hiegert.

Although it was a disappointing end to Valley State's championship reign, the Matadors were poised to take another crack at the NCAA title in 1972. "A lot of those kids [from the 1970 NCAA title team] carried over to play with Lyman in the '71 season, and some of them played through '72," recalled Hiegert.

Along with putting in a solid performance on the field in 1971 and becoming a team leader for Valley State, Lyman was also becoming a leader in other ways on the Northridge campus. As he worked on a degree in social psychology, he helped out kids near his home in Los Angeles, teaching them a little bit about baseball while also spending time as a mentor, reading to them. Lyman was becoming the type of young man his teachers at Manual Arts would brag about to younger students.

*　*　*

The 1972 Valley State baseball team underwent something of an overhaul. Much of the talent from the 1970 national championship squad and the 1971 West Regional squad had graduated, leaving Lyman, star pitcher Bob LoPresti, fellow outfielder Marty Friedman, and a group of hungry, eager youngsters remaining to fill the gaps.

"The '72 team was kind of a cleaning house. A starting over," said Hiegert. "The only kids who carried over from the '71 team was Lyman, a kid named Bob LoPresti, an All-American pitcher. Most of the rest of the kids who had played on the '71 team were graduated, or didn't make the '72 team."

It was a challenging off-season for Lyman leading up to the 1972 season at Valley State, as he dealt with an injury he had suffered the previous summer playing semipro ball. He spent the summer of 1971 between Los Angeles and the Chicago area, playing games regularly in both cities and finding solid competition in summer league games in and around the Windy City. He returned to Gary to spend time with his uncles, and, during one of many such trips, Lyman became close to one of his uncle's goddaughters. The young girl, named Joan, especially enjoyed having Lyman come over to read to her.

"I felt it would be a great thing for him to do is just get out, get himself involved in a full season, basically, after the '71 season," said Hiegert. "He played and he had a good summer. He was up in Chicago."

During one game, however, Lyman pulled up awkwardly during his running stride. A pulled groin would give him fits well into the fall and winter, right up to the time Valley State began making preseason preparations. He aggravated the groin pull during workouts at Northridge that winter, which slowed him down for several weeks at the start of the 1972 season.

"Lyman's year started off in '72 slowly," Hiegert continued. "He came back in the fall, and I had recruited a lot of kids. He had pulled his groin in the summer, and he kind of nursed it again all fall. And then he injured it again during winter workouts. So he couldn't run full-out for quite a while. He wasn't 100 percent until I think about the first of April."

Although Lyman had become injured playing semipro games in the Chicago area, he had also gained valuable experience. He had gotten bigger and stronger. He was completing his growth, developing from an awkward kid into a mature adult.

"When he came back from summer baseball in '71, before we started the '72 season, he came back more like a man than just a college kid," said Hiegert. "He had put on weight. He had gotten to play a lot. He was a lot more confident. And I think he knew his skills a little bit more.

"The '72 team, because we were practically all brand new, he came back with a pretty good attitude from the summer. He was feeling good about himself. He was in decent shape. He was a much more relaxed player—a much more engaged player—like he was as he went on in his career."

Although Lyman was limited early that season, the Matadors started hot in 1972, winning their first seven games.

In late February, Valley State traveled to San Diego for what became a marathon battle with San Diego State. With the score tied 7–7 at the end of seven innings, the game suddenly turned into a languid struggle of futility at the plate. Neither Valley State nor San Diego State scored for nine innings, leaving the game still tied at 7–7 heading into the top of the seventeenth inning. The Matadors finally took control in the top of the seventeenth, loading the bases and taking the lead on a sacrifice bunt. That set the stage for Lyman to put the game away with a two-run-scoring single, as Valley State went on to a 10–7 triumph.

After placing Lyman down near the bottom of the Valley State batting order for much of his first season with Valley State, Hiegert felt compelled to bat him higher up in the lineup in the spring of 1972, taking advantage of his consistent ability to come through at the plate with base hits.

"We were really, really loaded at the top in 1971. I think he hit fifth, sixth, and seventh that year," said Hiegert. "The next year when we came back, I had him scheduled to hit third. But because he couldn't run early in the season, we wound up moving him back to the fifth spot, the sixth spot. And then towards the end of the year we hit him in the second and third spot quite a bit."

Lyman was flexible, allowing Hiegert to make the best use of him. He believed, unlike more selfish ballplayers, that if he was in the lineup—anywhere in the lineup—he had a chance to make a difference in that day's game. And more often than not, he did make a difference for Valley State when he was in the lineup, no matter where he batted in the order.

"It didn't make any difference [where Lyman hit in the lineup]," said Hiegert. "The difference with Lyman and other players is other kids were really more upset if you moved them in a position or in the lineup than him, because he was still playing. As far as he was concerned, he got a chance to play, and he'd make the best of it. So we moved him around a lot."

While earning his teammates' respect with his personality and work ethic, as well as the way he fought through his nagging groin injury, Lyman was also becoming one of Valley State's leaders. "He really did take a leadership role with that team. He loved them. He was a leader on the team. He was a guy that people looked to. He was respected, because he worked hard. He had the respect of his teammates for sure, and they in turn earned his respect," said Hiegert.

* * *

On April Fool's Day, the Matadors headed to Pomona for a doubleheader with Cal Poly, the one program that had consistently proven to be trouble for Hiegert's powerful squad in conference play in recent seasons. Lyman slammed a double into the right-field gap to score Valley State's lone run in the opener; no other runs were scored until the bottom of the ninth, when Cal Poly prevailed, 2–1, on a walk-off homer. Valley State got revenge in the second game, winning 7–1, as Lyman crushed a home run over the right-field fence as the Matadors pulled away in the fourth inning. The victory improved Valley State to 11–1 in league play.

Lyman continued his spring power surge on April 14, belting another homer to pace a sixteen-hit ambush as Valley State crushed UC-Riverside on the road, 7–3. On May 5, the Matadors crushed Cal Poly, 10–2, to claim the conference title. Lyman had three hits in the victory, including a perfectly executed bunt single up the third base line in the seventh inning, when Valley State scored three insurance runs to put the game away. Lyman and many of the Valley State regulars sat out the next game, a 4–0 victory.

"We won the conference that year. We had a good pitching staff," said Hiegert.

Valley State's regular season ended with a 37–19 record. The Matadors had nearly two weeks off from game action leading up to the West Regional, providing Lyman and his teammates a chance to rest up and prepare for a run at the national championship. This time around, Lyman didn't have to report to jail, as he had managed to stay on the straight and narrow, focusing on baseball and his academic studies since his initial brush with trouble.

Playing at home, Valley State swept four games, beating Puget Sound twice, as well as UC-Irvine and Chapman, to advance to the College Division World Series for the second time in three seasons. Lyman belted a homer in Valley State's second win over Puget Sound. Valley State went on to score twice in the top of the seventh against Chapman, taking a 4–3 lead, and then held them off the scoreboard the rest of the way to earn their trip to Springfield, Illinois.

* * *

In early June, just as the Matadors were preparing for the College Division World Series tournament in Springfield's Lanphier Park, the school's name officially changed from San Fernando Valley State to California State University, Northridge. The Matadors nickname for its athletic teams would endure.

"We won the Regional. We hosted the Regional again and won that," said Hiegert. "We went to Springfield, Illinois. They moved the Division II World Series from Springfield, Missouri, to Springfield, Illinois."

Lanphier Park was an old minor league park in Springfield with a quirky outfield setup—light towers in fair territory, stationed in various spots along the outfield. "We played at a place called Lanphier Field. It's an old minor league ballpark—it may still be in existence today—but it had light poles inside the outfield fence. The light poles had this little chain link fence around them. And it was right near train tracks," said Hiegert. "So it was a very, very distracting place to play outfield, because you had to run around a post to catch a ball in left field, and the same thing in center field. And these trains were going by all the time."

For Lyman and his teammates, playing the Lanphier Park outfield properly could very well mean the difference between winning and losing the national championship.

"The light towers in the outfield were in left-center field and right-center field. And around them was a chain-link mesh thing. So if you didn't know what you're doing in the outfield, you could tear yourself running into the thing, number one," Hiegert said. "Number two, if the ball beats you, it could rattle around out there like Fenway Park, and by the time a kid picks the ball up, somebody could have scored."

Fortunately for Valley State, one of the higher-seeded teams still in the mix, their left fielder was fully healthy and playing the best baseball of his entire college career. "We went back there a pretty highly seeded team," said Hiegert. "Lyman finally got healthy in the warmer weather. He was just tremendous towards the end of the year, and when we got to the World Series, he was playing outstanding."

Things got off to a promising start for the Matadors in their opening World Series contest against Southern Illinois Edwardsville, as they broke out to an early 4–0 advantage. After scoring an early run in the second and tallying two more in the fourth, Lyman gave Northridge its 4–0 cushion with a towering solo homer in the fifth. The Matadors held on for a 7–6 victory, and were one game closer to the national title.

The next matchup was against Florida Southern, the defending national champions and the favorites to win again. The Moccasins jumped out to a 5–0 advantage in the first three innings. And despite a run Lyman scored in the fourth after drawing a walk and an RBI double he had in the eighth, the Floridians stayed in control, going on to a 10–3 victory over the Californians.

Hiegert's club would have to work their way through the loser's bracket if they were to gain a rematch with Florida Southern for the championship. Another showdown loomed with Southern Illinois Edwardsville before they'd get another potential crack at the Moccasins.

The Matadors were superb in their second game against Southern Illinois Edwardsville, as lightning and thunderstorms threatened above throughout the elimination battle. As Bob LoPresti held Southern Illinois off the scoreboard the entire way, Lyman doubled in the first inning and then scored on an errant throw to first base. Bob Canfield came up next and crushed a two-run homer, giving the Matadors a 3–0 advantage. Lyman also contributed to Northridge's four-run second inning, slamming a single to score two more runs for a 7–0 lead. Three more runs followed in the fourth for a 10–0 advantage.

By the top of the fourth inning, lightning and rolling thunder was becoming a major concern. Tournament officials informed both Hiegert and Southern Illinois Edwardsville manager Roy Lee that the game would be replayed in its entirety if it had to be called because of weather before five full innings were played. From that point on, Northridge labored to speed the game up, while Southern Illinois Edwardsville slowed things down, attempting to stall their way into a scratched game and a fresh start. While Northridge's batters tried deliberately to make outs, the Southern Illinois Edwardsville players threw balls around in the dirt, trying to extend the game and their chances of a rainout.

Fortunately for Northridge, they made it through five innings, and the remainder of the game, without any more runs scored and without a rain shower. Along with his prowess at the plate, Lyman was stellar in the field, making a diving catch and a couple other tough plays in the challenging Lanphier outfield. He and Marty Friedman together killed multiple potential Southern Illinois Edwardsville rallies with their big catches and pinpoint relays. The Matadors' 10–0 blowout set up another showdown with Florida Southern—its second elimination game of the day.

"Lyman made a great catch in left field. He went around the post and made a couple circus plays. He made some great catches. Lyman and the other kid, Marty Friedman, did just an outstanding job cutting balls off," Hiegert said.

Lyman's two runs and two hits, his stellar play in the outfield, and his performances in some of the earlier contests of the World Series tournament had caught the eye of Roy Lee, the man who had founded the baseball program at Southern Illinois Edwardsville in 1967.

Starting with a limited budget and no scholarships, Lee had quickly built a program that would make eight straight NCAA playoff appearances, as well as three World Series trips, in the late 1960s and early 1970s. Lyman had done quite a bit to knock Lee's team out of the tournament, and the veteran coach was thoroughly impressed with the young left fielder.

"The coach at Southern Illinois, Roy Lee, he came up to me," Hiegert recalled. "He was well-known. He had been coaching for a long time. He came up to me after a game we had played. We had eliminated Southern Illinois. We had beaten them. But they had stuck around and watched the [championship round] games, and this guy came up to me."

"Coach, I don't know anything about your program. But those two kids in the outfield—especially the left fielder—are going to be major league players," Lee told Hiegert.

"Lyman was the left fielder he was talking about," Hiegert continued.

"That kid is going be a major league player," Lee said of Lyman. "He is the best player I've ever seen."

"Not too often does a coach come after you and say, 'That's one of the best players I've seen in my life.' He went on and on and on," said Hiegert. "I thought he had just had a normal game. He was marveled at Lyman."

* * *

The Matadors returned to action just a couple hours after beating Southern Illinois Edwardsville and picked up a critical 3–0 shutout victory over Florida Southern to stay alive. Jeff Cherry hurled a two-hit shutout for Valley State—the first time and only time all season Florida Southern's potent lineup was shut out. Following the game, the crowd—estimated at around 1,350 spectators—gave Cherry and the Matadors a standing ovation. The Northridge players were a single victory from a national championship as they went to sleep that Sunday night. The next day the Matadors would meet Florida Southern once again for the title.

They awoke to a hot, humid Midwestern Monday morning. It hadn't been particularly easy sleeping the night before, as the Southern Illinois Edwardsville players—the players they had just eliminated—stuck around and partied following their season-ending setback to the Matadors.

"We were in Springfield, Illinois, in June. It had to be a hundred-plus that day, and the humidity was awful," recalled coach Hiegert. "They put us up in a college, where the teams were staying. Normally in a World Series, when you get eliminated you go home. When we started the tournament, there were four teams that were staying in these dorms on this college campus, and the campus was closed. The kids had gone home [for summer vacation]. That's not a good environment. You don't want to have teams bumping into each other, but that's how it was. A couple of the teams we eliminated went home.

"The coach of the Southern Illinois team, Roy Lee, who had come over and told me Lyman was one of the best players he had ever seen play was one of the guys there [in the dorms]. This older guy had no control over his kids, and they were drinking all night and raising hell. Our kids were trying to sleep. It's humid. It's hot."

That Monday morning, the Northridge players conducted a brief batting session before going back to the dorms to relax for that night's championship clash with Florida Southern. "It's the day of the championship game. We took them out there in the early morning for batting practice, about nine or ten o'clock. Then we came back. We were playing a night game, so we had four hours to kill.

"I said, 'Get off your feet. Try to stay as cool as you can,'" Hiegert remembered.

As he relaxed in his room shortly after the workout, Hiegert got a knock on his door. "My door is knocking. It's Lyman and the center fielder, Friedman, and a couple other kids," Hiegert said. The Matador players had come to their coach with a thought: "Coach, can we have the baseballs?" Lyman questioned.

"Why?" Hiegert asked.

"We're going to put on a clinic for some of the neighborhood kids."

"Okay, that's a good idea," Hiegert told his players. "So I give them the ball bag. And I said, 'Don't be long. Don't stay out in the sun.'"

"No, we're just going to play with some neighborhood kids. We won't be long. It'll be good," Lyman reassured his coach.

"They spent two or three hours with these kids out in the park," said Hiegert. "They were all neighborhood kids, a lot of black and Hispanic kids."

A few hours later, it was time to head over to Lanphier Park for the game.

"We take the kids to the park to hit. And I asked Lyman, 'Where's the ball bag?'"

"Right here," Lyman exclaimed.

"There was not a ball left in it. There wasn't a baseball left," Hiegert said.

Incensed at Lyman and his teammates' perceived irresponsibility, Hiegert demanded an explanation. "What the hell? Where are the baseballs?" the coach asked.

"We gave them to the kids," Lyman replied softly.

"What do you mean? We have batting practice!"

"They needed them more than we do."

The Northridge players and coaches were left scrambling for balls to conduct batting and infield practice. "We were looking for baseballs just to have batting practice before the game started," said Hiegert. "They gave away the baseballs, but that's Lyman. It was his idea to do a little clinic, and it was his idea to have a little fun with these kids and then wind up giving them the baseballs. You can't fault him. This is the reality of Lyman."

Friedman led off the title game with a walk for the Matadors and promptly stole second base. He advanced to third on an error by Florida Southern's catcher, providing a chance for Lyman to drive in the game's first run. Lyman tagged a deep blast to center field. It wasn't deep enough to leave the park, but it was deep enough to score Friedman and give Northridge an early 1–0 edge. That was the lone bright spot for the Californians. Florida Southern tallied four runs in the second inning, while adding an insurance run in the top of the ninth. Florida Southern All-American ace Jay Smith was tremendous, striking out thirteen Northridge batters and holding the Matadors to just four hits in a 5–1 victory.

"We lost the championship game to Florida Southern, finishing second place," remembered Hiegert. "We got beaten in the championship game."

Despite the loss in the title showdown, it had been a banner series for Lyman—one that helped raise his stock as a potential pro prospect. One of just three players to hit .300 or better during the championship round, Lyman was named to the all-tournament squad. In four contests, Lyman had gone six for fifteen with a homer, two doubles, and five RBIs. Lyman also earned a spot on the All–West Coast College Division second team for his .300 hitting in 1972, and Hiegert was named District 8 coach of the year.

"In '72 he was an All-West player," coach Hiegert said of his star outfielder. "I think he was voted the most valuable player on our team that year."

* * *

On Wednesday, June 7—the day after the Cal State Northridge baseball squad returned home from Illinois—the annual major league baseball amateur draft was held in New York City. There was hope around the Valley State baseball program that Lyman would be drafted, but nobody knew for certain. The big question was whether he'd sign or return to the Matadors for the 1973 season.

Four clubs had actually packed up and gone home by the time the number 595 overall pick came around that day. It was the sixth pick of the twenty-sixth round. The Minnesota Twins were on the clock. The Twins, having been dethroned as American League West champions the previous season, had selected six pitchers, five catchers, five outfielders, four third basemen, three shortstops, and two first basemen among its first twenty-five picks that day.

This time around, the outfielder from Northridge was their guy. The Twins made Lyman their sixth outfield selection of the 1972 draft. At the time, he was just the eighth player from San Fernando Valley State to be selected in the MLB draft since its inception in 1965. He was just the third player under Hiegert—and the Matadors' first position player—selected by a big league club.

"Lyman, he had come into his own," Hiegert said. "He was technically a sophomore eligibility-wise. He had two more years at school. The key for me with him was he was ready to play [professionally]."

From his own perspective, Lyman hadn't been drafted nearly as high as he'd expected. And, in later years, he would express resentment at the many scouts and franchises who had overlooked him. While it's likely that some clubs shied away from selecting Lyman earlier in the draft because of some of the off-the-field issues he faced in college, other franchises simply didn't familiarize themselves with the California small-college standout.

"They heard I had a bad attitude," he once said. "They were wrong."[4]

"I guess they weren't too high on me," Lyman would say in another interview. "But sometimes I think scouts do an inefficient job. They rely too much on what other people say. Scouts don't have enough time to see what guys really want to play baseball."[5]

A few days after the Matadors returned home and Lyman was selected by the Twins, he and his mother requested that Hiegert visit them down in Vermont Square to discuss the possibility of his signing with Minnesota.

"When we got home from Illinois—it was about the second or third week of June—Lyman and his mother called me. He put his mother on the phone," Hiegert remembered.

"Do you have time to come here? I need to talk to you," said Annie Bostock to her son's coach.

"Absolutely. What's the matter?" Hiegert responded.

"Nothing. Lyman has been contacted by the Minnesota Twins. And he wants to sign. And I'd like you to help him with that."

"Sure, I'll be happy to do that," the coach said.

With that, Hiegert headed south to help Lyman and his mother with impending contract negotiations with the Twins. "So I went down to their house in downtown L.A.," he said.

* * *

Jesse Sandoval Flores was born in 1914 in Guadalajara, Mexico. A hard-throwing right-hander, Flores was signed as an amateur free agent by the Chicago Cubs in 1938, though it would be another four years before he would make his big league debut. Just the third Mexican American in history to play in the majors, and the first pitcher, Flores appeared in four games for the 1942 Cubs before being traded to the Philadelphia Athletics. He would go on to pitch five seasons in Philadelphia before getting run out of town following a 4–13 record with the Athletics in 1947. After pitching two seasons for San Diego in the Pacific Coast League, Flores made his final major league appearances for the Cleveland Indians in 1950 before hanging it up. By the early 1970s, Flores was one of approximately twenty-five full-time scouts for the Minnesota Twins, scouring ballfields all over the United States and Latin America for talent.

In one of those legendary tales only baseball scouts can tell, Flores had gone to assess another player at a prep tournament one day in the late 1960s when he happened upon a talented young Dutch pitcher named Bert Blyleven. Flores successfully recruited and signed Blyleven for the Twins in 1969, and by the time Flores showed up at the Bostock residence in Vermont Square in June 1972, Blyleven had moved on to Minnesota's major league club. Though the Twins organization had shown little formal interest in Lyman prior to drafting him, Flores had been watching him since his days at Manual Arts. Flores and his son, Jesse Jr., sat quietly in the bleachers of local parks and at Harvard Playground, where Manual Arts played its prep games, and they also watched Lyman's college games at Valley State and other games throughout Southern California. Though Jesse Flores Jr. did much of the observation work, when it came time to negotiate and finalize a deal, the old man was always directly involved.

"I didn't think any team would draft me and I had never even seen a scout from the Twins," Lyman would say a few years later.[6]

"The scout that signed Lyman, Jesse Flores was the guys' name," recalled Hiegert. "A really, really good scout. A good guy. His son was helping him. [Jesse] didn't get around to many games, but his kid would go out and give the list back to his dad to go out and OK the deal, and try to sign them."

Hiegert arrived in Los Angeles on a warm mid-June day as the Flores father and son were working to lock Lyman in as a new member of the Minnesota Twins organization.

"They had drafted Lyman low in the draft. And Jesse was talking to him," said Hiegert. "So Lyman said, 'Can we go outside?'"

There were few, if any, men in Lyman's life that he trusted more than Bob Hiegert. He knew his college coach would give him the straight story.

"The first time I entered negotiations to sign my first professional contract coach Hiegert came to my house and made sure I was not taken advantage of," Lyman said.[7]

From Hiegert's perspective, it was important that Lyman be compensated well enough by the Twins that he would be covered through the rest of the calendar year and into the following year. Lyman would have plenty of time to impress the Minnesota organization and move up the ranks of the Twins' minor league system, but he had to live and put food on the table in the coming months. A short season, likely in Single-A ball, might not have properly covered his financial needs through the winter. So adding some kind of signing bonus was an absolute must.

"I wanted to make sure that he had enough money from the Twins when he signed that it would get him through the summer—because that was going to be a short season—and get him through spring training the next year," Hiegert recalled.

Walking out into the backyard, Lyman wanted to hear his coach's thoughts about whether he should sign. "Lyman said, 'What do you think?'" Hiegert recalled. "I said, 'You're in a good position. Do you want to sign? You've got two more years of school. And you've got next year as being draftable again. And you've still got another year to bargain. And you're coming off a great year.'"

"I think I want to sign," Lyman told him.

"OK. Then let's go back in and tell them that, and see what kind of offer they've got for you," Hiegert responded.

Lyman's mother was on the fence. She was interested, of course, in seeing her only child follow his dreams and begin making money playing baseball. But she also wanted him to complete his education at Northridge. She also wanted him to avoid signing an unfavorable contract, which is why she solicited Hiegert's advice.

"I think she really wanted Lyman to sign, but she didn't want to be taken advantage of," said Hiegert. "When she called and talked to me with Lyman on the phone, they told me what money had been offered."

"'That's not a lot of money,'" Hiegert remembers replying. "'Let's get to the bottom to the thing with them. Throw away the progressive bonuses. You get the money up front, because that buys you time.' And she understood that."

Hiegert insisted that they ask the Minnesota organization to pay for Lyman's education if and when he wanted to return to Northridge for his degree. "You want your college education paid for when you come back, and you want to tell them that when you get done with the minor league system that they'll let you go back to college if you don't play winter baseball and want to finish your degree," Hiegert advised. "And [Lyman] said, 'I do.'"

Taking charge, Annie began to negotiate directly with Jesse Flores and his son, insisting that they cover the cost of his education and allow him to return to complete his studies at Northridge. "She hammered all that out with the scout. 'I want you to pay for his education, and I want him to come back to school and finish his degree. It's very important to him and me,'" Hiegert recalled. "It was good. She was on track with everything. She didn't care about all the details but scouts do. I knew what was going on with that, and it helped Lyman out."

An agreement was reached, and the paperwork was signed. With that, Lyman Bostock was a professional baseball player.

"Both of them [Lyman and his mother], they had the mindset that he really thought he had a chance to be a big league player. So that was a really good discussion when we were down there. That worked out great for him," said Hiegert. "I left and went home, and Lyman called me later and said he and his mom had agreed to him signing with the Twins, and off he went."

4

THE PATH TO THE BIG LEAGUES (1972–1974)

Success is a journey, not a destination. The doing is often more important than the outcome.—Arthur Ashe, professional tennis player[1]

Less than two weeks after his final college baseball game, Lyman Bostock began what would be a meteoric rise through the Minnesota Twins farm system over a two-and-a-half-year period. Lyman had given up a chance to become an All-American at Valley State in 1973, as well as a chance to be drafted significantly higher than he was following his second season playing for Bob Hiegert and the Matadors. But the Twins were an ideal fit at the time for a young outfielder trying to rapidly move up the ranks to the big leagues.

"I think had he played one more year in college, he probably would have been drafted higher. I don't know if he would have gotten into the right organization," said Hiegert. "The Twins were absolutely the right organization for him when he signed, because they had a very weak minor league system. Most of the impetus was on pitching and position players that had played a little bit.

"He got a chance to move up a little bit quicker, and he needed that. He needed an opportunity, and had he gotten tied into a bigger organization, he might have gotten stuck in the minor leagues, Double-A ball or Triple-A ball for a couple more years, and may not have had the opportunity he wound up having."[2]

Lyman's first stop on the minor league trail was Charlotte, North Carolina, where he joined the Charlotte Twins of the A-level Western Carolinas League. He made his professional debut on the evening of Saturday, June 17, 1972, in Spartanburg, South Carolina. Lyman was uncharacteristically nervous in the hours and minutes leading up to his first professional game, and it showed when he took the field. In four at bats in his debut against the Spartanburg Phillies, Lyman hit into a double play, struck out a pair of times, and flew out.

"I was awfully tight," Lyman would say after the game. "I couldn't argue on any pitch because I knew I couldn't swing and I just knew I was going to strike out."[3]

Despite the pair of strikeouts and his hitless offensive performance, what really depressed Lyman about his pro debut was that he misjudged the very first fly ball hit his way. Losing the ball in the lights, Lyman dropped it—marking the first time he'd dropped a fly ball in a game that he could recall.

"You might say I had a bad night," Lyman said afterward. "Dropping that fly ball was just like someone dying in my family. I just couldn't believe it. I've never dropped a fly ball before. Sure, I've messed up grounders, but never a fly ball."

Along with having to adjust to improved pitching as he moved from the small college level to the minor leagues, Lyman had to get used to playing night games, having played almost exclusively day games during his career at Valley State.

"I've faced some pretty good pitchers in college, but I'm sure I will see a lot more in this league," Lyman said. "Another thing I have to get adjusted to is playing ball under the lights. I played about five games at night in the World Series last week, but that's all. Valley State didn't have any lights so we played in the daylight."

The Western Carolinas League was a six-team circuit consisting of two clubs in North Carolina—Charlotte and Gastonia—and four teams from South Carolina—Spartanburg, Greenville, Anderson, and Greenwood. Most played at local high school or community stadiums, usually drawing a few hundred fans each night. The Twins drew a remarkably scant crowd of approximately 150 spectators a night at Griffith Park. With so few fans watching him, Lyman didn't have to worry too much about high expectations from the home crowd or people booing him on the road.

Lyman went on to appear in fifty-seven games for Charlotte, showing impressive early plate discipline and on-base potential with a .294 batting average, ranking second on the team among those with at least a hundred at bats. Only two members of the '72 Charlotte Twins—Lyman and Rob Wilfong—would make it to the big leagues in the coming years. Wilfong's .295 average was the only one among Charlotte regulars to best Lyman's .294 clip. In addition, Lyman took advantage of marginal low-level minor league pitching by drawing a walk between every fifth and sixth time he came to the plate—the best walks per plate appearances average of his professional career.

The Charlotte Twins were a pretty bad ball club for the most part, finishing with an overall season record of 50–79. But most of those losses came in the first half of the season, when Lyman was still clubbing away as an All-West performer back at Northridge. The Golden State newcomer gave the Twins a lift with his bat, as well as with his hustle on the base paths and in the outfield, upon his arrival in Charlotte.

On July 6—the same day the big club in Minneapolis named Frank Quilici its new manager—Lyman got the game-winning hit for Charlotte in a 3–2 triumph over the Greenwood Braves, drilling a two-out, opposite-field liner to left field in the seventh inning. Four nights later, Bostock helped the Twins sweep a doubleheader over the Gastonia Pirates in front of former Pittsburgh manager Danny Murtaugh, who by then had become a scout for the Pirates.

The skipper of the 1960 and 1971 World Series champions must have been impressed with Bostock's bases-clearing double in the third inning, which drove in three runs in an eventual 10–1 blowout. In the second game of the doubleheader, Lyman's bunt single in the fourth inning preceded a three-run homer as the Twins won again, 4–3.

As Charlotte climbed to the top of its division for the second half of the season, Lyman kept on hustling and making things happen on the bases. On July 16, he scored the winning run in a 7–6 triumph over Greenwood. The game-winning run completed a four-hit day with two runs scored for the new Twins outfielder.

The following night, July 17, Lyman batted cleanup for Charlotte in its contest at Spartanburg. He doubled in the first inning, bringing home the game's first run, and then he scored himself, giving the Twins a 2–0 advantage. With the score tied 3–3 in the top of the ninth, Charlotte broke through with a pair of back-to-back doubles, giving the Twins a 4–3 advantage. Lyman then singled home another Charlotte run, completing a two-for-four game with two runs scored and two RBIs, as the Twins claimed a 5–3 victory.

While it was generally a very positive time for Lyman as he proved both to himself and his new organization that he could perform at the professional level, it wasn't all perfect. On July 23, he dropped another fly ball in center field that led to an unearned run in a game Charlotte wound up losing, 3–2. It was a continuing process for Lyman to learn the outfield at the professional level—developing the necessary skill and confidence to know when to go for the big play, when to stay back and be a little more conservative, how to play certain batters, and how to use depth perception to judge the flight of the ball against the backdrop of the sky and the seats around home plate.

Charlotte manager Bob Sadowski, who had played in nearly two hundred big league games as a utility infielder and outfielder with four different clubs from 1960 to 1963, gave Lyman a chance to work at all three outfield positions. In August, the organization provided Lyman, who had spent many of his early games playing center field and occasionally left field, an opportunity to see what he could do in right field, and he proved himself a versatile corner outfielder.

The Twins were holding out a winning record at 18–15 by August 5, just a half game out of second place in the second half standings. But by the final week of the season in late August, Charlotte was battling to stay out of the basement. Lyman saw sparse action in August, working in a platoon with a variety of other young Charlotte outfielders trying to prove themselves as pro ballplayers. Lyman's promotion to Double-A the following season was a sure thing—which couldn't be said for many of his Charlotte teammates—so Sadowski didn't wish to wear out the young professional newcomer.

Only 133 fans reportedly came out to Griffith Park on August 11, a Friday night doubleheader, to see the Twins split a pair of games with Greenwood. On August 18, the crowd at Legion Stadium in Greenwood was treated to the Clown Prince of Baseball, Max Patkin, who drew laughs from the seven hundred or so spectators in attendance, as well as the players, with his comedic skits and playful antics. Lyman didn't take the field that night; the club rested him after his busy spring and summer as Charlotte took a 5–2 loss to Greenwood.

The Twins won on August 24 over the Gastonia Pirates, 4–2, in the first game of the doubleheader to avoid last place in the league for the second half of the season. The club played a second game that Friday night and then finished out the next day with what turned out to be the organization's final game ever at Griffith Park in Charlotte. Barely a hundred spectators were there to witness it.

Lyman finished fifteenth in the Western Carolinas League in hitting that summer with his .294 clip. Two of his stats ranked in the top ten in the league: his on-base percentage (.419) and his on-base percentage plus slugging percentage (.804). All three stats ranked second on the Charlotte club. Despite his solid numbers, Lyman hadn't played in enough games to be listed on the Western Carolinas League All-Star team, voted on by the circuit's managers, general managers, and local beat reporters.

On September 15, 1972, the Twins announced that they were dropping both minor league franchises in Charlotte, ending a thirty-six-year relationship with North Carolina's largest town.

"We put some great minor league teams in Charlotte, but we finally moved the franchise to Orlando in 1973 because we didn't draw anybody," said George Brophy, a former official in the Twins system.[4]

* * *

During the winter of 1972, before he reported to Orlando for his second professional season, Lyman played semipro ball back home in Los Angeles. Lyman's team, named the Pittsburgh Rookies, featured a talented high school senior outfielder from Compton's Dominguez High School who would eventually become one of his future teammates in the pro ranks.

"I used to tell [Lyman] I wanted to play pro ball, and he knew because of how hard I was working," said Kenny Landreaux.[5]

Prior to Rookies games at Ross Snyder Park, an eleven-acre recreational facility along East Forty-First Street in inner-city Los Angeles, Lyman and Kenny would warm up together, throwing back and forth along one of the outfield lines. Kenny had known about Lyman for several years, since Lyman's stellar senior year at Manual Arts. He had played pickup ballgames around Los Angeles with Lyman during his college days and now imagined playing with him one day in the big leagues.

With Landreaux manning left field and Lyman playing center, the Rookies were one of the more talented semipro winter clubs in Los Angeles that off-season.

"It was extra incentive for me to think that maybe someday I might be on the same team with him again," said Landreaux. "He'd be in center, and I'd be in left."

The team was coached by Chet Brewer, who had played professional baseball for twenty-four years all over North America, South America, and Asia. Brewer, a right-handed pitcher with an excellent overhand curveball, was playing for the Kansas City Monarchs when Lyman's father broke into professional baseball in the early 1940s. By that time, Brewer had been playing professionally for fifteen years, since the mid-1920s. After playing in Mexico in 1944, Brewer briefly managed Jackie Robinson in a California winter league in 1945, just before Robinson made his start in the Brooklyn Dodgers organization. More than a quarter century after Brewer had seen greatness in Robinson, the lifelong baseball man recognized similar elite talent in Lyman. He implored Landreaux to learn from Lyman—to observe and emulate him.

"Chet Brewer, he used to tell me, 'You watch that guy,'" said Landreaux, pointing at Lyman. "He's going to be a major league ball player someday."

The longtime Negro League pitcher saw many similarities between Lyman and the elder Bostock in the way they carried themselves both on and off the field.

"Chet said he saw something in me like my father," Lyman would say years later. "They said [my father] could run and hit and field. And he was a gentleman. They said I had never heard him swear. I told them I swear all the time—but only on the field."[6]

In addition to playing semipro ball in Los Angeles that winter, Lyman also participated in an alumni exhibition back at Northridge, collecting two hits in three at bats and scoring a run in a 7–6 win over the Matadors' undergraduate squad. It was always important for Lyman, in those early days as an alumnus and especially in later years, to make his way back to Northridge, where Bob Hiegert had given him a tremendous opportunity that was changing his life.

"Lyman would come back in the off-season," Hiegert recalled. "He was finishing up his degree, as was his wife. He would come back and work out with us. I stayed pretty close with him at that time. He'd come back when he was in the big leagues.

"We had an alumni game each year, and he made it a point to come back to that. Whenever he had any time, he'd be out to practice. He'd talk to the kids."

After a productive and healthy off-season in Los Angeles, Lyman headed to Florida at the end of February, ready to make his next move on the path to the majors. The Orlando Twins, which had been a Single-A franchise in 1972 in the Minnesota farm system, became both the organization's new Double-A team for the 1973 season and the next rung in Lyman's ladder to the majors. Playing home games at Tinker Field, the Twins' spring training stadium in downtown Orlando, adjacent to the Tangerine Bowl, would help prepare Lyman for days to come.

Harry Warner, who had guided the Charlotte Hornets in 1970 and 1971 before taking the reins of Minnesota's Triple-A team in Tacoma in 1972, was named the manager of the Orlando Twins for the 1973 season. Warner, like Lyman, had been a left-handed hitter and right-handed thrower during his own playing days as a first baseman in the Washington Senators system in the late 1950s and early 1960s. Though he never made it higher than Double-A as a player, Warner impressed owner Calvin Griffith with his baseball acumen. Warner was an affable and popular manager with his players. His easygoing style meshed well with Lyman, who by that point had his sights set directly on Metropolitan Stadium and the American League.

* * *

The day before Orlando opened its 1973 Southern League schedule, Lyman was in the batting cages at Tinker Field, loosening up. After one particularly hard cut, he felt a burning sensation just below his armpit. The second-year pro had suffered a cracked rib, which would force him into a significant layoff.

Lyman was unable to join the Orlando club as an active player that April, as the cracked rib made following through on his swing impossible without searing pain throughout the right side of his body. It was a slow, meticulous process returning to where he could take swings comfortably and smoothly, like before.

Orlando got off to a respectable start in the early spring as Lyman recovered throughout April and May. The Twins were 5–4 on April 23, and they continued to hover just over .500 for much of Lyman's absence, sitting at 15–13 in mid-May. But in the days immediately preceding Lyman's return to action, Orlando fell apart, dropping fifteen out of their next eighteen games. By June 1 they sat at 18–28, in last place in the Southern League's Eastern Division.

Orlando's late-May swoon killed the club's chances of competing for a Southern League title upon Lyman's return, although the Twins showed immediate improvement once the second-year pro entered the lineup. An everyday starter by early June, Lyman gave the club a spark, getting on base, stealing, scoring runs, and playing solid defense. On June 11, shortly after returning to the lineup, Lyman belted two home runs, stroked a double, and scored three runs in a game in Asheville. Showing solid speed, he finished second on the Orlando squad with nineteen stolen bases. As was the case during his college days, Lyman was free to take off for second most any time after reaching first base. His aggressive leads off first base kept pitchers honest, regularly forcing them to throw over to keep him closer.

"Base running-wise, he had great instincts on the bases. He pretty much had a green light, but we sent him a lot more than other kids, because he was a good base runner," said college coach Bob Hiegert.

Bob Willis, Orlando's general manager, would later say that Bostock was farther along at that same point in his career than Rod Carew had been when he played in Orlando back in 1965. "Bostock was better than Carew, and we had them both at Orlando," Willis said.[7]

Although Lyman batted a healthy .313 for the Orlando Twins in eighty-five games following his cracked rib in early April, he couldn't help the club make a move for the Southern League title. Nor was he selected for the Southern League Eastern Division All-Star team that summer. The Twins were on the brink of reaching the .500 mark in mid-August but would finish 65–70, in last place in the Eastern Division. But Lyman finished the season strong, recording four hits and scoring five runs in an August 28 doubleheader in Asheville.

Though it hadn't been a very successful season for Orlando as a franchise, Lyman hadn't done anything but raise his stock in the eyes of the Minnesota top brass. He had overcome a major injury—and approximately two months on the shelf—to lead the Orlando Twins in both batting average and on-base percentage. Lyman was the only .300 hitter on the Orlando club among those with more than one at bat, and he added a .419 on-base percentage. He also finished third on the Twins in doubles, with eighteen, despite having two hundred fewer at bats than the two Orlando players who were ahead of him. Lyman's five homers and thirty-seven

RBIs were nothing to write home about, but he played a solid outfield, producing a .970 fielding percentage with 160 putouts and four assists against just five errors.

In the summer of 2013, the *Birmingham News* asked its readers to vote for an all-time team to mark the fiftieth season of the Southern League. Although Lyman didn't receive enough votes to join the likes of Reggie Jackson, Bo Jackson, and Jose Canseco in the first-team all-time Southern League outfield, he was listed among the top thirty outfielders in the circuit's first half century thanks to his solid efforts with Orlando in the summer of 1973.

Having proven himself as a productive and hard-nosed player at the challenging Double-A level, Lyman was set to make another move on his upward trajectory toward the majors.

* * *

On January 31, 1974, Lyman Bostock married Yuovene Brooks in a small ceremony back in Los Angeles. Since the day Yuovene caught Lyman's eye at Northridge in the late summer of 1968, she had been by his side. It didn't take Lyman long to realize that she was the one for him. She stood by him during his brush with trouble in college and was now following him on his quest to make the majors. Though she ran a tight ship, Yuovene did nothing but help Lyman, giving him much-needed encouragement and stability as he sought to make it big on the baseball diamond.

"She ruled the house. She got him under control, and channeled a lot of his energy into very positive things. Great lady," said Bob Hiegert of Lyman's wife.

Heading into the spring of 1974, Lyman was set to join Minnesota's top minor league franchise, the Triple-A Tacoma Twins of the Pacific Coast League (PCL). By the time Lyman was ready to make his assault on the PCL, the Tacoma franchise was managed by Cal Ermer, another baseball lifer whose own big league career evokes that of Archibald "Moonlight" Graham, made famous by the movie *Field of Dreams*. Like Graham, Ermer played in just one game in the major leagues—on Friday, September 26, 1947. It was the last weekend in another second-division season for Clark Griffith's woeful Washington Senators. On this particular day, the Senators hosted the Philadelphia Athletics for a doubleheader at Griffith Stadium. Starting at second base for the Senators in the second game of the doubleheader, Ermer reached base on an error in the bottom of the second inning, grounded into an inning-ending double play in the fourth inning, and grounded into a fielder's choice in the seventh inning of Washington's 4–3 victory.

Though he would play in the minor leagues from 1942 to 1951, excluding three years of military service in World War II, that late September day in 1947 proved to be Ermer's only chance to play in the big leagues. Despite his lack of star talent on the field, however, Ermer earned Minor League Manager of the Year in 1958 from *Sporting News* after leading the Birmingham Barons to a Southern League championship.

On June 9, 1967, Ermer got his shot at managing in the major leagues when Calvin Griffith hired him to lead his Minnesota Twins through a demanding American League pennant race. Ermer guided Harmon Killebrew, Rod Carew, Tony Oliva, Dean Chance, Jim Kaat, and the rest of the '67 Twins through one of the more legendary pennant races in American League history, with four teams—Minnesota, Boston, Chicago, and Detroit—all within three games of first place from August 19 through the final weekend of the regular season.

Ermer and the Twins came up short to the "Impossible Dream" Boston Red Sox that final weekend at Fenway Park, and then a 79–83, seventh-place finish in 1968 brought an end to Ermer's major league managerial career. He would return to scouting work and serve as an assistant coach for the Milwaukee Brewers' first three seasons from 1970 to 1972 before making his way to Tacoma in 1974, hopeful for another crack at managing in the big leagues.

Ermer was a low-key manager who knew how to get the most out of guys like Lyman. He played to their strengths, helped them relax, and avoided unnecessary discipline. He gave them the confidence to play without burdening them with nonsense.

"You have to get the players in the mood to do their best every night," Ermer said on his biography page in the Twins' official team program.

Lyman rewarded his manager's wisdom with his finest season yet in 1974.

* * *

The Pacific Coast League was a challenging circuit full of past and future big leaguers. Against such stiff competition, Lyman blossomed into a player ready for prime time. Despite the fact that Tacoma had the smallest population in the Pacific Coast League—much smaller than

THE PATH TO THE BIG LEAGUES (1972–1974)

league rivals such as Phoenix, Honolulu, and Tucson—the locals came out to see Lyman and the Tacoma Twins in 1974. The club drew nearly 175,000 fans to the 8,002-seat Cheney Stadium, the third-highest attendance among the PCL's eight franchises.

Cheney Stadium featured an interesting gimmick for players and spectators: a billboard from the city's *News-Tribune* newspaper offered a "$5,000 Hole." Any player who could hit a ball into a hole drawn onto a mitt on the *News-Tribune* billboard along the outfield wall would win $2,500, with a lucky fan in attendance also winning $2,500. While that spring and summer Lyman wasn't able to win $2,500 for himself or any of the fans, he would improve his skills across the board in Tacoma.

For one dollar, Tacoma fans could join the T-Twins Boosters, which granted them the privilege of purchasing seats on the team's chartered plane and joining the ball club on certain road trips. Hundreds of Twins fans joined the T-Twins Boosters, and several accompanied Lyman and his teammates on some of the more exotic trips throughout the PCL, including much-anticipated trips to Honolulu for the extended series the Twins played against the Hawaii Islanders. Lyman gave those T-Twins Boosters who made the trip with the club to Honolulu in mid-April something to cheer about.

On April 16, he led off a game with a long home run deep over the right-field fence of the biggest ballpark in the entire league, and finished the game three for five as Tacoma knocked off Hawaii, 4–2.

In contrast, Sacramento played in the smallest ballpark in the Pacific Coast League. Sacramento's park, in fact, was one of the tiniest ballparks you'd find anywhere in professional baseball at any point in history. Hughes Stadium, a high school football field with a track around it, had been converted for use as a baseball stadium by the Sacramento Solons. It was a scant 261 feet down the left-field line. And, predictably, balls sailed with regularity out of the tiny yard. Five games in, there had already been forty-one homers hit in the stadium.

Tacoma rolled into Sacramento on April 21, after the first Hawaii trip of the season, and knocked seven homers out of the tiny park on its way to a 16–9 blowout win. Lyman went a perfect five for five, taking advantage of the small dimensions for an opposite-field homer and finishing the day with four RBIs.

On Thursday, May 9, the Minnesota Twins came to Tacoma for the annual game with their top minor league club. With near-freezing eve-

Lyman enjoyed a stellar 1974 season at the Triple-A level with the Tacoma Twins, where he led the team in hitting (.333), stolen bases (13), and outfield putouts (242) on his way to the Pacific Coast League All-Star Game. (Tacoma Twins trademarks and copyrights used with permission; all rights reserved.)

ning temperatures swirling throughout the Pacific Northwest, the park was less than half full, with approximately three thousand spectators. Despite a first-inning homer by Minnesota legend Harmon Killebrew, Tacoma taught the big leaguers a lesson, taking a 9–3 victory.

Lyman continued to hit over .300 throughout the spring, and he found opportunities to produce in key moments. On May 19, Lyman ripped a two-out, bases-loaded double in the ninth inning, helping lead Tacoma to a 6–5 triumph over the Phoenix Giants in the first game of a doubleheader. Nearly two weeks later, on May 31, Lyman's sacrifice fly in the third inning brought home what turned out to be the winning run in a 4–2 victory over Albuquerque.

In early June, Twins owner Calvin Griffith addressed rumors that he might be shopping his club around when the franchise's lease with Minneapolis expired after the 1975 season. Cold weather and a sluggish start to the 1974 season had brought just 130,000 fans to the first twenty-two home games at Metropolitan Stadium. Despite the team's natural concerns about attendance figures, Griffith said he had no intention of leaving Minneapolis.

Looking at the team in Tacoma, he saw several players, including Lyman, Craig Kusick, and Sergio Ferrer, who would soon be playing in the majors. "We're very optimistic about the future," Griffith said. "We've got a lot of good young players."[8]

During his time in Tacoma, Lyman became good friends with Ferrer, a five foot seven shortstop from Puerto Rico who had spent the previous three years moving up the Los Angeles Dodgers farm system before being traded into the Twins organization. "I would call him 'Lee-mone' and he'd call me 'Cooch,'" Ferrer would recall a couple years later.[9]

Ferrer saw firsthand how much pride Lyman took in his ball-playing ability. "He was a good hitter, and he was proud of it," Ferrer said of his Tacoma teammate.

In an effort to instill confidence in himself as he prepared to step up to the plate or as he was running to the outfield, Lyman would repeat a phrase over and over. "'I can do it,' he'd say. 'I know I can,'" recalled Ferrer. "He was very good to me when I was with the Twins. 'Here, take my bat,' he'd say. 'It'll help you.'"

Tacoma was in the thick of the race in the PCL's Western Division as June arrived. At 29–23 following a June 5 doubleheader split against Sacramento, the Twins were just a game back of first-place Spokane.

Over the next month, Tacoma and Spokane stayed within a couple of games of each other, as Lyman continued to hit all over the league's parks. He had one of the more powerful games of his third minor league season back in Sacramento on Saturday, June 8, crushing two home runs, including a fifth-inning grand slam, and six RBIs as Tacoma defeated the Solons, 9–5. Lyman's tremendous play against the Sacramento club continued back in Tacoma two weeks later, as he scored three of the Twins' five runs in a 5–0 shutout victory.

On July 6, Lyman received his just due for a fantastic season to that point. He was selected as one of the Western Division outfielders for the Pacific Coast League All-Star Game, which would be held a couple weeks later at his home park in Tacoma. The next day, the Twins entered a tie for first with Spokane following a 9–3 win over Salt Lake City, as Lyman scored the go-ahead run in the fourth inning.

A week later, on July 14, Lyman stepped up to the plate in the bottom of the eighth inning of a 2–2 game with the bases loaded. It was the first game of a Sunday afternoon doubleheader in Tacoma against Albuquerque. Facing future Los Angeles Dodger Stan Wall, Lyman patiently worked the count and drew a walk, forcing in the winning run in a 3–2 Twins triumph.

The best of the Pacific Coast League converged in Tacoma on July 16, providing Lyman a chance to play his first professional All-Star Game in front of the home crowd at Cheney Stadium. Unfortunately, it was a rainy midsummer evening in the Pacific Northwest, and fewer than two thousand fans came out to see a game that would ultimately be called due to the driving rain after the sixth inning, following a little more than an hour and a half of action. Charlie Manuel, who thirty-five years later would lead the Philadelphia Phillies to a World Series title as manager, belted a solo homer in the first inning, followed by a two-run single by Bruce Bochte and a two-run blast by Rudy Meoli. The Eastern Division squad went on to an 8–1 blowout win. Lyman didn't factor into the game statistically, as the Western Division squad mustered just two hits.

Following the All-Star Game, Lyman's heroics continued in Tucson, as he belted a two-run homer in the top of the tenth inning of a 2–2 game to lead Tacoma to an eventual 4–3 triumph on July 17. His extra-inning blast was the culmination of a three-hit, two-run performance.

"I wasn't tired, but made just one bad pitch and that was that," said Tucson's losing pitcher Bill Parsons afterward.[10]

Tacoma and Spokane continued to battle neck and neck at the top of the PCL's Western Division heading into the dog days of August. The clubs met in a showdown of the division's top two teams. The first took place in Spokane, with Lyman homering in the first inning to give Tacoma the lead in a game they ultimately won, 9–6. Spokane and Tacoma met again August 13 in Cheney Stadium. The Twins broke out to a 3–0 lead, which was padded by Lyman's RBI single in the seventh. Spokane scored three times in the eighth inning, but Lyman's hit held up, as the Twins won 4–3 to pull within a game of first place with a 66–55 record.

As August wore on, however, Spokane slowly opened up a slight margin, taking a lead of three and a half games by the evening of Thursday, August 29. The season was nearly over, and Spokane could clinch the Western Division with a victory. But Lyman ripped a bases-loaded single for a 1–0 Tacoma win that kept the Twins' pennant hopes alive for at least one more day. In the end, however, Tacoma couldn't catch up. The Twins finished 75–66, just 2.5 games behind Spokane in the Western

Lyman rose quickly through the Minnesota Twins farm system, as the talented young outfielder needed just two and a half minor league seasons before he was ready to break into the big leagues. By the spring of 1975, Lyman was a starting outfielder for the Twins. (Photo used with permission of Minnesota Twins Baseball Club.)

Division. Spokane's Indians would go on to sweep a three-game championship series from Albuquerque to claim the Pacific Coast League's title that summer.

When the 1974 season was all said and done, Lyman led the Tacoma Twins in hits (158), batting average (.333), and stolen bases (13). He was third on the squad in games played (128), at bats (475), and doubles (17); fourth in runs (73); and sixth on the squad in RBIs (56). His .333 batting clip was good enough for third in the PCL, and his spot on the Western Division All-Star side that summer had been well-deserved.

On Friday, October 25, Lyman was one of eight players selected from Minnesota's minor league system for the big league club's expanded forty-man winter roster. This protected him from being snatched up during the off-season by another team and set the stage for him to crack the majors for real the following spring. After three successful seasons progressing up the ranks in Minnesota's system, school was about to be out for Lyman Bostock. All signs pointed to Lyman being considered seriously for a job in Minnesota's outfield once spring training arrived.

"My record wasn't that bad in the minors," Lyman would say a couple years later. "I hit .294, .313, and .333."[11]

"Outfielder Lyman Bostock is expected to make the club in 1975 from the Twins' Tacoma farm club," said Brent Kallestad of the Associated Press. "Bostock hit .330 in the Pacific Coast League and is called an exceptional defensive player and base runner by Twins officials."

"Based on his 1974 performance and the Minnesota scouting reports, Bostock figures to be a strong candidate to earn a spot on the Twins' roster next spring," added the *Valley News* of Van Nuys, California, which had covered Lyman since his college days.

"We need a little help," Calvin Griffith said in early October. "We've got an idea of what we need and we also expect some help from our farm system."[12]

5

A ROOKIE'S JOURNEY (1975)

> Baseball gives every American boy a chance to excel. Not just to be as good as someone else but to be better than someone else. This is the nature of man and the name of the game.—Ted Williams, outfielder, Boston Red Sox[1]

During the winter months between the 1974 and 1975 American baseball seasons, Lyman headed down to Venezuela, where he played with the Tigres de Aragua of the Venezuelan League. It was an opportunity to stay sharp in the months preceding one of the most important springs of his young life—where, in the Florida sunshine, he would attempt to earn a starting outfield spot with the Minnesota Twins.

Playing in Venezuela not only provided Lyman an opportunity to develop his skills against top-flight competition but also gave him a unique chance to see firsthand the passion that baseball evokes in that part of the world. He took time for the numerous young boys who frequented the ballpark, giving them hitting tips and attempting to converse with them in their native tongue.

"Everybody liked Lyman, especially the kids," said future big league infielder Doug Flynn, a winter-league teammate. "When we were in Venezuela, he'd always have time for them, talking baseball to them and trying to learn their language."[2]

Aided in large part by Lyman's bat and glove in the outfield, the Tigres de Aragua would win the Venezuelan League title in 1974–1975. But Lyman's time in South America wasn't entirely without drama.

One lazy afternoon, Lyman and four teammates—Flynn, Bill Campbell, Duane Kuiper, and Adrian Garrett—were riding down a country road, heading toward the small ballpark near town where the team played its games. Suddenly, they were run off the main path by a strange man speeding by in a green truck. A dust cloud billowed in the dry South American air as Flynn skidded off the road and swerved his way back, staying in control of the vehicle.

"From out of nowhere, this guy in a green truck comes up from behind and forces me off the road," Flynn would say later. "We wondered what was on his mind, but we kept going."[3]

Momentarily shaken, they players laughed off the incident and were continuing down the rural road when they were approached a second time by the man in the green truck. "A while later, this same guy in the green truck comes along again and drives me off the road a second time. I figured he either knew one of us, or else he was just looking for trouble."

Angered, Lyman and the other young players began to scream and yell obscenities at the crazy driver. "I caught up with him and we all yelled at him, wondering what the devil he was trying to do. We gave him a pretty good going over from the car," Flynn recalled.

But the travelers wound up biting off a little more than they could chew.

"Suddenly, without giving us any warning, this guy reaches down to the floor of his truck and comes up with a gun. It looked like a Lugar or something like that. And all the guys in our car, myself included, hit the floor when he stuck the gun out of the window and aimed it at us."

The episode stunned and frightened Lyman and his teammates, though they later were able to make light of their brush with an early death on a Venezuelan back road.

"We got out of there in a hurry. All of us were pretty scared," Flynn said. "Later, we talked about it a lot and wondered what made the guy do what he did.

"Lyman always kidded me about it afterwards. He'd say, 'Doug, there's a guy outside in a green truck looking for you.'"

Madman shooters left aside, Lyman was a young man on a mission when he reported to Minnesota's spring training complex in Orlando on Friday, February 28, 1975. Following a rapid ascent through the Twins' minor league system over the prior three seasons and coming off a successful winter session in South America, he knew he wasn't arriving in

Florida for a cup of coffee. A job was open in manager Frank Quilici's outfield, and he intended to earn it.

While Lyman had some stiff competition in spring training from the likes of Steve Braun, who came into the 1975 season with a .277 lifetime average, and Steve Brye, who hit .283 in a career-high 135 games in 1974 while leading all American League outfielders with a .9968 fielding percentage. Minnesota's 1975 preseason media guide, released to sportswriters and other members of the press that spring, reflected the club's optimism about Lyman's potential to stick with the big team:

"Lyman Bostock comes into his first big league training camp with a certainty of jumping with both feet into the outfield competition," said the guide. "A speedster who can hit one out occasionally, Bostock made remarkable improvement defensively after being switched to centerfield in midseason last year by Tacoma manager Cal Ermer.

"Although not selected until the 26th round of the free agent draft of June, 1972, Bostock's rapid progress as a pro more than bears out the confidence expressed in him by scout Jesse Flores, who'd followed him patiently since his days as Los Angeles' Manual Arts High School. Scouting reports from his play with the Aragua Tigers of the Venezuelan League last winter indicate that Lyman continues to progress, in fact at an accelerated rate."

Things couldn't have possibly gotten off to a better start for the ambitious newcomer: leading off the spring opener, Lyman belted a letter-high fastball over Tinker Field's right-field fence off Detroit Tigers starter Tom Walker. Lyman's leadoff homer unleashed a floodgate of power in a 13–4 rout. The next day, Lyman doubled in the ninth inning as the Twins beat the Tigers again, 5–0, in Lakeland.

He kept on hitting, rapping a double in the seventh inning of a March 14 tilt with the Montreal Expos. Two days later, Lyman had three hits against the Red Sox in a 5–1 Minnesota win in Orlando. Showing off his ever-increasing versatility, Lyman led off that particular game with a perfectly executed bunt single, and he later scored the winning run.

By the time March 18 rolled around, Lyman had done enough to earn strong consideration for a place not just on the big league club but in the Twins starting lineup. "I like rookie Lyman Bostock in center field," Calvin Griffith said in mid-March.[4]

Back in Minnesota, members of the grounds crew were working feverishly to prepare Metropolitan Stadium for its annual late winter conversion from frozen wasteland to big league ballfield in time for the April 15 Twins season opener.

"The sins of an old season are under the ice," wrote Joe Soucheray of the *Minneapolis Tribune*. "A splotch of oil, a dirty penny, discarded rolls of football film. The purples and yellow from the Vikings end zones are melting and running together like spilled soup along the third base path."

Much work had to be done, including draining the park of excess moisture from the winter snows, cleaning seats, reconfiguring the letters and numbers on the scoreboard from football to baseball, and recreating a pitcher's mound and infield through the delivery of truckloads of soil.

Lyman was hitting .342 through sixteen Twins spring training games, serving as a catalyst atop the lineup. But he was about to have a setback that set the tone for his rookie year in the big leagues. Playing in West Palm Beach against the Atlanta Braves, Lyman made an aggressive effort on a deep fly ball early in the game. He made an excellent catch but broke the index finger on his throwing hand in the process, limiting him for the remainder of the spring. That was the bad news. The good news was that the solid average he posted through the midway point of spring training earned Lyman a starting job in the Twins outfield come April.

"Bostock will be our center fielder," Griffith said in late March, a few days after Lyman's finger injury.[5]

Lyman, whom his teammates had started calling "Bos," was demonstrating the ability to hit to all fields, create havoc along the base paths, and serve as a youthful presence in a locker room filled with veterans.

"When he got a chance to play in the big leagues, he did a great job and took advantage of the skills he had," said college coach Bob Hiegert. "He had a good first couple of years [in the minors], and then he stuck with the Twins."

Hungry and cocky, Lyman was eager to prove himself with the Twins as the 1975 season approached. A chatty but friendly addition to the Minnesota clubhouse, everyone knew when Lyman was near because they could hear him talking about something.

"He was a young kid with a lot of talent," recalled Twins teammate Eric Soderholm. "He was cocky and expressed his views. He reminded me of a Muhammad Ali of baseball. He was loud, but he could back it up on the field."[6]

His sense of humor would keep his teammates, and the club's executives, on their toes. Once, when the Minnesota executives announced that they were painting the left-field fence instead of putting up protective padding, Lyman asked, "Is it soft green paint?"[7]

Minnesota didn't need their twenty-four-year-old rookie outfielder hitting home runs. They needed him on the bases, scoring runs, and making plays in center field. "I can pull the ball and hit home runs, but I'm not really a home run hitter. Not yet, at least," Lyman said just prior to opening day.[8]

As the Twins headed to Texas for their opening series of the season against the Rangers, Lyman was Minnesota's lone rookie starter. When asked what his thoughts were about his big league debut, he had one word: "Win."

* * *

The Texas Rangers and Minnesota Twins opened the 1975 baseball season on April 8 in front of a solid crowd of nearly twenty-nine thousand fans at Arlington Stadium. Batting second, Lyman stood in the on-deck circle, twirling his bat and focusing intently on the first big league pitcher he would face: Ferguson Jenkins, Rangers ace and one of baseball's more dominant pitchers over the prior decade. Lyman had come quite a long way from the wiry kid who climbed aboard a Greyhound bus with his mother seventeen years earlier for the golden land of California and an opportunity to live out his dreams. Now here he was, in the major leagues, preparing to face one of the game's top hurlers.

Lyman was surely nervous as he dug in, focusing his concentration on the tall, imposing right-hander, but he didn't show it. Jenkins scowled back, accepting Jim Sundberg's call behind the plate before going into his patented winding motion. Lyman took the first pitch—a ball—and patiently worked the veteran hurler, coaxing a walk. Bobby Darwin followed with a double to left field. Spinning his wheels at full steam, Lyman raced to third. The rookie would score on Tony Oliva's grounder to second base that was booted by Rangers second baseman Dave Nelson. Minnesota went on to score three runs in the top of the first.

Having batted around in the opening inning, Minnesota sent Bostock back to the plate in the top of the second with one out. Lyman got his pitch and roped a single to right field—his first big league hit. Following a Larry Hisle single, Oliva crushed a Jenkins fastball nearly four hundred feet into the right-field seats to give the Twins a 6–1 lead. Lyman jogged his way across the plate and then awaited Oliva at home plate to congratulate the veteran. Lyman Bostock was in the major leagues, and already he was proving he belonged.

* * *

In its early days, Metropolitan Stadium was considered one of the crown jewels of the American League. It had everything people wanted in ballparks of the 1960s. It was outside of the hustle and bustle of a congested urban center, but easily and relatively quickly accessible for people in the Twin Cities and surrounding communities. It had excellent sight lines. Nobody could complain about too few parking spaces, as they had in urban ballparks of the past such as Ebbets Field, which had been cramped into a single city block.

By the time 1975 rolled around, Metropolitan Stadium had become known as much for football as for baseball, thanks to the tremendous success of Bud Grant's Vikings, the two-time defending NFC champions who had appeared in three of the first nine Super Bowls. With a capacity of just under forty-six thousand for baseball games and over forty-seven thousand for Vikings games, the Met could hold large crowds. But it didn't have the distant feel of a cavernous football stadium, even though it often hosted as many as nine or ten NFL regular season and playoff games each year in those days, plus additional preseason contests.

In early April, the field still showed the battle stains of the Vikings' playoff battles the previous December with the St. Louis Cardinals and Los Angeles Rams on their way to Super Bowl IX. Cleat marks and tackle skids could still be seen in the thawing grayish-green outfield as Lyman prepared to play his first home games in the big leagues.

In Lyman's rookie year, the straightaway left-field and right-field distances were both 330 feet at Metropolitan Stadium. The left-field power alley was 350 feet, and the right-field power alley was 373 feet. The eight-feet-high outfield fence stretched to 410 feet in left-center and center field, leading out to the park's distant reaches—430 feet to right-center field.

A box seat cost $4.50 at the Met in the 1975 season. Seats in the left-field box and reserved grandstand were $3.50, and general admission was $2.00.

The nearly twelve thousand spectators who came out to Metropolitan Stadium for the Twins' home opener against the California Angels on April 15 had to weave their way through seven-feet-high piles of snow that had been piled throughout the parking lot in the hours preceding the first pitch. They mostly sat huddled under blankets in the lingering forty-eight-degree cold.

In the first week of the season, Twins manager Frank Quilici worked with Lyman to play a little farther back in center field. Always an aggressive outfielder—readily willing to sacrifice his body going back to his days playing the concrete wall at Northridge—Lyman was showing a tendency to play a little closer in, hopeful to snare opposing bloopers and line drives before they hit the ground in front of him.

"He plays a shallow center field," said *Minneapolis Tribune* writer Tom Briere the day of Lyman's major league debut. "He started that way as a youngster and moved in closer to the infield because he couldn't make the long throw."

But after Lyman made a couple catches over his head in the opening series at Texas, Quilici moved him back a little bit, hoping to avoid scenarios where he would be burned by deeper drives.

"The pitcher throws to every hitter differently, and it's hard for an outfielder, especially a rookie, to know how to play them," Lyman said that season. "It really makes me mad when they [the pitcher] look out to the outfielder when a line drive was hit where the fielder should have been able to reach."[9]

In his very first defensive opportunity in front of the home fans, Lyman badly misplayed a routine fly ball in center field. Playing very shallow, Lyman tried to run down Joe Lahoud's long drive from behind, but a leaping effort couldn't haul it in. Lyman chased it down, however, and held Lahoud to a double. "I didn't pick up Joe Lahoud's double soon enough because of the crowd background in the second inning," he would say after the game. "Otherwise, I'd catch the ball and save a run. I don't know all the hitters yet."[10]

Minnesota's home opener was Lyman's first-ever opportunity to face California ace Nolan Ryan, the fireballing Texan who had thrown three no-hitters over the previous two seasons and had set a new major league record with 383 strikeouts in 1973. Though Lyman poked a single the opposite way into left field in his first at bat against Ryan and then later walked, he also struck out looking in the sixth inning against the future Hall of Famer. Lyman struck out looking again in the bottom of the ninth inning, as California claimed a 7–3 victory.

Though initially Steve Braun and Steve Brye seemed the likeliest candidates to platoon in center field with Lyman, by mid-April Quilici was envisioning a scenario where Dan Ford would rotate in and out with the rookie, depending on who was on the mound.

"I'll stay with right-handed hitting Dan Ford in center field against the left-handed [A's starting pitcher Ken] Holtzman," Quilici said. "But we'll get left-handed hitting Lyman Bostock back against the right-handers."[11]

"Right now Bostock is going through a little rookie-itis," Quilici continued, still not entirely convinced of Lyman's ability to consistently hit left-handers or to play every day. "He's a little mixed up and pressing with the whole scene, including being badgered by the media. I've told him that it is all part of playing in the major leagues, and he'll be adjusted in a few days."

Lyman returned to Minnesota's starting lineup in the first game of a Sunday doubleheader in Oakland on April 20, batting second in the Twins lineup. He grounded out to second baseman Phil Garner his first two times up, but then lashed a single to right field in the sixth, giving the Twins two runners on with nobody out. But A's starter Glenn Abbott got out of the jam and went the distance in yet another 4–1 A's triumph.

Leading off the bottom of the eighth that Sunday afternoon, longtime A's shortstop Bert Campaneris blasted a deep drive toward the 380-foot sign in the far reaches of the Oakland Coliseum. Playing his usual, shallower-than-most center field, Lyman got on his horse and took off running at full speed. He managed to get around Campaneris's blast just as it was making its descent toward the center-field wall. Racing directly into the fence with no regard for his body, Lyman made one of the more spectacular defensive plays in baseball to that point in the season.

"It appeared to be out of the centerfielder's reach," wrote Dick Cullum of the *Minneapolis Tribune*. "But Bostock ran it down, leaped against the fence, made the catch and crashed to the running track. He held the ball while lying face down in the dirt."

Lyman had made an incredible catch, but he lay crumpled along the warning track. He had been knocked out cold by the force of his body crashing into the wall and the ground. "He did not recover consciousness for at least five minutes," wrote Cullum. "When he was helped from the field, the Oakland fans hailed him with prolonged cheers."

Lyman was taken to a nearby hospital, where doctors needed approximately a dozen stitches to seal up a large cut around his right eyebrow. The medical personnel also took x-rays of the dazed outfielder, attempting to determine if he had suffered any internal injuries or if he had suffered any damage to his right arm, which he was favoring. Those images came back negative. But as he remained hospitalized the following day, it was apparent something wasn't right with Lyman's right ankle. A soft cast placed on his foot, Lyman was released from the Oakland hospital and briefly spent some time in Los Angeles before returning to Minneapolis in late April.

As it turned out, Lyman wouldn't be returning to the Twins lineup for a while, as the rookie faced his first significant stretch on the disabled list as a big leaguer. Diagnosed with a chipped ankle, Lyman had surgery on Monday, May 5, in Minneapolis, during which loose bone fragments were removed from his injured right foot.

The Twins replaced Lyman on the big league club with Tom Kelly, the future Minnesota manager who was hitting .309 and coming off a grand slam he'd recently hit in a Tacoma Twins victory over Spokane.

It was a lonely, restless time for Lyman as he lay in a Minneapolis hospital bed—highlighted by Yuovene's regular visits—while the Twins were playing out their early spring schedule. But at least he hadn't been hurt even more severely when he crashed into the outfield wall in Oakland.

"Look at the beautiful weather. I should be out playing ball," Lyman said in discouragement from his hospital bed. "It won't be long, though. I figure three or four weeks. Sure, I'm disappointed in the number of times I've been hurt during my career. But I feel that I'm pretty lucky, because I could have been hurt pretty bad in Oakland."[12]

During his layoff in the hospital, however, Lyman had no intention to stop being the daring defensive outfielder that helped get him to the majors so quickly, and he was eager to be back soon playing for the Twins. "I'll probably bang into a fence again," he said. "I don't like people to hit triples against us. I think it makes the outfielder look bad.

"I earned a job fair and square in spring training," he continued. "I'll be back and the layoff isn't going to make much of a difference."

One of the things that irked Lyman the most as he lay in his Minneapolis hospital bed, aside from the injury he had suffered and the time he was off the field, was the way he was largely ignored by the Twins management. Neither Calvin Griffith nor anyone else from the Minnesota front office took the time to pay Lyman a visit in the hospital. This, after Lyman had put his body on the line making a tremendous catch, with the Twins losing substantially in the late innings. It was something that Ly-

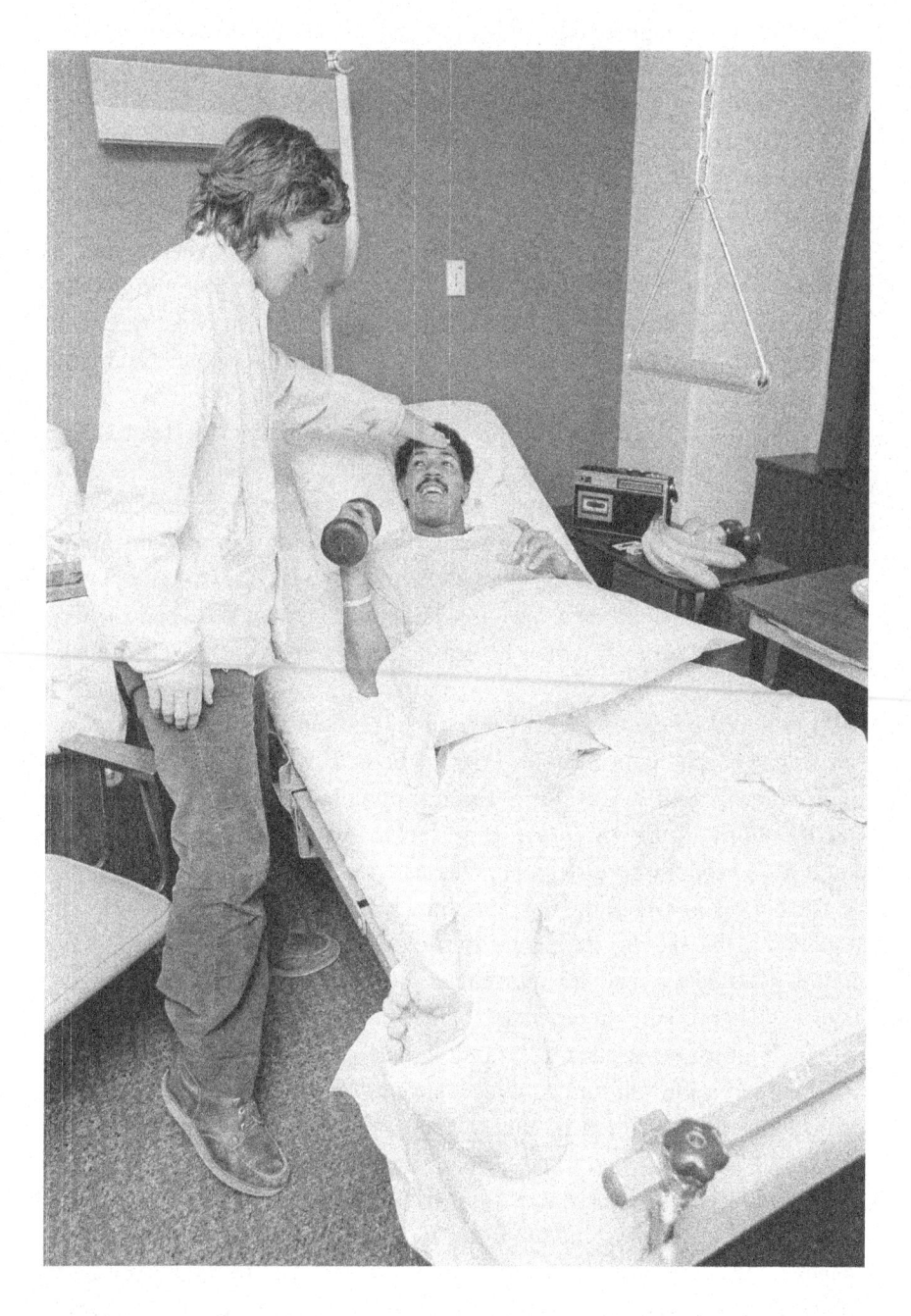

After earning a starting job in the Minnesota Twins outfield in the spring of 1975, Lyman broke his right ankle while making a spectacular catch in late April. Here, team batboy Tom Westcott (left) pays Lyman a visit in the hospital. (AP photo.)

man didn't easily forget—as was evident a couple of years later when he recalled his hospital stay.

"Back when I broke my ankle as a rookie, nobody from the front office came to see me in the hospital," Lyman said. "Some of the clubhouse kids did, but nobody from the front office. I don't recollect that anybody from the front office even called. That's a small thing but it carries weight. And it will carry over."[13]

* * *

After a layoff of approximately a month, Lyman returned to Tacoma on June 4. He was disappointed that he was sent down to Triple-A instead of returning directly to the Twins, who were facing multiple problems in the outfield early in the season, including the continued struggles of Bobby Darwin, who was getting booed badly by the Minnesota locals, and an elbow injury suffered by Larry Hisle.

Lyman wanted to be helping the big club in Minneapolis instead of rehabbing in the minors, and he even told Sid Hartman of the *Minneapolis Tribune* that he briefly considering quitting baseball altogether during this time. "I had made the All-Star team at Tacoma, was second in the league in hitting with a .333 average and had done everything you would think necessary to play in the majors," Lyman would say the following year.

Cal Ermer, who had helped develop Lyman over the prior season at Tacoma into a guy ready to play center field in the major leagues, inserted him in the starting lineup the day he arrived.

"Thanks to Cal Ermer, I got on the right track," Lyman would say. "Ermer took me in tow, put me in the Tacoma starting lineup the first day I got there and convinced me I had to play myself back into shape after being hurt."

Lyman shredded Pacific Coast League pitching over a three-week stretch, hitting .391 with thirty-six hits, sixteen runs, and thirteen RBIs in twenty-two games. On June 10, his RBI single proved to be the only run in a 1–0 Tacoma triumph over the Hawaii Islanders, completing a doubleheader sweep for the Twins. He added three more RBIs in a 9–6 loss to Spokane on June 13, and two days later he had another three-RBI game by clearing the bases with a double in the sixth inning of a 10–2 Tacoma victory. It was apparent during his brief stint back in Triple-A that Lyman was back in the groove at the plate coming off his layoff. He was about to return to the majors to stay, and he would make the most of the opportunity.

The Twins announced in time for a June 27 doubleheader at Texas that Lyman was returning to the Minnesota lineup. He had rejoined the big club the day before, as the Twins traveled to Tacoma for a Thursday-night exhibition game against their top minor league team. It was an embarrassing night for the major leaguers, as they suffered a humiliating 11–7 defeat to Tacoma. Lyman didn't play in the exhibition, but it was a perfect opportunity for him to rejoin the big club at a time when they desperately needed him.

Minnesota was struggling in the midst of a five-game losing streak that saw them fall below .500 at 31–36 as they headed to Arlington to play the Rangers again. The Twins were an injury-riddled bunch, as Lyman wasn't the only regular facing significant time on the disabled list. Lyman took Larry Hisle's roster spot when he returned to the Twins, as Hisle had succumbed to bone spurs in his elbow, making throws painful and forcing him into a stint on the DL. Hisle would go on the disabled list again in July and wouldn't return until early September.

The Minnesota outfield trio that was touted as one of the up-and-coming units in the American League during spring training had been decimated by injuries and subpar production. Bobby Darwin was never the same player after his breakout 1974 season. He struggled mightily out of the gate in 1975, hitting just .219 with five homers and eighteen RBIs in forty-eight games before the Twins decided to cut their losses and traded him to the Brewers in mid-June, while Lyman was still in Tacoma rehabilitating.

Although much of Lyman's rookie season had been lost to injury, now that Darwin was gone—traded for veteran utility man John Briggs—he wasn't going to have to worry about getting enough playing time. He became a regular fixture in the Twins outfield upon his return to the big club.

Lyman made his presence felt immediately on his first night back, doubling in a run in the second game of a twi-night doubleheader with Texas. The Twins won, 8–5, snapping a six-game losing streak. The following day the Twins faced off against Gaylord Perry, who had been traded to the Rangers by the Cleveland Indians earlier in the month. Perry cruised into the seventh with a 3–2 lead. But leading off the seventh, Lyman clubbed a triple off the veteran hurler. Rod Carew followed with a game-tying double, and Dan Ford drove in two go-ahead runs shortly thereafter as the Twins picked up another win over Texas, 5–3.

Lyman continued his productive hitting in the series finale on Sunday night, driving in a run with a base hit during a seven-run flurry by the Twins. Unfortunately for Minnesota, however, they had fallen behind 8–0 before pulling within one run at 8–7, and would go on to a 9–7 setback.

As June slid into July, the Twins were in fifth place, fourteen games back of front-running Oakland and gasping for air. With all the injuries and inconsistency, it was a testy time in the Twins clubhouse. Lyman would later say that he was disappointed that he didn't get more support and encouragement from the veterans after laying his body on the line for the Twins. "Nobody tried to help me after I came back up. It would seem like they would take more time with a rookie. I was hitting .190 for a while after I came back," he said the following season.[14]

The Twins limped into the final series before the All-Star break in Yankee Stadium, losing twenty of twenty-eight games going back to shortly before Lyman rejoined the club. A team hovering above .500 suddenly found itself ten games below .500 and in last place, with little hope of catching Oakland atop the Western Division. But Minnesota found some life against the Yankees, who were battling the Red Sox and Baltimore Orioles for supremacy in the American League East. After winning the opening game of the series, 9–6, the Twins crushed New York, 11–1, in the second game, with Lyman producing an RBI single in the victory.

In that 11–1 victory over the Yankees—the first game of a double-header—Lyman got upset with home-plate umpire George Maloney on a called third strike, continuing a trend that he kept up throughout his first few weeks in the majors. While Frank Quilici had been determined to position Lyman more effectively in the outfield early in his big league career, Rod Carew's primary objective for his rookie teammate was his specialty—hitting. Carew implored Lyman to be more aggressive at the plate: not to take so many choice pitches early in the count and especially not to bark at umpires over perceived mistakes in calling balls and strikes. Lyman was annoying Carew and other teammates with his brash approach, complaining about every pitch American League umpires were calling strikes that he didn't like.

"He's got a lot of talent, but he was taking too many pitches and complaining too much," said Carew of Lyman in July. "I made a deal with him that it would cost him a buck every time he squawked at the umps, and he's cut down on it quite a bit."[15]

"[Carew] just kept on me," Lyman said. "I was starting to think for a while that I couldn't play up here, and was taking my frustrations out on the umpires."

Reflecting on it after a year had gone by, Lyman owned his rookie immaturity. "I wasn't cool, man," he replied the following season. "When you're a rookie, you want to do everything in one week. It's hard to remember you've got six months to do it. Like I said, I wanted to do everything right away."[16]

"I wanted too much too soon. I wanted to be a star in one day," he added to Bob Fowler of *Sporting News*.

Along with his maturity issues, Lyman would later acknowledge some flaws in his technique at the plate—things that he had to work through with each passing at bat following his return from Tacoma. "After getting hurt, I was hitting off the toes of my front foot, raising the heel into the air instead of pointing," Lyman said.[17]

Minnesota dropped the last two games in the Bronx to head into the All-Star break 39–49, sixteen games behind Oakland and tied with California for last place in the American League West. Lyman was hitting just .195 at the break, having gone two for sixteen at the plate in the four-game set at Yankee Stadium. During his time in New York for the Yankees series, Lyman visited with an uncle—one of Annie Pearl Bostock's many brothers who were used to putting in long, hard hours in a regular job—seeking a sympathetic ear.

He was looking for someone to tell him that he was doing fine, that everything would be all right, and that he just needed to keep working through his rookie growing pains. If that's the speech Lyman was hoping to get, he was sorely mistaken.

"Bostock visited an uncle looking for sympathy. He didn't get it," wrote Bob Fowler of *Sporting News*.

"He told me to quit arguing with umpires and to shape up," Lyman recalled. "He was right. As long as I argued with umpires, they weren't going to give me a break on anything close to the plate."

Startled at first by his uncle's admonition, Lyman began to think about the first few months of his big league career. The many times he'd come back to the dugout grumbling about a perceived bad call by the umpire. The times he'd strutted around the Minnesota clubhouse like an All-Star, but only as a mask to shield himself, and others, from his daily bouts of insecurity. Lyman decided to take his uncle's advice to heart, and he came back for the second half of his rookie season with a fresh approach and entirely new attitude. His interviews began to reflect a more self-aware approach to his day-to-day activities.

"I decided to quit trying to win immediate acceptance. To quit trying to be a star overnight," Lyman said. "From then on, I played each game as well as possible and didn't worry about my average."[18]

* * *

Lyman started heating up after the All-Star break following the pep talk from his uncle, with three hits and three RBIs in a two-game series in Baltimore. He had a two-run single off Yankees southpaw reliever Sparky Lyle to cap a three-hit outing on July 21. Lyman had two more hits July 22 against Boston, pushing his average up to .248, a considerable jump from the struggle to stay above .200 earlier in the month. He produced an RBI double on July 23.

By the time the Twins flew out to Anaheim for a series with the Angels beginning on July 25, Minnesota was a full twenty games behind the A's—a hopeless deficit with just over two months left in the season. But the Twins still found something to take pride in, despite losses in fourteen of eighteen games. Before the first game of the Angels series, Rod Carew was named team captain—the first time a team captain had been named since the franchise moved from Washington, D.C., to Minnesota to become the Twins. Carew responded with four hits—raising his average to .385—to lead a seventeen-hit assault and a 12–1 Twins triumph. Bert Blyleven took a no-hitter into the sixth inning, while Lyman contributed three hits, a run, and an RBI in five plate appearances.

Lyman's solid hitting in late July was a prelude to the evening of July 28, as he enjoyed his best big league game up to that point in the opening contest of a series with the Kansas City Royals. It began with a leadoff double into the left-center-field gap. He picked up his second hit in the second, pulling a single into right field. Lyman's third hit came leading off the fifth, as he once again doubled, this time to right field. He scored his third run of the night moments later.

With the score tied 8–8 heading into the bottom of the ninth, the Twins loaded the bases. Up stepped Lyman with a chance not only to be a hero but to complete his first four-hit game in the big leagues. Lyman ripped an opposite-field liner that nicked the glove of a leaping Royals shortstop Fred Patek and bounded into center field, giving the Twins a thrilling 9–8 walk-off win. As he circled back around after touching first with the winning hit, Lyman was mobbed by a host of his teammates. It was one of the shining moments of Lyman's rookie season: four hits in six at bats, including two doubles, three runs scored, and the game-winning RBI.

"I'm hitting the ball very well," Lyman said simply after the game.[19]

Following his four-hit game against the Royals, Lyman was hitting .270, having brought his batting average up nearly a hundred points since his return from Tacoma.

"We'd always heard Lyman was a good competitor as he came through the system," said Quilici after Lyman's big game against the Royals. "He's started to get more confidence after being up here for a while."[20]

Quilici was clear: "I'll tell you, he's back in shape now."[21]

* * *

Although the Twins continued to slide farther and farther behind in the American League West standings, Lyman's sizzling rookie summer continued into early August. Lyman shot his average up to .282 with three hits and two runs against the Royals on August 4. In the third game of the series with Kansas City, he drove in two runs with a single, though the Twins dropped the game, 4–3.

After reaching on an error, scoring a run, and walking in Minnesota's 8–7 win over the Brewers on August 11, Lyman's surgically repaired ankle flared up and gave him some pain the following morning, so he sat out except for of a pinch hit groundout in Minnesota's 7–4 loss to the Brewers. He would play at less than 100 percent over the next couple of weeks. On Monday, August 25, Minnesota opened a series in Milwaukee, with the Twins taking the opener 6–3 behind Lyman's three-hit, two-RBI performance. He would get two more hits against the Brewers a couple days later.

Following the Twins' successful set at County Stadium, longtime *Minneapolis Tribune* sportswriter Dick Cullum provided his thoughts on Minnesota's emerging center fielder: "One man's opinion—mine—is that the next true star player to appear in the Twins' uniform will be rookie Lyman Bostock," the legendary newsman wrote. "Bostock has a special shine that is growing steadily brighter.

"A good thing about him is he has batting power but refrains from trying to stress power ahead of letting the hits fall where they are pitched," the eighty-one-year-old Cullum continued. "I think he will find his position in center field when he is no longer needed in right field. The Twins have been waiting a long time to find a man who can play center field exactly as it should be played. My guess is that Bostock will be the one."

As mid-September arrived and families in the Twin Cities settled back into their autumn routines, the crowds got smaller and smaller at Metropolitan Stadium for the season's final two homestands. The Twins drew just over 737,000 fans in 1975—worst of all American League franchises—and in the season's final month, Lyman and his teammates played in front of just two crowds of more than 10,000. On September 18, Lyman collected three hits against Kansas City, but the Royals would scratch across two runs in the seventh for a 4–3 victory in Harmon Killebrew's final game at Metropolitan Stadium.

The Twins finished the season 76–83, 20.5 games back of Oakland in fourth place. Lyman ended his rookie year with the Twins hitting .282, recording 104 hits in 369 at bats. The one stat that really suffered in Lyman's rookie year was stolen bases, as he swiped only two all season as he worked through ankle problems. But he had demonstrated his ability to place the ball in the gaps and down the foul lines with twenty-one doubles. He scored fifty-two runs and drove in twenty-nine more, while drawing twenty-eight walks. It wasn't exactly Rookie of the Year material—that distinction went to Lyman's former college rival from Southern Cal, Boston's Fred Lynn—but it was enough to show that he belonged in the big leagues as a fixture in the Minnesota outfield.

"[Lynn] hit .331 and deserved to be the Most Valuable Player and the Rookie of the Year," Lyman would say the following year. "But I hit .282 hitting with a broken ankle." [22]

Lyman Bostock's rookie season in Minnesota had been a mixed bag of injury, frustration, learning, redemption, and success. But as the off-season arrived, he was geared up to return to the Twins lineup in 1976, ready to build on his first season in the majors, and poised to become one of the top outfielders in the American League.

Healthy again coming off his early-season ankle injury, Lyman poses for photos with fans prior to the Twins game against the Oakland A's on Sunday, September 14, 1975. (Jeff Petty collection.)

6

THE GREAT BREAKOUT (1976)

You can't be afraid to make errors! You can't be afraid to be naked before the crowd, because no one can ever master the game of baseball, or conquer it. You can only challenge it.—Lou Brock, outfielder, St. Louis Cardinals[1]

Lyman returned to Venezuela in the off-season between the 1975 and 1976 seasons. There he picked up where he left off from the hot finish to the second half of his rookie campaign in Minnesota. Fortunately, this time around Lyman and his teammates managed to avoid the man in the green truck who had run them off the road and pulled a gun on them the prior winter.

By December 15, Lyman was in the thick of race for the Venezuelan League batting title, hitting a scorching .353. But he aggravated the right ankle injury he had suffered on that spectacular catch in Oakland the previous spring, the one that had forced him to miss more than two months of action with the Twins. Lyman returned to the United States frustrated about another ankle setback and elected to take it easy in the weeks leading up to spring training. He did, however, get himself into playing shape for the 1976 season by playing some semipro games back home in California, as he had done ever since his college days at Northridge.

"Some guys go home over the winter and eat," Lyman would say later that summer. "I go home and play baseball. That's the advantage of living in California."[2]

America's bicentennial year marked a new chapter in the history of the Minnesota Twins: owner Calvin Griffith had hired a veteran manager who was hungry to lead a winner after spending much of his career guiding losers. Gene William Mauch had his first crack at big league management in 1960 when he took over the Philadelphia Phillies. He'd enjoyed a long but largely unspectacular major league career, playing for six different clubs as a utility infielder from 1944 to 1957. In the two years prior to the introduction of the New York Mets and Houston Colt .45s into the National League, Mauch's Phillies were by far the worst club in baseball, going 58–94 and 47–107 back-to-back in 1960 and 1961.

Though the 1962 Mets would be remembered for their 40–120 record and unofficial title as the worst team in baseball history, the 1961 Phillies weren't too far behind, setting a modern-day baseball record with a twenty-three-game losing streak. When the run of futility finally ended, Mauch was hoisted facetiously onto the shoulders of a pack of Phillies fans back at the airport in Philadelphia. But within three years, by 1964, Mauch had built the Phillies into a club poised to claim the National League pennant. Mauch and the Phillies were teed up to meet the New York Yankees in the World Series, as they held a comfortable cushion heading into the final two weeks of the regular season. But in an epic collapse that many consider the greatest September choke in baseball history, the Phillies blew a six-and-a-half-game lead with twelve to play by dropping ten straight contests in late September, allowing the St. Louis Cardinals to surge past them and eventually claim the pennant.

Mauch would guide the historically inept Phillies to one of their best stretches up to that point in club history, producing six straight winning seasons from 1962 to 1967. But another shot at the World Series wouldn't come, and Philadelphia's fans couldn't bring themselves to forget the club's remarkable slide in the late summer of 1964.

Prior to the 1969 season, Mauch was hired away from the Phillies to lead the expansion Montreal Expos, where he learned how to do more with less. The 1969 Expos—the first Canadian club in the major league history—lost twenty straight games in their first National League campaign on the way to a 52–110 record, giving Mauch the unique distinction of leading two of the six longest losing streaks of the twentieth century in Major League Baseball and the two longest losing streaks in modern National League history. Though Mauch's Expos gradually got better, challenging for the National League Eastern Division title into late September 1973, he was eventually run out of Montreal following a disappointing last place 75–87 season in 1975. On Fan Appreciation Night in the final week of the 1975 season, Mauch walked out to a cacophony of boos in Montreal's Jarry Park. "The reason I decided to come out here is that I knew a lot of you would get a kick out of it," Mauch said to the spectators.[3]

Mauch symbolically ended his tenure with the Expos by telling the Montreal faithful that they would be cheering for this youthful group—talent that included a young Gary Carter and several contributing players—for a long time to come. A few days later, Mauch was let go by Montreal, setting the stage for Calvin Griffith to lure him to Minnesota with a three-year contract.

"It was the worst thing they could do," said Expos pitcher Steve Renko. "Gene Mauch is a super man and a super manager. I'll tell you one thing—he never, ever put the blame on any of his players. I think they fired him to cover up for themselves. Do they know as much about baseball as Gene Mauch?"

"Gene Mauch is one of the finest managers in baseball," Renko continued. "What did they expect us to do this year with all the young guys? We won 75 games with them and the most we ever won with experienced players was 79."

Mauch believed he could win big in Minnesota, where he inherited a ball club loaded with offensive talent. He liked to play the percentages, attempting to create favorable hitting and pitching matchups over the course of games. Mauch loved guys like Lyman who could get on base and score runs. Mauch preferred to manufacture runs by taking advantage of opposing pitchers' mistakes and errors, as well as the spacious dimensions of larger ballparks, to move runners along. The Twins weren't going to hit a ton of homers at Metropolitan Stadium, with its collection of left-handed hitters and the park's deep dimensions in right field. But with Lyman and Rod Carew getting on base frequently, Larry Hisle wouldn't have to lead the American League in home runs to challenge for the league lead in RBIs.

In their first spring working together, Mauch was looking to see if Lyman had fully recovered from the ankle setbacks that had derailed much of his first year in the big leagues. Mauch expected Lyman and fellow youngster Dan Ford to battle in spring training for the starting center-field job, with the loser likely relegated to right field.

"They'll have to show me in spring training and I have confidence they will," Mauch said in late January. "The players will make the decisions."[4]

Lyman came into the season unsigned and started spring training in Orlando without a contract, but in early March he agreed to a one-year pact with Minnesota for his second big league season. Lyman didn't feel comfortable going into the season without a deal in place, so he agreed to what the Twins offered him—essentially the same deal he had as a rookie. His pay didn't improve— he would once again play for just $20,000.

"I took what the man offered me," Lyman would say later that summer. "I signed right away to get it out of the way, off my mind."[5]

* * *

Lyman's second season in the big leagues, like his first, began in Texas, as the Twins took on Gaylord Perry and the Rangers in Arlington Stadium. Opening Day turned into a classic pitchers' duel between a pair of future Hall of Famers: Perry, in his second season with the Rangers, and Bert Blyleven, returning for his seventh season as Minnesota's ace. Bostock ripped a single up the middle into center field in his first at bat of the new season in the top of the second inning, but he was promptly caught trying to steal second base. Another single—this one to right field off Perry in the sixth inning—moved along Steve Braun to set up Minnesota's first run.

Perry went eleven innings for the Rangers through a 1–1 deadlock, retiring the last fifteen batters he faced without walking a single Twin the entire game. Blyleven was every bit as good, retiring sixteen straight from the fourth inning through the ninth as the contest went into extra innings. The Rangers finally broke through in the eleventh, as infielder Toby Harrah got the game-winning hit off Twins reliever Bill Campbell, giving Texas a 2–1 triumph. The loss served as a harbinger of what was to come throughout the first half of Minnesota's 1976 season.

The Twins were off to a sluggish 2–5 start by the time they faced Yankees ace Catfish Hunter in the final game of a three-game set at Yankee Stadium. Hunter was cruising, heading into the ninth inning with a 4–2 lead as the Bronx Bombers looked to put the finishing touches on a sweep of the struggling Twins. Hunter had held the Minnesota batters hitless from the fifth through the eighth innings, and got Steve Braun out

THE GREAT BREAKOUT (1976)

Coming off his injury-riddled rookie season, Lyman returned to the Twins outfield in 1976 and became a fixture in the starting lineup. It was Lyman's breakthrough season, as he spent much of the summer locked in a competitive race for the American League batting title. (Mike McCormick collection.)

to start the ninth. But Larry Hisle followed with a single, bringing Lyman to the dish. So far, Lyman had gone zero for three against Hunter, the burly six-foot-tall North Carolinian who had come to New York the year before as baseball's first big-money free agent. Hunter quickly got ahead two strikes, and it appeared his mastery of the seemingly overmatched second-year Twins outfielder would continue. But then the legendary right-hander made a rare mistake, dropping an off-speed pitch right into Bostock's wheelhouse. Connecting squarely with all his might, Lyman watched as his high drive sailed over the blue-padded wall in right-center field—just over the 353-foot sign—for a game-tying home run.

Prior to 1976, Yankee Stadium had spent two years undergoing extensive renovations, as new owner George Steinbrenner brought the ballpark up to modern big league standards. He also sought to erode the iconic stadium's reputation for overly expansive power alleys by bringing in the outfield walls, dramatically shortening the playing field. No longer were the statues of Babe Ruth, Miller Huggins, and Lou Gehrig in deep center field in fair territory. And no longer did a batter have to crush a pitch well over four hundred feet to have it leave the ballpark in the right-field power alley. What might have been a routine flyout a couple years before—or an extra-base hit, at most—became the first home run of Lyman Bostock's big league career. And off the pitch of a future Hall of Famer, no less. Lyman had played in just over a hundred big league games to that point, with just under four hundred major league at bats. His first homer couldn't have come at a better time or against a more challenging opponent.

"I didn't think it was going out," Lyman said afterward. "A guy who doesn't hit any home runs doesn't know when the ball is gone."[6]

"[Yankees catcher Thurman] Munson wanted the next pitch in the dirt, but I reared back and tried to put a little extra on a breaking ball and threw it right down the middle," added Hunter. "I give up a lot of guys' first home runs. I'm used to it. It used to get me mad, but you can't do anything about it except try and get the next guy out."

Butch Wynegar followed Bostock's game-knotting blast with a shot of his own that barely cleared the new outfield fence, lifting Minnesota to a 5–4 victory. It was the first loss of the season for the much-improved Yankees, who would prove to be a thorn in the side of everyone in the American League for the next few years.

Following a two-hit, two-RBI game against the Milwaukee Brewers on May 1, Lyman's average was up to .311. He was proving his worth as Minnesota's everyday starting center fielder and leadoff man to Mauch, who preferred having him farther down in the lineup against left-handers.

"I like leading off because that's my position," Lyman said after Minnesota's 9–5 win over the Brewers. "There's a big difference when you're up here for your second season. "You feel a lot more comfortable and know what's expected of you. You have to do it every day here."[7]

He continued his solid hitting a couple nights later in Detroit, banging out two hits, including a stolen base, in a 5–4 Minnesota win over the Tigers.

After a tough rookie season, in which Lyman stole only two bases because of his lingering ankle issues, he increased to twelve in 1976. "It takes time and it takes patience," Lyman would say about stealing bases at the major league level. "You have to study the pitchers and learn their motions to first base. I'm studying. I think in about another two years I should be where I should steal thirty bases a year with confidence."[8]

Lyman's batting average was up to .345 when Mauch elected to give him a day off in Milwaukee on Saturday, May 8. The Twins exploded for fifteen hits in a 13–2 wipeout of the Brewers. Lyman returned to the leadoff spot in the lineup the following day and blasted three more hits, his average creeping up to .365.

It was getting more and more difficult for Gene Mauch to justify keeping Lyman out of the starting lineup, but he did so again on May 10 as the Twins met Kansas City in Royals Stadium. He entered the game in center field in the bottom of the eighth, with the Twins leading, 4–3. Kansas City tied the game in the bottom of the ninth, and Lyman came up for the first time in the top of the tenth with two runners on. The Royals intentionally walked Rod Carew to face him, but Lyman got his revenge, snapping off a single into left field to score the game-winning run, as the Twins claimed a 5–4 victory over one of the favorites to win the American League West.

Two more hits came for Lyman a couple nights later against Kansas City, and his average ticked up to .384. An eleven-game hitting streak finally came to an end May 14 in Anaheim with a zero for five outing against the Angels.

Lyman hit a slight lull in mid-May after a torrid start to the season, but he always enjoyed hitting in Comiskey Park and picked up three hits off Goose Gossage in a 3–2 loss to the White Sox on May 20, bringing his average up to .344. Per his usual routine when the Twins came to the Windy City, he stayed with his uncles in Gary, and they chauffeured him back and forth from their homes to the South Side of Chicago for each game and then took him to the airport for the flight back home to Minneapolis.

NBC's "Game of the Week" telecast made its way to Metropolitan Stadium for the Saturday afternoon matchup on May 22 between the Royals and Twins, and Lyman had one of his better games of the spring, driving in three runs as the Twins prevailed, 5–3. After the game, Lyman was humble about his solid outing.

"I just don't know, but I think it's the day games," he replied. "I really don't think most players think too much about televised games. And most players, or at least hitters, seem to prefer playing in the day."[9]

* * *

Minnesota sat 21–21, four games back in fourth place in the Western Division, at May's end. On June 1, the Twins faced off against California's Nolan Ryan, who was in the midst of a rare rough patch. Ryan entered the contest with a 3–6 record, having gone winless since May 1. Lyman led off against the fireballing right-hander with a leadoff double—extending his streak to ten games—and scored following a single by Larry Hisle and a groundout by Rod Carew. Ryan dominated the Twins from there, holding the home club scoreless until the bottom of the seventh. He struck out a total of six Twins in a complete game 6–4 victory. Lyman went one for three with two runs scored.

That same day, the Twins struck a deal with one of their Western Division rivals, the Texas Rangers, to relocate the unhappy Bert Blyleven, combining him with shortstop Danny Thompson and shipping the pair to the Lone Star State in exchange for journeyman starting pitcher Bill Singer, minor league pitcher Bill Gideon, third baseman Mike Cubbage, and shortstop Roy Smalley. The Twins had rejected a potential trade with the Rangers for Blyleven during the previous off-season, but with Blyleven eager to relocate, the Twins elected to get something of tangible value for the star pitcher before he hit the open market. Most importantly from Minnesota's perspective, the Rangers' free-spending owner, Brad Corbett, added $250,000 to sweeten the deal for the cash-strapped Calvin Griffith. Blyleven would agree to a three-year, $550,000 contract with the Rangers, making him Texas's highest-paid player.

"The last two years or so have really been tough," said Blyleven, who won ninety-nine games in his first stint with the Twins.[10]

In his final game at Metropolitan Stadium as a member of the Twins, Blyleven extended his middle finger at some Minnesota fans that had been heckling him.

"I think without any question Blyleven will pitch the way he is capable of at Texas," said a disappointed Gene Mauch. "His record is impressive, and now his mind is clear having all his monetary problems behind him."

Blyleven's departure was a sign of things to come for the Twins, as the club would watch much of its talent dwindle away to American League rivals in the coming years.

Of all the players involved in the Blyleven trade, Smalley would make the biggest impact for Minnesota, playing ten seasons for the Twins between 1976 and 1987, with a brief stint with the Yankees sandwiched in-between. Smalley would be one of the few bright spots during the Twins' sharp decline of the late 1970s and early 1980s, earning a starting appearance at shortstop in the 1979 All-Star Game and helping lead the Twins franchise to its first World Series title in 1987.

Gideon would never make an appearance with the Twins. Cubbage became a regular in Minnesota's infield rotation over the next few seasons, though he would never hit any higher than .282 at the major league level. Thompson would play out the 1976 season with Texas, but, tragically, he died from leukemia on December 10 at the age of twenty-nine, leaving behind a young wife and two daughters.

Blyleven would eventually make his way back to Minnesota in 1985, earning an appearance in the All-Star Game that year at the Metrodome and leading the American League in strikeouts and shutouts. Two years later, Blyleven joined Smalley on the Twins' 1987 championship squad. In the near decade that passed between his stints in Minnesota, Blyleven pitched a no-hitter in 1977, won a World Series with the 1979 Pittsburgh Pirates, reached the three-thousand-strikeout mark, and earned enough victories to merit selection in the Hall of Fame on his fourteenth attempt in 2011.

By June 5, Lyman was in the midst of a twelve-game hitting streak, and his average had crept up to .341, which ranked in the top five among all hitters in the American League. Despite a hitless performance against Cleveland's Dennis Eckersley on June 8, which snapped his latest thirteen-game hitting streak, and then a game out of the lineup on June 9, Lyman carried a .331 average back home to Minnesota for a ten-game homestand against the Red Sox, Yankees, and Tigers. Lyman would miss six straight games during this period as he struggled with some leg issues, and the Twins went just 3–7 during the homestand, falling ten games back in the American League West by June 20.

* * *

With Lyman ailing and the pitching staff struggling, the Twins had fallen below .500. The second-year outfielder was exercising daily, taking care of himself and his leg issues. All season he worked to stay healthy and in the Twins lineup.

"He knows he has to work hard to take care of his legs because he doesn't have the more durable legs in the world," Mauch said that summer. "He is doing exercises that will take care of this situation."[11]

By Sunday, June 27, when Lyman returned to action in Oakland after missing five more games, Minnesota was in fifth place, 9.5 games behind front-running Kansas City. Things clearly weren't going according to plan in Mauch's first season in Minnesota. But whatever drama may have been unfolding with the Twins paled in comparison to the turmoil in the A's clubhouse. Owner Charlie Finley saw the impending dismantling of his championship A's club after the 1976 season, when most of the team's core would be hitting the free-agency market simultaneously after not signing contracts. Finley had sold Joe Rudi and Rollie Fingers to the Red Sox, and Vida Blue to the Yankees, for $1 million apiece earlier in June. But commissioner Bowie Kuhn nixed those deals, and Rudi, Fingers, and Blue returned to Oakland. Finley vowed to bench the three stars; in response, the other A's players said they would strike if he made good on that threat. Finley acquiesced five minutes before the third and final game of the weekend series with the Twins.

After his second extended layoff of the month, Lyman pinch hit in the top of the sixth inning, with the Twins trailing, 4–0. He came through against Oakland's Dick Bosman, nailing a single into right. A pinch runner promptly substituted for him to avoid aggravating the leg issues that had slowed him down the last few weeks. The Twins rallied late, but Rollie Fingers came on for the save and Oakland prevailed, 5–3.

As the Twins returned home for a series with first-place Kansas City, Mauch decided to return Lyman to the starting lineup, but further down in the batting order. The center fielder batted sixth in the opening game against Royals starter Dennis Leonard. Leading off the top of the second, Lyman singled and eventually scored the game's first run following two more Minnesota hits. After a rain delay of approximately an hour, Lyman drew a walk against Mark Littell in the top of the eighth.

Up stepped pinch hitter Tony Oliva, who received a standing ovation from the Metropolitan Stadium faithful. One of the last links to the Twins glory days of the mid-1960s and early divisional play, Oliva had undergone seven operations on his tattered right knee over the years. The three-time batting champion could barely get around the bases anymore, but he could still be relied upon to come up with a clutch hit. It was a perfect scenario for the veteran talent. "Can you think of many people you'd rather see hitting in the clutch?" said Mauch after the game.[12]

Oliva crunched a Littell offering off the wall in right field. With the crowd cheering him around, Lyman turned on the afterburners, racing around to score from first to tie the game, 3–3. Larry Hisle followed two batters later with a sacrifice fly, and the Twins had a 4–3 win over the divisional leaders. But the Twins would lose two straight to the Royals after that, falling even farther behind in the divisional race.

As July arrived and the nation's bicentennial approached, Lyman was still among the top hitters in the American League, holding above .330 in fourth place. He was behind only George Brett, his Kansas City teammate Hal McRae, and Detroit's Ron LeFlore. Lyman was making a strong case for his first All-Star appearance. He had worked through his hitting issues as a rookie and was stroking the ball purely and with purpose. He was hitting the ball to all fields and proving to be a very difficult man to get out.

"After getting hurt last year, I hit off the toes of my front foot, raising the heel into the air instead of pivoting. Now I've got it straightened out," he said that summer.[13]

At the All-Star break, Lyman was third in the American League in hitting, at .332. Only Royals teammates George Brett and Hal McRae were hitting higher. Based on that number alone, he deserved a spot on the American League squad for the All-Star Game at Philadelphia's Veteran's Stadium.

But playing most of his games in Bloomington, Minnesota, in an era long before games could be streamed coast to coast through cable television and the Internet, Lyman wasn't able to get the necessary attention from America's baseball fans to start in the Midsummer Classic. Plus, there were too many established outfield talents around the American

League to gobble up those precious few reserve spots not filled by the leading vote-getters.

Due to his nagging leg issues, Lyman wasn't playing every day that spring and early summer, when voting was nearing its peak. And the Twins weren't getting the pitching and key hits they needed to get over the hump and in the Western Division pennant race, which could have brought Lyman and the club more national exposure. But the fact that Lyman failed to make the top ten vote-getters among American League outfielders that summer didn't go completely unnoticed in the media.

Rod Carew, the much more well-known Minnesota Twin, made another start at first base for the Junior Circuit, and Butch Wynegar also earned a spot as a backup catcher, though his .294 average at the break was well behind Lyman's. But with Minnesota out of the race in the Western Division, even the presence of Gene Mauch on the American League coaching staff couldn't get three Twins on the squad. Lyman had to settle for watching the National League's 7–1 victory on television back in Minneapolis.

* * *

The Twins opened the second half of the season at home with a four-game series against the Cleveland Indians. In the second game of the set, on July 16, the Metropolitan Stadium spectators, and the players themselves, were unwitting subjects to a tiny piece of baseball history. The Indians thoroughly outplayed the home team for eight and a half innings, taking a 7–3 lead into the bottom of the ninth. But then the Twins rallied, scoring three runs on a Butch Wynegar homer with two outs off Cleveland closer Dave LaRoche.

Indians manager Frank Robinson elected to keep the left-handed LaRoche in the game to pitch to Lyman, and he responded with a rope into the left-field gap, putting the tying run on second base for the Twins. Robinson decided to do something drastic following Lyman's double: he brought on starter Dennis Eckersley to pitch to pinch hitter Phil Roof. Eckersley had rarely been used in such situations before. But Robinson was desperate to get his team back in the win column after five straight losses. Roof swung through three Eckersley fastballs, stranding Lyman on second and giving the Indians a 7–6 win to snap their losing streak.

The save was just the third of Eckersley's big league career up to that point—and the only one he would get throughout the entire 1976 season. Eckersley, in fact, wouldn't get another save for more than a decade, until

Tony La Russa reinvented the tall, hard-throwing right-hander and transformed him into a Hall of Fame closer with the Oakland A's in the late 1980s. "It's only the first time this year, maybe the second, we've used Eckersley in relief," said Robinson after the game. "I thought it would be a good tuneup for him."[14]

Although Lyman had spent much of his life without a great deal of interaction with his father, the pair crossed paths in the midsummer of 1976. In a unique event, the two men played on the same field on the same day. On July 17, the Twins hosted an Old Timers' Game at Metropolitan Stadium. It was a chance for the locals to pay homage to the recently departed Harmon Killebrew and other members of the American League championship team of 1965. Several Minnesota stars of recent years made their way to Bloomington, as did numerous Negro League standouts of the 1940s and 1950s who had played in the Man-Dak League. Lyman Bostock Sr. was one of those invited to play in the game.

"Tonight's appearance of Harmon Killebrew, Bob Allison, Earl Battey, Don Mincher, and Tony Oliva in the uniforms of the 1965 Minnesota Twins will bring back memories of the days when the Twins had real home run hitters in the lineup," wrote Sid Hartman of the *Minneapolis Tribune* the day of the Old Timers' Game.

On the afternoon before that Saturday evening's game, Lyman accompanied his father and many other former Twins and Negro Leaguers to a St. Paul movie theater to view a comedy opening that weekend featuring Billy Dee Williams, James Earl Jones, and Richard Pryor. Titled *The Bingo Long Traveling All-Stars & Motor Kings*, the film depicted the nomadic life of barnstorming black ballplayers in the 1940s—a world that Lyman's father knew very well. Sitting in the dark theater, sharing laughs and enjoying the film, Lyman Bostock Sr. fondly remembered his own playing days. For the younger Lyman Bostock, it was a chance to momentarily wipe away vivid recollections of a bitter past and to embrace with pride the career his father had put together in baseball, long before the sport accepted men of their race as equals.

"I've tried to learn what I could about what his life was like in the Negro Leagues in those years," Lyman said later. "I have a few clippings about my father. I've asked a number of the guys who played against him in those years. They say he could have played in the major leagues if they had let him."[15]

Nearly sixty years old, Lyman Bostock Sr. stepped onto the field at Metropolitan Stadium that Saturday evening wearing a Twins uniform. He was one of the oldest participants in the game, which featured a collection of former pros called the "All Stars" going up against the former Minnesota Twins players. During batting practice, the sting of the ball connecting with bat stunned the former Negro League star. "Whew!" he said, shaking his hands. But once the game started, Lyman Sr. showed he still had some pop at the plate, ripping a clean hit into center field over second base. As the old man reached first, the base coach, Twins manager Gene Mauch, was waiting with a big smile on his face.

Lyman's father also showed he could still use the glove over at first, completing multiple putouts. "In the top of the second inning the elder Bostock, playing first base, stopped a throw in the dirt from third baseman Jim Davenport of the All-Star team," wrote Gary Libman of the *Minneapolis Tribune*. "The ball dribbled in front of him and Bostock sprawled out, his nose in the dirt and his posterior in the air. But he grabbed the ball with his free hand and touched the bag for the out. The crowd cheered loudly."

"He was fifty-eight then," his son recalled. "He was playing with all these guys—Tony Oliva and Zoilo Versalles—and he hit a line-drive single up the middle. There was a throw in the third to first base and he came up with it easy as could be."

"I felt it was an honor for me to have him there," Lyman continued. "And I was so pleased that he got the recognition. People who had never heard of him before got to know who he was. It was great for him and for me to see him get the credit after all those years."

Though Lyman was happy to see his father recognized for his own playing career, he fell short of admitting that his dad was better than he was as a ballplayer. "Who is better, you or your father?" someone asked Lyman after the Old Timers' exhibition at the Met.

"I am," he confidently replied.

"I don't know about that," retorted Lyman Sr.

"We called it a draw," the younger Bostock would say later. "He [my father] did say I progressed faster than he did. He said, 'You're a helluva player.' Coming from your father, that means a lot."[16]

A few weeks after the Old Timers' reunion, Lyman spoke about his father to Ken Nigro of the *Baltimore Sun*. While acknowledging his father's prior greatness on the field, Lyman added that things might have been much different had Lyman stayed in his birth state of Alabama instead of heading to California with his mother. "He played in the '40s and '50s and he was one of the best around," Lyman said of his old man. "But I really don't think I would have played baseball if I had stayed with my father. He's a perfectionist and I'm too much like him."

While Lyman may have been proud of his father's baseball exploits, he remained angry that his father had played such a minimal role in his life up to that point. Lyman truly believed, through his family background, that he was destined to play big league baseball. As he commented to one reporter, "The way I look at it, some guys play baseball because they don't want to work and other guys play because they were born to. I was born to."[17]

At the same time, he resented the fact that so many young ballplayers in the era of the Negro Leagues learned from the veteran slugger, but none of his father's vast baseball knowledge was ever passed on to him.

"My father helped teach Willie Mays," Lyman once recalled to Dave Anderson of the *New York Times*, referring to the Hall of Fame outfielder, his dad's Negro Leagues contemporary with the Birmingham Barons in the late 1940s, "but he never taught me."

"I never met his father. Lyman rarely talked about his father. I don't ever recall him mentioning his dad," said Lyman's college coach, Bob Hiegert. "I think the separation between his mother and his father was not good. I never heard him speak of his father, or his father's baseball background at all. The majority of the family he went back to was his mother's side in Chicago."[18]

* * *

While the Old Timers' spectacle brought a momentary pause for reflection, the Twins continued their struggles against Cleveland over the weekend, dropping a pair of games to the Indians. Lyman went one for three in both games.

On July 20, another spectacle awaited the fans of Metropolitan Stadium, as Tigers manager Ralph Houk threw starter Mark Fidrych, who had become the biggest draw in the entire sport of baseball. Coming in at 10–2, Fidrych was bringing in the crowds wherever he went. After only 5,005 spectators watched the Twins and Tigers play the night before, more than 30,000 fans jammed into the Met to see "The Bird." The reported paid attendance of 30,425 was the best of the entire 1976 season for the Twins organization and more than three times the club's nightly average. There were, in fact, so many people waiting in line outside the park that officials elected to delay the first pitch by fifteen minutes so they had time to get inside.

Several days prior to the game, Calvin Griffith had contacted the Tigers, hoping to hear that Fidrych would be pitching while they were in Minnesota.

"Half a dozen other clubs have called to see if he would be pitching when we played them," said Tigers general manager Jim Campbell. "Hell, if I was on some other team coming to Detroit, I'd be calling too. That's just good business practice. Their fans all want to know if he's going to pitch there.[19]

"It's unbelievable how much interest there is in him. But you've got to try to be fair with the fans and let them know if he's going to pitch or not."

In a silly pregame ceremony, the Twins released more than a dozen pigeons at the pitcher's mound while a mascot in a bright yellow bird suit pranced around on the Twins dugout.

The Twins got after Fidrych early, jumping out to a 3–0 lead. Lyman, who was settling into the fifth spot in the Minnesota lineup, singled and scored in the fourth inning as the home club built its early cushion. But later in the game, the Tigers slugged it out against four different Minnesota pitchers, and Rusty Staub and Ron LeFlore both belted home runs. As a team, Detroit pounded out fourteen hits. A four-run sixth inning and a three-run seventh paved the way for an 8–3 Tigers win that improved Fidrych's record to 11–2.

The Twins were at a low point, sitting at 41–48 overall, 14.5 games out of first place. But the club was about to hit its stride and play its best baseball of the year as the dog days of August approached. In the meantime, Lyman put together his third double-digit hitting streak of the season, stretching it out to eleven games by July 22. That night at the Met, Lyman had two RBIs off Luis Tiant, coming on a sacrifice fly and a walk with the bases loaded, and poked a ground-ball single up the middle off Reggie Cleveland in a 5–1 win over the Red Sox. Following that night's game, Lyman went home to his nearby condo and finished packing for another trip to Chicago.

For Minnesota's July 24 tilt against the White Sox, Gene Mauch decided to mix things up, batting Lyman cleanup. It was the first time in his brief big league career that he was hitting in the four hole, and he rewarded his manager's confidence by having arguably the greatest game of his career that day. On a perfect Saturday afternoon for baseball on the South Side of Chicago—with clear skies and temperatures in the mid-seventies—nearly fifteen thousand spectators came out to see one of the biggest offensive outbursts of the entire season, as the Twins cruised to a 17–2 blowout win.

After drawing a walk and scoring a run in the first inning off White Sox starter Jesse Jefferson, Lyman blasted a deep drive in the second inning into the distant reaches of Comiskey Park's center field, over the head of center fielder Ralph Garr. The ball managed to bounce around long enough for Lyman to reach third with a two-run triple. Lyman faced his third pitcher of the game in the fourth inning and ripped a Chris Knapp fastball over the fence in right field for a 360-foot home run, his third of the season, to give Minnesota a 6–0 lead. Batting again in the sixth, Lyman had a golden chance for even more RBIs with runners on first and third. Though he got under one, his fly ball to White Sox left fielder Jorge Orta was deep enough to bring home Roy Smalley for his third RBI of the day and an 8–2 Minnesota lead.

Knapp was still pitching for Chicago in the eighth inning, and Lyman led off the frame by plugging the right-field gap with a double, his third hit on the afternoon. After an error by Alan Bannister at shortstop moved him up a base, Lyman scored on a single by Mike Cubbage. With a 15–2 lead in the top of the ninth, the only drama at hand was whether or not Lyman could get a single off Blue Moon Odom to hit for the cycle. It was business as usual as Lyman stepped into the batter's box and slipped into his familiar crouched stance. And then it happened, as Lyman caught an Odom offering and dumped a base hit into right field for his fourth hit of the day.

When it was all over, Lyman had contributed four hits, four RBIs, and three runs scored to Minnesota's seventeen-run explosion. He was one of just six players around major league baseball that season to hit for the cycle in a game.

"I didn't bother looking at the lineup card today," Lyman said afterward. "And when somebody told me I was hitting cleanup I couldn't believe it. Never batted No. 4 before, never went for the cycle, either.[20]

"Any success I'm having I've got to attribute to more confidence in myself in my second season with the Twins," he added.

To that point in the 1976 season, the Twins were 32–24 in games Lyman started in center field. In games he didn't start, they were a dismal 13–24. Mauch kept Lyman out of the starting lineup for the first game of a doubleheader the next day, as the Twins once again tore up White Sox pitching in a 13–8 victory. Lyman entered the game in the sixth, replacing Steve Brye in center field. He wound up walking twice and grounding out on a questionable call at first base, ending his thirteen-game hitting streak. He promptly banged out three hits in the second game of the Chicago doubleheader.

Thanks to his huge games against the White Sox, Lyman moved briefly into second in the American League batting race at .347, behind only George Brett's .362. Lyman had driven in ten runs in eight games after producing only nineteen RBIs through his first sixty-one games of the season. He had hits in seven of his last ten at bats.

"I was trying to do too much with men on base before," he said in late July. "If they played me to pull and pitched me inside, I'd try to hit the ball to left field to cross them up. Now I'm just trying to hit the ball hard anywhere, and there's a lot less pressure on me."[21]

"When I'm leading off, or when a man is on third base, I hit the ball where it is pitched. But in a few situations with men on base you have to place the ball. With men on first and second base, for example, you hit it to the right side to advance the runners," Lyman continued in a later article. "I got in a little trouble early this year when I tried to place the ball in every situation with men on base. That's one reason I only had a few runs batted in for the first half of the year. I was trying to do too much."[22]

All of a sudden, Lyman wasn't just having a solid second season with the Twins; he was blossoming into one of the top hitters in all of baseball. "A lot of that success comes from desire," he said. "When you're a ballplayer, you haven't got a sideline. So why not be the best ever? That's why I put a lot of time into it. I want to be the best.

"I made up my mind that this year I'm not going to be overshadowed by anybody. If I get the publicity on my side, fine. If I don't, that's fine, too. But this is the year that people are going to remember me."

* * *

Minnesota headed home to close out July and open August with nine games at Metropolitan Stadium against Texas and Oakland. It was tough sledding in the opening game of the Rangers series, as former Twin Bert

Blyleven got sweet revenge against his former mates. In a supreme effort that must have been intensely satisfying for the Dutch right-hander, Blyleven stymied the Twins, striking out nine and allowing just two hits in a 3–0 shutout victory. Batting fifth, Lyman went zero for three against his old teammate.

After a rainout on July 27, the Rangers and Twins returned for a Wednesday doubleheader at the Met, and the Minnesota bats came back to life after being shell-shocked by Blyleven earlier in the week. The Twins broke off eight runs in both games in a doubleheader sweep, with Lyman going five for eight on the day with three runs, three RBIs, and a walk in nine plate appearances, lifting his batting average to an even .350.

"Everything went wrong last year. Now it's just the opposite," Lyman said. "Late in the season one gets a little tired. So I know I'm not going to keep up this pace at bat. I've got a lot of confidence now and I feel I can hit almost anybody.

"When I was leading off early this season, I made the mistake of trying to place the ball. Now I'm just hitting it hard and fortunately, the ball is falling in the right place."[23]

"It shouldn't shock anyone too much what I'm doing," Lyman also said. "The big thing is that I'm not a rookie any more like I was last year. I know the pitchers better and I'm hitting with a lot more confidence."[24]

Lyman was banging on the door of George Brett, whose lackluster five for twenty-four effort on a recent trip to the West Coast brought him from over .360 to the mid-.350s. But even more importantly from Lyman's point of view, the Twins had gotten back around .500. "My job is to win ball games. That's my goal," Lyman said following the doubleheader sweep of Texas. "In my whole life, my only goal is to be a winner. Batting titles come. But everyone can enjoy a championship."[25]

At the end of July, only a few points separated Lyman from Brett: Lyman stood at .349, Brett at .353. The Twins were playing well, winning six straight and twelve of fifteen in late July and early August. Lyman was making a believer of everyone keeping an eye on the Twins. After platooning and working through leg issues for much of the first half of the season, Lyman was once again an everyday fixture in the Minnesota outfield. Even when he wasn't starting, he was one of Gene Mauch's more trusted options as a late-inning pinch hitter or defensive replacement.

"You've got to play every day to be good," Lyman said in early August. "I've had some problems with injuries, but now I hope that's all behind me."[26]

Although Lyman went a hitless zero for four in the second game of the August 1 doubleheader against Oakland, the Twins prevailed once again, 6–2, for the club's seventh straight win. They would make it eight in a row the following day, completing a five-game sweep of the stumbling A's. But then the Twins were swept by the front-running Royals, and Lyman batted just three for eleven from the plate against Kansas City.

Leading up to a series in Baltimore, Lyman had been in a minor slump, though he was still hitting .330. "I have a tendency to get a little tired toward the end," Lyman explained to Ken Nigro of the *Baltimore Sun*. "My timing is not there and neither is my concentration. I'm starting to guess a lot at home plate. Maybe I reached my peak too early. I don't hit homers, so I can't afford to go into a slump. Lately I've been hitting too much to right field. If you want to be a .300 hitter, you have to hit to the whole park.

"I'm learning that the only difference being up here is the people in the stands and the lights," he added. "I played against these same guys in the minors. If they're smarter now, so am I."

Leading up to the two-game set at Memorial Stadium, Lyman still didn't feel that he was receiving his due from the East Coast media for his breakout season. But given that he was just a second-year player, he knew it would take a little more time. "Sometimes it upsets me that no one seems to notice me," Lyman told Nigro prior to the Orioles series. "But some guys have played up here for four years and no one knows them. I've only been playing for two, so I don't think it's too bad."

Lyman would go one for seven against the Orioles, his average slipping to .326, though he did single in the first inning and score Minnesota's first run in a 2–0 victory on August 11.

As mid-August arrived, Lyman and Rod Carew, the winner of the previous four American League batting titles from 1972 to 1975, were running neck and neck for the Twins team lead in hitting. Though Lyman led the Twins with a .326 average after his two-hit game on August 14, Carew had a two-hit game of his own in a 9–8 win over the Yankees, pushing him to .325 compared to Lyman's .324. It would be a nip-and-tuck battle all the way down the stretch.

That August, a reporter suggested that Lyman's smooth swing was reminiscent of Carew's. "I wish," Lyman said simply. "Carew is still the best, and to me he's still the man to beat in the batting race."[27]

Lyman's respect for Carew went beyond his lofty hitting figures; he closely watched the veteran first baseman. He observed his movements in the batter's box, how he made adjustments at the plate, and how he studied opposing pitchers, eager to find weaknesses and ways to exploit them.

"If I'm going to be compared to someone, it might as well be Rod Carew," Lyman added in another interview that summer. "But I'd like to be remembered as just Lyman Bostock, and have other players compared to me. Maybe if I play a little longer it will happen."[28]

* * *

Lyman had earned the respect of his manager and his teammates for his consistency, his patience in dealing with his early-season ailments and being moved around in the batting order, and his work ethic. He might have been chatty and joking around before the game—he often was—but his heart was in the right place.

"Lyman is batting around .330," said Butch Wynegar. "But he talks about 1.000."[29]

"He's the talkingest one man I've ever run into," added Larry Hisle. "How that man loves the sound of his voice."

But at the same time, everyone knew he was all business once the game began and that he came to the ballpark every day ready to pour his heart out for the team.

"If there's a harder worker, a man who concentrates any more on the job he has to do—outside of Rod Carew—I don't know where he's playing today," said Gene Mauch. "Lyman has excellent hand-eye coordination, great hitting ability, and a ton of confidence."

The Twins would split four games with the Orioles, and Lyman went just one for ten over the first three games of the series. His average was down to .317—having slipped more than thirty points in the span of a month—but he would play a key role in Minnesota's series-splitting win over the Orioles, drawing a bases-loaded walk in the sixth inning to give the Twins a 5–4 edge. It would turn out to be the game-winning RBI.

"I'll take it," Lyman told reporters in the locker room later. "I haven't been winning many with base hits lately or helping this club much. But driving in the winning run with a walk might get me going again."[30]

Lyman emerged as a bona fide star for Minnesota in 1976, with a .323 batting average that ranked fourth in the American League. Lyman was thriving in the Twins clubhouse, where he was regarded as a hard-working player with a gregarious, larger-than-life personality. (Author's collection.)

THE GREAT BREAKOUT (1976)

It hadn't been an especially great homestand for Lyman in mid-August, so he didn't mind hitting the road for ten games at Detroit, New York, and Cleveland to close out the month. Though he went hitless again in the first game of a Friday doubleheader at Tiger Stadium in Detroit—his slump continuing to just one hit in his last fifteen at bats, his average falling to a summer low of .312—Lyman snapped out of it with eight hits over the last three games of the series in Motown. His average was back up to .321 as the Twins left the Motor City with three wins in four games.

On September 1, Lyman played a unique part in Minnesota's 3–2 win over Milwaukee. Batting in the bottom of the twelfth of a tie game after Rod Carew led off with a single, Lyman laid down a solid sacrifice bunt in front of the plate. Brewers catcher Darrell Porter turned to throw to first base, but his toss sailed past George Scott into foul territory down the right-field line. Carew scampered all the way around from first for a freak walk-off victory. Three more hits followed Lyman the next day against the Brewers, as he singled home a run in the third, led off with an opposite-field double and scored a run in the fifth, and then hit another RBI single in the sixth as the Twins pulled away en route to an 8–4 win.

As his average continued to soar in early September, Lyman rapped two hits with two RBIs in an 11–1 win over the White Sox, and then went four for four in Texas on September 8 to lift his batting average to .331.

"I would call this my second-best night," Lyman said following the outing against the Rangers. "I hit for the cycle in Chicago."[31]

"Bostock works at it pretty hard," added Gene Mauch. "He works at making contact and doesn't try to hit it big—although once in a while he'll hit one over the centerfielder's head like he did tonight. He doesn't worry about driving it over the outfielder's head. He's having a remarkably consistent season."

"I've had some trouble with my legs early this year, but I've felt fine in the second half. We're only five and a half back of Oakland and my only worry right now is whether we can get into second place."

Just five days after their eighteen-run outburst against the White Sox, the Twins remarkably did it again on September 10, crushing the Royals, 18–3. Lyman again collected three hits to continue his scorching September, pushing his average up to .335.

* * *

The American League hitting race was still very tight heading into mid-September, with Hal McRae and George Brett essentially tied at .337

(McRae's average was slightly higher at .3377 to Brett's .3374) and Lyman in third at .335. For his part, Lyman wasn't worried about where he finished in the batting race. As far as he was concerned, the only race that mattered was the race for the American League West's playoff spot.

"I'm not trying to catch George Brett or anyone else," Lyman said that summer. "The only thing being chased around here is the Kansas City club."[32]

Unfortunately for Lyman and his pursuit of an American League batting title, he would slip off the pace, falling below .330 as the season dwindled into the last couple weeks. Although he was unlikely to win the batting crown as the Twins headed to Chicago for one last series with the White Sox, Lyman very nearly duplicated his cycle from late July, providing the Comiskey Park spectators a late summer thrill.

Back hitting leadoff for the first time in a while, Lyman responded by starting the game with a single and scoring the first run of the night. Returning to the plate in the second inning, Lyman poled an other-way shot into left field, good for an RBI double. After walking in the third, Lyman came back up in the fifth inning and rapped an RBI triple, which gave Minnesota an overwhelming 10–0 lead. He recorded his fourth hit, a single, in the seventh.

Strolling confidently to the plate in the top of the ninth inning, Lyman dug his right hand into the dirt near the front of the left-handed batter's box, rubbing his hands together before reaching to pull down his right pants leg. He then spit into one hand and rubbed his hands together before settling into his stance and looking in. Lyman needed only a homer to hit for the cycle for the second time at Comiskey Park that summer.

Batting in front of a near-empty late-inning crowd, Lyman stepped into the box knowing that at least two spectators—his uncles—were still there watching him and rooting him on.

"I was conscious that I was going for the cycle my last two times up," Lyman replied after the game. "After you've done it once, you can't help but know that you're going for it again."[33]

"Bostock has raised his average six points tonight, with four out of four," said White Sox announcer Harry Caray as Lyman stared in for the awaiting pitch. "He's in contention now. He's third in the league in hitting right now. Bostock has gone ahead of Carew."

Lyman didn't hesitate, swinging at White Sox rookie reliever Larry Monroe's first offering. "There's a pitch, swung on! A long drive! Deep right field if it stays fair!" exclaimed Caray. "Foul by half a foot!"

"Oh boy! That's how close he came to his fifth straight hit. That ball just kept tailing off. The wind helped blow it foul," Caray continued.

"My last time up I definitely was trying to hit a home run, and I almost got it," Lyman said about his first-pitch swing against Monroe.

He accidentally swung at what would have been ball four, meekly tapping it foul along the first-base line. But then Lyman managed to lay off a high, inside fastball, drawing a walk for his sixth consecutive at bat reaching base. The Twins went on to a 13–6 win. The solid game against Chicago gave Lyman hits in eleven of fourteen plate appearances.

Afterward, a reporter asked Lyman if there was some secret he had to hitting well in Comiskey Park, the oldest ballpark in baseball at that time. "No, I don't have a secret to hitting here," he said. "Some guys just do well against some teams and not so well against others."

He admitted that staying with his uncles over in Gary and having their support at games made it easier for him to play in Chicago than in some of the other ballparks around the American League. "I like playing here. I have relatives and friends in Gary who like to come out and see me play," he said. "They always invite me to stay with them, and I'm able to pick up a good home-cooked meal or two."

Following his huge Tuesday night performance and nearly hitting for the cycle for the second time that season at Comiskey Park, Lyman fell back down to earth the last two games of the set. He went zero for four on September 22 as the Twins picked up another win over the White Sox, 6–3. While Lyman had a rare struggle, it was a big night for Rod Carew, who homered into the right-field seats at Comiskey Park and tripled, finishing with three RBIs. Carew's big night helped him continue to creep up the hitting standings—moving ahead of Lyman for the moment at .329 to Lyman's .326.

Another hitless game awaited Lyman the following night, though the Twins completed a sweep of the White Sox with a 3–0 victory. Eight straight at bats without a hit at the end of the trip to Chicago seriously damaged Lyman's chances of winning the batting title, but he wasn't out of the running entirely as the Twins headed home for the final four games of the year at Metropolitan Stadium—two weekend games against the Angels and two midweek games against the Rangers.

The last Saturday home game at the Met on September 25 brought out only 4,942 fans, as most folks in the Twin Cities had moved on to football season despite the strong finish the Twins had put together in the second half. Though it had been an off season by Nolan Ryan's lofty standards, with a 15–17 record coming into the game, the California hurler had a chance to make history that afternoon. No man had ever previously thrown three hundred or more strikeouts in a season four different times. Ryan needed nine strikeouts to reach the three hundred mark, and he got off to a solid start, fanning three in the first two innings, including Rod Carew looking to end the bottom of the first and Lyman swinging to lead off the second inning.

Dan Ford broke through against the big right-hander with a solo homer in the third, and Lyman came through five batters later by running out an infield dribbler just behind the mound, scoring Steve Braun to give Minnesota a 2–0 lead. After giving up two more runs in the fourth, Ryan was sharp the rest of the way, throwing seven innings of three-hit baseball. He struck out the side in the Twins' half of the sixth—the last strikeout victim, Bobby Randall, gave Ryan his fourth three-hundred-strikeout season. He whiffed two more batters in the seventh inning to finish with eleven strikeouts for the game.

But Ryan was upstaged by Dave Goltz, who completely dominated California. Goltz struck out eight Angels, but, even more importantly, he went the distance without giving up any runs. Lyman singled a second time in the eighth inning and then scored on Larry Hisle's double as the Twins prevailed, 6–0. With the victory over the Angels, Minnesota assured itself a .500 season, picking up its eighty-first win.

"I don't think we can be overjoyed at .500," Mauch said. "But considering all the things that happened during the season, it really isn't a failure."[34]

The last day of the regular season dawned with three men—McRae, Brett, and Carew—still in position to win the batting title. Lyman had fallen off the pace, though he was still in the top five among American League hitters. Because Lyman did not have a statistical shot of winning the batting title on the final day, Gene Mauch gave him a second straight game off to close out the season. Royals manager Whitey Herzog would have preferred to sit out Brett and McRae once again that last day to get additional rest before taking on the Yankees in the upcoming American League Championship Series. But with both players sitting at .331 and

THE GREAT BREAKOUT (1976)

Carew nipping at their heels at .329, he had no choice but to let both guys battle it out with the Twins veteran for the batting title that Sunday afternoon.

Carew left it all out on the field, finishing two for four in another solid outing. It wasn't enough for a fifth straight batting title, but Carew didn't let go of the crown without a fight. Carew's .331 finish could have led to a three-way tie atop the batting list had Herzog not played Brett and McRae. But Brett rose to the occasion on the final day, going three for four with an RBI double in the fourth, another double to right field in the seventh, and an opposite-field, inside-the-park home run in his final at bat of the season in the ninth. McRae grounded out following Brett's makeshift homer in the ninth, which gave Brett the batting title. McRae's two-for-four outing left him one point behind, at .332. Carew's .331 clip was good for third.

The 1976 Twins finished the year with an overall mark of 85–77. It had been a very impressive finish for Gene Mauch's club, as Minnesota went 44–29 over its final seventy-three games from July through early October.

Had the Twins not gotten off to a 41–48 start—had they been able to get a few more timely hits and more consistent pitching in May and June—they may very well have made it interesting down the stretch. But they were never realistically in the playoff hunt that summer. As it was, the Twins' sweep over the Royals in the final regular-season series only brought Minnesota within five games of the divisional winners, who would go on to lose in devastating fashion to New York in the ALCS on Chris Chambliss's walk-off homer in the decisive fifth game at Yankee Stadium.

Despite the third-place finish, there were plenty of positives to take away from the Twins' 1976 season, and plenty of reasons to be optimistic about the club's future. The 1976 Twins won twenty-three of their last thirty-two games. The Twins led the American League, while setting a new franchise record, with a .274 team batting average. They also led the American League in hits and runs, setting new Twins team records for triples, stolen bases, and sacrifice hits. The pitching staff set new team records for fewest home runs allowed and fewest balks.

There were some deficiencies, of course, as the team hit only eighty-one homers—last in the American League and worst in club history to that time—while hitting into 182 double plays, which also set a new team record for futility. Minnesota didn't play a lot of slugfests in 1976, as the Twins pitchers rarely gave up homers and the Twins didn't hit many.

Lyman's .323 batting average was ten points behind George Brett's .333 pace that earned the Royals' third baseman his first batting crown. But Lyman had done well enough to finish fourth in the American League. The breakthrough season put Lyman on the map as a shining star in Major League Baseball. The Twins headed into the off-season confident not only that they were going to be in the hunt for a Western Division crown in 1977 but that they had one of the top emerging young outfielders in Lyman Bostock.

7

SOMETHING TO PROVE (1977)

> Hitting is an art, but not an exact science.—Rod Carew, Minnesota Twins first baseman[1]

In the off-season between the 1976 and 1977 seasons, Lyman once again played winter ball in South America to fine-tune his skills. Heading down to Mexico, he played for Mazatlan under Maury Wills, the one-time record holder for stolen bases in a single major league season. His former Twins teammate Tony Oliva coached another team in the league, Los Mochis. In the playoffs, Oliva's squad faced off against Mazatlan, where the three-time American League batting champion got a taste of what it felt like to be on the other side of Lyman's onslaught of line drives.

"[Lyman] had received permission from Calvin Griffith to play for Maury Wills' team. In return, Wills promised to return and teach Bostock and Danny Ford how to steal bases," Oliva told *Sporting News* after returning from Mexico. "In the first round of the playoffs, we had 18,000 people in Los Mochis lined up inside the fences. Some of the American players were shaking. They thought, if we lost, the fans would kill them."[2]

"Bostock hit two home runs in the seventh inning of two games to tie the score," Oliva continued. "We lost one, 2–1, and lost the other, 3–2, in extra innings. He really enjoyed it, but he isn't supposed to be a home run hitter."

After having made just $20,000 for his outstanding 1976 season, during which he spent the entire spring and summer among the American League's top five hitters, there was no doubt that Lyman had earned a bigger contract heading into the 1977 season. The question was how much and whether it would be with Minnesota or with some other club.

Arriving in Orlando three weeks later for Minnesota's spring training, Lyman was healthy and feeling great. He had shed approximately 15 pounds during the off-season, arriving for workouts a svelte 170 pounds. He was lighter on his feet and appeared a half-step quicker. But as he quickly would demonstrate, the weight loss hadn't affected his hitting. On the third day of workouts with the full forty-eight-man squad—facing well-rested teammates who were throwing near full speed—Lyman sprayed the ball all over Tinker Field, consistently plugging the gaps in left and right field with frozen ropes. And he kept right on hitting as the Twins started playing spring training contests.

As the season approached, Calvin Griffith and the Minnesota executives were growing increasingly uneasy about whether they'd be able to sign Lyman. But Lyman was far from their only concern. By early March, the Twins had signed just fifteen of the thirty-seven athletes on the big league roster. No other major league club had as many unsigned players heading into spring training games. Although Lyman and his agent, Abdul-Jalil Al-Hakim, knew that the open market could yield potential riches far beyond what the Twins would ever pay, the outfielder was prepared to show long-term loyalty to the Minnesota organization.

Lyman wanted $200,000 a year for a four-year arrangement from 1977 to 1980, plus a healthy signing bonus. It was the same annual money that his former Twins teammate, relief pitcher Bill Campbell, had gotten from the Boston Red Sox, but obligated Lyman and the Twins for one fewer season. All things considered, it was a more-than-fair way for Minnesota to gain a long-term commitment from one of the top young hitters in baseball. With his late twenties approaching, the next four years figured to be quite productive for Lyman.

But Calvin Griffith wasn't prepared to accept that deal—at least not yet. Griffith was willing to more than double Lyman's 1976 salary to $50,000, but he couldn't abide a long-term contract. With Hisle and many others on the club in a position to leave in the coming months, it wasn't the right time for the tight-fisted Twins owner to meet Lyman's demands.

As an unsigned player who could become a free agent after the season, Lyman was the subject of considerable trade speculation throughout spring training. The press covering the club in Florida that March heard rumors that Minnesota would probably move Lyman around the June 15 trading deadline, and in the meantime they'd seek the best offer they could get for the outfielder, since "Bostock does not appear to have any intention of signing with the Twins."[3]

Lyman was mentioned as the focus of a potential one-for-one trade with the New York Mets for southpaw ace Jerry Koosman, who was coming off a twenty-win season in 1976. Rangers manager Frank Lucchesi said in mid-March that it would take a player the caliber of Lyman Bostock or Larry Hisle for him to agree to a trade involving young Texas hurler Len Barker. Still another rumor had Lyman heading home to Los Angeles to play for the Dodgers in a trade for hurler Doug Rau. The clubs interested in trading for Lyman hoped that the Twins would somehow, someway sign him that spring and then offer him up for a deal later that summer. That spring, the Twins brass didn't make it any real secret around the league that they'd offer up Lyman for the whole season for the right price. But other franchises were naturally wary of a scenario in which they'd give up significant personnel for what amounted to a one-year rental if they couldn't sign Lyman and he participated in the reentry draft after the season.

Lyman turned up the heat on Griffith and the Twins on Friday, March 25, telling reporters he wanted a contract by the start of the regular season or there wouldn't be a negotiation beyond that point. "I'm giving them a chance now," he told reporters. "I gave them a good year in 1976 and now they have to pay me for it."[4]

"He's only had one good season," Griffith countered. "We want to make sure that wasn't just a one-shot thing."

"He doesn't want to be bothered by salary negotiations in the season," chimed in Twins vice president Howard Fox. "I would have to say I don't blame him."[5]

"I didn't want to have to play under the pressure of trying to perform and negotiate at the same time," Lyman would say later that summer.[6]

The same Friday afternoon he issued his public ultimatum to the Twins, Lyman belted an RBI double in Minnesota's 4–3 victory over the Toronto Blue Jays. The following day he had another RBI hit in a 3–2 setback to the Houston Astros, pushing his spring batting average to .361. On Sunday, Lyman and Abdul-Jalil Al-Hakim met with Fox to discuss his demands. While they agreed on a figure at which to start negotiating, the meeting didn't accomplish much more than that. "I didn't tell them the figure I wanted," Lyman said. "I told them what I wanted to start negotiating at."[7]

"It was a very amicable discussion," Fox added. "At least we know now where we stand, and if we can work something out."

The old man seemed much less optimistic. "He wants to be traded, or something like that," replied Griffith. "I don't know."

The contract negotiations continued behind the scenes. The Twins bent a little, offering Lyman a two-year deal, just half of the four-year deal Lyman desired, and the dollar amounts the Twins were throwing around were nowhere close to what the third-year outfielder and his agent thought he deserved. "I never did ask them for any money. I wanted him [Griffith] to make me an offer competitive to modern-day athletes of my ability. I asked him what I was worth to the Minnesota Twins," Lyman would say the following year. It would later be reported that the Twins offered $150,000 a season—nowhere near the salary Lyman could command on the open market.[8]

By April 8, after one more meeting with Howard Fox the day before the season opener, it was evident that Lyman wasn't planning to sign with the Twins. Speaking from Oakland, his agent's base of operations and the site of Minnesota's opening series of the regular season, Lyman made good on his threat to play out his option and leave the Twins after the season. The negotiations were over as far as Lyman was concerned.

"Regardless of what they offer after today, I am not going to sign with the Twins," he said. "I set an expiration date and they failed to settle. Their last offer wasn't even close."[9]

"We were looking for a four-year deal with fairly good increases—an average of 18 percent over the last three years of the contract," added Al-Hakim. "We feel the compensation offered would not be a fair compensation of a player of Lyman's caliber."

A Twins spokesman established the ball club's position, stating, "Of course we thought it was a good offer, and felt it was an honest effort to sign him. We have great confidence in Lyman, but he's only had one year in the major leagues. I hope we can continue negotiations and eventually get him signed."

"I'm doing this [turning down Minnesota's offer] to set an example to the next young ballplayer coming along," Lyman said to Scott Ostler of the *Los Angeles Times*. "Somebody's got to make a stand somewhere."

Multiple early April reports suggested that the new American League expansion franchise in Seattle, the Mariners, might land the Twins outfielder in a trade. Lyman was fond of the Pacific Northwest, having had a positive experience playing in nearby Tacoma for parts of two earlier seasons in the minor leagues. "I can make a new start [in Seattle]," Lyman said, adding that he preferred a team on the Pacific Coast.[10]

In another interview, Lyman said that he had indicated his interest in Seattle to the Twins management, in case a trade might happen. "I explained to him [Howard Fox] that I'd like to play in Minnesota. But if I can't, I'd like to play in Seattle."[11]

Lyman said he preferred Seattle "because the situation there is about the same as in Minneapolis."

Although the ground was shaky going into 1977, Calvin Griffith was getting quite a collection of talent at a tremendous bargain. Heading into the new season, the combined payroll of the Twins starting lineup and opening-day pitcher, Dave Goltz, was $565,000. It was the fourth-lowest figure in the American League, behind only two expansion teams, the Seattle Mariners and the Toronto Blue Jays, and the Cleveland Indians. Rod Carew, having just re-signed for three years in 1976, earned $165,000 for what would turn out to be one of the greatest hitting seasons in the last half century of major league baseball. Hisle would earn $85,000 for an MVP-caliber season of his own, and Dan Ford got paid $60,000.

Lyman was set to get a raise, from $20,000 to $25,000, for the 1977 season. That was still far from what he was worth, and the 20 percent raise was the last thing on Lyman's mind that spring as he sought a long-term deal. But because he hadn't signed a new deal with the Twins, Calvin Griffith elected to dock Lyman's pay from $25,000 to $20,000— the maximum 20 percent deduction allowed by baseball owners. Lyman would make the same paltry salary he'd made his first two years in the bigs.

* * *

On April 15, the day of Minnesota's home opener back in Metropolitan Stadium against Oakland, Associated Press Twins beat writer Brent Kallestad sympathized with a couple of the Twins' emerging young stars and their frustrating preseason contract negotiations. With New York Mets slugger Dave Kingman demanding a multimillion-dollar pact, and many other players around both leagues seeking significantly more money than the third-year Twins outfielder, the deals that Lyman and Larry Hisle were willing to sign to stay in Minnesota into the 1980s seemed quite fair by comparison.

"Many major league baseball observers feel the four-year, $800,000 financial package being sought by Minnesota outfielder Lyman Bostock is reasonable on today's market," Kallestad wrote. "Almost no one except Twins owner Calvin Griffith argues with Larry Hisle's request for $100,000. Hisle, who does his own negotiating, would also like some security in the form of a multi-year contract."

In the sixth inning of the home opener against Oakland, Lyman came up with Carew, the tying run, on first base after a single. "Let's see how much you are worth now!" yelled one spectator, annoyed at Lyman's contentious preseason negotiations with the Twins management.

Lyman didn't come through that particular time, grounding to Oakland first baseman Dick Allen, who threw to shortstop Rob Picciolo to force Carew at second. He came up again in the eighth, after Carew had homered to cut Oakland's lead to 3–2, and once again grounded out at first as the A's held on for the one-run victory.

On April 18, the Twins began a three-game set with the defending Western Division champion Royals for their first road series of the spring in Kansas City. The Twins were a ho-hum 5–5 out of the gate, but Lyman came up in the first inning and crushed a Dennis Leonard offering deep into the Midwestern night, well over the center-field fence near the park's massive scoreboard and innovative sprinkler and waterworks system. Lyman's two-run, 420-foot blast gave the Twins an early 2–0 advantage, and then he provided an RBI single in the fifth inning, pulling a shot into right field to tie the game at 4–4. The Twins would go on to an 8–6 triumph, with Carew going four for five with a run and two RBIs.

"It seems like every time we come to town, it's a slugfest," Lyman said of Minnesota's battles with the Royals. "I'm down to 170 [pounds] and I feel lighter, and better. But losing weight shouldn't make you have more power."[12]

While Rod Carew was still the top dog on the Twins roster and in the clubhouse, Lyman had emerged as one of the bona fide standouts in the Minnesota lineup. As he settled into his third season in the Twins clubhouse, Lyman was becoming more and more of a team leader with his friendly nature, his ability to calm his teammates and keep them laughing through conversation and humor, and his consistent performance between the lines, which, more than anything else, commanded his teammates' respect. Lyman was also earning the respect of local reporters for his bubbly personality and his willingness to speak frankly on a wide range of topics.

"When he saw reporters he liked, he smiled in anticipation of the conversation," wrote *Minneapolis Tribune* executive sports editor Gary Libman. "And he was effervescent. He commented on everything.

"The comments were never malicious. Sometimes they made no apparent sense or seemed childish, but more often they were rich in insight or humor. Usually the sentences flowed quickly, running together in machine-gun fashion. Often they loosened up the clubhouse."

He joked with teammates about how ugly they were. He would go on and on in the locker room, both before and after games, with idle chitchat about anything that came to mind. Sometimes serious. Sometimes not so serious. "We called him Mr. Logic," said Dan Ford. "There was a reason for everything, and he knew it."[13]

"He would talk to anybody, anytime, about anything," added Roy Smalley. "It may have gotten on your nerves sometime. But he was liked for it, because that was Lyman."

He constantly played pranks on Hisle, who was his best friend on the team. The two had condos in the same complex in Minneapolis. Their wives were friends.

"I talk to the players all the time because I think it's good," Lyman once said. "Talking to each other keeps a team loose."[14]

* * *

After taking two out of three in the series at Royals Stadium, the Twins headed to Texas for another divisional matchup. Lyman and the Minnesota bats showed no signs of jet lag in the opener, as the Twins routed Gaylord Perry and the Rangers, 11–4. In his second at bat of the game in the third inning, Perry fooled Lyman with one of his patented breaking pitches. Checking his swing, Lyman plugged a looper above third baseman Toby Harrah's head in left field, scoring the first run of the game. Lyman would then score himself on another opposite-field double by Mike Cubbage.

"I was fooled and the ball sunk," Lyman said afterward. "I checked my swing, and it went out to left field. I don't plan those kind of hits. But I was robbed over there in Kansas City the other night, so it kind of evens out."[15]

By the time he returned to the plate in the fifth, Minnesota held a 4–1 lead. Lyman clubbed a Perry pitch deep over center fielder Juan Beniquez's head, driving in Carew for the Twins' fifth run. Lyman scampered to third for a triple and would score another run on a Mike Cubbage sacrifice fly. Lyman drove in his third and fourth runs of the night in the sixth, pulling a Paul Lindblad offering into right field to give Minnesota a 7–2 edge. The Twins would score four more before they were done.

Following his impressive game that late April night in Arlington, Lyman demonstrated the humility that made him one of the more popular players in the Twins clubhouse. "I don't think I should be called the star of the game just because I had three hits and four RBIs," he replied. "We are all stars out there when we win. Sure, I got three hits, but what would those hits have been if Carew and [Roy] Smalley hadn't been on base?"

Lyman got a chance to play the hero again the following day against an old teammate—Bert Blyleven. It started out a tough night for Lyman against the future Hall of Famer, as the Dutch master used his devastating curveball and assortment of other pitches to strike the Minnesota center fielder out in each of his first three at bats. With one out in the top of the eighth, Lyman came up with Blyleven still on the hill, a 1–1 score, and Roy Smalley on. He quickly fell behind 0–2.

The tiring Blyleven made one of his few mistakes of the game, offering Lyman a hittable pitch that he stroked to the opposite field. Left fielder Willie Horton and center fielder Ken Henderson gave chase, but it was no use. The ball settled into the left-field bleachers, giving the Twins a 3–1 lead. Butch Wynegar followed Lyman with a solo homer, and the Minnesota bullpen held off the Rangers the rest of the way for a 4–1 triumph.

"I was so confused I had to ask what pitch I hit," Lyman said after the game. "After those three strikeouts, if I didn't get him that time, I would have been through with Bert for the rest of the year."[16]

Through Minnesota's first eighteen games in April, Lyman was hitting .322 with three homers and fourteen RBIs. He was once again earning his paycheck and then some. When pressed by writers about his frustrations about not reaching a deal with Calvin Griffith before the start of the season, he couldn't help but tell them how he really felt. "I do get bitter sometimes," he admitted. "I think I've been fair and why can't the world be fair to Lyman Bostock? I gave the Twins all winter and spring to sign me. I didn't wait to give them a good season."

"I don't want $3 million like some of these guys are talking," he continued. "I want to be reasonable, but I want to get what I think I'm worth."[17]

Lyman reiterated that he didn't intend to sign with the Twins, no matter what they offered him. "The Twins can make me the highest offer and I will not sign with them. I'll do everything I can to help them this year because you don't often have a chance to be a contender or winner and we have a chance this year."

Griffith didn't have much to add by that point, saying, "I guess we can only hope Lyman helps us win the division."

"Remember, it was Mr. Griffith who made the decision," Lyman added. "They knew what I wanted and it was fair. Now I just hope we can win this year."

Part of the reason Calvin Griffith couldn't offer Lyman more money was the poor attendance at Metropolitan Stadium, particularly early in the season. It had been four years since the Twins had drawn a million fans over the course of a season, and only 3,170 fans came out on Wednesday afternoon, April 27, to see the home club take on Seattle. Throughout the season, Griffith ran a series of television commercials in the local media market. The spots were intended to lure more spectators to Metropolitan Stadium and also to improve the image of the Twins in the community. In mid-April, Griffith had posted a full-page ad in local papers around the Twin Cities, asking for feedback from the general public about how to make the Twins a better team and how to make the game-day experience better at the Met.

Interestingly enough, the most frequent complaint Griffith received that spring had nothing to do with the team or the players. It had to do with the parking outside Metropolitan Stadium. Since Griffith hadn't built the ballpark and didn't own the land, the Twins didn't benefit financially from the parking fees that enraged local fans. "You've be surprised, but the biggest complaint is the parking and we have nothing do with the $1.50 charge per car. That's the Metropolitan Sports Area Commission. It's distasteful to everybody and we'd like to get a change. The people think we get the parking money, but we don't get a darn thing from it."[18]

* * *

Though Lyman's father had spent some of his last years in baseball north of the American border in Winnipeg in the early 1950s, the Twins' trip to Toronto for a weekend series in early May was Lyman's first-ever baseball trip to Canada. Minnesota was off to a solid 15–10 start and was sitting in first place, half a game ahead of the White Sox.

On an unseasonably warm fifty-seven-degree evening in Toronto, more than twenty-six thousand fans came out to Exhibition Stadium—the home field of the Canadian Football League's Toronto Argonauts, converted into a makeshift baseball facility—to see the spanking-new Blue Jays do battle with Minnesota's offensive talent. It was no contest in the opening game, as the Twins banged out ten hits, picking up three runs each in the fourth and ninth innings, to claim a 7–2 victory. Lyman's two-for-five outing, which included an RBI and two runs scored, pushed his batting average up to .315.

The Twins didn't wait around the following day, scoring three runs in the top of the first inning as part of a 4–1 win, and then they completed a three-game sweep with a 5–4 triumph to close out the series. It was a tremendous series in Toronto for Lyman, as he went seven for fourteen with five runs scored and an RBI, shooting his average from .310 up to .337. In the meantime, the Twins improved to 18–10 on the young season. Rod Carew's four-for-four Sunday against Toronto pushed his average up a full twenty points, from .340 to .360.

By the time the Twins headed to Boston in late May to face off against the Red Sox, Lyman ranked eighth in the American League at hitting, holding steady at .331. Carew was hitting second in the league, off to a stellar .367 start. Lyman went two for six in a 13–5 victory in the opening game of a May 25 doubleheader at Fenway Park, doubling off the Green Monster in left field in the third and then doubling a second time to the opposite field in the final inning, scoring Carew to make the score 11–5. He would then score himself two batters later on Dan Ford's two-run homer for Minnesota's last two runs in a twenty-four-hit slugfest.

In the second clash of the day-night doubleheader, Lyman would make baseball history in a way that neither he, nor anyone else, could have possibly expected as the two clubs warmed up on the field between games. In a remarkable demonstration of defensive consistency, Lyman tied a major league record by catching twelve fly balls, constituting nearly half of Boston's total putouts in the game. Though Lyman only had one outfield play in the game's first two innings—a sacrifice fly off the bat of Steve Dillard—he made two catches in the third inning on a pair of flies by Carlton Fisk and George Scott. After making one grab in the bottom of the fourth, Lyman caught three straight fly balls in the fifth, retiring Fred Lynn, Jim Rice, and Carl Yastrzemski in succession.

"Jim Rice's ball in the fifth inning was hit kind of funny," Lyman said later. "The wind played tricks on it. The ball was hit to my right and I ended up catching it on my left."[19]

By the sixth inning, the Twins held a 9–4 lead that would hold out to the end. Lyman went two for three, pulling a RBI single into right field as part of the Twins' two-run first inning, and then he added a second single and scored a run as Minnesota batted around and tallied six runs in the top of the third. Lyman caught a George Scott fly ball in the sixth for his eighth putout of the night and made his ninth catch in the seventh, retiring Fred Lynn to end another frame.

Around this time, the fans in the Fenway Park center-field bleachers were becoming aware that Lyman was within striking distance of Earl Clark's major league record of twelve putouts, which he accomplished as a member of the Boston Braves in May 1929. Between innings, a few of them yelled out to Lyman, letting him know that he might have a chance of making baseball history.

"There were none of the catches I couldn't get to," Lyman said.

Dwight Evans hit a straightaway drive with two on in the bottom of the eighth, but Lyman came through again for his tenth catch. Moving into Boston's half of the ninth, Butch Hopson popped out to center field for Lyman's eleventh catch.

With two outs and one last shot at history, Fred Lynn hit a short fly into center. Playing shallow as usual, Lyman took a few steps in and snagged it—his twelfth catch of the game. This final catch—coming after nearly seven hours of baseball at Fenway that evening—tied Clark's major league record. Combined with his five catches in the first game of the day-night doubleheader, Lyman set a new major league record with seventeen outfield assists in a doubleheader.

"After exchanging embraces and soul handshakes with his teammates following the game-ending catch Wednesday night, he whirled and threw the ball 300 feet to fans in Fenway Park's center-field bleachers," wrote the *Minneapolis Tribune* in its account of the record defensive effort.

"I figured they had kept up with the record," Lyman said of the Red Sox fans that he threw the ball to. "It's cool for me to keep it, but it's more fun for them to have it because whoever got it can remember it wasn't just a fly ball. It was a record."

Twelve outfield assists by one player in a major league game wouldn't be matched again for nearly thirty-two years, when Jacoby Ellsbury of the Red Sox made twelve putouts in a 2009 game that, like the other two twelve-putout games in baseball history, was also in Boston and also in late May.

* * *

After slugging their way to twenty-two combined runs in the pair of victories against the Red Sox in the Wednesday twi-night doubleheader at Fenway Park, the Twins stood 27–14, 3.5 games in front of the pack in the Western Division. Gene Mauch's club was making a strong case as the breakout team in the American League. Though the Los Angeles Dodgers had gotten off to a fantastic 31–11 start as they looked to dethrone the two-time defending World Series champion Cincinnati Reds in the National League West, the Twins had the second-best record in baseball as they headed to Baltimore for a four-game Memorial Day weekend set.

During the spring of 1977, filming began on a new weekly show that would become must-watch programming for serious baseball fans throughout the United States. In an effort to draw on the tremendous success of NFL Films' Ed and Steve Sabol, who over the previous decade and a half had turned professional football highlights and bloopers into a new art form, major league baseball sought to put together a weekly show that would not only feature the best plays and top performances around the big leagues but also present the lighter side of the game. "This Week in Baseball" premiered in early June, featuring games played over the last several days of May. Legendary New York Yankees broadcaster Mel Allen, the show's host, provided a unique combination of baseball knowledge and homespun charm. Allen's unmistakable Southern-accented voice, laid behind a collection of great catches, key hits, and goofy moments, was a marriage made in baseball heaven.

Five minutes into the premiere episode, Allen heaped praise on Lyman and the Twins for their fast start to the 1977 season. "Lyman Bostock and the Twins have been winning ball games with their bats," said Allen behind a wide shot of Lyman kneeling in the visitor's batter's box at Baltimore's Memorial Stadium.

"This Week in Baseball" was an immediate and long-lasting success, becoming a staple around big league ballparks in the hours preceding games. Players could often be seen observing the highlights and bloopers themselves as batting practice commenced in those ballparks that had video scoreboards.

The Twins had arrived in Baltimore for a series with the Eastern Division leader as the most productive offensive team in the American League. But the Orioles had an answer in veteran southpaw Rudy May, who handcuffed Minnesota in a six-hit 6–0 shutout. Lyman was given the night off against the left-hander. Despite a rare hitless night against May, Carew had taken over the lead in the American League hitting race with a .378 mark, and he would stay at the top. At .336, Lyman had moved into the top five.

In front of a huge crowd of more than forty-seven thousand Saturday-evening spectators, Lyman and the Twins faced Jim Palmer, the reigning Cy Young Award winner who was on his way to leading the league in wins for the third straight season. Though Lyman led off the game with a shot up the middle for a single, it was his only hit of the day. The Twins could only muster one run off Palmer; the Orioles scored three runs in the seventh, for a 3–1 win.

Sunday's third contest of the Baltimore series was one of the stranger games of the early part of the season around the American League. Lyman went hitless, striking out twice against Baltimore southpaw Mike Flanagan. The game featured a sequence, replayed for years, demonstrating how not to catch a fly ball in the outfield. With two outs in the top of the second inning, Roy Smalley tagged a long fly ball around the warning track in left field. Orioles left fielder Pat Kelly backed under it, ready to make what appeared to be an easy catch just in front of the chain-link outfield fence, which was covered by a thin green tarp. Going for a one-handed play, Kelly not only dropped the ball but watched it deflect behind him over the fence. As Kelly stared at the wall in stunned disbelief, lowering his head, the umpires gave Smalley credit for a home run since the ball never touched the ground. The gift gave Minnesota an early lead.

In the eighth, following Lyman's second strikeout, Orioles manager Earl Weaver goofed, thinking Larry Hisle was at the plate instead of Dan Ford. Flanagan began to intentionally walk Ford before Weaver finally realized what was happening. Baltimore wound up walking Ford anyway, setting up Hisle to hit a hard liner right back at the mound, off Flanagan's foot. The ball bounded toward shortstop Mark Belanger, who had no play. Glenn Borgmann scored to give Minnesota a 3–0 lead, and the edge held as the Twins picked up a 3–2 win.

In a weird quirk of baseball scheduling back in the late 1970s, the Twins and Orioles jumped on planes and flew to Bloomington, where they would play two more games against each other on Memorial Day and the day following. In a rare appearance in the number eight spot in the Twins lineup, Lyman got a chance to bring home Minnesota's first run on a single to left field in the second inning. He finished two for four on Memorial Day evening, though the Twins suffered a 9–7 loss to the Orioles.

After dropping three of four to the Eastern Division frontrunners, the Twins put it all together and outplayed Baltimore in the final showdown of their five-game home-and-home series. Lyman led off with a single in a 1–1 game in the bottom of the fifth. He then scored the go-ahead run on Rod Carew's groundout. Minnesota would score four more times in the sixth inning and go on to an 8–3 win.

Up three games in the Western Division on June 1, the Twins welcomed defending American League champion New York. It was the first of twenty-two home games Minnesota would play that month at Metropolitan Stadium. The Yankees had an early 3–0 lead until Lyman came through with a single to left field to bring home Jerry Terrell. Billy Martin's club still led 3–1 until the bottom of the ninth, when three straight singles off a tiring Ron Guidry compelled the Yankees manager to bring on Sparky Lyle for the save.

The Twins were within a run, trailing 3–2 with nobody out, when Lyman stepped up against Lyle, who would go on to win that year's American League Cy Young Award. He couldn't leg out a grounder to Bucky Dent at shortstop, but the play moved Terrell up to third and Butch Wynegar to second. After Lyle struck out Bob Gorinski for the second out of the inning and walked Roy Smalley, up stepped Rod Carew. Though Carew had walked twice previously that evening, he was hitless in nine consecutive at bats as he walked up to the plate with the game on the line. Lyle hung a slider across the dish and Carew plugged it over Dent's head into left-center field, giving Minnesota a dramatic walk-off 4–3 win.

"Rodney's a great hitter," Martin said afterward. "He may be the best hitter in the history of baseball."[20]

Carew came into the following night's game against the Yankees hitting .364, and a four for five performance improved his average to .376. Lyman was two for three with a walk against Ed Figueroa, singling in the first and seventh innings. Unfortunately for the Twins, however, the Yankees exploded for five runs in the fifth and three more in the seventh, as Lou Piniella drove in three runs and Thurman Munson and Graig Nettles brought in two apiece as the Yankees split the series, 10–3.

In came the Red Sox, and the Twins got back in the win column with a 6–2 victory, as they continued to beat up the Boston pitching staff. Three more hits for Carew—two triples and a single—moved him all the way up to .383, while Lyman added an RBI single to score Carew in the first inning and then tripled Carew home in the third inning off Red Sox starter Bob Stanley to give Minnesota a 3–0 lead. Lyman would score on a Larry Hisle single, and then Dan Ford homered to give the Twins a 6–0 cushion.

"I don't know that we have any preferences [regarding who we play]," Lyman said after the game. "We like hitting against anybody."[21]

Dave Goltz allowed two runs in the fourth but picked up his fifth win of the season in the victory over Boston.

"A surprise leader in the American League West, the Twins' outstanding hitting has been bolstered by good pitching like Dave Goltz, who beat the Red Sox in a series opener," said Mel Allen in the second episode of "This Week in Baseball." "Everyone knew the Twins would get good hitting, but few thought they'd get good pitching. That element has helped them stay around the top of the American League's Western Division."

"In Minnesota, there's been talk of hitting records, which means talk about Rod Carew," Allen continued. "Carew just missed getting his fifth straight batting title last year, and just might hit .400 someday.

"Baseball's perfect master with the bat. He makes it look so easy—like swatting summer flies. And Carew can really fly around those bases, too, in case you didn't know. Carew leads the league in batting average, hits, triples, and pitchers' nightmares.

"But the Twins have other hitters who make pitchers toss and turn, like Lyman Bostock—Carew's most ardent disciple."

After the Red Sox left town, Chicago and Kansas City came in for a pair of two-game sets to complete an eleven-game homestand for the Twins. The White Sox and Royals were both trying to knock Minnesota off the division pedestal. After dropping three of four to the Red Sox, the Twins' lead in the West had slipped to just two games.

Although Minnesota lost, 9–5, to the second-place White Sox on June 6, both Lyman and Carew continued their hot hitting. Carew went three for six with two runs scored. Lyman had been hit by a pitch and grounded out twice when he strolled up in the bottom of the ninth, the Twins trailing, 5–3. The Twins had runners on second and third with one out against Chicago's Lerrin LaGrow.

Lyman got his pitch, plugging it into center field. Two runs scored, and the game was suddenly tied, 5–5. He had a chance to be a hero again in the eleventh, as he came through with a two-out triple. Some thought later that Lyman should have taken a chance for a game-winning inside-the-park homer on his shot into right field, but he held up at the last second.

"From where I was sitting, it sure didn't look like he could make it," said White Sox manager Bob Lemon after the game.[22]

The winning run was just ninety feet away, but Roy Smalley struck out to end the frame. Chicago would score four runs in the twelfth for the win.

The White Sox were poised to join Minnesota atop the Western Division if they could win on June 7, but Lyman doubled, singled, and scored twice as the Twins claimed a walk-off 6–5 win in eleven innings. Another walk-off win came for the Twins the following day against the Royals, though Lyman went hitless in two at bats after entering the game in the sixth inning.

Carew was still tops in the league in hitting at .381, and Lyman was holding fourth at .331, as the Twins concluded their long homestead with a second game against Kansas City. Hitting eighth, Lyman went hitless in four at bats against Andy Hassler and Steve Mingori, including the final out of the game on a grounder to first baseman John Mayberry, as the Royals claimed a 7–2 final score.

* * *

As the June 15 trade deadline approached, Lyman, hitting around .330, became the source of considerable speculation around Major League Baseball, as various teams attempted to see what it would take to lure him away from the Twins and to sign him long-term.

One team potentially interested in a midseason trade was the New York Mets, who had fallen on hard times after reaching two World Series in a five-year period from 1969 to 1973. The Mets organization had been willing for several months to trade one of its longtime aces, left-hander

Coming off a 1976 season in which he hit .323, and then a .336 season in 1977, many believed it was only a matter of time before Lyman won his first American League batting title. (Author's collection.)

Jerry Koosman, to the Twins. The Associated Press had written a story back in early February indicating that Koosman was interested in being traded to Minnesota to play in his home state and that the Twins had offered Lyman straight-up for the veteran left-hander.

But there was a caveat on the Mets' side. Instead of waiting around to bid on him in the open market following the season, the Mets wanted the Twins to do the legwork of signing Lyman to a long-term deal that they could inherit.

Lyman, of course, caught wind of all the scuttlebutt, both before and after it was made public. And while it didn't affect his play on the field that spring and summer, the way the Twins handled his contract negotiations—making it abundantly clear that he was expendable—permanently soured his relationship with Calvin Griffith and the rest of the Minnesota front office.

"Those things leak out," Lyman would say later to Dave Anderson of the *New York Times*. "I found out that the Mets were willing to trade Koosman for me, but only if the Twins signed me at any cost. But when I found out about that, I wasn't going to sign. I don't like to be manipulated. I don't like to be plotted against."

"I think there is more of a chance at this time to sign the others before Lyman," Griffith admitted a couple weeks later. "Hell no, I don't want to lose Lyman. At the same time, I don't want to do something to jeopardize my thinking with lots of other people."[23]

Lyman and his agent, Abdul-Jalil Al-Hakim, had broken off talks with the Twins after spring training, and the two sides had gotten nowhere over the first ten weeks of the season. "I don't think we'll even talk to Minnesota again this season," said Abdul-Jalil in early June.[24]

Known as Randy Wallace before his conversion to Islam, Abdul-Jalil Al-Hakim was an Oakland-based agent who, at age twenty-six, already counted Lyman and San Diego Padres star Dave Winfield among his clients. A former three-sport athlete in high school who had once been a member of the freshman basketball team at the University of California, he had begun managing players shortly after his college days.

"He was very personable," said Dave Maggard, Abdul-Jalil's college coach at Cal. "The guys were attracted to him. He has a flair for that kind of thing. He's not afraid to ask. He's confident. I can see him asking for anything."[25]

"Lyman's agent, he was a very interesting man," added Lyman's college coach, Bob Hiegert.

A sharp dresser who was well-known around baseball circles for his excellent cooking skills, Al-Hakim liked to stroll around Oakland and the San Francisco Bay in one of two Rolls-Royces he owned. "I wanted to be a millionaire by the time I was 30," he once said.

Despite his growing popularity among young African American players, Al-Hakim had his detractors. Following a contentious series of negotiations with Atlanta Braves management regarding Junior Moore, one local reporter said Moore was under the influence of "black militancy." Calvin Griffith considered the agent a menace to the sport, which only enhanced his stature in the eyes of the Minnesota players and made Lyman bristle.

True to his nature, Lyman expressed a united front—and fierce loyalty—when the subject of Al-Hakim came up in his interactions with the media. "A lot of people say that he's trying to wreck the game. Just because you're an orthodox Muslim doesn't mean you're racist or militant," said Lyman. "Why don't they ever say Jerry Kapstein and the Jews are trying to wreck the game?"

Al-Hakim already anticipated that Lyman would be among the top free agents in the upcoming off-season, but that didn't stop him from hyping the Twins outfielder and his other clients as being gutsy for playing the 1977 season without contracts in place. "They're under pressure because they know they must have good seasons if they're going to be free agents. They're proving how good they are," Al-Hakim said.[26]

Griffith admitted later in the season that the lofty numbers Lyman and Larry Hisle were putting up were probably partially because they needed to have great seasons to get new deals elsewhere. "That's one reason, I suppose, we're doing so well," Griffith said in late July. "My kids are working their tails off because they're hungry, and I'm sure some of them want to see what they can get in the open market after a good season."[27]

Since the Twins weren't in position to sign Lyman long-term, they weren't able to trade him for any significant return. No club would give away very much for what could amount to only a half season of Lyman's services. So the June 15 deadline came and went without any activity.

"They know they are going to lose me, so I am surprised they didn't work out a trade," Lyman said later that summer. "If [Calvin Griffith] thinks I am worth that much, why couldn't he pay me in the same manner?

"It is funny he could want so much for me and offer so little. I don't understand why we had to get to this situation before anything could be done."[28]

* * *

On June 14, the California Angels came to Bloomington, and Lyman had a huge night, banging out four hits, including two triples and two singles, to improve his average to .343. But California cranked out seventeen hits, including two Joe Rudi homers and five hits from Mario Guerrero, in a 12–9 victory. The win helped the Angels continue to creep toward Minnesota. California was now just 3.5 games back.

Lyman struck out in his only plate appearance June 15, though the Twins claimed a 3–2 win over the Angels to improve to 35–25. Minnesota now held a three-game lead in the Western Division, and Lyman was up to third in the batting race, behind only Carew and Boston's Carlton Fisk.

Though Lyman raised his average up to .349 by late June, the Twins had dropped fifteen of twenty-four games since reaching their high-water mark of 27–14 in late May, and had relinquished their stranglehold of the Western Division. More than ten thousand fans came out to see the Twins and Rangers face off on June 22—mostly to boo and yell unfavorable comments at former Twin Bert Blyleven, who was on the hill that evening. "I wanted to beat them in one inning," said Blyleven later. "I'm glad the fans come out to boo me. Maybe enough of them will show up to help Calvin sign Hisle."[29]

Lyman had two hits as the Twins pushed Blyleven out of the game in the fourth inning, but the Rangers won, 10–8. It was a low point not only for the Twins' bullpen but also for the club as a whole. After more than fifty days in first place going back to late April, the second setback in three games to Texas knocked Minnesota out of the top spot by a game.

"If we remain a contender depends on how long we can tolerate this," Lyman said later of Minnesota's pitching issues. "We're at a point where we're second guessing ourselves. We don't know if we can score five runs and win anymore."

Though they had fallen out of first place, the Twins salvaged a split of the Texas series by winning the final game of the four-game set, 12–2. Continuing his charge toward the magical .400 mark, Rod Carew had three hits to trickle up to .395, while Lyman walked and scored a run in Minnesota's decisive six-run first inning.

"There's a long way to go," said Carew after the game. "I don't really want to be thinking about .400 right now."[30]

* * *

A big late June weekend awaited in Bloomington, as the Chicago White Sox came to town in a first-place tie with the Twins. The crowds were some of the biggest and best that the club had enjoyed in years. Gene Mauch penciled Lyman in the leadoff spot against Chicago southpaw Wilbur Wood, and he responded with an opposite-field single to left. He later scored on a hit by Larry Hisle. It was part of a five-RBI night for Hisle, who now had the major league lead with seventy runs driven in. Lyman returned to the plate in the bottom of the eighth, with the score tied, 6–6. Lerrin LaGrow laid a pitch over the middle, and Lyman crushed it. The ball sailed over the right-field fence, giving Minnesota an eventual 7–6 victory.

Lyman went hitless the next day, an 8–1 Chicago win, to fall to .346, while Carew got one hit to sit at .396. After more than 21,000 fans shuffled their way into the Met for the Friday evening and Saturday afternoon games against the White Sox, an even larger crowd awaited on Sunday. A reported paid attendance of 46,463 fans jammed through the turnstiles—the biggest crowd ever for a regular-season game at Metropolitan Stadium.

"The largest crowd in Twins history came out Sunday to see Carew reach for the .400 hitting barrier, and the hot hitter came through with four hits to push his average to the magic mark," said Mel Allen on "This Week in Baseball."

It was quite a festive day at the Met as the Twins banged out a club record nineteen runs. Glenn Adams had a grand slam, three hits in total, as well as eight RBIs. Carew's four-hit performance included a homer, double, and two singles. He scored five times and drove in six. Lyman also had a banner day feasting on Chicago pitching, singling in the third, walking twice, and scoring three runs, as the Twins returned to first place by a game.

As Carew ran around the bases following a two-run homer in the eighth, which gave him four hits on the day, the right-field scoreboard "Twins-O-Gram" spelled out a message: "That is .400 for Rod!"

"In the last three decades, Rico Carty, Hank Aaron, Willie Mays, and Stan Musial all reached .400 in mid-June, but Carew is the first batter in that period to approach July with that mark," said Mel Allen. "Hitting .400 under the tough conditions of modern baseball might rate as the greatest batting feat ever."

"It's possible that Rod Carew can do it," Allen continued. "It's certain that if he moves at his present rate, he will surpass George Sisler's record of 257 hits in one season."

From June 20 through June 26, Carew went seventeen for twenty-eight at the plate, scoring eleven runs and driving in twelve more, to move over .400.

"Not only is Rod hitting .400, and after that all-time hit record, he also leads the league in triples, run scored, and moved into second place on the league's RBI list. And he stole home this week for the 16th time in his career. Carew is having a season for all seasons," added Allen.

All of a sudden, Rod Carew was the talk of baseball. His pursuit of the magical .400 plateau was expanding beyond the parameters of the sport and becoming national news. Though he had been toiling for years in Minnesota as one of baseball's most consistently productive players, it wasn't until the 1977 season, and his flirtation with .400, that Rod Carew finally got his due as one of the elite players of his generation.

George McKenzie of KMSP-TV, a Minneapolis-based ABC affiliate, did a feature on the Twins first baseman that summer as he gave chase to history.

"I don't really try to do things I'm not capable of doing. I know my capabilities, and how far I can go, and what I can do with the bat," Carew said in the interview.

"I've disciplined myself over to the years to know that I'm not a home run hitter, so I'm not going to swing for the fences. I try to use the whole field, because I think I can get more hits this way instead of just trying to be a pull hitter, and hitting the ball in one place."

"Everybody knows that Ted Williams had the greatest pair of eyes that had ever been tested in the Naval cadet program. And Rod Carew has eyes of that caliber," added Gene Mauch. "I've been told by doctors that people who are under great stress don't have the benefit of their best eyesight. Both of these players—Ted Williams and Rod Carew—are so extremely relaxed, and so confident, because they acknowledge the fact that they are great hitters, that they operate daily at their best level of efficiency as far as their eyesight is concerned. I believe in that."[31]

"Hitting .400, it's a great feat," Carew continued. "Guys are going to hit home runs every day. But when you get 240, 250 hits throughout a season, I think it's an amazing feat to accomplish. I'm not going to just come right out and say yes, it's going to happen. But it might happen if things go my way, the way they have been going the first half of the season."

"Making a lot of baseball history with his magic bat," Mel Allen said of Carew in the fifth episode of "This Week in Baseball." "It isn't sorcery. Just more pure hitting talent than anyone has seen in a long, long time."

Carew's incredible all-around play was certainly the biggest draw to Metropolitan Stadium in the spring and summer of 1977, but Twins fans were also caught up with Lyman's thrilling efforts and slugger Larry Hisle's long drives.

The club was playing an exciting brand of baseball—scoring runs, collecting big hits, and staying in the hunt in the American League West. Despite his outstanding season, however, Lyman was once again snubbed by America's baseball fans, who selected the starters for the All-Star teams. As of late June, Lyman had collected more than a half million votes, but he still ranked eighth in the outfielder voting, lagging far behind Chicago's Richie Zisk and Boston's Carl Yastrzemski, who had over a million votes each. Carew, on the other hand, was the game's leading vote-getter. He would eventually receive more than four million votes to start the upcoming All-Star Game at Yankee Stadium.

"Minnesota's Rod Carew, top vote getter in the majors, with well over 4 million votes. That's enough to win the governorship of Minnesota," joked Mel Allen that summer on "This Week in Baseball." "They should at least offer Rod a seat in the Senate if he finishes the year at .400. Rod has always been popular with the voters. This will be his tenth All-Star Game."

"It's given me some respect," Carew said of his large vote totals. "It's great, you know, because I go up there, and I know that the guys don't think I'm an easy out. They're going to do everything they can to keep me from getting a base hit, and hurting their chances of winning a ball game. I try to use the whole diamond to hit. I hit the ball to left, up the middle, left center, right center, and pull the ball down the right field line."

Milwaukee came to town for a three-game series, the last series of June and the last three games of Minnesota's ten-game homestand. The Twins got back to their high-scoring ways, and Carew got three more hits, improving his average to .408, as Minnesota blew out the Brewers, 10–3. Lyman pinch hit in the seventh and struck out in his only at bat of the game.

The Twins struck again the next game, winning 8–3 behind two RBIs each from Glenn Adams and Dan Ford. Carew hit into his tenth straight game to keep his average well above .400 at .407. Lyman went one for five. He grounded to Brewers second baseman Don Money leading off the bottom of the first, and he reached on an error. He then scored Minnesota's first run. Lyman singled again leading off the seventh, though he would be thrown out at home on a force play.

Still in first place by a single game, the Twins ran into a buzz saw in Brewers youngster Lary Sorensen, who pitched eight innings of six-hit shutout ball. Lyman, who was dealing with a bruise at the base of his left thumb from a wayward swing earlier in the week, was unable to get a hit off Sorensen, going zero for three in the Twins' loss.

"His hand is beaten to a pulp," said Gene Mauch of his star outfielder.[32]

"It hurts when I just touch it, and these things take time to heal," Lyman said afterward.

As June came to an end, Lyman had proved over the first three months of the season that his outstanding 1976 campaign was no fluke. As he continued to rip line drives to both fields all over the American League in the spring of 1977, it was abundantly clear that someone would have to pony up some serious money to attain his services for the following year.

8

SETTLING INTO STARDOM (1977)

> I'm a human being. I'm not a piece of property. I am not a consignment of goods.—Curt Flood, outfielder, St. Louis Cardinals[1]

As July 1 rolled around, Rod Carew was still hitting well above .400, sitting at .411. Lyman ranked fourth in the American League, hitting .331, with Cleveland's Paul Dade and Boston's Carlton Fisk lying between him and Carew in the rankings.

In first place by just one game over the White Sox, the Twins made their way to the Windy City for a four-game weekend set with Western Division supremacy on the line. Lyman got the Twins off to a good start, leading off the opener with an opposite-field triple into left-center. Carew followed with a triple two batters later, and the Twins led, 1–0. Lyman got six hits in the four-game set, but the Twins were swept four straight by Chicago. Losers of five straight, and twenty-two of thirty-seven since late May, the Twins were just six games over .500, at 42–36, as they headed to Milwaukee.

Although Lyman's vote total for the All-Star Game surged over six hundred thousand around the Fourth of July, he still remained far back of the top vote-getters in the American League outfield, among them Boston's Carl Yastrzemski, who had over a million more votes than the third-year Twins talent.

Following the sweep on the South Side of Chicago, the Twins got back on track with a pair of important wins at County Stadium over the Brewers. California came in for a two-game set in Bloomington following the road trip to Chicago and Milwaukee, and the two teams played to a 3–3 draw through seven innings in the opener. Lyman led off the bottom of the eighth for the Twins off Angels reliever Paul Hartzell, who tried to sneak a fastball past him. Striking like a cobra, Lyman got all of it. His line drive shot landed in the bullpen in right-center field, about four hundred feet away from home plate, for his fifth dinger of the season. It was one of the longest homers of the year for Lyman, and it was the last run of the game as the Twins prevailed that night, 4–3. But the wins weren't nearly as plentiful as they had been earlier in the year.

As July 10 dawned, the Twins suddenly found themselves 4.5 games out of first place. Things were rapidly slipping away from the club. But they put it all together against Seattle in a 15–0 domination of the expansion team. As Geoff Zahn tossed a three-hit shutout, Roy Smalley and Butch Wynegar combined for seven RBIs as part of Minnesota's sixteen-hit attack. Lyman's bases-loaded single in the sixth gave the Twins an 8–0 advantage. He added a single in the fourth and another RBI single in the seventh to finish three for six, pushing his average back up to .333. Though Carew got a hit to keep his average above the magical barrier at .401, Carew's average had fallen ten points in recent games as he sought to continue his torrid pace.

* * *

By midseason, following the Twins' five-game homestand against California and Seattle, Metropolitan Stadium had welcomed approximately 150,000 more paying customers than at the same point in the 1976 season.

"Upper Midwest baseball fans have returned to the Met in 1977 to watch one of the highest-scoring teams in major league history," wrote Brent Kallestad for the Associated Press that summer. "The Minnesota Twins, who haven't reached the one million mark in attendance for seven years, are a cinch to easily surpass that figure this year. The popularity stems from winning. And contradictory to baseball truisms, the Twins are winning with hitting rather than pitching.

"They are also one of the top attractions in other American League cities, which puts additional charge into the Griffith coffers—money which can be used to keep the centerstage performers," the article continued. "Perhaps 1977 won't be the Twins' year, but the heart of the club is reaching its professional maturity, giving Minnesota backers a potential contender for many years."

Minnesota's solid gate to begin the 1977 season was part of a trend around major league baseball. Americans were flocking to parks all over the big leagues that summer, with a combined total of more than thirty-seven million spectators taking in games that season.

While the Twins organization was doing better financially in the summer of 1977 in comparison to the year before, that didn't necessarily improve Lyman's mood about his situation with the club. Despite his excellence at the plate, it was a frustrating early summer for the third-year Twins outfielder. Frustrating because the Twins didn't take his contract demands seriously. Frustrating because despite his excellent hitting and batting average, he was once again, for the second straight year, snubbed as a selection for the American League All-Star team. Frustrating because the Twins were reeling, having fallen out of first place. Frustrating because he wasn't playing what he felt was his natural position, center field, every day. He was also upset that the Twins organization hadn't done more to help his wife find work in the Minneapolis area and that he and other Minnesota players had been forced to stand on the team bus so members of the front office could have seats.

Lyman knew he was vastly outperforming his paltry contract and spent much of that summer with a burning rage building inside him. He had shown maturity from his rookie year on the field itself, refusing to get caught up in embarrassing showdowns with umps over called strikes. He also refused to let his annoyance with Twins management affect the way he treated his teammates. But by the time July rolled around—with no certainty he was going to sign a huge contract—it was simply the winning, the hitting, and the camaraderie with the guys that kept Lyman happy day-to-day in the Twins clubhouse.

Unable to suppress his feelings any longer, he made his frustrations public. Knowing he wasn't going to be with the club but a few more months, he let his thoughts be known. Lyman spared few people, criticizing Minnesota's ownership, management, and fans.

"I have a lot of pride in myself and my family," Lyman said to Tracy Ringolsby of the *Long Beach Independent-Press-Telegram* in an early July interview. "I'm not going to be humiliated like he [my father] was. Times have changed. He had no choice. Now, every player has the right to determine his destiny. I'm going to determine my own."

"I'm tired of playing for a second-class organization. The money is no longer an object. Happiness is what I'm looking for," Lyman added in another interview.[2]

Calling Twins fans "front runners," Lyman suggested they weren't engaged with the club unless the team was winning. "They're ignorant about baseball. They know nothing about the subtleties. It's really the organization's fault for not educating them."

Turning the criticism to his manager, Lyman expressed anger that Mauch was platooning him against some of the American League's tougher left-handers and, at times, making him play left field instead of his preferred center field.

"The way it was put to me was why should they play me in center field if I am not coming back to the organization?" Lyman said to Ringolsby. "They say it is an experiment, but I feel like it is a demotion. A center fielder has to do more work, backing up on almost every play," Lyman continued.[3]

When the local media in Minneapolis criticized him for his stance on playing left field instead of center field, Lyman had a ready response: "Ain't I got a right to say that?"

Lyman was still bitter several months later about the outfield situation—one of the few aspects of Gene Mauch's managerial style that he didn't agree with. "People think the Twins moved me to left field because I couldn't play center. They moved me because they felt that gave them a better chance to sign Hisle. I still ran the outfield from left field," he would say the following spring.[4]

Lyman felt that the Twins management was toying with him by not moving him in a trade. "They're playing with my mind. They figure if they can't keep me, they can try to ruin me any way they can," he replied to Ringolsby in the July interview. "But they are just trying to drown a fish. I'll be okay. I can't stop playing just because I'm going to be gone. Nobody wants a quitter. I'm a challenger and I have a job to do so I'll do it the best I can."

A couple days after Lyman's comments were published, Calvin Griffith responded. It was clear the venom going back and forth in the papers between the two strong-willed men was seriously challenging any hope of reconciliation that would result in Lyman's signing with the club for 1978 and beyond.

"Bostock is a bitter man because we won't give him a four-year contract for $1 million," Griffith said. "I don't happen to believe he's worth $250,000 a year."[5]

Calling Lyman "a cancer on our club," Griffith threatened to complete a waiver deal with a second-division team to cast Lyman off to someone else. But nothing ever materialized on that front.

Although many of the Twins players sympathized with Lyman's complaints and tended to agree with him, they were put in a difficult spot. Do they agree with Lyman and bite the hand feeding them, trashing the organization paying their salaries? Or do they keep their mouths shut and let him take the heat for all of them? The Minnesota players, for the most part, stayed quiet on the subject.

Refusing to rock the boat any further, the players let Lyman take the brunt of the criticisms alone—much like the Birmingham Black Barons players had thirty years earlier, when Lyman's father had demanded an extra dollar for meal money from the team's owner after he returned to professional baseball in the late 1940s following his service in World War II.

"We wasn't makin' no money. The best I ever pried 'em out of was 'bout five or six hundred a month," Lyman Bostock Sr. said to Brent Kelley for his oral history of the Negro Leagues. "I came in a great big out-of-shape fella [after the war] and we wasn't gettin' but two dollars a day for eatin' money. I called a meetin' on [Black Barons owner] Tom Hayes. To make sure they got the message, we came before him.

"He said, 'I understand you're havin' a meetin' down here.' I spoke 'cause them guys wanted to stay at home and I didn't give a hoot where I played. So I said, to make sure he got the message, I said, 'Mr. Hayes, the cost of livin' is up. In the face of the economic situation, I think we would like for you to give us a dollar [more] come May the twelfth.' The season starts in May. I say, 'As of now, we're not askin' that, but when that time come, we expect to get three dollars. We play in them doubleheaders and hard games on Sundays. We need that.'

"Hayes said, 'Ah, I see Bostock is your spokesman.' Nobody said nothin'. I got the message. I was traded to Chicago. He [Hayes] later said, 'Bostock will cost me money.'"[6]

Calvin Griffith certainly wasn't the only one who disagreed with Lyman's position. Syndicated columnist Murray Olderman took a shot at the Twins outfielder in late July: "Every time I hear about the unhappiness of ball players with their lot—the latest are Lyman Bostock of Minnesota and Dave Parker of Pittsburgh—I wonder what they'd do if they had to work 9-to-5 at one-tenth the pay," Olderman wrote.

After spraining his ankle on a stolen base attempt against the Angels earlier in the month, Lyman sat out and rested his sore foot on July 12 as the Twins were shut out on just four hits by Nolan Ryan and his eight strikeouts. Following another day off his tender ankle, Lyman was prepared to return to the Twins lineup for the last game of the series in Anaheim. Prior to that Wednesday night's game against the Angels, Gene Mauch sat down with Lyman to clear the air. The veteran manager told Lyman that all the griping wasn't going to help him in the free-agent market. The two men reconciled, though Mauch would defy Lyman down the stretch by repeatedly playing him in left field instead of center.

Carew arrived in California hitting .401. But after going just two for thirteen in Anaheim, he had fallen to .391. Unfortunately for the future Hall of Famer, he wouldn't get back to the lofty .400 perch. Despite his slight slip, however, Carew still easily led the league in hitting as of July 15. Toronto's Bob Bailor was holding second at .341, while Lyman was nipping at his heels at .338.

As Carew, Larry Hisle, and Butch Wynegar packed up and prepared to head to New York City for the All-Star Game following Minnesota's last game of the first half in Oakland, Lyman and the rest of the Twins gathered their things, left the Oakland Coliseum clubhouse, and headed out for three days of rest and relaxation before returning to action the following week in Bloomington. At the All-Star break, with seventy games left in the regular season, Lyman ranked third in the American League in hitting, third in triples, and fourth in hits. But he wouldn't be at Yankee Stadium, taking what many felt was his rightful place among the game's greats.

* * *

Dealing with inside pitching was something Lyman had gotten used to over the course of the 1977 season. As more pitchers around the American League faced him—and more at bats led to more scouting opportunities around the circuit for the various clubs—the book on Lyman Bostock was to jam him. Crowd him. Make him swing at pitches that he couldn't extend the barrel of the bat on. Make him beat you by feeding him inside.

"It's something teams try," Lyman said of the inside pitching. "They change pitching outside when a hitter has it going good and switch to inside. I guess that's what they are trying with me."[7]

"Gosh, that Bostock can hit," said Angels manager Dave Garcia. "Right-handers. Left-handers. I don't think it makes any difference. When he's hitting like this, it's hard to get him out. He will help whatever team he's with a great deal."

After belting homers in back-to-back games in mid-July against the Angels, Lyman's average was up to .334 in the days following his controversial statements to the media. Though he lined into a triple play in the California series—the only time that happened during his major league career—the hits kept coming.

Acting like a man with something to prove, Lyman got three more hits on July 24 as the Twins picked up a win over Oakland in the first game of a Sunday doubleheader at the Met. In the second game of the twin bill, the A's and Twins slugged it out, combining for eighteen runs over the first nine innings and going into extra frames tied, 9–9. Lyman had produced an RBI double in the third inning to contribute to Minnesota's score. Leading off the bottom of the twelfth with the game still tied, Lyman stepped up confidently. He had been seeing the ball remarkably well in recent days. By the time Lyman strolled into the batter's box, approximately half of the more than thirty thousand fans who had filed in for the first game of the doubleheader had gone home. They had dealt with a brief thirty-minute rain delay and the hot, muggy midsummer heat that followed. Settling into the box, Lyman stared ahead at A's reliever Doug Bair, who made a mistake, lofting one over the heart of the plate. Lyman tagged it. The ball flew off the outfielder's bat on a high trajectory before it settled into the right-field bleachers, 403 feet from home plate. Lyman's solo blast—the first walk-off homer of his big league career—gave Minnesota reliever Tom Johnson his eleventh win in his last fourteen decisions.

The third-year Twins outfielder got another clutch hit the following day, as Minnesota completed a much-needed three-game sweep of the last place A's for its seventh victory in eight outings. Though Lyman had reached base on an error in the first inning and drew a walk in the sixth, he was hitless on the day when he came up in the bottom of the eleventh of a 1–1 game. Facing Oakland's Rick Langford, Lyman pulled a single into right field on a hit-and-run, which allowed Rod Carew, who had led off with a single, to reach third. Larry Hisle brought victory to the Twins two batters later, singling into left for a 2–1 Minnesota win.

"We're not out of it, but we've been on vacation," Lyman said after the game.[8]

Remarkably, Dave Goltz pitched all eleven innings for the Twins, allowing eight hits to pick up his twelfth win in his last sixteen decisions.

"Dave Goltz now knows what it takes to win in the major leagues," said Mauch after the game.

"Experience and confidence," Goltz added. "And a good team doesn't hurt."

Lyman finally cooled off on July 27, going zero for four in a 4–1 Twins win over the Seattle Mariners. Carew went two for four with an RBI in the victory, his average improving to .387. As Lyman's seven-game hitting streak was snapped, his average slipped to .341. But he had largely justified his outspoken comments earlier in July, going fifteen of thirty-one at the plate with three homers, nine RBIs, and eight runs scored in the span of a week.

* * *

The Twins began August with a seven-game homestand against the Royals, Tigers, and Indians, and Lyman had a huge night in the opening game of the stand against Kansas City, bumping his average to .343. After opening with a walk in the first inning, Lyman nailed a Jim Colburn pitch for a two-run homer, giving the Twins an early 3–2 lead. With his sudden midsummer power surge at the plate, the free-swinging outfielder was becoming more and more familiar with trotting around all four bases instead of merely strolling to first with a base on balls.

"I've always thought you swing at anything in the strike zone," Lyman said later. "I don't give the pitchers much of a chance to walk me."[9]

"Tony [Oliva] still kids me that I'm a dumb hitter. I know he's right, too. Anything near the strike zone and I swing."[10]

In the sixth, with Minnesota still leading, 6–5, Lyman ripped a single into right-center field, scoring Roy Smalley to make the count 7–5. Then in the eighth he got his third hit, poling an opposite-field double to right to bring home Butch Wynegar for Minnesota's ninth and final run. The Twins took the game, 9–5.

"We've got to show them we aren't afraid of them on our home grounds," Lyman said of the Royals.[11] "A whole season, that's what it's about. We're working hard."[12]

"Lyman is one of finest hitters in the game," Mauch added to Bob Greene of the Associated Press. "There is absolutely no restriction in his swing. He's a very intense player."

"We're playing good, but we have to," Mauch continued. "I really think that for the first time in 1977, there's a little heat on Chicago. They've been in first place long enough now and people know they're for real."

With the win over Kansas City on August 1, the Twins had suddenly reeled off victories in twelve of sixteen contests—moving ahead of the Royals into second place and pulling within 4.5 games of Chicago. At night's end, Lyman was a full twenty-two points ahead of Boston's Jim Rice in second place in the American League hitting race. Though he wasn't going to catch Carew, who was hitting .382 at the time, Lyman did have an outside chance of catching his teammate in hits, runs, and triples with a strong finish. As it was, Lyman was in the top three in the American League in four categories—second in hitting (.343), second in runs (75), second in hits (136), and third in triples (10). Carew was leading in all four statistics.

Lyman had back-to-back two-hit games against the Cleveland Indians August 5 and 6, as the Twins continued to make their assault on first place in the Western Division. The Twins broke out the big guns in the first contest, setting a new franchise record with eleven runs in the fourth inning of a 14–10 victory that sounded more like a football score. Lyman contributed to Minnesota's huge inning by doubling in a run and scoring on a bases-loaded walk. The Twins completed a three-game sweep of the Indians the following day—Minnesota's seventeenth win in its last twenty-two games—to move within a half game of first place. Lyman got an RBI single off Dennis Eckersley in the fifth, giving Minnesota a 4–0 lead, after Rod Carew dragged a bunt for a hit and stole second. Carew went a perfect four for four, moving his average back up to .387.

"They beat our brains out," said Indians manager Jeff Torborg. "They hit the best we had to offer in this series. The way Minnesota is swinging the bats, I don't think it would matter much who was pitching."[13]

With the Royals completing a home sweep of the White Sox that same afternoon in Kansas City, there was suddenly a logjam atop the American League West. Heading into the second week of August, there were four teams within three games of first place. Chicago still led Minnesota by a half game with the surging Royals 1.5 games back and the Texas Rangers just three games back in fourth place.

"The Twins, in a burst, make a move towards first," said Mel Allen on "This Week in Baseball." "Out in Minnesota's Twin Cities, Rod Carew and his crew have been stroking and smoking. The nod not only goes to Carew, but to the whole Twins team, which moved to within one game of the top.

"The Twins top the majors in runs scored, and what remains to be seen is if they can top the White Sox, Royals, and Rangers in that zany race for the Western Division title. A lot of fish in a small pool. So who will sink and who will swim in this wild Western race?"

While Minnesota's surge into the Western Division race was reigning supreme on Lyman's mind that August, so was his impending contract situation. Though he had decided not to negotiate during the season, he was willing to discuss it when the subject came up that August. He candidly gave beat reporters his thoughts.

In early August, Bostock announced, "Now I want to see what I'm worth on the open market. Maybe no one will pay very much for a line drive hitter."[14]

One reporter prophetically responded, "Someone probably will."

"Lyman Bostock, a la Hubert Humphrey, loves to talk in the third person," wrote AP writer Brent Kallestad in August. "Lyman, like the Minnesota senator, seldom refers to himself in the first or second person." Kallestad was referring to Lyman's recent comments suggesting he might have an about-face with the Minnesota Twins if they'd improve their offer.

"'Lyman Bostock wants to play with the Twins,' he had said. 'Right now it's up to the man [Calvin Griffith], not Lyman Bostock.' The fleet outfielder probably plays with more detectible enthusiasm than anyone in the American League."

Though Lyman may have been perplexing—and even annoying—to reporters with his third-person speech and his antimanagement commentary that summer, he was still making plenty of friends among those who loved the sport of baseball and appreciated players who played the game well with a smile on their face, as he did each and every day out on the field.

* * *

During the summer of 1977, an assistant principal at a high school in Vancouver, Washington, by the name of Bill Click embarked on the journey of a lifetime with his teenage sons. Setting out in the family's 1973 Ford station wagon, the Clicks' mission was to visit every major league stadium—twenty-six at that time—in the span of a month. Beginning in Seattle, the trio drove south into California and then east, stopping in Houston before watching a game in Atlanta. They then headed to the Midwest, and after that the Northeast, taking in games at stops along the way. Along the way, the Clicks got to hang out in the dugout with the Los Angeles Dodgers before a game at Dodger Stadium. They were put up in the Plaza Hotel in New York City by a local television station. They received field passes throughout both leagues. They even saw a topless Sally Rand, the seventy-two-year-old former burlesque dancer, while making an appearance on a talk show. But of all the Click family's memorable experiences that summer, they unanimously agreed that their best moments on the road were their interactions with Lyman Bostock.

"He's all of our favorite," said fifteen-year-old John Click.[15]

While the Clicks were in Minnesota taking in a game at Metropolitan Stadium, Lyman took several minutes of his pregame time chatting with the family. He asked them about their wild journey, which consisted of approximately fifteen thousand miles of driving and a month on the road.

"He just stood there on the field and talked to us for about 20 minutes while dad was photographing us," John added. "We talked about the trip and photography, everything."

A few nights later, when the Twins were at Exhibition Stadium taking on the Blue Jays, Lyman recognized the Clicks, and went over and talked with them before the game.

"Yeah, then we saw him again in Toronto and he recognized us right away and came over to say hello again," added Carl Click.

An August 16 Twins game in Baltimore turned into an epic series of rants by Orioles manager Earl Weaver, who got tossed from the contest in the eleventh inning. Weaver's frustration with the umpires began in earnest in the sixth, when the game was delayed by more than ten minutes by the Twins as Butch Wynegar had a moth pulled from his right ear. At that point Weaver brought an official protest, but things would only go downhill from there. In the ninth, Lyman came up with a runner on first and nobody out. He attempted to bunt Carew, who had led off the inning with a single, into scoring position, but a perfect strike by Orioles pitcher

Tippy Martinez forced Carew at second base. Lyman would eventually reach third, where, with Jerry Terrell at the plate, the Twins went for a suicide squeeze. Terrell was unable to make contact, and Ken Rudolph successfully picked Lyman off third. The Twins would botch another suicide-squeeze attempt in the tenth inning.

Weaver had been rankled by Lyman's suicide-squeeze attempt in the ninth, thinking that Terrell had gone around on the fateful pitch that resulted in Lyman being picked off. Though Terrell struck out anyway, Weaver's frustration was reaching a boiling point by the eleventh, when Lyman returned to the dish. With Scott McGregor on the mound for another inning of relief work, the Orioles hurler threw an inside fastball that Lyman tried to avoid. The ball brushed closely against Lyman's body, close to his right arm. After claiming he was hit by the pitch, Lyman was awarded first base. Weaver lost it: the veteran manager ran onto the field and chastised home-plate umpire Al Clark, earning a quick boot. Before he left the field, Weaver threw his cap several feet into the air, buried home plate under several mounds of dirt, and even attempted to make a pitching change before the umpires insisted he go to the clubhouse.

Despite his frustration with Lyman that particular night, Weaver couldn't deny his greatness. "[Bostock will] win four batting titles in the next seven years," the Orioles manager would say of Lyman.[16]

Finally, in the thirteenth, a single by Doug DeCinces ended the game, the Orioles victorious, 6–5.

As August 20 dawned, Lyman was more than fifty points behind the front-running Carew atop the batting average, but he remained firmly in second place at .331. After Lyman went one for four with a third-inning single in Minnesota's 6–2 setback in the second game of the Baltimore series, the Twins finally got it together offensively and ran the visitors out of the ballpark in the third contest.

Playing in front of a solid Sunday afternoon crowd of more than twenty-three thousand fans at the Met, Lyman batted eighth and played left field. His sacrifice fly in the bottom of the second gave the Twins an early 3–2 lead, but that was just the start of one of Lyman's better games of the season. Batting with one out and runners on first and second in the bottom of the sixth, Lyman pegged one up the middle into center field, breaking a 5–5 tie. Then, in the eighth, Lyman belted a homer off Dennis

Martinez for Minnesota's final run in a 9–5 triumph. He finished two for three with a run and three RBIs.

"I felt so good at the plate, I could see myself hitting a home run," Lyman said after the game. "The hard thing is not to try something new if things aren't going so well. Playing every day helps any hitter. I just hope I'll feel this good the rest of the way."[17]

Ron Schueler, who pitched four and a third innings of one-hit relief to help lead the Twins on the mound, was all too eager to celebrate with Lyman as he put to bed his brief lull at the plate. "The day he broke out of a slump, I grabbed him and threw him all over the place," said Schueler.[18]

The Twins headed to New York just a game out of first place, but they ran smack into a red-hot Yankees club that was battling its way toward a second straight American League pennant. Billy Martin's club had won fourteen of sixteen games coming into the Minnesota series. And behind a four-hit complete game by Catfish Hunter and four home runs by various Yankees, the home team won in an 11–1 wipeout. Lyman led off the game against Hunter with a line drive into right field, which he turned into a triple. He scored the Twins' only run of the night moments later on a Roy Smalley sacrifice fly.

As the Twins were getting throttled in the Bronx, Kansas City was winning its eighth straight game—setting a new franchise record—with a win over Milwaukee. Minnesota was now two games back, and they wouldn't get any closer to the galloping Royals.

Despite a nine-game hitting streak, Mauch elected to sit Lyman on August 27, as the reeling Boston Red Sox, who had lost eight of nine games, hosted Minnesota in front of an overflow Saturday afternoon crowd of nearly thirty-five thousand fans at Fenway Park. Red Sox manager Don Zimmer switched up his rotation, throwing Bill Lee at the Twins. In the top of the eighth, with the Twins trailing 5–3, Lyman pinch hit with one out and runners on second and third. But all he could manage this time around was a popout in foul territory to Butch Hobson at third base, ending his latest hitting streak in Minnesota's 7–5 loss. The following day, despite Lyman's three hits, the Twins lost once again to the Red Sox, 6–5. Following another highly disappointing loss for his club, Mauch's frustration finally boiled over. Walking into his office, Mauch began throwing things off his desk at the adjoining walls.

Pitcher David Johnson made six starts and had thirty appearances for the 1977 Twins, producing a 2–5 record and a 4.58 earned run average in

72.2 innings of work. In late August, he spoke with reporter Mark McDonald from his hometown newspaper, the *Abilene Reporter News*, about his teammates and their contract situations.

"Some of the guys say they're tired of messing with [Calvin Griffith] and they're going to go through with playing out their options," Johnson said.

"If we lose Larry Hisle and Lyman Bostock, you can kiss the Twins goodbye for a few years," the reliever continued. "These guys are not making much money, so it has been sort of a common cause to rally around. It's making us play harder than a bunch of millionaires. We want to make some big bucks, too."

* * *

As September arrived, the Royals and Twins were about to race off in different directions, like two locomotives passing in the night. There would be no pennant race this time around for Minnesota. Starting with a win over the Rangers on August 31, the Royals wouldn't lose another game until September 16—a sixteen-game winning streak. From there, Kansas City reeled off eight more wins for an incredible stretch of twenty-four wins in twenty-five games.

Kansas City's incredible finish in the late summer of 1977 took the wind out of Minnesota's sails, but the Twins were their own worst enemy, dropping ten of twelve contests from August 31 to September 13 to slip a full ten games in the standings. From August 27 to September 13, when the Twins lost their sixth straight game, Minnesota dropped twelve out of sixteen contests and had fallen twelve games back—ruining any hopes of a late pennant run and pushing them within a few losses of mathematical elimination.

Lyman went four for eighteen at the plate to begin September, and he sat out his first full game in months on September 4, a 4–0 New York Yankees victory over the Twins that completed a sweep. He was just two for seven against the Yankees pitching as New York continued its rise to the postseason.

On September 5, Lyman was still holding strong in second place at .337, eleven points ahead of Baltimore's Ken Singleton in the American League batting race. And while he would go just two for eleven at home against Texas, he scored a couple runs and drove in four more during the series, including an RBI in all three games.

On September 9, in the middle of Kansas City's epic winning streak, the Royals made their way to Bloomington for the final road series of the season against their Western Division rival. Lyman's recent slip to .334 dropped him briefly to third in the American League batting race, as Singleton had slithered past him to .338.

Though the Royals outplayed Minnesota in the opener, 6–3, for Kansas City's tenth straight victory, Lyman did his part for the Twins, nailing a shot into the gap in left-center field for a double in the first inning. He would later score as part of a two-run inning. Lyman was in left field in the top of the fourth of a 2–1 game as John Mayberry of the Royals hit a slicing line drive in front of him. In a lot of ballparks, with a lot of left fielders, Mayberry's shot would have undoubtedly been a single. But playing shallow as usual, Lyman took off after it, dove to his right, and snared the ball in front of his body with both hands, rolling over once in the process. He got up and jogged off the field, having ended Kansas City's half of the fourth.

"Good timin', Lyman!" said Mel Allen on an episode of "This Week in Baseball," featuring his catch as one of the top defensive plays of the week.

Kansas City finally broke through in the seventh, taking the lead on back-to-back hits by Darrell Porter and Amos Otis off Paul Thormodsgard and then breaking it open on a three-run homer off the bat of George Brett, completing a five-run inning. Though the Twins were swept by the Royals—falling to fourth place, eleven games back—Lyman came back with a big game on September 11, singling off Andy Hassler up the middle in the second inning, coming through again with a hit in the fifth, and then singling again into right field in the ninth, though he failed to score any runs.

Heading off to Chicago to play the White Sox, Lyman had a rare struggle in Comiskey Park, picking up just one hit in the first three games as the Twins endured the franchise's longest losing streak in the last two seasons. The Twins would manage a series split, however, with Lyman getting three hits in the last contest of the four-game set.

At .332 on September 20, Lyman was still slightly behind Ken Singleton's .335 for second place in the American League batting standings. Gene Mauch typically gave Lyman the night off against Kansas City's challenging southpaw Paul Splittorff. But with the season fading away, he elected to give his third-year outfielder a shot against the Royals starter. He finished hitless in three at bats in Kansas City's 4–2 victory, though he drew a walk.

The Royals were poised to clinch at least a tie for the Western Division crown on September 21. But Lyman would put together another four-hit game in an attempt to keep Kansas City from clinching the division on his watch. After singling in the first and third innings, Lyman belted a deep home run off Jim Colburn, his third hit of the night, in the fifth. Finally, in the seventh, Lyman got his fourth hit, a single to left field. Though he wouldn't get his fifth hit in the ninth inning, the Twins outfielder did drive in his second run of the day on a fielder's choice groundout. But despite his best efforts, the Royals clinched a tie of the Western Division title with a 10–4 victory.

In a classy move, Lyman walked through the bowels of Royals Stadium after the game to the Kansas City locker room, where he congratulated the Royals players for a season well played. With a big smile on his face, he shook hands with George Brett, one of the biggest catalysts in Kansas City's run to its second straight divisional title.

Returning home for the final homestand of the season at Metropolitan Stadium, Lyman had moved back into second place in the American League hitting race. His four-hit game in Kansas City had pushed him into a statistical tie with Ken Singleton at .333. But in Minnesota's next outing, Lyman firmly staked his claim for the American League's second-best hitting season. Only forty-seven hundred fans came out on a Saturday afternoon to see Lyman get another three-hit game, Dave Goltz's nineteenth win of the year in a victory over the Milwaukee Brewers. The following day, one last doubleheader at the Met, Lyman once again led off with a single, but it was his only hit of the day. Lyman sat out the second game of the Sunday double-dip with Milwaukee—his average holding at .335 as the Twins ensured another winning season with an 8–4 triumph heading into the final week.

An interesting story in the *Minneapolis Tribune* that last week of September indicated that the Twins began the 1977 season with approximately $1.5 million in cash and were now sitting on significantly more as a result of the presence of more than a million spectators at Metropolitan Stadium, the addition of the Blue Jays and Mariners to the American League schedule, and increases in ticket and concession prices. The feature suggested that the Twins had the necessary reserves to pony up more

SETTLING INTO STARDOM (1977)

to players like Lyman and Larry Hisle. It incensed Calvin Griffith and the Minnesota front office.

"The figures are totally inaccurate," said Twins spokesman Tom Mee. "This is the worst kind of journalism."[19]

"I have no idea how much we've made," added Griffith.

"Baseball fans are taking a negative feeling towards Larry Hisle, Lyman Bostock, Tom Burgmeier, Jerry Terrell, and Ron Schueler, who are playing out their options with the Twins this year," wrote Cliff Morlan, a Twins beat reporter from the *Bemidji Pioneer*, about Minnesota's projected free agents. "I hope that Griffith can get Lyman to sign his contract with the Twins. The others can be replaced."

Sitting at .336 as the White Sox came in for the final pair of contests in Bloomington, Lyman picked up two more hits, a single and a double, though the Twins suffered another loss, 8–6. In what would be his final appearance at Metropolitan Stadium as a Minnesota Twin, Lyman went

Lyman, seated second from left, joins five of his Twins teammates who remained unsigned heading into the summer of 1977 and would be eligible to become free agents after the season if they didn't sign. From left, pitcher Tom Burgmeier, Lyman, outfielder Larry Hisle, pitcher Ron Schueler, infielder Jerry Terrell, and pitcher Dave Goltz. (Associated Press / Jim Mone.)

hitless in four at bats on September 28 against the White Sox in a 4–3 loss.

Some among the reporters in the house that Wednesday afternoon suggested that Lyman and Larry Hisle wouldn't be missed very much, but others saw things differently. "Seems that Larry Hisle will be gone for sure," wrote Cliff Morlan. "Lyman Bostock is also on the market. These two will be missed. The way Hisle played the outfield Wednesday and Bostock drew the horse collar at the plate, there were mutterings in the press box that indicated they wouldn't be missed."

With the final series of the season at hand in Milwaukee, Lyman put it all together for one final flurry, going five for seven at the plate with two runs and two RBIs in his final two appearances of the 1977 season. In the top of the third inning, Lyman crushed a Moose Haas fastball for his fourteenth homer. His two-run shot tied the game, 3–3. He would go on to double in the fourth inning of a game that was halted by weather after five innings, with the Brewers leading, 7–5.

The next day, Lyman and his mates got one last chance to put together a power surge. Behind Hisle's twenty-eighth homer and a combined six hits between Carew and Lyman, the Twins rolled, 9–1. Lyman would single in each of his first three plate appearances, scoring in the first for the opening run of the afternoon.

Minnesota starter Dave Goltz went out the final day looking to get his twentieth win, and he got it, as the Twins won 6–2 over the Brewers. Lyman had a sacrifice fly in the fifth inning, tying the game before Minnesota pulled away. He finished out at .336, the second-best average in the American League behind only Carew. But going hitless four times on the last day of the season, Lyman would finish with 199 hits, one shy of the 200 plateau.

Although .400 wasn't meant to be for Rod Carew, he got three hits on the last day to finish his greatest season at .388. He ended the year with 239 hits—the most in major league baseball since Detroit's Heinie Manush collected 241 hits back in 1928—and 100 RBIs. Carew's .388 mark was the closest anyone had yet come to Ted Williams's historic .406 season of 1941, though George Brett's .390 season a couple years later in 1980 was another strong run at the .400 barrier. No major leaguer has managed to surpass even the .380 threshold in the last thirty-five seasons.

"All I can say is I did my best," Carew said the final week of the season. "My only complaint is I wish we had done better. It's frustrating when you don't win."[20]

Demonstrating remarkable consistency, Lyman hit an identical .336 at home and on the road in 1977. As he did throughout his career, he hit well against right-handers, with a sizzling .342 clip. But he hit nearly as well against southpaws, going .324. The 1977 season forever put to bed the notion that Lyman could only hit right-handers. Hitting .331 during the first half and .341 during the second half, Lyman had 101 hits on the road and 98 at home. Lyman saved his best performances for the best teams, hitting .389 against the eventual world champion New York Yankees and going .346 at the plate against the division champion Royals. There were only three teams in the American League that Lyman hadn't hit .300 against: the Oakland A's (.292), the Texas Rangers (.268), and the Detroit Tigers (.229).

When it was all said and done, in 1977 Lyman finished second in the American League in hitting, fourth in runs scored, fourth in total hits, and fifth in triples. He had established himself not only as a bona fide star in major league baseball but as a young man worthy of a massive new contract.

9

A LIFE-CHANGING NEGOTIATION
(1977 OFF-SEASON)

> If you think that one player could win for you—make you a contender and put you in the World Series—sure, I'd spend some money for that.—Gene Autry, actor and California Angels owner[1]

As one of the all-time great American League Championship Series between the Royals and the Yankees played out in the Bronx and in Kansas City in October 1977, Lyman Bostock was back home in California, preparing to become a very wealthy young man. Lyman had been one of twenty-three players around the majors who had played without a contract in 1977, which made him eligible for the second annual Major League Baseball reentry draft, to be held in the ballroom of New York City's Plaza Hotel on Friday, November 4.

It was a stout crop of free-agent talent hitting baseball's open market. Along with Lyman were his soon-to-be former Twins teammate Larry Hisle, who had just led the American League with 119 RBIs; reliever Goose Gossage, who saved twenty-six games for the Pittsburgh Pirates; Dave Kingman, who had mashed twenty-six homers for four different clubs; and Chicago White Sox teammates Richie Zisk and Oscar Gamble, who had combined to hit sixty-one homers with 184 RBIs.

By the time the 1977 season concluded, following Reggie Jackson's epic three-homer performance in game six of the World Series in Yankee Stadium against the Dodgers, Lyman was considered a favorite to land one of the more lucrative off-season deals. Calvin Griffith and his assistants had lowballed Lyman and his agent the previous spring, prior to his second straight huge season. They had offered him around the major leagues as trade bait before attempting to negotiate with Lyman and his agent, eventually throwing out a six-year contract for more than $2 million toward the end of the 1977 season.

"That was way more than enough money," Lyman would say the following spring. "If they had offered me that at the beginning of the season, I'd have signed. But by the end I just didn't want to stay there."[2]

Griffith knew that he couldn't compete on the open market for Lyman's long-term services. So the longtime Twins owner took advantage of the outfielder's skills for one more spring and summer in 1977, then prepared to move on without him in 1978. And it was just as well, since Lyman didn't plan to do any more negotiating with the Twins.

"I don't think Calvin Griffith can match the highest offers of other teams, and I don't think he would want to," Lyman replied. "It hasn't been a joyous three years with the Twins. It's been joyous on the field and with the fans, but we have no relationship with the owner. All the other teams seem to have that. They come around and see what's going on and how they can rectify situations. I couldn't play under the same circumstances with Calvin Griffith."[3]

"Griffith never got close."[4]

"I wanted to stay in Minnesota. I loved the city. The fans were good. But I didn't want to play for Calvin Griffith anymore. He's not reasonable. He doesn't care about his players. And he doesn't pay them like modern ball players," Lyman said to Steve Dilbeck of the *San Bernardino Sun-Telegram*. "Eleven guys left the team this year. That's evidence somebody is doing something wrong.

"It's like a job. You want to be able to talk to your employer. I don't want to be going into his office every day. But I want to feel like I can talk to him.

"It's a give-and-take situation. A lot of people perform better when they're appreciated. You want a little extra out of your players, that's a good way to get it—showing them you care."

Lyman's biggest regret as he prepared to leave the Twins was that he would lose the day-to-day company of men who had grown to be his close friends, such as Larry Hisle and Rod Carew. "I'll miss Larry Hisle, who was my main man," Lyman said to Dave Anderson of the *New York Times* a few months later. "We were each other's shadow."

He would miss his many conversations about hitting with Carew and Hisle, as well as with Tony Oliva, who had gone from teammate to trusted batting instructor during Lyman's time with the Twins. "Rod really helped me a lot," Lyman said. "We were always talking about hitting, about the other pitchers. I talked to Tony Oliva and all of us, Rod and Larry, and me were always talking hitting. I'll miss that. I'll miss Gene Mauch, and I'll miss the fans, too. The fans were good to my family there. I felt very free there. The people there [in Minneapolis] don't know how lucky they are to be in a crime-free area. If it wasn't for the owner, Minnesota would be a great place to play."

Taking one final jab at his former owner, Lyman prepared to move forward without the Twins. He said, "I just wanted to get away from Calvin Griffith. He felt he only needed me when the pressure was on him to sign me. I hope he misses me more than I'm going to miss him."

* * *

Owners like Calvin Griffith had enjoyed decades of prosperity, without the burden of an expensive open marketplace for prime talent, through a reserve clause in every player's contract. The reserve clause specified that a club had a right to "reserve" a player's services on a year-by-year basis, essentially for the player's entire career, unless they traded or released him.

Free agency in American professional baseball was made possible through a few monumental legal decisions that had gone in the players' favor—specifically, the rulings by arbitrator Peter Seitz on December 23, 1975, in regard to pitchers Andy Messersmith and Dave McNally. The legal question at hand was whether the reserve clause was perpetual. Did the one-year renewal language bind a player to a certain club into perpetuity, regardless of whether a signed contract had been executed by both player and owner every single year? In the cases of Messersmith and McNally, both of whom had played without contracts in 1975, Seitz determined that since they hadn't signed an agreement with the clubs they had played for that season, they weren't required under the reserve clause to negotiate solely with that team the following year. Therefore, they were free to sign with whichever team they chose.

By playing without a contract in 1977, known at the time as "playing out his option," Lyman was given the same consideration and, along with the others who had played without a signed agreement, was declared a free agent. There was concern about both competitive balance and the possibility that teams couldn't sustain the expected rapid spike in salaries around the two major leagues. The fighting between the players and owners would only escalate in the coming years.

"It is clearly a source of concern for the business side of baseball," commissioner Bowie Kuhn said that off-season. "The stronger teams are the teams with more financial resources and if they become even stronger through this system, what happens to competitive balance? If you lose the competitive balance, the attractiveness of the game is affected. That's the side that worries me."[5]

"It's going to be the ruination of baseball," Griffith quipped during the fall of 1977. "One of these days the owners are going to get hit with a sledgehammer and see what damn fools they are."[6]

The first reentry draft in 1976 had been a curious affair. Inside the smoke-filled Terrace Room at the Plaza Hotel, the various owners and team officials attempted to rein in their growing concern about free agency. Watching his Oakland A's get dismantled player by player, Charlie O. Finley called the event a "den of thieves."

Not much had changed by the following year, though two additional American League franchises, the Toronto Blue Jays and Seattle Mariners, participated. Although the reentry draft was designed to provide some organization for the impending bidding war, the event, in hindsight, didn't make much sense. The rules were obscure and not easily explained.

A player could be drafted by half the major league franchises—twelve of twenty-four teams in 1976, which was bumped up to thirteen of twenty-six teams in 1977 with the addition of Toronto and Seattle. Only those franchises, along with the club each player had played for the previous year, had the right to negotiate for the player's services. No matter what round a team drafted a player, they could negotiate with him, so long as he wasn't off the board by having already been drafted by thirteen other teams.

Although the reentry draft was conducted like traditional drafts of amateur talent—with the worst teams getting the earliest picks—there wasn't much advantage in taking a player early, since up to twelve other franchises could select the same player.

Not everyone participated in the reentry draft. The Cincinnati Reds, the two-time defending world champions of 1975 and 1976 who had represented the National League in four of the seven World Series played to that point in the decade, refused to make selections.

As the 1977 reentry draft neared, it was clear that Lyman would be one of the more popular selections. He had emerged as one of baseball's best hitters, and he had done so earning a paltry salary compared to other ballplayers of his caliber. While some of the richest teams in the big leagues were convinced they could reel Lyman in, some of the clubs in smaller markets were equally convinced that they could sign him for less than some of the other free agents. Soon, there would be open warfare among numerous teams for Lyman's services.

"It is not so much money that I am concerned about," Lyman had said to Tracy Ringolsby and the *Long Beach Independent-Press-Telegram* the previous summer. "It is finding somewhere that I feel I am going to be happy, where Lyman Bostock can be Lyman Bostock."

* * *

With the November 1 deadline approaching for the Twins to work out a deal with Lyman prior to the reentry draft, Calvin Griffith continued to put up a good face in the media. Though Minnesota was allowing nine of its eleven players from the 1977 season to play out their options without trying to re-sign them, the Twins were still optimistic they could find a way to sign Lyman and Hisle.

"It's imperative that we have one of the two back on the ball club," said Griffith of Lyman and Hisle. "We still have a chance."[7]

Though on a few occasions the Twins owner felt that Hisle was close to re-signing, he didn't get that same impression from Lyman. Though things had gone fairly well on field in 1977, Lyman and the Twins had gotten no closer to negotiating a new deal. "Nobody knows how far away you are with Bostock," Griffith replied. "He never committed himself one iota."

Calling his efforts to retain Lyman and Hisle "fantastic offers," Griffith said, "I don't think they will be offered as much money as we offered, to tell you the truth. That's the way I look at it."[8]

No deal would be struck between Lyman and Griffith in the latter days of October or on November 1, as Lyman prepared to see which teams would be interested in bidding for his services for the 1978 season.

November 4 finally arrived, as representatives of all twenty-six big league franchises convened at the Plaza Hotel for the second reentry draft. It would be an exciting day for the players, who knew they were about to get huge raises. On the other hand, it would prove to be a nerve-wracking day for owners and other team officials who had to ensure they selected the right guys to negotiate with and had to deal with losing players to other clubs.

Lyman's agent had prepared him for the strong possibility that his name would be called early and often. But Lyman and his agent, Abdul-Jalil Al-Hakim, had to be pleasantly surprised by how much attention the young outfielder got from various clubs in the early phase of the reentry spectacle.

The Toronto Blue Jays, who had gone 54–107 in their inaugural season in 1977, made Lyman the number one overall selection of the draft. After the Atlanta Braves selected pitcher Mike Torrez, who had just helped lead the Yankees to their World Series triumph, the Oakland A's and New York Mets each selected Lyman with the third and fourth picks, respectively. In all, eight franchises—the Blue Jays, A's, Mets, California Angels, Chicago White Sox, Texas Rangers, Pittsburgh Pirates, and Baltimore Orioles—selected Lyman in the first round.

The San Diego Padres, Milwaukee Brewers, and New York Yankees also earned the right to negotiate with Lyman by selecting him in the second round. Two others, the San Francisco Giants and Kansas City Royals, took him later. The Royals became the last franchise eligible to negotiate with Lyman. Lyman was one of eight players, including Torrez, Hisle, Oscar Gamble, Rich Gossage, Ross Grimsley, Terry Forster, and Rawly Eastwick, selected by the maximum thirteen franchises in the forty-four-round draft.

"They gathered a few steps off Central Park South to open this year's market on unsigned, unattached, or unwanted talent," said Joseph Durso of the *New York Times*. "And in three and a half hours under the crystal chandeliers, the roll of teams was called 43 times, a total of 89 players went on the auction block. 44 were 'drafted' for future consideration. 45 were not. And a $20,000-a-year outfielder named Lyman Bostock became the hottest property in the business."

After the reentry draft, much was made in the national media about the fact that Lyman had made only $20,000 during his breakout 1977 season in Minnesota. "The intensive early interest in [Lyman] almost assures that the bidding will produce a seven-figure contract for the 26-year-old outfielder," read the Associated Press the day after the draft.[9]

Back in Oakland, Abdul-Jalil Al-Hakim began fielding interest from the various franchises on Saturday, less than twenty-four hours after the draft.

"The attention paid to Lyman is a tribute to a deserving player," Al-Hakim said.

"Lyman will be fully involved in any and all phases of the negotiations. There are a lot of factors involved here. After you get so much money, there's a certain diminishing return. That's when you have to be concerned with the other things like organization, management, city, and the rest."[10]

"We just plan to sit back, rub our hands and wait for the money to fall into them," Al-Hakim added to Joseph Durso of the *New York Times*.

Suddenly, the world seemed to be at Lyman Bostock's feet. He was in a unique position. He could sign with half the teams in major league baseball and decide where he wanted to live among numerous attractive destinations, including New York, Chicago, Southern California, Northern California, Dallas, and even Canada. But what did he really want to do?

There was Toronto, a new expansion franchise seeking a team leader, but in a foreign country with cold weather. Fellow American League East rivals Milwaukee and Baltimore could use one more essential piece as they attempted to catch the Red Sox and Yankees. Milwaukee would provide the opportunity to continue playing with Hisle, who had all but decided to sign with the Brewers. But would the Orioles or Brewers be in position to pony up the money it would cost to attract Lyman and his agent?

He could play anywhere he wanted in the American League West with exception of Seattle, who hadn't bothered to pick him. Though Lyman had expressed an initial interest in the expansion Mariners at the start of the 1977 season, the franchise didn't have the resources at that time to sign Lyman, and hadn't selected him in the reentry draft.

The White Sox offered Lyman the chance to play regularly in front of his adoring uncles and cousins in a large ballpark friendly to hitters, against many of the same pitchers that he had grown accustomed to in recent seasons. Lyman had always hit well at Comiskey Park, which for a time in the 1970s was also known as White Sox Park.

Two other Western Division rivals, Texas and Oakland, were like trains passing along a rail line. One club, the Rangers, was spending big bucks for top talent, as owner Brad Corbett was rapidly using his fortune trying to turn the team into a winner. The A's, in turn, were breaking apart piece by piece because of Charlie Finley's resistance to paying his players fair market value. Though it seemed logical that the Rangers could throw an appealing offer Lyman's way, would Oakland? Or did the A's think they might be able to get Lyman for a bargain since he only made twenty grand the previous three years in Minnesota? In addition, the Royals, a veteran-laden club, might be able to use Lyman as an additional ingredient in a championship recipe.

Lyman also had the option to move to the National League—to play for a Pittsburgh club trying to get back to the top of the National League East, or to head to San Francisco to surge the Giants to competitiveness in a tough National League West.

San Diego was even closer to home than San Francisco, and the Padres were building on a young nucleus centered around talent like Dave Winfield.

He had the choice of either New York franchise. The Mets had been floundering in recent seasons, and the previous summer they had traded away the face of the franchise, Tom Seaver, for a collection of Cincinnati Reds youngsters that included his old Venezuelan winter-league buddy, Doug Flynn. With the Mets, Lyman would be the undisputed star of a team hoping to rise in the coming years.

And then, of course, there were the Yankees, who offered the allure of New York City, the opportunity to play for the defending World Series champions, and a team widely considered a favorite once again in the American League in 1978. George Steinbrenner was quickly building a winner in the Bronx by paying for the best talent money could buy. Steinbrenner had helped institute big money in free agency by offering Catfish Hunter $3.5 million over five seasons after Hunter had led the Oakland A's to three straight world championships from 1972 to 1974. The year after acquiring Hunter, Steinbrenner spent nearly $3 million to land another former Oakland star, Reggie Jackson. The pair of future Hall of Famers, along with many others, had helped the Yankees rapidly rise to the top of Major League Baseball.

In the weeks immediately following the Yankees' World Series triumph, it was no secret around baseball that Steinbrenner wanted Lyman, despite already having a loaded outfield unit. They'd figure out the outfield rotation once Lyman arrived. He could play left field every day, moving Lou Piniella to a full-time designated hitter's role. He could split time in center field with Mickey Rivers, or even give Reggie Jackson the occasional day off or designated hitting opportunity by playing in right field. Or Rivers and Piniella could platoon in left, opening up center field for Lyman as he preferred.

The Yankees could even perhaps make a move—trading either Piniella or Rivers for more pitching—to free up room in the starting lineup for Lyman. The Bronx Bombers were stockpiling talent, and they wanted a proven hitter with a professional clubhouse presence to join them.

"If the Yankees acquire outfielder and relief ace Rich Gossage, next year's pennant race will be as good as over before spring training even starts," wrote Red Sox beat reporter Sam Weisberg of the *Lowell Sun* prior to the reentry draft.

Finally, there were the Angels. The Angels represented home. The allure of returning to Southern California, where so many of his friends and family were located, was certainly appealing to Lyman. So was being in a position to take care of his mother day-to-day, to see her on a much more regular basis.

"Los Angeles is a big city," Lyman had said a few months earlier. "There is room for lots of people out there."[11]

The Angels not only offered the draw of home, but also plenty of cash. Like Steinbrenner, California owner Gene Autry had decided to use his vast financial resources to improve his ball club. A former singing cowboy, Autry had starred in his own series—*The Gene Autry Show*—for nearly twenty years before embarking in another highly successful career as a businessman and investor. Autry had been awarded the California Angels expansion franchise in 1961. And like the ball club's legions of fans, the longtime owner was impatient for a championship following another disappointing season in 1977.

"I consider myself a fan probably before I'm an owner," said Autry in the Angels' twenty-fifth anniversary special, *Heaven Can't Wait*. "And there's times I've second-guessed the managers, and I've second-guessed players a lot of times. Every owner that I know, that is his primary ambition—to win the big one. And I don't think I'm any different than anyone. I would like to win not only for myself, but especially for the fans."

"He's the only owner I've ever seen who keeps his own boxscore. Putouts, assists, everything," said Angels scout Frank Lane to journalist Milton Richman in a United Press International article.

It hadn't worked out for Autry and the Angels in 1977, as the club underachieved despite expensive pickups in Joe Rudi and Bobby Grich. And as California started negotiations with Lyman in the days following their selection in the reentry draft, it appeared that the Angels might blow their chances with the hometown hero, as general manager Harry Dalton extended an offer that was far below the outfielder's market value at that time. Calling the offer "insulting," Lyman's agent later told journalists, "I wouldn't even tell Lyman what it was."[12]

When Dalton made the decision soon after to accept a job as the new general manager of the Milwaukee Brewers, Autry set out to find one of the top executives in baseball to replace him. The hire would go a long way in determining Lyman's upcoming decision.

* * *

Emil Joseph Bavasi had seen it all in a lifetime of baseball. A boyhood friend of former National League president Ford Frick's son, Fred, Bavasi had gotten his start in his early twenties with the Brooklyn Dodgers. Leaving the Dodgers to serve his country in World War II, Bavasi served with distinction in the Italian Campaign, earning a Bronze Star as an infantry machine gunner. Returning to the United States after the war, Bavasi, who had gotten the nickname of "Buzzie" during his youth, was directly involved in Branch Rickey's effort to integrate the major leagues.

Bavasi had witnessed firsthand the years-long battle that Walter O'Malley fought with New York City's powerful urban visionary, Robert Moses, in an effort to bring a downtown stadium to the people of Brooklyn. Buzzie was heavily involved as O'Malley made plans to move the Dodgers to Southern California—around the same time that Annie Bostock was making plans to raise her young son in Los Angeles.

Bavasi was there the day a wrecking ball, painted like a baseball, started tearing down Ebbets Field in the winter of 1960. He was there alongside Roy Campanella, who he'd helped find a home in the minor leagues, after he was paralyzed in a devastating car accident on an icy strip of New Jersey highway the winter after the Dodgers moved to Los Angeles. He had been smack in the middle of the contentious negotiations between Dodger pitching sensations Sandy Koufax and Don Drysdale in the mid-1960s—the first prominent multiplayer unified holdout in big league history.

Buzzie had helped start an expansion franchise just down the road in San Diego, getting the Padres off the ground in the late 1960s under eccentric owner C. Arnholt Smith. He was in the house the night in June 1970 that Pittsburgh Pirates ace Dock Ellis no-hit the Padres while, according to his own claims, high on LSD.

Bavasi was exactly the type of man Gene Autry wanted running his club: seasoned, savvy, knowledgeable, compassionate. As time went on, Buzzie didn't resent the new salary escalation, as many owners and executives did. Like Autry, he saw it as the price of doing business. Now, Buzzie was being asked to get the California Angels over the hump in the American League West. While the Angels had developed a passionate group of fans throughout Southern California, they could always be counted on to let down their supporters. The franchise had failed to make a playoff appearance through its first seventeen seasons of existence heading into 1978.

And then there were the tragedies. The Angels knew something about tragedy. No other club in baseball had been beset with so many strange and horrific events. It began just a few years after the Angels had been founded and began playing games down the street from Lyman's house. Dick Wantz, a talented young rookie pitcher, began struggling with chronic headaches in the spring of 1965. Diagnosed with a brain tumor, the twenty-five-year-old died in May after slipping into a coma. Five years later, in the spring of 1970, standout relief pitcher Minnie Rojas was driving on U.S. 1 around Key Largo, Florida, when a truck plowed into his vehicle. Two of his daughters were killed, and Rojas suffered paralysis and never played baseball again. Just three years earlier, in 1967, Rojas had saved twenty-two games for California with a 2.60 earned run average. In the winter of 1972, former Angels infielder Chico Ruiz died in a car accident on Interstate 5 in San Diego.

Two years later, in March 1974, Angels pitching prospect Bruce Heinbechner was involved in a head-on collision in Palm Springs, where he was attending California's spring training, trying earn a spot on the big league club. Scheduled to make a start the following day, Heinbechner had pitched two scoreless innings in his Angels spring debut.

Just after the New Year, in early January 1977, the Angels were stunned again by another automobile accident, as Mike Miley, the team's number one selection in the 1974 MLB amateur draft, was killed. A former college quarterback at LSU, Miley was known as "Magic Mike" in Louisiana and his native Mississippi. Miley was back in his old stomping grounds in Baton Rouge when he misjudged a sharp rural curve late at night and overturned; he was killed instantly. A first-round draft selection for the Angels in 1974, Miley made his big league debut in early July 1975 and wound up playing in seventy games that summer and another fourteen games for California in 1976. Miley had reached the Angels at the age of twenty-three and was expected to be a big part of the franchise's long-term plans at shortstop before his untimely passing.

Yes, the California Angels as a franchise knew a great deal about tragedy. But with an owner willing to spend as much as it took to rise to prominence, there was a lot for Angels fans to be excited about that offseason. California had several pieces already in place, and now they were going to do their best to secure Lyman Bostock and bring him home to Los Angeles.

* * *

Lyman's negotiations were played out largely in the public spotlight. Even if the figures weren't specifically announced as Al-Hakim, Lyman, and the various clubs went back and forth, details and rumors about the negotiations were splashed across newspapers nationwide that autumn. The Pirates and Royals were quickly eliminated, according to Lyman's agent, because of their low offers. "You can't ask a player to consider signing for $1 million less with one club than he can get from another," said Al-Hakim. "Right now, we have five offers of over $2 million and three offers that are better than what Reggie Jackson signed for."[13]

A few other clubs quickly made it apparent that they weren't going over a certain dollar figure—effectively eliminating themselves from the bidding. The New York Mets were one of them. "We're not going to have a shootout at O.K. Corral with our pocketbooks," said Mets chairman of the board M. Donald Grant to Murray Chass of the *New York Times* following the reentry draft.

"A lot of clubs have eliminated themselves by not being competitive," said Al-Hakim. "There's no sense negotiating with someone who's not really interested."

By mid-November, Lyman was almost ready to narrow his options to six. But by then, it was fairly evident that only two clubs were really in the running—the Yankees and the Angels. The Yankees went all out for

Lyman, sending executives Gabe Paul and Cedric Tallis to Los Angeles for conversations, while Steinbrenner stayed in contact over the telephone. The Yankees even had World Series hero Reggie Jackson, "Mr. October" himself, dial up Lyman and try to talk him into coming to the Big Apple.

As it turned out, Lyman had been watching the 1977 Yankees closely. Though immensely talented, the eventual world champions went through a season of turmoil and drama, which made an impression on Lyman a thousand miles away in Minnesota. Lyman recalled the June encounter at Fenway Park when Jackson and Billy Martin nearly came to blows in the dugout and had to be separated. He knew that if things went bad in New York, they could go really bad. And he would be in what he called the "dog-eat-dog lifestyle" of the Big Apple, a continent away from the people who loved and cared for him most.

But the Yankees offered the chance to win. A lot. Without Lyman, the Bronx Bombers had just claimed the franchise's first World Series title in fifteen years. They were set up to be championship contenders for the foreseeable future. With Lyman, the Yankees could become an even greater team, and he could also be a breath of fresh air in a clubhouse filled with gigantic egos—a humble man with humble aspirations. He just might be the glue to make the Yankees a juggernaut well into the 1980s.

With Lyman in their outfield, working alongside the rest of the team's core, the Yankees could potentially get back to the glory days of the late 1940s and the early 1950s, when the franchise won five straight World Series crowns.

A week or so after the reentry draft, Lyman made his way over to Anaheim to meet with Gene Autry and Buzzie Bavasi. The two men rolled out the red carpet for Lyman—something he wasn't used to from his years in Minnesota.

"The Angels showed me more respect in the few hours I spent at the stadium than in all six years I spent in Minnesota," Lyman would later say to Dick Miller of *Sporting News*. "When I met Mr. Autry, he approached me and introduced himself. Buzzie asked if the team could do anything for my wife, who was in the hospital. When I was in the hospital in Minnesota with a broken ankle, nobody from the front office visited me."

"Two years ago Calvin Griffith said he hadn't been in the clubhouse in twenty years. Now what in the hell is that?" the former Twin continued.

"You have to talk to people, find out why the operation is not working. I was there six years and everything was just helter skelter, almost like they condition you to be unhappy. Why do you think the Dodgers are so advanced? It's the relationship the front office has with the players."

Lyman's meeting with Bavasi and Autry made a huge impression—enough to make the Angels the clear frontrunner. For their part, the Angels were supremely confident that they were about to sign Lyman after his visit to Anaheim Stadium.

"Maybe they thought the fact that I had said I'd like to play near home would be enough, but things turned around when Buzzie Bavasi became involved in the negotiations," Lyman would say.[14]

"We are close to a deal," Bavasi indicated in mid-November. "[Al-Hakim] has been fair with us and we have been fair with him. He mentioned a figure and we responded and said it was acceptable. He said he would talk to Bostock and get back to us."[15]

"What more can you do than give them what they ask for?" the Angels executive continued.

While the Angels tried to zero in on Lyman, the Yankees were still trying to figure out exactly what it would take to sign him. "Somebody from the Yankee organization was in touch with us every day. Sometimes it was four and five times a day. They offered and offered and offered," Al-Hakim would say later to Loel Schrader with the *Long Beach Independent-Press-Telegram*. "Finally, they just asked, 'What the hell do you want?'"

Another phone call rang in. It was the Angels, increasing their offer.

"Stop it. Stop it," Lyman said. "Let me sign. Somebody else is going to offer me another million and I'll look like a fool if I don't take it."[16]

Al-Hakim smiled broadly. He was getting his client exactly what he wanted, but the agent still wanted a little bit more for Lyman.

* * *

As Lyman's twenty-seventh birthday approached, George Steinbrenner was ready to come out to Los Angeles to close the deal personally. And then on November 20, the Twins finally stepped up with a competitive offer to keep Lyman in Minnesota. By then, however, it was far too late, both for the Yankees and for the Twins. Lyman had made up his mind, once and for all. Lyman called Steinbrenner to tell him the news. He was going to be a California Angel.

"I offered him more money than he got from the Angels," Griffith would say a decade later to Claire Smith of the *Hartford Courant*. "Unfortunately, our farm director and his agent had a fight, and [Bostock] never knew of our offer."

"Mr. Steinbrenner was going to come out, but I told him not to waste that trip—that I'd decided. I'm not a flashy guy. I'm not Joe Namath or Clyde Frazier," Lyman later explained to journalist Dave Anderson.

"He told me what he wanted," Bavasi said of Lyman's agent. "We consummated the deal in five minutes. We shook hands and that was it. Everything was above board. The agents know what they want, and the teams know what they can afford."[17]

"It was a difficult decision to make," Lyman would say to Frank Mazzeo with the *Valley News* in the coming days, "but it all came down to my family and my mother living here alone. I also feel I can do more for the community where I grew up."

"New York wanted me as a player. California wanted me as a player and a person," he told another journalist.[18]

While it was a relief for Lyman and his family that his decision was made, he couldn't help but be a little sad that Sunday evening. Sad that he was leaving Minnesota. Sad that he was walking away from countless friends, as well as from all the Twins fans who had embraced him and accepted him as one of their own.

Lyman, Yuovene, and his mom were initially going to have a celebratory dinner out. But Lyman was in no mood to celebrate that night, even after agreeing to a life-changing contract. "We were supposed to go out and celebrate," Lyman said later that evening. "My wife, my mother, and I. But I'm going to miss Minnesota. I have a lot of memories there. I wanted to be alone with that feeling for a while."[19]

* * *

On the day prior to his birthday, Lyman signed with the Angels in a ceremony at Anaheim Stadium. As Lyman, Yuovene, and Abdul-Jalil Al-Hakim got off the elevator on the second floor of the ballpark, they were greeted by numerous Walt Disney characters, including a large poster of Mickey Mouse. There were also some pictures of various Angels players. But the idea that the cartoon characters were interspersed with the ballplayers was a little unsettling to Lyman's agent.

"Are you sure you want to sign with this organization?" Al-Hakim said, half-jokingly, to his client.[20]

Some of the media covering the press conference joked that while Texas Rangers owner Brad Corbett was treating reporters to a hearty meal at a country club to formally announce signing Richie Zisk and Doc Medich, the Angels offered only peanuts and beer. The joke was that the Angels were undergoing a little budget austerity to pay their new outfield star and the other talent that had cost Gene Autry approximately $8 million over the last year.

"Some people question whether I was an actor," said Autry at the press conference. "But when I was in the motion picture business, I used to get all the money I could. So I can't blame baseball players for getting all they can."

Al-Hakim applauded Autry's remark, despite the fact that the Angels owner struggled throughout the event to get his name right. Initially, Autry said he wouldn't even try. But then he botched it once, calling Abdul-Jalil Al-Hakim "Jabril," and then mixing it up again before finally settling on "Leo."

Sitting alongside Yuovene at a table to the immediate right of the podium, Lyman placed an Angels hat on his head and smiled broadly as Autry and Bavasi explained their good fortune in landing one of baseball's top young stars. The Angels later indicated the contract was for $2.25 million. The reported annual salary would be $400,000 over five years, along with a healthy signing bonus of $250,000. In an effort to provide long-term stability for himself and Yuovene, Lyman agreed to defer $205,000 of the annual salary. According to Al-Hakim, Lyman and Yuovene would receive deferred compensation in the amount of $195,000 per year until 1994.

For his part, Lyman was shy about the numbers, saying the day of his signing, "I'd rather not say. I'd rather not have any ballplayers get mad at a line drive hitter."[21]

While the figures did not make Bostock the highest paid of the free agents in 1977, he was among the top five. Former teammate Larry Hisle went to Milwaukee for six years for over $3 million with a $650,000 bonus, while Rich Gossage signed a contract with the Yankees with a $750,000 bonus and a salary of $333,000 per year for six years. Hisle, who focused in fairly quickly on the Brewers and their lucrative offer that off-season, knew deep down that the Angels were Lyman's destiny.

"He liked Minnesota, but according to Lyman, no place could touch California," Hisle said in 1988 to Patrick Reusse of the *Minneapolis*

On November 21, 1977, the day he signed a five-year contract with the California Angels for $2.25 million, Lyman poses with Angels owner Gene Autry. (Associated Press / Jeff Robbins.)

Tribune. "It had the best baseball, the best football, the best basketball, the best beaches, the best sun, the most attractive people. California was it."

In the months after signing, Lyman was willing to explain in detail to the press why he chose the Angels over the Yankees. He claimed it had nothing to do with money—though the compensation the Angels had agreed to pay Lyman was more than ample.

"There are a lot of other things involved, though," he said. "My mother lives in Southern California and she's getting up in age. New York offered me more money but I was concerned about the other things such as my mother."22

Lyman and his agent would speak regularly about the Yankees that off-season, indicating just how close he'd come to heading to the Bronx to play for the defending American League champions. "Their [California's] offer wasn't the best by far," Al-Hakim said. "If I had accomplished what Lyman Bostock has, I'd be wearing pinstripes right now, instead of a halo. How can you compare the Yankees, with their World

Series pennants, the all-star games, the media exposure. How can you compare anything with that?"[23]

"If you knew what we gave up by not signing with the Yankees, ooeee," Al-Hakim added. "What we gave up, someone else would have been happy to sign for. But that's Lyman—he wanted to play here. Besides, you get to a certain point in bargaining, money doesn't mean anything. You have enough. Heck, Lyman doesn't have to worry about money the rest of his life with this contract."[24]

"I was very close to signing with the Yankees," Lyman told Anderson of the *New York Times* in the late winter of 1978, just as spring training was getting going. "They offered me more money than the Angels did. But with all that controversy, I thought I might wind up being a vegetable. I couldn't take all that controversy in the clubhouse."

"I was going to New York," Lyman added to Miller of *Sporting News*. "New York is a nice place to play baseball. But I had to do a little soul-searching. I would have gone to New York if there wasn't all that controversy. They had all those problems last year. I couldn't go through another year like that with reporters taking everything that is said and blowing it out of proportion."

"My mind was almost made up to go to New York. They have the glamour and the lights. I don't think I could take another year of controversy. New York seems like a big Peyton Place. I mind my own business and I don't condemn anyone on my own team."[25]

Despite his openness in describing why he chose the Angels over the Yankees, Lyman wouldn't disclose the specific financial details of his new contract. "You have to look at all the provisions in my contract," Lyman would say a few weeks later to Miller. "All things considered, I possibly could be the highest-paid player. I won't say at this time what they are. They don't show up right off the bat.

"I really don't care to be the highest-paid ballplayer. You become the center of attention. I love a low profile. I don't want to be where people look at me as the highest-paid player. Reggie Jackson is the kind of guy who can use a lot of publicity. That is how he made his name, the things he has said and done."

While Lyman left it to others to ponder the fine print of his contract, his agent was all too willing to speak. Although no dollar figure was released on November 21, the day the signing was announced, Lyman's agent indicated that the total package exceeded $3 million—which would make him the highest-paid player in baseball, and the contract the most lucrative in baseball history to that time. Although Hisle was in the $3 million club, his contract was for six years rather than the five years of Lyman's deal with California.

Abdul-Jalil Al-Hakim was asked about the discrepancy between Lyman's reported earnings—he had indicated they were in the $3.2 million range, but they were listed by the Angels as $2.25 million—and those of American League contemporaries such as Hisle, Gossage, and Gamble.

"Two and a quarter million? That's ridiculous. That's quite a bit off. He gets more than that. Much more than that," said Al-Hakim approximately two months after the deal was struck. "We've got things in there that are worth much more than that. I don't know how those rumors got started."[26]

"We could have named our own price either with the New York Yankees or San Diego Padres," Al-Hakim said in an interview with Don Merry of the *Los Angeles Times*. "If I had been Lyman Bostock, I would be wearing pinstripes now. What we gave up by not signing with the Yankees, most players would willingly sign for."

Al-Hakim indicated that the deal Lyman signed with the Angels was a quarter of a million dollars less than the offer submitted by the Yankees—something the Yankees organization vehemently denied. "That's an out-and-out lie," said a Yankees spokesman. "Our offer is nowhere near the figure the Angels offered Bostock."

"If he [Lyman's agent] said that our offer was higher than the Angels, then he's a liar," the spokesman told another reporter. "We offered him nowhere near what was paid Hisle or Zisk. If our offer was the highest, there's no way Lyman is the highest paid player in baseball."[27]

Others in the national media would challenge the claims of Lyman's agent about the real value of the contract. While it was clearly a highly lucrative deal for the times, there was a clear discrepancy between what was officially reported by the Angels and what Abdul-Jalil Al-Hakim purported the deal's full amount to be.

"When Abdul Jalil, a.k.a. Randy Wallace, discusses the contract of his main man, outfielder Lyman Bostock, he tends to inflate its value, so he can advertise Bostock as the highest-paid player in baseball history, which he isn't," wrote Ray Kennedy in a *Sports Illustrated* article in 1978. "If enough players hear that Bostock signed with the Angels for $3,262,000, as Jalil has said—instead of $2,250,000, which is what Bostock really got—they will want Jalil to represent them. And pretty soon he will be the highest-paid hustler in baseball history."

Lyman had a ready answer for those who thought that no ballplayer was worth $400,000 a year. "Some people look at athletes' salaries and say they're ridiculous. They don't bother to look at singers and dancers, people like Elton John, who makes $17 million a year," Lyman said in a very compelling argument. "If a baseball player is worth $2.5 million, which I am not saying is what my contract is for, he should get it. Some people point out that ballplayers get more money than the president of the United States. Evidently, more people support ballplayers than they do the president."[28]

"If Jimmy Carter could hit .336, he'd be making more money, too," quipped Bavasi.

* * *

With the stroke of a pen, Lyman had cashed in handsomely. Money would no longer be a concern as he played out his professional baseball career. He was locked into a long-term deal that would provide comfortably for his family for the rest of their lives. And who's to say he wouldn't be in position to sign another lucrative deal five years later? He was only twenty-seven years old. His career was just getting going.

As the holidays approached that winter, Lyman could sit back and relax. He enjoy a few days of rest with Yuovene and Annie around Christmas and New Year's before getting back on the field and in the batting cage for preseason training in early January. As he prepared for his first season back home with the Angels, Lyman could now turn his entire focus to winning a championship and doing something worthwhile with his newfound wealth.

10

THE BIG SLUMP (1978)

> The big money was out there to get. People ask me all the time how I could get the money when Willie Mays and Babe Ruth and all the other guys didn't get this kind of money. I tell them, Don't ask me if I'm a better base stealer than Maury Wills. I have to say no. Don't ask me if I'm a better base stealer than Lou Brock. I have to say no. Am I a better outfielder than Roberto Clemente, Willie Mays, or Mickey Mantle? Again, I have to say no. But if you ask me if I was in the right place at the right time, I have to say yes.—Lyman Bostock[1]

Lyman surely had to be happy to finally get out on the field as the California Angels began spring training in March 1978. The talk about his hefty contract continued to draw attention that he didn't feel comfortable with.

Early that spring, Lyman took part in a stunt that likely made him feel particularly uncomfortable. *Sporting News* was doing an extensive feature on baseball's newest big-money star, and the magazine wanted a cover photo of Lyman taken by celebrity photographer Frank Worth. There, splashed across the front page for newsstands nationwide, was Lyman, flashing his big smile in his new Angels home uniform, wearing dark sunglasses with white dollar signs painted over the eyes. In that same issue of *Sporting News* was a feature on Curt Flood, who had challenged baseball's reserve clause and paved the road for players like Lyman to cash in nearly a decade later.

During his contentious negotiations with Calvin Griffith and the Twins the year before, Lyman cited the example of Curt Flood, who had essentially thrown away his career in an effort to change the long-standing dominance that owners had over players in salary negotiations and trades. Lyman saw leaving Minnesota and exploring the open market as a matter of principle. "I'd be defeating the purpose of what Curt Flood has done for the players. He wanted everybody to be able to enjoy the beauty and freedom of the game," he said to Dave Anderson of the *New York Times*.

That he'd wound up back in Southern California, which he and his mother had long called home, and that he'd gotten a pile of cash at the same time were just bonuses. "I think the people here appreciate me a lot more because I'm from the area. And I hope I can please the people here," he said on "This Week in Baseball" in September.

Having grown up without affluence, Lyman wasn't going to let his new financial position change who he was and how he took care of business on the diamond. Finances weren't something he particularly enjoyed talking about. He'd rather talk baseball than money.

"Some guys are born to be doctors, some to be musicians. I was born to play baseball. I love to play the game. I don't think about my bank account," he added that spring to Scott Ostler of the *Los Angeles Times*.

"Me, I'm not really interested in what people write as long as they are not bad, negative things. I don't live off newspaper clippings. I live off what I do."[2]

"Money is something I've never had in abundance. I'm not going to let it go to my head."

Instead of purchasing a Rolls-Royce or fancy sports car, Lyman rolled around Los Angeles in a Saab. Instead of buying an expensive mansion, Lyman purchased a modest $155,000 condo for himself and Yuovene.

"Sure, money changes you to a certain degree. With the money I'm making now, I've got a chance to pay off a few bills. But if you had never lived an extravagant life it is hard to start wasting money. I don't feel that spending a lot of money is going to make me a much better person," he said. "It won't make me more important if I go out and buy Rolls Royces and quarter-million dollar houses."

"Everyone was expecting me to buy a Rolls Royce? Why?" Lyman added in his interview with Ostler. "It blows their minds when I don't be the person they want me to be.

"But my grandmother always told me, 'Don't never let your wants overrule your needs.' The last thing I told my wife was, 'Don't spend money just because you've got it.'"

Lyman did spend some of his money right away, but certainly not on himself. He made a large donation to the Vermont Square Methodist Church in Los Angeles, where he and his mother had worshipped since moving to California over twenty years earlier. The church had been vandalized around the time Lyman cashed in with the Angels, and the outfielder ensured that necessary repairs could be made quickly.

"He was the kind of man who never forget his old neighborhood church," said Vermont Square Methodist secretary Orrie Hamilton in a *Los Angeles Times* article by Earl Gustkey. "He gave us $10,000 to rebuild our Sunday school. Vandals had broken in and nearly destroyed it. He wanted the money to specifically go to new carpeting, windows, painting, and general restoration."

"Lyman wanted the money spent on constructing a prayer room and a special youth section on the second floor of the church," added another church member, Albert Williams, to *Jet Magazine*. "Not only that, but money was taken out of the fund periodically to buy game tickets for about 60 neighborhood kids who would be driven to the game."

Lyman purchased sporting equipment, from bats and balls to gloves, for the youth clinics he was planning to host. Throughout the off-season, Lyman conducted a handful of sessions, helping youngsters in the San Fernando Valley and South Los Angeles with their skills on the field. "Too many people grow up taking from a community and it is not every day you can go back to that community when you have fame and fortune," he commented. "You have to think about the people you grew up with."[3]

Lyman gave money to local groups that were trying to keep neighborhood kids off the streets, off drugs, and out of the reach of the spreading gang influence in inner-city Los Angeles.

"I've given some money to the Teen Challengers—guys who are strung out on drugs," he said to Dick Miller of *Sporting News*. "We're building a new housing complex. I'm donating some money there. When I was in college, I was affiliated with a lot of groups."

"One of the reasons we went after him was because of his off-the-field activities," said Angels owner Gene Autry.[4]

"He believed in helping," said Lyman's uncle Tom Turner, years later, to K. C. Johnson of the *Chicago Tribune*. "We always talked, and he had big ideas, especially for kids."

In February, a couple of weeks before he reported to Angels spring training in Palm Springs, Lyman made an appearance at Marshall High School, where his former head coach at Manual Arts High School, Fred Scott, was now coaching. Lyman gave the high schoolers a stirring pep talk. "He gave a talk to my players," said Scott to Gustkey. "You could have heard a pin drop. They loved him."

Around the same time, Lyman also returned to Northridge for the annual alumni game that Bob Hiegert had continued. At the game Yuovene got into it with a spectator in the bleachers who criticized Lyman's skill, as well as his huge new salary, in front of a group of onlookers.

A self-reflective man who was supremely honest with himself, Lyman openly pondered the question of his own mortality during his first spring with the Angels. "People always say, 'What if you die tomorrow?' But what if I live tomorrow?" he said. "I dress well, but people notice me by the things I do, not what I wear or drive."[5]

In hindsight, Lyman and those around him reflected on his first spring with the Angels as one of nonstop activity: interviews, photo opportunities, and events that took his focus away from the field and from what awaited him with the Angels. Never one to shy away from reporters or fans before his huge deal, Lyman now worried that some might consider him aloof and unapproachable with his newfound wealth.

"I never really had a spring training," he would say later that year. "Every day, there were reporters and photographers around. It was like that day after day. I never had time to concentrate. I needed some concentration. A lot of times, I didn't feel like talking, but I was afraid people would say that I'd changed as far as talking to people was concerned because of my big salary."[6]

"He was on every talk show there was. And I don't think he really gave himself a chance to focus totally on himself and baseball. He was trying too hard, working too hard, got himself involved in every little thing," added Bob Hiegert.[7]

* * *

The Angels entered the 1978 season not just hoping to win, but expecting to win. Although the Angels had limped to a 74–88 record in 1977—10.5 games behind the Twins and 28 games behind the division champion Royals—things seemed much different as spring training convened in Palm Springs.

Injuries to free-agent signees Joe Rudi and Bobby Grich had derailed the team's prospects the previous year, but both players returned in the spring of 1978 healthy and ready to play. With Lyman also in the mix, much of the pressure to perform that had been on Don Baylor in the 1977 season would be spread among the club's veteran talents.

"I hope I can thrill the fans here as much as I did in Minnesota," Lyman said to Tracy Ringolsby of the *Long Beach Independent-Press-Telegram*. "And I'm going to try to keep the people healthy so things won't happen to me like they did to Don Baylor. I don't feel the guys had a fair chance because they [Grich and Rudi] were hurt early in the season, and a lot of pressure fell on Don Baylor."

Despite the power in the California lineup with guys like Baylor and Rudi, the Angels needed a singles hitter like Lyman, who could consistently get on base and be in position to score runs, hitting ahead of those sluggers in the lineup. Throughout its history to that point, the Angels had only two batters hit over .300 in a single season: Alex Johnson, who hit .329 in 1970, and Albie Pearson, who hit .304 in 1963. In the seven years since Johnson's team-record .329 campaign, the Angels hadn't had a single player bat more than .290 over a season, much less .300. But there was little doubt that spring that Lyman would finally change that record.

Although veteran slugger Bobby Bonds had enjoyed one of the best seasons of his career in 1977, hitting thirty-seven homers with a career-high 115 RBIs for California, Lyman's signing made the veteran outfielder expendable in the Angels' lineup. On December 5—just thirteen days after Lyman had signed with California—the Angels struck a deal with a divisional rival, sending Bonds, outfielder Thad Bosley, and California's first pick in the 1977 amateur draft, right-hander Richard Dotson, to the South Side of Chicago. In return, the Angels received a pair of tall righties—Chris Knapp, who stood six foot five and had gone 12–7 with the White Sox in 1977, as well as Dave Frost, who stood six foot six and had made three big league starts heading into 1978.

Knapp would settle into California's rotation behind Nolan Ryan and Frank Tanana, while Frost would emerge as an effective spot starter. With Ryan and Tanana leading the rotation, California had two guys who could outmatch anyone on any given day. Knapp and Don Aase were quality starters on the back end of the rotation, and Dave LaRoche was a first-rate closer.

But the biggest pickup in the Bonds trade for the Angels was Brian Downing, a twenty-seven-year-old veteran of five big league seasons. Along with his aggressive playing style and solid hitting ability, Downing was an excellent defensive catcher who would make only five errors in 128 games throughout the 1978 season.

The Angels were loaded with talented position veterans, along with a solid supporting cast. Lyman was just another piece of the puzzle.

"He was a tremendous acquisition," Downing said of Lyman ten years later to *Los Angeles Times* reporter Mike Penner. "A great signing. He was a real solid hitter, always making contact, hitting the ball all over the ballpark."

With Bostock and Downing on board, along with the other returning players, things looked quite promising for the Angels that spring in Palm Springs. In that regard, Lyman didn't arrive back home in Southern California feeling that he needed to be the savior of the Angels. Reporters left and right wanted to speak with him that spring, and he was his usual friendly, talkative self, filling their notepads with copy.

"I've got to play baseball the way Lyman Bostock can play. I ain't no messiah. I can't rescue the team all by myself," Ostler reported Bostock as saying that spring. "I don't have to do anything fancy to prove I'm worth it. I'm going to leave a little blood out there on the field. I did it for six years with the Twins, and I'll do it here."

"People point their fingers at me and say, 'You've got to do good now. You're making all that money.' But one man can't resurrect a ball club," Lyman added in another spring interview. "One man can't save a business. He can contribute ideas. But he can't do it all. If that was the case, they wouldn't need nine ball players."[8]

"I don't anticipate any pressure. The pressure was last year when I played without a contract at Minnesota. I think playing with a contract is easier than playing without one."[9]

Lyman quickly ingratiated himself with his new Angels teammates, earning their friendship and trust for his workmanlike approach to the game, his friendly chatter, and his playing ability.

"We paid a lot of money for Lyman Bostock and it didn't seem to affect the other players negatively," said owner Gene Autry. "Lyman was a great asset for the younger players and veterans alike. They all felt he could help the team win, and if they can win it means more money for all of them."[10]

Lyman's old semipro buddy from Los Angeles, Kenny Landreaux, had been California's first-round draft pick in 1976, following a solid career at Arizona State. Landreaux had gotten a cup of coffee in the majors in 1977, hitting .296 in twenty-three games, and was expected to challenge for a spot on the big club in 1978. In many ways, Landreaux was Lyman Bostock three years removed. Like Lyman back in 1975, when he was a gifted newcomer trying to find a spot on a veteran Minnesota Twins club, Landreaux was trying to work his way into a crowded Angels outfield that was full of speed, power, and hitting. Like Lyman, Landreaux had gone to college before getting drafted, earning valuable experience and discipline.

Despite all the talent in California's camp that March, Landreaux was determined to stick around and make the team. He quickly realized that to have the best chance of earning a spot on the club, he needed to watch Lyman. So he did.

Landreaux watched Lyman in the batting cage, observed him shagging fly balls in the Palm Springs sunshine. He began warming up with him again, like in the old days at Ross Snyder Park.

"It was the first time since '72 that I'd seen [Lyman]," Landreaux reflected later to the *San Bernardino Sun-Telegram*'s Steve Dilbeck that spring. "When he came over [to the Angels] it made me even more relaxed."

"I used to help Kenny Landreaux when he was in high school and here we are playing on the same team," Lyman added. "I like to see that. I like to see a kid put a lot of effort into his goal in life."

Landreaux, in fact, was so obvious in his efforts to learn from Lyman and to play like him that Angels teammates starting jokingly calling him "shadow." In Kenny Landreaux's world that spring, Lyman Bostock's shadow wasn't such a bad place to be.

* * *

As was the case during his days with the Twins, Lyman made no bones about wanting to be the Angels' center fielder. It had been a point of contention throughout the summer of 1977, as Gene Mauch played him more and more often in left field as it became apparent that Lyman was in his final season with Minnesota. Lyman would have competition in the Angels camp from Rick Miller, whom California had picked up from the

Red Sox. But Lyman felt center field was where he belonged, and he didn't mind stating it publicly.

"[Angels manager Dave] Garcia has told me he would try me in center field," Lyman said to Ostler of the *Los Angeles Times* that spring. "You put me in right field, and you're going to hurt the team. I want to play center field. I can play center field with the best of them.

"You look at my errors over the last three years and it won't amount to over ten. [Fred] Lynn and Miller can't outrun me. Not many people play as shallow as me."

There couldn't help but be talk about a potential batting title for Lyman, coming off back-to-back seasons hitting .323 and .336. "You have to like Lyman Bostock [in the batting race]," said Mauch. "He's the second-best hitter I've ever seen [behind Rod Carew]. Without a doubt, he will lead the league in hitting soon. Maybe this year."[11]

"When the Angels signed Lyman from Minnesota, we all felt he would be the next Rod Carew," added Dick Enberg. "There's no question he had the skill to be a potential AL batting champion."[12]

Despite the lofty expectations, Lyman downplayed the batting-title talk as premature. "You don't go out and say you're going to win a batting title," Lyman told Miller of *Sporting News* that spring. "There are too many guys in this league who can do it. Some player might get confidence like George Brett did two years ago and beat out Carew."

There were some who felt that Lyman would suffer without the benefit of Carew hitting in the same lineup. Lyman scoffed at that notion while also hinting that some of the media back east were ignoring ballplayers from small-market clubs like Minnesota.

"Rod Carew is my man," Lyman said to Ostler. "But that story is more asinine than anything. Where was Rod Carew in Venezuela and in Mexico, and in triple-A and double-A? Why was it that Rod made me famous and not Roy Smalley and all those other guys?

"The press in New York and Boston has made their guys out to be superman outfielders. Other guys don't get the publicity."

With the season approaching, Lyman was confident that the expectations wouldn't overwhelm him. "What do I have to prove?" he asked Dilbeck that March. "I played three years in Minnesota and I had three good years. I might have a bad year, but I think I can perform up to my half of the contract."

"From what I've seen so far, the Angels are a first-class organization. But I don't want to make any predictions about the club. I don't want to say I'll be happy here because I'm getting paid well. I'll have to wait a year and see how it goes."

Although Lyman was the talk of Major League Baseball throughout spring training because of his lucrative off-season contract and the high expectations both on himself and on the Angels in 1978, there were still a few people who didn't know who he was.

One was an eleven-year-old boy, Rob Swift, a Chicago White Sox fan who was out west that March hunting autographs of big league players as they conducted spring workouts. One sunny March afternoon, Rob saw Lyman around the Angels dugout as the club conducted batting practice. He went up and asked for Lyman's autograph, which he happily provided.

"You got it champ!" replied Lyman.[13]

The boy starting flipping through the baseball cards in his hands, trying to figure out exactly who this player was and which card needed to be signed. Finally, the kid swallowed his pride and asked the ballplayer for his name.

"Who are you?" Rob asked.

"My name is Lyman. What's your name?"

"Rob."

"Well, Rob, there's my card right there."

Embarrassed, the boy apologized for not knowing who he was. Looking the boy in the eyes, Lyman said, "Rob, don't worry about it. I'm glad you came out to the game today and hope you have fun!"

Lyman signed the card, "To my new friend Rob, Lyman Bostock."

"I didn't appreciate how much that little moment of my life would mean to me in the future," said Swift over a quarter century later. "I did realize though how cool Bostock was on that spring day in 1978. And even though I was a Chicago White Sox fan, he automatically became my newest favorite player."

"As I look back on it now, it amazes me how nice he was to a little kid he had never met," Swift continued. "It would have been so easy for him to just blow me off and walk away. It would have been so easy for him to just stand there and say his name when I asked him. It would have been so easy for him to just have signed his name on the card and forget about it."

* * *

Lyman could get away neither from the talk about his huge contract that spring nor from comparisons about his father, who might have had talent comparable to his son but didn't have the bank account to show for it.

"My father played in those [Negro] Leagues for nothing," Lyman said wryly one afternoon to Ostler and the *Los Angeles Times*. "I'm not going to perpetuate the humiliation of my family."

That same evening, Bostock shared time with a few teammates and sportswriters around the pool at the team's spring quarters in Palm Springs. It was a jovial time, with Lyman sharing jokes and stories from his past experiences in baseball.

"He was a great guy," recalled Bob Hiegert. "Infectious personality. People just liked being around him. And extremely competitive. A great competitor once the game got started. Great teammate. The kids loved him. He liked the team concept. He got that part of it better than most kids did."

Lyman and the Angels seemed to be right on track, getting off to a 10–5 start that spring following a victory over the Chicago Cubs on March 19. California pounded out sixteen hits against Chicago pitching, with Lyman and four other teammates all getting two hits apiece. Everything seemed to be going right all at once as Lyman's fourth big league season commenced. But as anyone who has been around baseball long enough knows all too well, appearances can be deceiving.

* * *

Through the first three games of the season, Lyman was hitless with one RBI and one run scored. It wasn't yet time to hit the panic button, but certainly it was far from the start with the Angels the fourth-year big leaguer had hoped for. Though Lyman was making contact in the opening series with the Oakland A's—failing to strike out a single time—he was hitting the ball right at people.

After Oakland left town, Minnesota rolled into Anaheim. It was Lyman's first matchup against his former Twins teammates. One-time Twins pitching coach Don McMahon, who at that time represented a sporting goods company, decided to play a little prank on Rod Carew at the struggling outfielder's expense. Carew walked into the Anaheim Stadium visitor's locker room to quite a surprise on April 10—a copy of Lyman's *Sporting News* photograph with the dollar signs over his eyes.

Below the image was a note: "0–11. Rod, Help Me!—Lyman"

Carew laughed at Lyman's so-called message, knowing full well that it was only a matter of time before his former teammate broke out. "Lyman's going to hit," Carew told the *Los Angeles Times*' Rich Roberts. "There's no doubt about it."

California's fourth game of the season started out as another nightmare for Lyman, who grounded out to third baseman Larry Wolfe in the first inning, flew out to right fielder Bombo Rivera in the fourth, and ended the bottom of the sixth inning with a two-out fielder's choice groundout to shortstop Roy Smalley. As Lyman approached the plate in the bottom of the eighth, he was zero for fourteen in an Angels uniform. Finally, the veteran outfielder got some redemption, as Lyman slammed an offering from his old pal Dave Goltz into right field for his first hit of the season. Bobby Grich, who had led off with a single of his own, raced to third. Joe Rudi followed with an opposite-field single to right field, bringing home Grich for the third and final run of the game. The Angels shut out the Twins, 3–0, with Ken Brett pitching a complete game, five-hit shutout.

As Lyman walked down the Anaheim Stadium tunnel and into the Angels dressing room, he was met with a carpet of his teammates' making—a series of white towels strung together from the dressing-room entrance all the way to his locker. In an act of total selflessness, Ken Brett—who had just pitched one of the best games of his entire career—gave Lyman a game ball for finally getting a hit. Another teammate, Terry Humphrey, presented Lyman with a red rose.

"I guess I'm on the team now," Lyman joked to reporters. "They've been on me the whole time about when I was going to get a hit."[14]

Ten games in, Lyman was sitting at .051—just two hits in his first thirty-nine at bats of the season. When things were at their worst, Lyman would sit in his car outside Anaheim Stadium, sometimes for as much as an hour before games. For the first and perhaps only time in his life, it wasn't fun for Lyman to come to the stadium.

"I'd drive to the ballpark about 4 pm and just sit my car," Lyman recalled later in the season. "I didn't want to come to the clubhouse. I figured it would just be another bad day. I didn't know if I'd ever come out of it."[15]

"Toward the end, I was almost hallucinating, seeing myself step out of my body at the plate. It's the way some people think they see Martians," he added.[16]

A week later, Lyman joked about the Martians comment. "I don't think I ever really said Martians," he joked. "Oh hell. People will just think I'm a little crazier than I am."

After yet another hitless game, Lyman was moving along a Los Angeles freeway late one April night when he pulled his Saab next to another vehicle. The driver of the other car, a local reporter, was stunned to see the Angels outfielder driving parallel to him, honking to get his attention. Rolling down his window, the reporter asked Lyman how he was doing.

"Still tryin'," Lyman said simply before driving off into the Southern California evening.[17]

* * *

Lyman benched himself prior to the April 19 game against the Mariners in the Kingdome. He knew something was wrong, and he needed a day off to figure it out.

"I might have snapped at the plate last night. The adrenaline was so high and the tension so tight, it was like blowing up a balloon as tight as you can, then deflating it, having it drop back to nothing. I was really hallucinating," Lyman told journalists. "I felt myself standing outside my body up there at the plate, then jumping back into it just before the pitch. Everything was just a big glare in front of my face."[18]

"You try to blot everything out when you're up there, but things run through my mind like a ticker tape. I couldn't hold a thought. I couldn't concentrate on anything. I looked out there and I was seeing eighteen men instead of eight," the veteran outfielder continued.

Lyman sat and watched from the cozy confines of the Angels dugout as his teammates suffered a 6–1 setback to the Mariners under the roof.

"I did this [benched myself] once in college and sat out a game and came back swinging the bat. When you sit out you see a lot of things you don't see when you're playing. You can internalize the game a lot more," Lyman said after the game.

It was reminiscent of the spring of 1972, when a hobbling Lyman had been held out of the Valley State lineup by Bob Hiegert for a few days as he recovered from a groin pull.

"He was a 100 percent guy—he was full out. If he was running the bases, he'd run through somebody to break up a double play," said Hiegert. "But he just was not the same kid. I knew something was wrong with him. We had a doubleheader the next day."

"What's the matter with you?" Hiegert asked his young left fielder.

"My leg is bothering me," Lyman replied.

"What else?"

"Oh, that's it. I can play through it."

"No, you're not. You're not going to play through it," Hiegert retorted.

"So I sat him down, and it was nothing more than any other kid in exactly the same situation. But he was honest enough to say, 'My leg hurts,'" Hiegert continued. "Most kids aren't going to do that, or wouldn't do that, because they fear they'll never get back into the lineup. But he knew he was hurting the team, and hurting himself. He wasn't playing well."

Six years later, and Lyman wasn't playing well. He was hurting the Angels. And he knew it.

"The thing that was different with him than most players is he was never out of the baseball game. Lyman was focused on what's going on in the ball game," said Hiegert. "When he sat out of a ball game, he knows what's going on. He's watching signs. He's totally involved. I think that was part of his problem when he got with the Angels."

"I think a lot of the stuff with him was he had the weight of the world on him when he did not take the Yankee contract, and moved to Anaheim," Hiegert continued.

One night during one of California's early road trips, Lyman called Hiegert back in California.

"He called me one night," Hiegert recalled.

"Coach!" Lyman exclaimed.

"Hey, what are you doing?"

"Can I talk to you?"

"Sure. How's it going?"

Lyman explained to Hiegert that he was having out-of-body experiences at the plate. "Last night I just felt that my spirit jumped out of my body. I'm standing in the batter's box, and I felt like I left. And I'm still standing there," Lyman replied.

Immediately sensing the problem, Hiegert intervened.

"Chill out. Take a little pressure off yourself," he said.

"As things kind of settled in, he finally started figuring that out a little bit. He was really close to reaching his potential," Hiegert added.

By the end of April, Lyman was hitting just .147. As May 1 arrived, the outfielder was just eleven for seventy-five at the plate on the season. Around Major League Baseball, Lyman's story became something of a cautionary tale of how things can go woefully wrong when a player arrives on a new team with abnormally high expectations and then fails to deliver in the beginning.

"The free agency thing kind of scared me at first," said Alan Trammell of the Detroit Tigers. "I think a lot of guys got the big money and it put too much pressure on them.[19]

"Lyman Bostock, for example. He hit .330 the year before the Angels signed him as a free agent, and because he got a million dollars everybody thought he should hit .380 or something.

"You could see he was really pressing when he got off to a bad start. He was saying to himself, 'What can I do? What am I doing wrong?'"

"If a guy suddenly gets three times as much money as before, how is he going to improve his performance three times?" Trammell continued. "Is he all of a sudden going to hit 50 homers, drive in 130 or 150 runs?"

Lyman's desperation had turned into feelings of guilt. He didn't feel like he was earning his large paycheck. "I let it get out of hand," Lyman would say a couple months later. "I regretted having the money, having come to the Angels. I wanted to give it all back and call it even."[20]

"He was offered one of the richest contracts in pro sports and he didn't feel comfortable about it. He was almost embarrassed," added Hiegert.

Lyman felt so bad about the situation that he was willing to do something very unique: he offered to give the Angels back his April salary—approximately $40,000. "If I don't do well the rest of April, I'm going to ask Mr. Autry not to pay me for the month," Lyman told reporters in the Angels locker room toward the end of April.[21]

"I feel I'm receiving money and I should produce. I want to give him his money's worth. If he won't keep the money I'll ask him to give it to some kind of organization that can use the money."

"I realize I haven't earned my salary," he said, according to Jim Hawkins of the *Detroit Free Press*. "I don't feel I've done enough for the money I'm making."

Lyman wasn't bluffing. It wasn't some shallow ploy for public sympathy. He genuinely intended to give his April salary back to the Angels. He walked into Buzzie Bavasi's office in Anaheim Stadium and made his declaration official.

"He came into my office and told me he was reluctant to take his salary," Bavasi later said to Penner of the *Los Angeles Times*.

"I'm not doing my job," Lyman told the Angels executive.

"I won't let you do that," Bavasi replied, refusing to take Lyman's money back.

"Why not?" the outfielder responded.

"What if you hit .600 next month?" Bavasi said. "You're sure as hell not getting any more money out of me."

"That floored me," Bavasi added. "I never knew a .200 hitter who didn't think he deserved a raise. I never heard of a ballplayer wanting to give $40,000 away."

"It was a legitimate offer [to give his salary back]," added an Angels spokesman to Gustkey of the *Los Angeles Times*. "He and Buzzie Bavasi talked about it. Then Gene Autry talked to Bostock and told him, 'We wouldn't pay you any more if you were doing better than expected, so you don't owe us anything.'"

"I appreciate very much the way you feel and what you said, but we'd never do anything like that," owner Gene Autry told the struggling outfielder.[22]

"Listen. Don't worry so much about your base hits," Autry went on. "That's the way this sports thing works. I've been around moving pictures long enough and I've seen when things wouldn't go right there, too. Just take that nice easy swing of yours, and it'll come back to you."

"Maybe you're trying too hard. I've seen that happen too," Autry added.

"He got off to such a terrible start in '78. I think he tried to donate his first half the seasons' money to charity, and Gene Autry wouldn't let him do that," said Carney Lansford.[23]

Although the Angels ultimately refused to take back Lyman's salary, the outfielder wound up dispersing the money throughout the Los Angeles community.

"I'm definitely going to give it up," Lyman said. "I still don't feel like I've done enough for this month."[24]

"I'm not that type of person to take money, and I know I'm not doing well," the new Angel continued. "Especially that type of money that I'm receiving. I don't feel like I gave Mr. Autry a full month's work. If I can't perform to my capability, then I don't think I deserve the money."

Letters poured in to Lyman from all over the United States after he announced he was giving away his April pay. Some were children, simply seeking an autograph. Others came from various civic groups and private citizens. "I've received a lot of mail from all over the country," Lyman replied. "I'll spread it around."

The situation of less fortunate children always pulled at Lyman's heartstrings. It was why he gave away all of Valley State's baseballs before the national championship game in the summer of 1972. It was why he spent so much time with the local children at the Venezuelan ballpark where he played winter ball before making it big with the Minnesota Twins. It was why he had bought sporting goods equipment for his off-season clinics in and around Los Angeles. So now, in a moment of supreme frustration, Lyman intended to make some good of what had been an unqualified disaster so far in his career with the Angels.

"I'm investigating the causes now," he said to Hawkins of the *Detroit Free Press*. "I might donate $5,000 here and there, to polio and sickle cell anemia and things like that, to people who have been affected by disease."

"I mainly want to do something for kids—give a little here and there," he replied. "I'm really looking toward orphans. Maybe I can buy some tickets from the club to get them into ball games."[25]

Lyman was less impressed by the efforts of grown adults to seek a handout. "One guy wrote and said he lost his business and is about to lose his family because of it, and needs $20,000," Lyman replied. "He's got the wrong idea. I'm talking about charities, not just giving it away to individuals."

Naturally, there were some who called Lyman's motives into question. Some suggested his action was just a way to deflect attention from his poor performance. Others suggested it was a way for Lyman to curry favor with Angels fans.

"A lot of players thought he was crazy to do that," said former Twins teammate Ron Schueler to Dave Nightingale of the *Chicago Tribune*. "But if you knew Lyman as well as I did in Minneapolis, you knew that he was sincere, you knew that he did donate it."

For his part, Lyman continued to ignore the doubters, as he'd done throughout his baseball career. "I don't really care what people think," Lyman would say. "I'm not doing it for the publicity, just for the satisfaction I'm going to get."

The move was unprecedented, before or since. Since when has a ballplayer ever offered to give back his pay?

"He had a miserable April, couldn't buy a hit," said Dick Enberg. "But to his credit, he humbly met with Gene Autry and Buzzie Bavasi, insisting he not be paid a salary for the month. He said he didn't deserve or earn it. Can you imagine today's millionaires being so honest to themselves?"

"He wanted to earn his money, and if he didn't earn it, he didn't want it," said his uncle Tom Turner in ESPN's *Outside the Lines*.

"That showed the type of integrity he had," added Brian Downing to Penner of the *Los Angeles Times*. "He was one of the first wave of free agents, and there was a lot of pressure on the big money guys. That [giving the money away] was how he dealt with it. He had a lot of personal pride. He got off to a horrendous start, but he fought so hard to get out of it."

"You know he wanted to give his salary back 'cause he wasn't doing with the Angels what he thought he ought to be doing. He was in a slump," said his father, Lyman Bostock Sr.[26]

As it turned out, Lyman's slump would bring father and son together in a way that hadn't been the case throughout most of their lives.

* * *

As Lyman struggled through the first month of the 1978 season, he was desperate to find a way out of his dreadful slump. Lyman was, in fact, so desperate that he did something he had rarely done—he called Birmingham to get advice from his father. In a moment where absolutely nothing was working at the plate, the younger Lyman Bostock swallowed his pride.

He had humbly come to the conclusion that perhaps the man who had given birth to him—though absent throughout much of his life—could help him out of the worst and longest-lasting slump of his entire baseball career.

"He called me once about his hitting," said Lyman Sr. about the conversation he would have with his son.

In order to help his son out, Lyman Sr. recalled a piece of advice he once heard from "Candy Jim" Taylor, the man who had pulled him from obscurity nearly forty years earlier and given him a spot with the Birmingham Black Barons. Back in the 1940s, Candy Jim, or "Uncle Jim," as some of his players referred to him, once used a simple approach, which Lyman Sr. had overheard, to get one of his Chicago American Giants sluggers out of a prolonged slump.

"Mule Miles lived in San Antone, Texas. He was strong and he could hit. Miles got in a slump, wasn't hitting the ball, and Jim Taylor—on the team we called him 'Uncle Jim'—was a great manager," explained the elder Bostock. "We were playing in Chicago then."

Miles had gotten the nickname "Mule" from his manager after a game in which he had belted two home runs. Taylor exclaimed that Miles "hits like a mule kicks." But during this particularly unproductive slump, Miles was struggling even to make contact with the ball. The elder Bostock recalled that Taylor had advised Miles to stop trying to hit the ball out every single time he went up to the plate, and instead to take what the pitcher gave him. Shortly thereafter, Miles broke out and began hitting the ball again.

"He [Taylor] said [to Mule], 'Miles, stop looking at that goddamn fence! Every time you look at the fence, you hit the ball two hops to the pitcher.'"

As the American Giants toured the East Coast in the late 1940s, they often played teams who brought in former big leaguers as temporary ringers. They were competitive games, but Mule proved to be the better man with a flurry of long-ball power as he emerged from his slump.

"[Later] we had to play 10–11 games out there in the East. They had old major leaguers all the time. We played 11 games and Miles hit 11 home runs!"

The younger Lyman Bostock wasn't a slugger. But in his own way, Lyman Sr. attempted to convey to his own son the same message Candy Jim had passed along to Mule Miles. "I wanted to tell my son the same thing. I told him just to hit the way they was pitching it. And he did and he went on [from there]."

Lyman finally starting hitting, slowly but surely coming out of his funk. It all began May 2 with an opposite-field RBI triple he ripped off Detroit's Milt Wilcox. Lyman stayed patient, sat back, and dropped a hard shot down the left field line, legging it out to third. Though the

Angels got slaughtered, 10–2, Lyman had taken what Wilcox had given him, didn't rush himself or overthink things, and got back to taking the ball the other way instead of pulling everything on the ground. It was a critical moment for the Angels outfielder.

"A .230 team batting average," said Angels manager Dave Garcia afterward, shaking his head. "It's got to go up before it goes down. It's just one of those things. We didn't just forget how to hit. Hitting is like riding a bicycle. One you learn, you don't forget."[27]

The *Detroit Free Press* ran a poll in its sports section that first week of May, asking its readers to call in and tell them if they would have donated their salary for a month to charity.

"If you felt you hadn't earned your pay would you do the same?" the poll asked.

After Lyman went one for four in a loss to the Tigers the following day, Dave Garcia closed the clubhouse door to reporters to have a talk with his underachieving club. It was the twenty-first time in twenty-three games to begin the season that the Angels had ten or fewer hits.

"Water will seek its own level," Garcia told reporters later. "If a guy has batted .280 for five years in the big leagues, you know he is going to hit .280. If someone told me that Lyman Bostock is a .175 hitter, I would look him in the eye and say he is crazy."[28]

The following day, Lyman announced that he had made his final decision regarding which charities would receive a piece of the approximately $40,000 he was donating. True to his nature, Lyman preferred to keep those fortunate recipients of his money private.

"The entire matter is now closed," he would say. "I'm deeply appreciative of all who forwarded words of encouragement and for those fine charitable organizations who contacted me. For the remainder of the season my only concern will be to help the Angels win games."[29]

* * *

Lyman put together a seven-game hitting streak, including three hits May 9 in an Angels win over the Detroit Tigers. On May 26, Lyman crunched a hard line drive into the seats along the right-field line at Anaheim Stadium in the sixth inning. Inching his average up to .224 with his first homer of the season, Lyman's blast gave the Angels a 5–4 lead, which eventually turned into a 6–5 victory over the Milwaukee Brewers. Lyman returned to his locker after the game to see a pot of flowers that had been delivered by some encouraging Angels fans.

"Everything seems to be against you for a time," Lyman said to a huddle of reporters. "But it's like swimming. When you get a cramp you don't fight it, or you drown. But if you know what to do, you get over it. You just have to relax."[30]

While Angels fans may have been frustrated at Lyman's early struggles, most stood behind him. Sure, there were some isolated boos here and there. But while certain California players couldn't get away from the barrage of boos and jeers hurled upon them, Angels supporters, by and large, treated their new outfielder with kid gloves that spring.

"The biggest surprise of the Anaheim sadists this season has been their treatment of Lyman Bostock," Steve Dilbeck of the *San Bernardino Sun-Telegram* wrote in late May. "Despite his disappointing start, his ears have hardly been treated to a single boo."

"The fans have been very fair to me," Lyman would say. "At least I haven't had any signs on my car saying, 'Go Back to Minnesota.'"

After going hitless on May 29 to slip to .215 at the plate, Dave Garcia sat Lyman out the next day until calling him as a pinch hitter in the eighth inning. Afterward, Lyman walked into Garcia's office. He was beyond frustrated at his performance so far. It went beyond living up to a contract. He felt he was hurting the team. "I didn't call Bostock in. He came in to talk to me," Garcia said later. "He felt he isn't helping the club. I told him to forget what has happened so far and not to worry about hitting .350.[31]

"I told him he'd have to hit over .500 the rest of the season to reach .330. I told him to hit .300 from now on and everything would be all right."

"It wasn't a big deal," Lyman replied. "We're just losing and things are not as serious as people think they are. This time of year the guys get a little tired.

"It was just a manager-player conversation."

As it turned out, Lyman and his teammates would have a new manager within forty-eight hours.

11

REDEMPTION AND HAPPINESS (1978)

One of the beautiful things about baseball is that every once in a while you come into a situation where you want to, and where you have to, reach down and prove something.—Nolan Ryan, pitcher, California Angels[1]

Despite their losing May, the Angels actually gained a half game in the Western Division standings and were just 1.5 games back of the surprising Oakland A's going into a weekend series at Anaheim Stadium against the Boston Red Sox starting June 2. Lyman had moved his average up from .147 to .209 by the start of the month. It was still way below his high standards, but a marked improvement from the dreadful start he'd had.

As the Angels took a day off on June 1 leading up to their series with Boston, they were in the midst of a five-game losing streak climaxed by their 17–2 pummeling at the hands of the White Sox. Gene Autry had decided to make a move, and that afternoon Dave Garcia was informed that he was being fired as the Angels manager. Garcia's replacement was thirty-six-year-old Jim Fregosi, who had just retired after appearing in twenty games that spring as a member of the Pittsburgh Pirates.

"We felt the Angels needed more motivation and we feel very strongly that Fregosi is the type of individual to fill that bill," Autry said to Steve Dilbeck of the *San Bernardino Sun-Telegram*.

Lyman's early-season difficulties that spring—as well as the problems that some of California's other high-priced free agent acquisitions had in prior years—were giving Autry second thoughts about shelling out his cash on the open market. "I doubt seriously if we will try to sign any free agents in the future," Autry said later in the season. "I won't say we won't."[2]

"I think there were players not playing up to their capabilities, but I think they were trying to do their best," Garcia replied after being notified of his firing. "For instance, nobody can tell me that Bostock is a .200 hitter after watching him the last three years when he was a .300 hitter."[3]

"I can't explain it," the terminated manager said to Dilbeck in another article. "When people get into a batting slump, how do you get them out of it? The California Angels that have been hitting poorly will begin to hit. I know Lyman Bostock is a good hitter."

"Lyman Bostock hit .300 for three years at Minnesota. Now he is hitting .200. Maybe there was something I didn't do to get him in the right frame of mind," Garcia explained.

For his part, Lyman accepted the news with a tinge of shock. He had, the night before, had a conversation with Garcia that went reasonably well. "It was a big surprise," he said the following day. "I didn't think it would happen. Not this soon."[4]

A couple weeks later, however, Lyman admitted that the ball club needed a charge. "I'm going to play hard regardless of who's manager," he said. "I like Dave Garcia, but he left too much for the players to do. We needed a manager who would fight for us. A few of the guys thought some things should have been fought for by the manager."[5]

Fregosi was an original Angel whom Lyman had grown up watching and rooting for at Wrigley Field, Chavez Ravine, and Anaheim Stadium. He held ten Angels batting records at the time of his retirement, and he brought a player's perspective to the California clubhouse. The players liked and respected him because he was one of them. Fregosi knew what made ballplayers tick, what set them off. He knew how to handle a nervous rookie pitcher as well as he knew how to handle a prima donna slugger.

"The players are going to do one thing," Fregosi said to Dilbeck. "They're going to play hard, or they won't play at all. I think the one thing that has to be built up is motivation. I was always proud to be an Angel."

"Fregosi's a fiery guy. Maybe that's what it takes to get a team going," Lyman replied. "I think a pro motivates himself, but some players need to be motivated."[6]

REDEMPTION AND HAPPINESS (1978)

In Lyman's case, Fregosi saw a classic example of a player that was putting too much on himself at the plate. "A guy doesn't hit .336 one year and .209 the next," said Fregosi. "He came here as a high-salaried free agent and probably tried to do too much, probably tried to carry the whole thing."[7]

Fregosi's perception was widely accepted around baseball, and Lyman openly agreed as the season moved on. "I don't think attitudes of players change. They play hard no matter who it's for. In fact, sometimes they play too hard. Look at a kid like Lyman Bostock. He signs for all that money and he tries so hard to earn it. He presses trying to show he's worth the money and he has trouble," said St. Louis Cardinals Hall of Famer Red Schoendienst to Associated Press columnist Barry Wilner.

"I wanted to do so well, not so much for the money, but playing here for the first time," Lyman said of his dreadful early start. "They are not paying me for this year. They pay you for what you did in the past, but I wanted to earn it this year."[8]

Though the Angels were crushed 6–1 by Boston in Fregosi's debut, Lyman welcomed his new manager with a tremendous outing, collecting four hits and bumping his batting average up .19 percentage points in a single evening.

Showing confidence in Lyman, Fregosi batted him third right out of the gate against the Cuban sidewinder Luis Tiant. After pulling a single into right field in his first at bat off Tiant, he dropped singles into center field in the fourth and sixth innings. He came up again to face Dick Drago in the bottom of the ninth and completed his perfect night with another single into right field.

"I went four-for-four that day," Lyman said later in the season to Dilbeck, looking back on Fregosi's debut. "I'll never forget it."

"There are pluses even in a loss," Fregosi said following his first big league game as a manager. "I got to see my team for the first time. Lyman Bostock got four hits. He ran hard, breaking up double plays. There were some bright spots. The main thing I want to do is take a look at everybody on this club before I start changing things."[9]

While Fregosi brought a much-needed burst of youthful energy to the Angels locker room, hitting coach Bob Skinner focused on the task at hand—restoring Lyman's confidence and swagger at the plate.

"If he was more disciplined at the plate, he would hit .350," Skinner had said of Lyman during spring training to *Sporting News* reporter Dick Miller. "He has amazing intensity."

In Lyman's conversation with Gene Autry earlier in the season about giving back his April salary, the owner had advised him to work closely with Skinner, and it proved to be wise counsel.

"You're probably getting all kinds of advice," Autry had said to Lyman. "If I were you, I'd take one man's advice. You seem to like what Bob Skinner can do for you, so I'd listen to him."[10]

"[Skinner was] a big help," Lyman would say that summer. "He didn't just wash the season off. He kept talking to me, telling me I was a better hitter, reminding me of the things I was doing wrong."[11]

The former big league manager stuck with the veteran outfielder, giving him pointers and generally helping him relax at the dish.

"He's just Lyman now," Skinner said. "I don't know who that was the first part of the season. He's more patient now. He was trying to do too much in one at-bat before."

"Skins stayed with me every day," Lyman added. "You don't get a chance to study yourself. Skinner has done a heckuva job in terms of getting me back on the right track. He's worked with me every day."

Although Lyman never admitted publicly that his father had given him sage advice, Lyman Sr.'s suggestion to relax and take what the pitcher gave him was also beneficial to his emergence from the slump.

"I know why I wasn't hitting. I found out the day before Jim Fregosi became our manager. I just wasn't aware before that. It had nothing to do with anything on the field," Lyman would say. "I'm not going to say why. I just don't feel like I want to make the reason public. But I'm convinced I know the answer."[12]

"I had some problems off the field," Lyman added. "It's something I will never talk about."[13]

"I found out what it was and who it was and did something about it. But I don't want to say because it's complicated and involves too many people."[14]

Starting with his four-hit game at home against Boston on June 2, Lyman embarked on an eleven-game hitting streak over the next week and a half. Lyman had twenty-four hits in forty-eight at bats, raising his average all the way up to .274.

"[After the slump] he then hit like we all expected and, as I recall, was batting close to .300 later in the season," said Dick Enberg.

The old Lyman Bostock—the fun-loving, gregarious, talkative Lyman that everyone loved and enjoyed being around—was back. Aside from winning games and hitting well, few things in baseball could bring Lyman any more happiness and satisfaction than simply hanging out in the locker room, teasing his teammates, telling jokes, engaging in horse play.

"No teammates ever thought Bostock crazy," wrote Thomas Boswell of the *Washington Post*. "He was the sort of superstar that any player, even a scrub, could grab in a bear hug or a headlock. He loved the humor, the needling, the wrestling, the constant energy and chatter of the baseball clubhouse. It was his favorite atmosphere—his perfect frenetic habitat."

"There were never enough hours in the day for Lyman. We called him 'Jibber Jabber' because he was always talking. Everyone was crazy about him because he was so outgoing and friendly, always 'up,' always looking on the bright side," said Angels second baseman Bobby Grich.

As Lyman began to hit again, the Angels fans were all too eager to cheer him with each successful connection at the plate. While a few hecklers had given him a hard time at home during the deepest depths of his April slump, Lyman was pleased with the way the California fans supported him as he emerged from his cold spell.

"I can't say enough good things about them," Lyman said to Ross Newhan of the *Los Angeles Times*, referring to the Angels fans who stuck by him during his slump. "They were super. I kept getting letters and tapes, all kinds of positive suggestions and messages of support."

The way the fans in Southern California reacted to Lyman's struggles reminded him of his difficult decision the previous off-season and why he was better off with the Angels than the Yankees. "I couldn't help but think of how it might have been if I had signed with the Yankees and gone through that kind of slump. The Yankees were really my first choice. The glamour and bright lights. But they wanted me only as a player. The Angels recognized my value as a person, too.

"I now know how fortunate I am. I have to think that if I had gone through that kind of slump in New York I'd have been mugged on my way to the park. I'd be dead by now."

***

For those who see artistry and poetry in baseball, Lyman's swing had something more to it. Like a fine wine, like an exquisite painting or sculpture, Lyman's swing had a certain beauty that couldn't be easily duplicated. It had panache. Standing in, hands parallel to the letters on the front of his jersey in an easy, effortless crouch, knees slightly bent, Lyman would peer at opposing pitchers. Not menacingly, but with purpose.

"Hit the ball hard somewhere every time," Lyman once said of his philosophy at the plate. "I don't like the high pitch. Mostly I like the ball from the knee to the thigh."[15]

Thanks to his outstanding eyesight, Lyman could decide on pitches in fractions of a second that would determine the angle and location of his impending cut. More often than not, Lyman's swing came across the middle of the plate in a straight line. Because he swung on such a level trajectory, he was much more prone to hard grounders and line drives than short popups or deep fly balls—results more typical of power hitters that tend to get under the ball.

Lyman liked to let go of the bat with his left hand—the top hand in his stance—during his follow-through, especially when he made good contact. When he swung and connected, the bat would swirl out in front of his body with his right hand and then whip back behind him in a sweeping, one-handed, split-second flash before he'd let go and race off toward first.

"He had this beautiful, level swing," wrote Jim Murray of the *Los Angeles Times*. "His hits seemed to jump off the bat. I supposed he got his share of cheap hits, but the ones I saw were screamers. Stan Musial type hits—catch me if you can. Frozen ropes."

"I like to hit," Lyman once said. "That's something a guy should always like to do. It's the most exciting part of the game."[16]

Though he would need to hit .330 the rest of the way to finish the season as a .300 hitter, it was an attainable goal for Lyman as June set in. He had hit .330 back-to-back the previous two seasons in Minnesota; if he stayed patient and let things come his way, it could happen again.

"I still think I can hit .300 this season," he said in mid-June in an Associated Press article. "Hitting .300 is going to be tough, but I'm a tough hitter. If I keep my sanity, I've got a shot at it."

Lyman singled twice in California's 10–7 win over Oakland on June 8, as his average improved to .261. He was now hitting a full hundred points better than his .147 April and had been hitting his customary .331 over the Angels' last thirty-two outings. A couple days later, Lyman scored the winning run as the Angels outlasted the Yankees, 4–3, at the

Big A. After coaxing a leadoff walk from Goose Gossage in the Angels half of the 12th inning, Lyman advanced to second on a Joe Rudi sacrifice bunt. Following a Don Baylor groundout, Ron Jackson poked a seeing-eye single up the middle, which bounded off the glove of Yankees second baseman Willie Randolph into short center field. Lyman raced all the way from second and beat Randolph's throw home, pumping his fists and clapping as he ran out to congratulate Ron Jackson for the game-winning hit. The following day against the defending world champs, Lyman drove in California's first run with a first inning single and then nailed another RBI single the following inning, tying the score at 3–3. The Angels would rally for six runs over the fifth and sixth innings on their way to a 9–6 victory.

"The Lyman Bostock playing center field for the California Angels in June bears little resemblance to the Lyman Bostock who was out there in April," wrote the Associated Press in its account of the Sunday, June 11, contest. "After hitting .147 in April and being so embarrassed he donated his monthly check to charity, Bostock is playing so well now a raise might be in order."

"The first month of the season, I could have hit right-handed and done better than I did, and I've never switch-hit in my life," Lyman said at the peak of his hitting streak. "A lot of the guys have helped me. They used examples of players who had gotten off to horrible starts and still had big years. It gave me a lot of hope."[17]

"I'm human like anyone else. I questioned my abilities. I wanted to know what was going wrong. It just took me a long time to realize what it was."

Unfortunately, the Angels didn't really capitalize on Lyman's hot hitting in early June, as they barely held above .500 and actually lost six of Fregosi's first eleven contests as manager. Lyman put together a hitting streak of fourteen games that was finally snapped on June 18, as he had a hitless night in Yankee Stadium against Ed Figueroa. Though he failed to pick up an RBI in three games back at Metropolitan Stadium against the Twins, Lyman went four for thirteen at the plate as the Angels swept three straight. The sweep allowed them to move into a first-place tie in the American League West on June 22.

Moving on to Texas, California's yo-yo season continued as they were taken down four straight times by the Rangers at Arlington Stadium. After going one for three off Fergie Jenkins in the opener, Lyman got two hits the following night, improving his average to .279. Rangers hurlers Jon Matlack and Doc Medich would shut out the Angels the last two contests of the four-game set, as Lyman finished up the series just one for eight.

The Western Division was truly wild in late June, with four teams, including the Angels, within four games of first place. Texas slid past California into a first-place tie with the Royals, while the A's were slipping, dropping out of first place and below .500.

All the while, Lyman kept on hitting. Two hits against Kansas City on June 26. Two more hits two days later, along with an RBI single to score California's first run, in a 9–5 victory over the Royals. Another hit-and-run the following day, coming off Royals southpaw reliever Al Hrabosky, as California caught Whitey Herzog's club with a 3–1 win.

The Angels were now tied with Kansas City in second place, and just a game behind the Rangers. Two more hits to close out June. On the last day of the month, Lyman got RBI singles in the third and seventh innings, scoring California's first two runs in a 4–2 victory over Texas to move back into a first-place tie.

"I got used to this kind of race at Minnesota," Lyman said afterward. "It's a lot easier to come to the park when you're fighting for the lead."[18]

* * *

As July 1 arrived, Lyman had hit safely in eleven of the Angels' last twelve games, and twenty-five of the last twenty-seven contests. In recognition of his .404 batting clip over the month of June, Lyman was nominated for American League Player of the Month but lost out to Yankees southpaw Ron Guidry, who was having the season of his life on the way to the Cy Young Award. A move to right field was helping both Lyman and the Angels, as he could now play without all the pressure of defensive action in center field. Plus, the move allowed Jim Fregosi to insert both Lyman and Rick Miller in the lineup at the same time. Miller had a nice offensive streak for California in late June and early July, hitting in sixteen of seventeen games.

Another hit on July 1 against Texas gave Lyman a seven-game hitting streak on top of the fourteen-game streak he'd put together in early June. The next day he singled home a run, extending his new hitting streak to eight games and improving his average to .287 as the Angels claimed a 4–3 walk-off win over the Rangers.

The Angels headed off to Kansas City for a huge four-game series with the Royals before returning home, and Lyman cooled off a little, going just three for seventeen as the Western Division foes split a quartet. From there, California returned to Anaheim Stadium and continued its assault on first place, taking three of four from the Seattle Mariners. Lyman drove in the Angels' first two runs in a 9–5 victory on July 7, and then went three for eight in a July 8 twi-night doubleheader, scoring two runs and driving in another as California picked up two more wins.

Not only were the Angels winning, they were hitting. Over a stretch of thirteen games in late June and early July, California batted .315 as a team. Lyman gave the credit to Jim Fregosi for his no-nonsense approach to the ball club.

"I know one thing," Lyman said to *Los Angeles Times* reporter Scott Ostler. "We didn't have no fiery instinct to come back [before]. With Fregosi, you know he's a fighter, so nobody goes dead on him. If you've got a guy who will fight for you, you've got a good chance to come back. Garcia might have been too nice."

California won two straight from the Toronto Blue Jays, with Lyman belting a solo homer in the sixth inning, his second of the season, to tie the score on July 14. The home run improved Lyman's recent hitting streak to nine games. He would increase it to ten games the following day with a first-inning single in an eventual 2–0 win over the Detroit Tigers. Lyman's single against the Tigers gave him hits in thirty-seven of California's last forty games.

On the afternoon of Sunday, July 16, Lyman was honored in a pregame ceremony at Anaheim Stadium as Honorary Big Brother of the Year. The annual award was based on Lyman's work in the Los Angeles community, including his efforts with the Teen Challengers in the church back in Vermont Square where he grew up.

"Working out with boys since 1972 lets me watch certain groups progress," he said. "It gives them self-determination, not only for baseball, but to achieve other goals."[19]

Although the Angels suffered a 4–0 loss to the Tigers that afternoon, Lyman collected a pair of bunt singles to stretch his latest hitting streak to eleven games. In addition, Lyman scaled the Anaheim Stadium fence in the fifth inning, reaching up to take a two-run homer away from Detroit's Jason Thompson. The more than twenty-one thousand fans who came out to see Lyman be recognized as Big Brother of the Year pushed the Angels' 1978 attendance to over a million fans at Anaheim Stadium. Never before in club history had the team drawn a million fans at such an early point in the season.

Though the Angels lost, 4–3, on July 17, Lyman picked up three more hits—an opposite-field double in the third, a single to right field in the fifth, and another hit into left field in the seventh. The hits gave Lyman a twelve-game hitting streak and hits in thirty-nine of forty-two games since Jim Fregosi had been named manager of the Angels. His average shot up to .291.

"He got off to the worst start I've ever seen a ballplayer get off to," said Angels teammate Merv Rettenmund to Brian Hewitt of the *Chicago Sun-Times*. "And he battled back. He was a real battler."

While Pete Rose's incredible National League record forty-four-game hitting streak caught the attention and fascination of baseball observers throughout the summer of 1978, Lyman's streak of hitting in thirty-nine of forty-two games wasn't too far behind the Reds superstar. Of course, few outside Southern California were paying attention to what Lyman was accomplishing.

Lyman finally came crashing back to earth on July 18, going zero for five against Cleveland pitchers Rick Waits and Jim Kern, including a strikeout to end the game in the ninth inning. His twelve-game hitting streak was over, but Lyman was still very much on track for his third straight .300 season. It wouldn't be long before Lyman got back on track. After getting a hit against the Indians in an Angels victory July 19, he would collect three hits in the first game of a doubleheader two days later at Detroit's Tiger Stadium.

Lyman had become a staple at the number three spot in the California lineup since Jim Fregosi's hiring. But prior to the July 19 game against Cleveland, Fregosi penciled youngster Carney Lansford in the number two spot—a move that would prove beneficial to both players.

"At a certain point when Jim Fregosi took over halfway through the season he moved me right into the number two spot, and Lyman hit third," said Lansford in *Remembering Lyman Bostock*. "It got to a point where he felt so confident that he would tell me in the on-deck circle, 'Hey, when you're on first base, if you see me step out of the box and I tuck in my shirt, take off. Hit and run.'"

Along with hitting behind Lansford and providing the youngster numerous run-scoring opportunities, Lyman also took time with the talented Angels infielder, giving him advice and little pep talks to show he cared.

"I was the only rookie on an all-veteran major league team, and he paid attention to me. And he would talk to me," said Lansford. "Him and Joe Rudi were really the two guys that paid attention to me at all my rookie year on that team. He just really took care of me."

After Lyman collected an RBI single in a loss to the Tigers on July 22, the Angels and Tigers played their second doubleheader in three days. He would go four for eight with a run scored in the doubleheader split, pushing his average a bit closer to the .300 plateau at .294. Lyman would cool off a little bit as the month wound down, going hitless in three straight games against the Indians and Brewers before getting back in the hit column July 27 against Milwaukee.

As he worked through a minor concussion suffered on a stolen base attempt—his head rammed into Kiko Garcia's knee—Lyman played a minimal role in California's series in Baltimore to close out the month. But Lyman did get hits in both of his official plate appearances. As August arrived, Lyman was hitting .289 after a one-for-two performance against Oakland.

* * *

While Lyman heated up throughout the summer of 1978, one of baseball's premier left-handed hitting stars of the previous two decades—Lou Brock of the St. Louis Cardinals—endured a dreadful July with four for twenty-seven at the plate. Brock, who had set a new major league stolen-base record the previous season, wasn't far from three thousand career hits. But as his slump progressed, he couldn't help but sympathize with Lyman and what he had done earlier in the season.

"I've got a feeling like Lyman Bostock," Brock said to Neal Russo of the *St. Louis Post-Dispatch* upon receiving his July paycheck. "I feel like I ought to give this check to charity."

Up in Boston, MVP candidate Jim Rice was engaged in intense contract renegotiations with the Red Sox. While Rice's lawyer, Tony Pennacchia, was bent on having the star outfielder surpass Lyman and all other big leaguers with the richest contract in the game—paying approximately $800,000 per season—Rice had some trepidation about being the game's highest-paid player.

"The more you're paid, the more they [the fans] want you to do," Rice would say in August to the *Los Angeles Times*. "The more they get down on you. Look how they were on Lyman Bostock's case. I don't want that."

August 2 would prove to be another banner night for Lyman, as he collected three hits with four RBIs in an 8–2 win over the A's. Before the game, Lyman had elected to go fishing out at Seal Beach, providing him a brief opportunity to relax.

"I went fishing today and caught a few fish," Lyman would say later to the *San Bernardino Sun-Telegram*'s Dilbeck. "I figured if I could have good luck out there that I'd be all right at the ballpark."

"When Dave Garcia left and Jim Fregosi took over, I found out the same night who was causing me problems. It's nice to have good nights, but I remember the bad."[20]

"I don't get really up for these games," Lyman continued with Dilbeck. "Sure, it's nice to have a good night and help the team win. But it doesn't make up for my April or my half of May. If I'd had that kind of start in New York they would have mugged me.

"It eats you apart. It'll tear you down. If there's a really cocky person and he has an April like I did, it will straighten you out, mellow you out. I don't know if it was the change of scenery or what. There were a lot of people who were hoping I'd flop. I had relatives who were hoping I'd flop—and that's bad."

Though the Angels were three games back of Kansas City, they were holding firm in second place. "It's going to go down to the wire with Kansas City," Lyman stated. "It's kind of exciting for us to be as close as we are. I think we've got things squared away right now."[21]

After getting another hit and scoring two runs the following day in another blowout win over Oakland, and then going two for four with a run and an RBI August 4 against his old club, the Minnesota Twins, Lyman had another injury scare. Lyman left in the seventh inning of California's 4–3 loss to the Twins on August 5 after straining a tendon in one of his knees. He would be limited for the next several days.

"It happens every year," Lyman said afterward. "Your knee turns one way but your spikes dig in. Now it'll take rest. You just can't run. You have to let it go."[22]

Five days later, on August 10, Lyman showed that he was back and ready for a strong late summer push. As the Angels crushed Oakland,

16–5, Lyman picked up three hits, scored two runs, and had his second four-RBI game of the month against the A's. As mid-August approached and the Angels headed to Seattle for four games in the Kingdome, Lyman's assault on .300 was coming to fruition. An RBI hit on August 11 moved him back to up to .293. Two hits with a run in the first game of a doubleheader the next day increased his mark to .295. Lyman finished up his Pacific Northwest tour with another four-hit game on Sunday, pushing him up to .298. However, the Angels could only manage to split four games in Seattle and left town a game behind the Royals in the Western Division race.

After a day off, Lyman finally returned to the .300 ranks on August 15, as he got three hits against Dennis Eckersley in a 5–2 Angels win, viewed by a sellout crowd of more than forty-one thousand at the Big A. He singled in the third, fifth, and seventh innings, his average inching up to .303. Over the previous twelve contests leading up to his rise over .300, Lyman had gone an astounding .438 at the plate.

"It feels good," Lyman said after his three-hit performance against Eckersley. "But not as good as beating a team like the Red Sox. A batting average is an individual thing. But a win like this, everyone can share."[23]

Lyman's average would shoot up to .305 with two more hits the following day against Boston, but he also made a huge play with his glove. In the eighth inning of a 2–2 game, the Red Sox had Jim Rice on third base with two outs when Dwight Evans nailed a slicing shot into right field that looked like it was going for extra bases. Lyman refused to give up on the play, racing to his right and diving in the right-field gap, near where the grass meets the warning track. Sliding headlong into the dirt of the warning track, Lyman not only seized Evans's deep shot in the gap but also managed to hang onto it, temporarily saving the game.

As late August arrived, Lyman was back in a customary place—hitting over .300, sitting in the top ten of the American League batting race, and battling daily to help the Angels win their first-ever American League West title.

"I really feel he's got it together," said Angels hitting coach Bob Skinner. "He's a relaxed hitter who's going to all fields, which has always been his strength. The man is not just a .300 hitter. He's a .320 hitter."[24]

On August 22 and 23, the Yankees strolled in for a two-game set in Anaheim. New York had cut Boston's massive fourteen-game lead in the

American League East nearly in half, heading into the August 22 contest tied with the Brewers for second place, 8.5 games back of the Red Sox. Prior to the August 23 game, Yankees slugger Reggie Jackson came out for batting practice when he noticed a large sign bearing his name hanging from the railing along the third deck: "Go Home Reggie and Don't Come Back!"

"Here I am," Jackson said to Yankees manager Bob Lemon. "Love me or hate me, but you can't ignore Mr. Excitement."[25]

Lyman took some of the wind out of Mr. Excitement's sails in the second inning of that evening's game, as he came up throwing following a single Jackson had struck into right field. Reggie had turned a little too far toward second base, and Lyman's pinpoint throw to first base nailed the future Hall of Famer for an assisted putout. "After what Reggie did tonight, all the mustard in the world couldn't cover him. He hit a single to right, and as he rounded first he gave one of his stares at Bostock in right as if to say, 'Go ahead, challenge me, mother******.' Bang, Bostock fired the ball in and picked him off first base. Challenge me, my ass," wrote Sparky Lyle in his bestseller *The Bronx Zoo*. After going two for four with an RBI in the first game against the Yankees, Lyman had a hit and scored two runs—his average holding steady at .302—as the Angels managed a split of the two-game set.

Lyman scored California's first run in the win on August 23, coming home on a sacrifice fly with a brilliant slide around Yankees catcher Thurman Munson, beating the throw by Reggie Jackson from right field. Remarkably, Lyman had hit .352 since Jim Fregosi had been named manager of the Angels. And, suddenly, it wasn't crazy talk to place Lyman Bostock and American League batting title in the same sentence once again.

"I don't think there's any doubt that I'll finish high, in the top ten," he replied. "As for the batting title, it's hard to pick up points in a hurry when you have as many at-bats as I do. Also, to win, I have to catch Rod Carew. And he's simply the best hitter I've ever seen."[26]

Asked that summer for the *San Bernardino Sun-Telegram* article "Angel Notes" what it would take for him to win a batting title, Lyman had a simple response: "Rod Carew to retire."

Lyman went just three for twenty-one at the plate over five straight losses to the Red Sox and Yankees in Boston and New York, his average slipping to .295 as September arrived. California headed north to Toronto for a three-game set starting September 1. They were just 1.5 games back of first place as they arrived at Exhibition Stadium. Lyman enjoyed the spacious right field of the Blue Jays' home park and feasted on the team's marginal pitching. He collected two hits, scored two runs, and belted a solo homer in the fourth inning as the Angels won the opener over Toronto, 6–4.

After sweeping the Blue Jays in Toronto, the Angels were just a game out of first place on September 4, but they would lose seven of twelve contests between September 6 and September 15 leading up to a huge series in Kansas City. California headed to the Midwest 3.5 games back of the front-running Royals. Lyman played reasonably well during this stretch—a two-run single in a 7–6 win over Texas on September 7, a three-run homer off Royals reliever Al Hrabosky on September 8, two hits in a doubleheader sweep of Kansas City September 9. Two hits, two runs, and two RBIs on September 10, as the Angels pulled within a half game of first place.

As the Angels completed their strong series against the Royals, beating Kansas City three out of four times, a teenage Angels fan named Carl Patten and a friend of his waited outside the players' gate at Anaheim Stadium, hoping to get an autograph or two as the California players left the ballpark for their cars. Lyman was the last player to leave the California dressing room that particular evening. By that time, the parking lot was almost completely empty.

Most ballplayers would have kept walking to their cars, oblivious to the fans and their problems. But that wasn't Lyman. As he saw the young boys hanging out unsupervised, Lyman grew concerned for their welfare. Stopping to greet Carl and his friend outside the players' gate, Lyman signed autographs for them and asked them if their parents were around. Learning that their parents were nearby but had not quite gotten there, Lyman took matters into his own hands. He walked them across the street to a nearby restaurant, where he waited with the two boys until Carl's father arrived to take them home.

"I was at the last game of the homestand," Patten would recall years later to MLB.com's Tom Singer. "My friend and I waited after the game. It was really late. Lyman came out last, signed my card and walked us to Charlie Brown's restaurant. We didn't have a ride and he waited until my father picked us up. That's the kind of guy he was."

* * *

Starting a twelve-game road trip in Arlington, a devastating blow was struck to California's playoff chances as they dropped three straight in Texas, with Fergie Jenkins pitching a 1–0 shutout in the opener. Lyman failed to get a hit in three at bats against the man he'd faced in his first major league game three and a half years earlier. Though the Angels had to respect Jenkins's three-hit pitching, as well as the fact that he moved into the top ten pitchers in major league history in career strikeouts, the California players felt robbed. In the fourth inning, Lyman ripped a fastball deep into the Texas evening sky. But the ball fell a little short as Juan Beniquez caught it at the warning track.

"Whoever built this place, they ought to cut off his fingers so he could never build nothing else," Lyman said dejectedly after the game in reference to Arlington Stadium, a notoriously unfriendly ballpark for hitters. "I can't hit one any harder [than the one in the fourth inning]. It's the worst hitter's park in baseball. The grass is bad and the wind is bad."[27]

"They hit three balls that might have been out if Mother Nature hadn't been on my side," Jenkins said afterward. "But that's always been a part of this ballpark."

Lyman got back on track the following day against the Rangers, lining a single into center field in the first inning to drive in California's first run. He singled again in the fifth and then crushed a double to right field in the seventh. Though the Angels lost again, 7–5, Lyman was up to .295. Two more RBIs came Lyman's way the following day after he roped an opposite-field shot into the left-field gap. But the Angels lost yet again, slipping 3.5 games behind Kansas City in the Western Division standings.

California finally got some measure of revenge against the Rangers on September 14, picking up a 16–1 win behind a major league record thirteen-run top of the ninth inning. Texas would need five pitchers to get out of the frame, as Lyman came up twice in the frame and singled both times to drive in three runs.

"Well, we found out we can score in this park," said Fregosi. "Like I said last night, anything can happen. This is incredible."[28]

Trailing by 3.5 games with fourteen left to play, the Angels headed to Kansas City, where they needed to win at least two of three to set themselves up for the final stretch. After the Angels dropped a 3–2 walk-off decision in the opener, tempers would flare the following night as California attempted to challenge the Royals' supremacy in the division.

Trailing 3–1 heading into the top of the eighth of the second mid-September showdown at Royals Stadium, the Angels prepared to face Al Hrabosky, who had emerged as Kansas City's top reliever.

Hrabosky, like Lyman, called Southern California home. He had been drafted from Anaheim's Savanna High School two different times by the St. Louis Cardinals in the late 1960s. He had been a productive reliever for the Cardinals throughout much of the 1970s, leading the National League in saves and winning percentage after going 13–3 with twenty-two closes for St. Louis in 1975. Hrabosky made his way to Kansas City prior to the 1978 season as additional bullpen depth to help the Royals be even more competitive in the late innings. For the most part he had done just that. But Lyman had been hitting him well and had homered off him just nine days earlier. Lyman was confident as he waited his turn in the on-deck circle that eighth inning, as Carney Lansford stepped in. Bobby Grich and Rick Miller represented the tying runs on first and second base. Lansford had been playing well since moving in front of Lyman to second in the Angels batting order, and he was also feeling good as he stepped up against Hrabosky.

Hrabosky uncorked a high, hard fastball over the heart of the plate, and Lansford caught it, belting the pitch deep over the left-field wall and out of Royals Stadium. The Angels now led, 4–3.

Lansford's homer unmoored Hrabosky's emotions, as such events often did. Known throughout baseball as the "Mad Hungarian," Hrabosky was well-known for his mound antics, as well as for his unpredictable, sometimes boorish behavior when entering games. With his familiar long hair and imposing Fu Manchu mustache, Hrabosky liked to turn away from opposing batters for a moment—clutching the ball tightly while facing second base—before turning back toward home plate with a loud smacking of the ball into his glove. Though these kinds of gimmicks made Hrabosky popular among fans of the teams he pitched for, they earned him derision among opposing players.

"I don't care if he does somersaults and runs around the bases before he pitches," Lyman told Steve Dilbeck for his September article. "That's fine. If it works for him. But when a guy is throwing intentionally at me, that's a different story."

Hitting directly behind Lansford in the Angels lineup, the California right fielder would take the brunt of the Mad Hungarian's frustration after allowing the go-ahead homer. On the opening pitch, Hrabosky threw a wayward ball high on the left side, several feet over Lyman's head. It caromed on a fly against the top of the backstop, dropping to the ground several feet behind Royals catcher Darrell Porter. Lyman didn't respond to this clear message pitch. He simply watched it sail over his head.

Without leaving the batter's box or taking any steps backward or forward, Lyman casually spit in front of the box and briefly dropped his head before staring back at the Kansas City southpaw, twirling his bat as if nothing had happened.

Hrabosky's next pitch was harder, straighter, and directly at Lyman's face.

"The first pitch was a spitball that had too much spit on it," Hrabosky said later in the evening. "The second was a Hungo—or was it the other way around?"[29]

The outfielder ducked at Hrabosky's second pitch and then turned toward the Royals reliever, slowly walking toward him. Taking a brief glance at his dugout and the on-deck circle, he saw his teammates standing, ready to charge the infield.

Lyman took off in a flash toward Hrabosky, who had stepped in front of the mound, almost daring the Angels outfielder to come after him. The Royals reliever threw down his glove and hat, and charged Lyman. Hrabosky tried to tackle him, but Lyman was too quick.

Sidestepping Hrabosky's initial advance, Lyman jumped on top of the mercurial left-hander and muscled him to the ground. The two were rapidly enveloped by players from both sides moments after the initial confrontation. Lyman got up and tried to get back at the thrashing Hrabosky, but they were kept from reengaging. Order seemed to be restored for a brief moment. But then words continued to be exchanged between Hrabosky and Lyman, both of whom were just getting up from the initial brouhaha.

"It wasn't over," Lyman would say after the game to Dilbeck. "He wanted some more and I wanted some more."

Suddenly, the two charged each other, about to go at it again, before they were finally separated for good. Both players were ejected from the game.

"On the mat we will go. And on the mat they did go. Hrabosky versus Bostock. Everyone joined in. Typical baseball fight, though. A lot of shoving. A lot of pushing. A lot of ejections. But absolutely no one was hurt," said Bryant Gumbel the following day during a break in NBC's Sunday National Football League coverage.

"I can understand him throwing one pitch inside to let off some frustration," Lyman said after the game. "But when a guy is playing with my life and my family, that's a different story. I don't throw my bat at him when I strike out."

"I wanted to let him know if he's going to throw at me again I would go after him again," Lyman continued. "I told him, 'You're going to have to learn there's some people you can throw at, and some you can't.'"

The Mad Hungarian was a little less direct in his postgame response. "Darrell [Porter] and I were just discussing, I'm hoping it'll rain tomorrow so my grass will grow and he's hoping it won't rain so he can go catch some catfish. And that's about it," Hrabosky replied.

"I think they know we'll be ready with our bats or fists," added Don Baylor about the following day's series finale. "We beat them in their own park with their so-called ace reliever pitching."

"I'll tell you one thing," chimed in Porter. "There's going to be a game tomorrow. And I hope if another fight breaks out, I'm not near Don Baylor."[30]

* * *

Lyman would go hitless the following day as the Royals picked up a huge swing win, 5–0. Instead of leaving Kansas City just 2.5 back with eleven games left, the deficit was a significantly more challenging 4.5 games for California. The Angels packed up their gear and left the clubhouse at Royals Stadium to head to Bloomington for two games against the Twins at Metropolitan Stadium.

Despite his feelings toward Minnesota's management, Lyman always enjoyed his return trips to Bloomington, where he got a chance to catch up with former teammates and friends within the Twins organization and also with members of the media in the Twin Cities.

"Bostock was in the visitors clubhouse at the start of the series, pantomiming his early slump for a Twins Cities sportswriter," wrote Patrick Reusse of the *Minneapolis Tribune* in 2008. "'I was the original April fool,' Lyman said. 'I watched some videotape of myself. I was pumping my leg, lunging forward, almost falling down. Man, did I look funny. I looked like [Japanese home run king] Sadaharu Oh.'"

"You didn't look that good," said teammate Don Baylor, hanging out nearby.

Spending some time with him prior to one of the games in the series, Twins outfielder Willie Norwood recalled how happy Lyman was. Having finally gotten through his horrific early-season slump, he had settled in well with the Angels and was still hopeful that a playoff berth was in the cards for California.

"When he was here, it was probably the happiest I'd ever seen the man," said Norwood. "He was just happy with life. He always had a good grip on life. He always knew what he wanted. He knew what it took to get it."[31]

Only 2,278 fans came out on a brisk Monday evening to see Lyman collect two hits and produce a run with a bases-loaded walk in the sixth inning of California's 10–4 win. A few more folks—about 3,700 or so—came out the next evening to see Nolan Ryan put together one of his finest pitching performances of the season. Going all the way, Ryan allowed just one run on six hits, striking out ten Twins batters. Lyman stepped up in the sixth inning of a scoreless game with two runners on. Facing Roger Erickson, Lyman lined a rope into center field, giving California a 1–0 lead. He would then rip a double into the left-field gap in his last at bat in Metropolitan Stadium.

"The Angels closed the series with a 4–1 victory behind Nolan Ryan," wrote Reusse. "Bostock went 2-for-4 and drove in a run. He saw the sportswriter on the way out of the ballpark, shouted, 'Take it easy on my boys, Poison'—meaning Willie Norwood and Hosken Powell, two outfielders who had been forced into the Twins lineup that season after the free agent losses of Bostock and Larry Hisle."

Following the two-game set in Minnesota the Angels returned home, where they got a rare two-day break on Wednesday, September 20, and Thursday, September 21. On Wednesday, the Angels conducted a brief workout at Anaheim Stadium before the club's final road trip of the season in Chicago. Lyman took batting practice and shagged a few fly balls while his college coach, Bob Hiegert, looked on.

"Before Lyman left for that trip [to Chicago], we were down at Anaheim Stadium. If he was in town and I was recruiting, I would call him and get tickets. We went into the locker room and went down and watched them take batting practice," Hiegert recalled. "Around that time, Dick Enberg walked up."[32]

Enberg always had a soft spot for the baseball program at San Fernando Valley State, renamed Cal State Northridge, where he had spent time the previous decade coaching and teaching. "Lyman came to San Fernando Valley State College after I had left as an assistant baseball coach and assistant professor. Hiegert had taken the head coaching job from Stan Charnofsky, with whom I coached in the early 1960s," said Enberg.[33]

After his time in the batting cage, Lyman approached Hiegert and Enberg with an idea that had been on his mind for quite some time—a scholarship fund for the Northridge baseball program. "I was down on the field with Dick Enberg. We were down there at Anaheim Stadium, and Lyman came over," Hiegert recalled. "Enberg was standing there with me when we were talking about this."

"I want to get this scholarship thing set up. I want to give some money to the program, and I want to help the kids in the inner city," Lyman said to Enberg and his former coach. "I really want to help. Another kid in my situation, I want to be able to give him a scholarship."

"That would be a great thing," said Enberg.

Lyman had only one stipulation. "It has to be anonymous," the outfielder told the two men.

"Yeah, we've talked about that before. We can fix that up," Hiegert told him. "When you get back, we'll all get together and get it all squared away."

Lyman shared some time with Hiegert that night over a couple beers, telling old stories and talking more about the proposed scholarship fund at Northridge. "That was a Wednesday night. That's how we left it. They got on a plane and headed to Chicago on Thursday," Hiegert added.

The Angels flew to Chicago to conclude their twelve-game road stand still technically in the Western Division race, but they needed the Royals to collapse epically while they themselves played nearly flawlessly. Lyman had always hit well at Comiskey Park, and he relished another chance to hang out with his relatives in Gary, which he had done going back to his days with the Twins.

"Bostock didn't stay at the hotel when he was in Chicago," said Buzzy Bavasi the following Monday. "He stayed at his relatives' home. That's normally a violation of club rules, but he received permission from the manager and the traveling secretary to stay with his cousins."[34]

As Lyman headed to the Windy City with his teammates, he was the second-highest hitting player in the American League from June through late September, with a .331 batting clip. He was picked up at the airport by his uncle, Tom Turner, who drove him to Gary and then back to the South Side for that Friday night's game.

Though Lyman would go zero for three on Friday night, the Angels got a much-needed win, 3–2, scoring all their runs in the third inning. That same evening in Bloomington, the Royals split a pair of games with the Twins. Kansas City had won nine of twelve games in mid- to late September and had stretched their lead to five games. As the weekend approached, it appeared that California was all but done for in the Western Division race. But as he drove back into Gary that late Friday evening and hopped into bed at his uncle's house for a good night's sleep, Lyman had every reason in the world to feel confident and happy about the way things were going in his life.

12

ANOTHER DAY IN COMISKEY AND GARY (SEPTEMBER 23, 1978)

> When you arise in the morning, think of what a privilege it is to be alive, to think, to enjoy, to love.—Marcus Aurelius (Roman emperor), *Meditations*

On the morning of Saturday, September 23, 1978, Lyman woke up in a great mood at his uncle's house in Gary, Indiana. He had a lot on his mind, including two very important games against the White Sox that weekend, his conversation a few days earlier with Bob Hiegert and Dick Enberg about a scholarship fund back at Cal State Northridge, and thoughts about the off-season to come. But it was a time of joy for the Angels outfielder as he spent the morning laughing, telling jokes, and listening to music with his uncle and cousins. Pulling one of his uncle's records out, Lyman danced around in Edward Turner's living room, jamming to a favorite song that he said got him into a rhythm and helped him hit better.

"He was really happy Saturday, playing a record that we like, a Chuck Mangione record that plays about 11 minutes—'The Land of Make Believe' by Esther Satterfield," Turner said the next day. "He put it on before we left for White Sox Park."[1]

It had been a banner four months for Lyman since he had pulled out of his horrific early-season slump. From early June through that day's game against the White Sox, Lyman had been the second-best hitter in the American League. Although he wasn't quite at the .300 mark—coming into that Saturday's game at .294—a solid final week would likely get him there.

"No telling what the man would hit if he got off to a good start for once," wrote Jim Murray of the *Los Angeles Times*.

The Angels had won two straight games—one in Minnesota and one the night before against the White Sox—to stay in the Western Division race despite a sluggish September. Heading into that day's battle at White Sox Park, the Angels were 82–72, five games behind the Royals with eight left to play.

There was a nip in the air as the Angels and White Sox took batting practice and warmed up—a light but steady breeze moving through the trees behind the park. The outfield seats were largely empty in the old stadium on Chicago's South Side as the two Western Division clubs continued to wrap up a long season that Saturday afternoon. The Angels got something going immediately in the top of the first against White Sox starter Rich Wortham, as Bobby Grich walked and Carney Lansford singled to right field, moving Grich to third. Lyman came up and took a wild pitch, which allowed Grich to score the game's first run and Lansford to move up to second.

The veteran outfielder then swung at an inside pitch from the Chicago left-hander and dropped a single the other way into left field, allowing Lansford to reach third. Lansford went on to score California's second run on a sacrifice fly by Don Baylor. Lyman returned to the plate in the top of the third and promptly ripped a Wortham offering into the right-field power alley for a double. Another wild pitch allowed Lyman to reach third, but he was once again stranded after Baylor was picked off first base following a walk.

As he stood on third base in the third inning, Lyman engaged in a brief chat with White Sox third baseman Eric Soderholm, a former teammate with the Twins his rookie year back in 1975. Soderholm, watching from afar, had been impressed with the way Lyman had worked through his slump and had gotten back on track. The Chicago infielder asked him what his secret had been. "Eric, I got my life straightened out off the field," Lyman told him. "And that turned it around for me on the field."[2]

Soderholm had cut California's early lead in half, 2–1, on a long second-inning leadoff homer to left field. The White Sox then took the lead in the bottom of the third on an RBI triple by Chet Lemon and a sacrifice fly by Lamar Johnson. The Angels quickly came back to tie the score at 3–3 in the top of the fourth, as Ron Jackson doubled and Brian Downing drove him home with a single to right field. The game would remain tied until the bottom of the seventh, when the White Sox reclaimed the lead on another RBI hit by Lemon. Lyman led off the top of the eighth for California, with the Angels trailing, 4–3. He had grounded out in the fifth inning to Chicago first baseman Mike Squires, but this time around he drew a walk, forcing Rich Wortham out of the game. Jim Willoughby came on for the White Sox to pitch, and Baylor welcomed him with a base hit to left field, advancing Lyman to second. After Joe Rudi was hit by a pitch, Ron Jackson singled to left off another Chicago reliever, Lerrin LaGrow, scoring Lyman and tying the game at 4–4.

The Angels had new life, but it wouldn't last long. The White Sox scratched across a run off Dyar Miller in the bottom of the eighth, and the game went into the top of the ninth with Chicago leading, 5–4. Pinch hitter Ron Fairly grounded out to first base to lead off the California ninth, but then Rick Miller reached base on an error by right fielder Rusty Torres. Danny Goodwin, pinch hitting for Bobby Grich, hit a hard grounder to second baseman Greg Pryor, who flipped the ball to shortstop Harry Chappas for the second out of the inning. Carney Lansford came up as California's last hope as the small crowd of spectators, spread out around home plate and the baselines, rose to their feet and began to cheer. LaGrow reached back for what he hoped would be the game-ender, but Lansford had other plans, drilling a single to right to move Goodwin to second. Lyman came up again, this time with a chance to be the hero. It was a moment ballplayers live for—ninth inning, game on the line in the middle of a pennant battle. A hit would give the Angels hope in a divisional race that they were losing. Trailing by a run but with two runners on, an extra-base hit could potentially give the Angels the lead.

It wasn't to be, however. Lyman bounced a hard grounder up the middle, right to LaGrow at the pitcher's mound. The Chicago reliever fielded the grounder cleanly and threw Lyman out easily at first to end the game. And with the game went California's realistic hopes of catching Kansas City.

With the loss, California fell to 82–73. The Royals would take down Lyman's old squad, the Twins, in Metropolitan Stadium later that night, giving Kansas City a six-game lead with just seven games to play. The Angels weren't mathematically eliminated yet. But now California would need to win out, and the Royals lose out, in order to win the Western

Following his dreadful early-season slump in the spring of 1978, Lyman was the American League's second-best hitter from May to September. On September 23, he recorded two hits against the Chicago White Sox—improving his average to .296—though he also made the final out in a devastating 5–4 loss, which all but ended California's postseason hopes. (Bettman/Corbis.)

Division crown outright and reach the playoffs. The Angels, barring a miracle, simply weren't going to catch Kansas City.

* * *

Quite understandably, Lyman wasn't happy at all after making the final out in such an important game. As he jogged off the field, stormed through the Angels dugout, and proceeded to California's dressing room, it was becoming more and more evident with each passing second that his fourth major league season, like the three before it, would conclude without an appearance in the American League Championship Series. Angrily sauntering into the Angels dressing doom, Lyman balled up his uniform

ANOTHER DAY IN COMISKEY AND GARY (SEPTEMBER 23, 1978)

and chucked his jersey and pants into the corner of his locker. Before many of his teammates had entered the locker room, Lyman abruptly headed out to his uncle Thomas's waiting car for the ride back to Gary.

One of Lyman's best friends on the Angels, Don Baylor, has spoken to a number of sources about that afternoon's events. Baylor had been around the majors since 1970, when, as a precocious twenty-one-year-old, he had appeared in eight games with the eventual world champion Baltimore Orioles. In his days with the Orioles, and later with the Oakland A's and the Angels, Baylor learned through observation and experience how to interact with veteran ballplayers—when to engage them and when to leave them alone. As Baylor undressed and collected his things in the locker room that Saturday afternoon, he knew that the best thing he could do in that particular moment was to leave Lyman alone.

"I can remember seeing him walk out of the locker room that day. He had grounded into a game-ending play at first base," Baylor said in the Angels' twenty-fifth anniversary documentary, *Heaven Can't Wait*.

"He was so pissed, I'm not sure if he even took a shower," Baylor said in another interview about the day's events. "After the game he dashed by me wearing a sport coat and dripping wet from sweat or a shower. "He didn't say a word. He just bolted by."[3]

"Veterans know enough to leave other veterans alone. So when Lyman walked by, I didn't say a thing."[4]

Reaching his uncle's gray Buick Electra, Lyman hopped in and pulled the door shut. Edward and Thomas Turner were among a number of family members who had made the short trek to Chicago, and they had been among the 7,953 patrons that Saturday afternoon for the Angels' setback to the White Sox. The Angels were heading back to Los Angeles following the next afternoon's rubber game. Tonight was Lyman's last chance to see his uncles, aunts, and cousins in Gary until Memorial Day weekend the following year, the next time the Angels would be playing the White Sox in Chicago. He would spend the evening in Gary and, as always, be driven back into the city the following day for the last game of the series and the ensuing trip back to California.

Earlier in the day—before making the last out and angrily storming out of the ballpark—Lyman had invited multiple teammates to join him after the game in Gary, including one of his closest friends on the Angels, Ron Jackson, and youngsters Carney Lansford and Kenny Landreaux. Lyman enjoyed taking teammates with him to Gary, where they were always treated like royalty by the Turners and their neighbors. But this time, none of the other Angels took Lyman up on the offer.

"He invited me to his place in Gary. He wanted me to meet his family and come to dinner that night. I was just a rookie and I just wanted to get my rest and finish the season, so I turned him down," said Lansford.[5]

"I was tired, and I didn't really feel like going out," added Ron Jackson. "Had I gone, I imagine I would have been in the car with him."[6]

Kenny Landreaux had just missed Lyman after the game. "He [Lyman] told me, he goes, 'K.T. Wait for me after the game. We're going to ride back to the hotel together. My uncle is going to take us back and we're going to go out and eat.' and I said, 'OK.'

"I went back downstairs to see if Lyman had showed up yet. They said, 'Yeah, he had already came. He was looking for you, but nobody knew where you were. So he left.' And that's how that night went down."[7]

Lyman didn't have much to say as he rode east out of South Chicago and into Indiana with his uncle Tom. Lyman's uncle Edward, along with other family members, had joined Thomas and Lyman in a caravan of cars heading back to Gary from the South Side. It wasn't in Lyman's nature to stay upset very long—and certainly not around his family. After Lyman and Tom visited another cousin in Chicago, they were headed back to Gary for a family meal and an evening of reflection and happiness. The plan was to get up bright and early Sunday morning and return to Chicago for the final game of the series with the White Sox.

"He was just supposed to stay for the night," Lyman's uncle Thomas said to Jeff Pearlman. "Have a little dinner and talk about old times. That's all he was supposed to do."

Since his dreadful April when he went eleven for seventy-five, Lyman had been hitting .318—easily outpacing all his teammates on an Angels ball club that didn't have anyone else hitting .300. Lyman's two-for-four performance that Saturday afternoon pushed his average up to .296 with seven games to go. Lyman had found a winning team to play for in California. And though they weren't quite on par with the Royals and the Yankees just yet, they were a relatively young club with many pieces in place to contend for years to come in the American League West.

While 1978 may not have been the year that Lyman got to play in his first ALCS or World Series game, he had plenty of reasons to feel good—as well as plenty of reasons to see good things coming in the future—as he and his uncles slid into Gary around dusk that Saturday evening. For a night, Lyman could forget the pressures of a fading pennant push and shed his identity as Lyman Bostock, the professional ballplayer. He could be Wesley, as many of his relatives on his mother's side called him.

"Gary is like a second home. I have relatives and friends there who always come out to the ball park to encourage me. I'm able to get good, home-cooked meals. It makes coming to Chicago a pleasure," Lyman had said the year before.[8]

But the Gary that Lyman visited that Saturday evening was a lot different than the one he had fled to with his mother as a little boy in the mid-1950s, when Annie Bostock left her native Birmingham for a fresh start.

*　*　*

In the Eisenhower years, the city of Gary experienced a remarkable cycle of continued upward growth, fueled by America's post–World War II position as the world's leading steel producer. Founded by U.S. Steel in 1906, during the second year of Theodore Roosevelt's second presidential term, Gary had risen to be one of America's top industrial centers in the first half of the twentieth century, providing tens of thousands of good-paying jobs to the town's citizens.

By 1960—when Lyman was a grade schooler getting settled with his mother half a continent away in Los Angeles—Gary was a bustling city of nearly 180,000 people. It was a beacon of America's postwar industrial strength, and one of the more thriving communities in the entire Midwest. For many African Americans of the time, Gary was a marked improvement from the denigration and lack of opportunities they faced in the Jim Crow South. They came in droves, Annie Bostock's brothers among them, to work in the town's many steel mills.

But when Lyman arrived in Gary as one of baseball's brightest young stars on that early fall Saturday night in 1978, he was entering a different place—a place that was decaying and growing more dangerous with each passing day. U.S. Steel lost steam starting in the early 1960s, amid a more competitive global steel market. By the late 1970s, Gary was more well-known for its poverty and high crime rates than for its place in world industrial history. Between 1970 and 1980, the median income of Gary's residents fell by 20 percent.

A generation later, in 2014, fewer than eighty thousand residents inhabited Gary—a hundred thousand below its peak population a half century earlier—and the city employed only about 20 percent of the steelworkers it had employed in the early 1960s. Approximately one in five homes in the town was abandoned.

Many among the townspeople of Gary still around by the late 1970s were angry, and prone to criminal activity, following the losses of their jobs in the great steel collapse. Untold thousands fell into the emerging urban trap of drug and alcohol dependency, as crack cocaine and heroin became cheaper and more prevalent on the streets and liquor stores popped up on street corner after street corner. Burglaries and vandalism became commonplace throughout Gary. So did gun violence, as more and more residents took out their frustrations through the blast of a firearm.

Leonard Smith was one such angry young man living in Gary in the early autumn of 1978. A lifelong resident of Gary, Leonard was unemployed from the steel mills and in an unraveling marriage that Saturday evening. While Lyman may have been pissed off after making the last out against the White Sox a couple hours before, his anger paled in comparison to the rage burning inside Leonard. Leonard's mother, Mildred, divorced his father when he was young, leaving him with a cycle of stepfathers who abused and mistreated him. Leonard had seen the lives of two of his sisters destroyed by mental illness, with one committing suicide. Leonard had been arrested at least seven times over the decade and a half since 1964. Despite all the arrests, however, he had been formally charged just once, for second-degree burglary in 1967. He avoided a conviction in the burglary case but continued to walk the line between law-abiding citizen and rogue malcontent.

Leonard was prone to fits of rage. His wife, Barbara, was often the primary recipient of his angry tirades. Leonard and Barbara had been together for approximately a decade, had been married four years, and had two daughters together. But she was exceedingly unhappy in the relationship. Just a month earlier, in August, Leonard had struck Barbara in the face when she arrived home at a time he deemed too late. He had reportedly pulled a gun on his wife less than a week earlier when they got into yet another argument. Having finally had enough of the abuse, Barbara had filed for divorce from Leonard just four days earlier, on Tuesday, September 19. Barbara had also recently filed a restraining order against Leonard and had moved in with her sister in an effort to end the tumultuous cycle of domestic violence.

Leonard was desperate to make amends with his wife that weekend, but it seemed futile. Naturally, he opposed the divorce. Earlier that very Saturday, Leonard had reached out to Barbara in a desperate effort to compel her to come back to him. His efforts failed. Before leaving Barbara, he issued a fresh barrage of threats and communicated a cryptic message to his young daughter.

"He followed her every chance he got. He had been to her home early that evening and made a threat," said Gary police corporal Charles Hicks a few hours later.

"It won't be long before you'll be living with me," Leonard said to his little girl before walking out to his car and driving off into the early evening twilight.[9]

* * *

Lyman ate a hearty meal of cube steak, crowder peas, okra, sliced tomatoes, and blackberry pie that evening with Edward, his wife Lillie, Tom, and some cousins at Edward's house, sharing laughs and catching up on old times, telling stories and sharing reminiscences. It was a happy time for Lyman's relatives sitting around the dinner table, relishing their brief opportunity to spend time with their beloved nephew and cousin. Although he couldn't resist talking baseball around them, any lingering resentment Lyman had about making the final out against the White Sox earlier in the day had dissipated around his family members.

"We tried to cook something he liked," said Edward Turner in regard to his nephew's visits. "He liked vegetables and pies, maybe blackberry pie or peach cobbler. Everybody would be looking forward to him coming. A lot of friends stopped by."[10]

"He was in a real good mood," Lyman's aunt Lillie added. "He was talking about the game. He said, 'I gave a little defense Friday. Then today I gave a little offense. Tomorrow, I'm going to get a little defense and offense.'"[11]

Lyman simply didn't have to be there in Gary that night. He could have joined any number of his teammates in an entertaining evening in the Windy City, a nice dinner and maybe a drink or two before hitting the hay. He could have stayed at the Water Tower Hyatt and rested, saving his energy up for another crack at the White Sox and a .300 season the following afternoon. He could even have even spending the evening with Yuovene. Lyman's wife had given serious thought to surprising him that weekend with an impromptu trip to Chicago. But with a variety of things going on back home in Southern California, she had elected at the last minute to stay home.

"I thought about going to surprise him. And I didn't. I was just going to show up. But it didn't happen," she said in *The Lyman Bostock Story*.

So there Lyman was, signing autographs for local kids in the Turners' neighborhood in Gary after dinner that Saturday evening, sharing more laughs and stories with his uncles' other guests. That Lyman was willing to go back to Gary and spend time with his relatives, even on such a limited basis, during the middle of a September pennant race, was a source of admiration for his uncles, aunts, and cousins, along with everyone in the neighborhood that knew about his visits.

Following dinner, as his friends and family members sat around talking, Lyman recalled another old friend. A goddaughter of his uncle Tom, she used to live next door to him, and Lyman used to read to her when he made his summer trips to Gary back when he was at Manual Arts High School and Valley State. Lyman hadn't seen her in several years and was interested in seeing her if possible in this, his last trip of the calendar year to Gary.

"Tom, whatever happened to Joan Hawkins, that girl I used to read to? I'd sure like to see how she's doing," Bostock asked his uncle.[12]

"She lives right across town. I'll take you to see her now," Turner replied.

Tom called Joan's home to see if she was around, but reached her sister instead. Her sister, a young woman named Barbara, indicated that Joan wasn't there right then but would be returning soon. Edward Turner, Lyman's other uncle in the room, playfully suggested that his nephew couldn't roam the streets of Gary that night and expect a strong performance the following day against the White Sox.

"You can't stay out all night and play ball!" Edward told his nephew.

"I'll be right back," Lyman said with a smile.

With that, Lyman and Tom walked outside and got back into the Buick for the short drive across town to Joan's residence. Tom Turner sat in his car as Lyman went in and caught up with his old friend and met her sister. Shortly thereafter, the two women asked Lyman if they could get a ride across town to their cousin's house. Lyman, of course, was obliging, and so was his uncle.

"I sat in the car and [Lyman] went in," said Tom Turner about the visit to Joan Hawkins's house. "And then when he came out, he said, 'Tom,

Barbara and Joan want me to drop them off over to their cousin's house. Is it OK?' I said, 'Sure, I don't mind.' They got in the car and we drove off."[13]

As Lyman, Barbara, and Joan walked out of Joan's house and toward Tom's car, Leonard Smith sat nearby in his Ford, seething with anger. Beside him, in the passenger seat, lay a .410 bore shotgun. Leonard had driven without notice over to his sister-in-law's house, hoping to speak with Barbara for yet another desperate chance at reconciliation. He was well-known for following his estranged wife around. Despite the divorce filing, the restraining order, and his earlier threats that very same day, he still hoped to talk her into going out with him that night for a late dinner and conversation. But by the time Leonard arrived—just after 10:30 p.m.—Lyman and his uncle were already there. They had no possible way of knowing that Leonard had threatened Barbara just a few hours earlier, or that he was lurking just a few feet away from them.

Smith stalked the group from inside his vehicle, watching their every move but failing to alert them of his close presence. As Lyman opened Joan's front door and walked outside with the two women, Leonard watched on, his anger intensifying with each passing second. It was one thing that his wife had chosen to file divorce papers earlier that week. It was another thing entirely that, in his own mind, she was flaunting the fact that she was seeing other men.

While he couldn't have had any clear idea about the nature of Barbara's relationship with this man, seeing his soon-to-be ex-wife walking to another car with this charming, attractive, well-dressed guy pushed Leonard over the edge.

* * *

Lyman and the two women finished their brief walk from Joan's house to Turner's Buick, and they all hopped in. With Tom driving, Joan in the front passenger seat, Lyman in the backseat on the passenger side, and Barbara to Lyman's left in the backseat on the driver's side, the quartet headed toward downtown Gary. As Turner drove away, Smith pulled away as well, slipping closely behind. It was now around 10:40 p.m. Lyman, his uncle, and their two female companions rode carelessly down Fifth Street, heading east into the downtown area. They were engaging in friendly conversation.

When Gary had been founded more than seven decades earlier, its downtown streets were laid out in a grid, like many urban towns across the country. The east-west streets were numbered (Fourth, Fifth, Sixth, and so on), and the intersecting north-south streets were named after American presidents, starting with the nation's second president, John Adams. The fifth north-south street in the grid, heading from west to east, could have been named after Adams's son, the nation's sixth president, John Quincy Adams. But the obvious conflict of having two Adams Streets within a few blocks of each other led Gary's city planners to name it Jackson Street instead, after Andrew Jackson, the nation's seventh president.

They moved slowly down Fifth Street, past Roosevelt and McKinley Streets, past the busy thoroughfare on Grant Street, past Lincoln Johnson Park to their left. Finally, a red light forced Turner to stop at the intersection of Fifth and Jackson Streets. In the fall of 1978, the corner of Fifth and Jackson was still a reasonably thriving part of Gary. It wasn't paradise by any means, but there were still signs of life in the area, such as the Bi-Lo grocery store on the corner, as well as a number of other nearby businesses and homes.

It was 10:44 p.m. as Turner rolled to a stop at the light. A handful of pedestrians were moving about the adjoining sidewalks. There were later newspaper reports that Tom Turner had engaged in a daring high-speed chase with Leonard Smith through Gary, but the individuals in the car denied that account in subsequent interviews over the years.

"We were just riding down Fifth Avenue, normally, talking, no big deal. I stopped at the red light on Fifth and Jackson, where a Bi-Lo retail store used to be," said Turner.[14]

Leonard pulled along the right-hand side of Turner's car. No one will ever know exactly what he was thinking at this moment. Rolling down his driver's side window, he stuck out his small-gauge shotgun. Barbara Smith would later say that she saw Leonard look into the backseat of the Buick with a smirk on his face. Aiming at the right-side opera window of Tom Turner's Buick, located behind the primary passenger window, Leonard fired a single shot. The blast exploded a vibrant flash of orange in the evening darkness, tearing into the adjacent car in a cascade of flying glass. The unmistakable pop of the shell's discharge gave Lyman's uncle the initial impression that he was going to have to change a tire.

"I thought our tire had blown out," said Turner.

It didn't take long for Tom to realize that he had heard an entirely different sound altogether. Lyman, sitting closest to Leonard in the passenger-side backseat, took the brunt of the shotgun blast along the right side of his head, near his temple. The blast violently thrust him to the left, knocking him down into the backseat. Barbara, sitting next to Lyman, was also struck in the face by buckshot pellets, but her wounds were not life-threatening. She would be treated at the hospital and later released.

"Tom, I seen him! Go get him! That's my stupid old husband!" Barbara yelled to Tom, who looked up just in time to see Smith's Ford speed off into the night.

Barbara's second instinct, after spotting Leonard, was to tell Tom that Lyman had been hit. "Tom, your nephew has been shot."

Turner peered into the backseat, where he saw his nephew lying motionless. "That's when I looked around and he had slumped. I was just, I couldn't believe it," said Turner.

A circular hole, about an inch wide, could be seen piercing through the shattered glass in the right-hand passenger-side opera window. Working through the immediate shock, Tom snapped into action. He jumped out of his car and ran into the Bi-Lo store on the corner, yelling to the clerks at the front entrance to please call an ambulance. An employee quickly jumped on the phone and called 911.

A Gary fire department paramedic crew was on the scene quickly to carefully pull Lyman's body out of the backseat, which was sprinkled with tiny shards of glass. The paramedics gingerly grasped Lyman's arms, legs, torso, and head, avoiding the shattered glass, and lifted him onto a stretcher.

St. Mary's Mercy Hospital was only three blocks away, so Lyman would be getting rapid medical attention. But as Tom and his goddaughters stood helplessly on the curb just after a quarter to eleven in the evening—cars backing up behind the Buick stalled in the middle of the street, a small crowd of curious onlookers starting to gather on the sidewalk as Lyman was ushered into the ambulance and secured for the race to the hospital—the minutes must have seemed like years.

13

PASSING INTO LEGEND

You expected to be sad in the fall. Part of you died each year when the leaves fell from the trees and their branches were bare against the wind and the cold, wintery light. But you knew there would always be the spring, as you knew the river would flow again after it was frozen. When the cold rains kept on and killed the spring, it was as though a young person died for no reason.—Ernest Hemingway, *A Moveable Feast*

Although Gary had been in a significant economic downturn for more than a decade by the early fall of 1978, there was still work to be had in the local steel mills for those willing to put in the long hours—and\ put themselves in harm's way. The jobs weren't nearly as plentiful as they had been for the post–World War II generation of working-class northwest Indiana natives. But plenty of men in Gary and in surrounding communities still made their way daily to the U.S. Steel facility and other local mills.

One such man was Paul Hutchins. A resident of nearby Portage, Indiana, Hutchins drove the daily ten-mile commute to Gary to work as a switchman, doing his part to help ship newly forged steel out of town as quickly as it could be loaded onto train cars. It was a steamy day in the summer of 1978 when the dangers of the job finally caught up with Paul. Performing work on a car during a routine shift, he accidentally was pinned between two large steel shipping containers. Paul was attended to and carefully removed from between the train cars, and was rushed by ambulance to St. Mary's Mercy Hospital in downtown Gary, where he would spend the rest of the summer recovering.

While Lyman and his Angels teammates were doing battle on the South Side of Chicago against the White Sox in late September, Hutchins was struggling with continued medical complications at the hospital in Gary. Although a month had passed since his initial injury, a bleeding ulcer had forced Paul into intensive care.

Paul's bed was located directly beside the large swinging double doors of the intensive care unit's entrance, adjacent to a long corridor leading to the emergency loading and unloading dock. This dock was where the many victims of Gary's violent crimes—including all gunshot victims—were initially rushed into the hospital. Paul was often awakened or distracted by these all-too-common occurrences throughout his long hospital stay.

A few minutes before eleven that Saturday night, Paul was lying in bed trying to sleep in spite of his assorted injuries and considerable pain. Suddenly, he was jarred awake by a loud noise down the hallway, a noise that grew louder and louder as an entourage of doctors, nurses, medical personnel, and police officers made its way directly toward him. They surrounded yet another victim of a gunshot wound in Gary. But this victim was much different.

* * *

It had been a very short ambulance ride from the corner of Fifth and Jackson to the hospital, which was located along Tyler Street. In the short trip from the shooting scene to the hospital, the technicians quickly determined that Lyman had a pulse and was breathing, but he made no indication of recognizing them. Hundreds of buckshot pellets had penetrated his skull and entered his brain tissue. And while he wasn't killed instantly by the close-range blast, severe damage had been done.

As the ambulance sped down Sixth Street for three blocks before reaching the emergency entrance at St. Mary's Mercy, the EMTs wound gauze and bandages around Lyman's head, attempting to control the bleeding from its right side. Within a few minutes, the ambulance arrived at the hospital. As the wounded ballplayer was pulled from the back of the emergency vehicle and hoisted onto the loading dock of the emergency room, multiple police cars who had trailed behind the ambulance—their sirens blaring their presence on the scene—screeched to a halt. The officers jumped out of the vehicles and moved their way inside.

PASSING INTO LEGEND

Around 10:45 p.m. on the evening of September 23, 1978, Leonard Smith fired a single shotgun blast with his .410 bore shotgun into the backseat of Tom Turner's Buick Electra in Gary, Indiana. The blast pierced the passenger-side opera window, striking Lyman in the right temple and mortally wounding him. (Bettman/Corbis.)

Giving a few minutes to get Lyman's body on a stretcher and into the ambulance, and the short ride to the hospital, Lyman's arrival at St. Mary's Mercy that night would have been between 10:55 and 11:00 p.m., ten to fifteen minutes after the moment he was shot.

The noise, growing louder and louder, grew closer and closer to Paul Hutchins and the others in the intensive care area as Lyman, laid out on a stretcher, and the large contingent made their way down the hallway. Suddenly, they burst through the swinging double doors and into the room.

"They wheeled this guy in. His head was all bandaged up and his face was swollen," Paul recalled. "There were a lot of people. Hospital personnel. Policemen. He was surrounded by police officers and doctors and nurses. His head was almost completely bandaged."

Paul wasn't a huge baseball fan. And like the young White Sox fan back in Palm Springs during spring training whose baseball card Lyman had signed, he didn't recognize this young black man with the goatee at first. Paul's nurse, who had been his companion throughout that Saturday afternoon and evening, had caught wind of the hospital's famous new patient from a fellow employee. He explained to Paul who this man was and the magnitude of the moment at hand.[1]

"What's going on? Who is that?" Paul exclaimed.

"That's Lyman Bostock!" the nurse told him.

"Who's Lyman Bostock?" Paul questioned the nurse.

"He's one of the best ballplayers in the American League. He plays for the California Angels. He was sitting in a car when some guy pulled up beside him and shot him.

"He was shot by a jealous husband. He was shot in the head with a shotgun," the nurse solemnly explained.

"He's alive, right?" Paul inquired.

"Well, technically," said the nurse.

Although it had been less than a half hour since he had been shot, Lyman's face was rapidly swelling as the effects of Leonard Smith's single blast took hold. While Lyman's head and face were intact, the buckshot pellets that had entered his skull had severely diminished his brain function. The resulting hemorrhage filled Lyman's skull cavity with blood that had no place to go, resulting in rapid swelling of his head. Upon an initial examination of the wound, the doctors in the intensive care ward realized rather quickly that there wasn't much they could do for Lyman. Saving his life wasn't going to be possible. He had suffered too traumatic an injury.

"I heard one of the doctors say he caught almost the whole load from the shotgun, and there's nothing they could do," Paul remembered.

All the medical personnel could do to make Lyman's final minutes on earth as peaceful, and painless, as possible before he inevitably died. Lyman was prepared in a bed directly beside Paul inside the intensive care unit. As the minutes ticked away, Lyman's heart monitor marked time, intermittently beeping, slower and slower, with less and less regularity as Saturday night turned into Sunday morning.

"After a few minutes, they had him settled in and everyone left," Paul remembered. "After a little while, everyone had left, or was asked to leave because after all, it was intensive care.

"He was right next to me. His face looked as if it was bloated. All I could hear was the sound of his heart monitor. I just laid there and stared at him.

"There was really nothing chaotic about it. It was just another shooting in Gary, Indiana, in 1978."

* * *

They heard about it in different ways from different people. The astonishing news of what happened in the streets of Gary made its rounds rather quickly, from the halls of St. Mary's Mercy Hospital to downtown Chicago and to Los Angeles, among Lyman's teammates, coaches, friends, and family members. Though it didn't spread with the lightning-fast intensity of modern twenty-four-hour news channels and social media, word was getting around to those who were closest to the Angels outfielder within an hour after the shooting.

After making his way to the hospital and getting an update on his nephew's bleak status, Tom Turner, almost in a state of shock, made a panicked phone call to Yuovene. Back in Los Angeles, Lyman's wife was preparing for a Bible study session with the wives of other Angels' players. Lyman's mother, Annie, was also over that evening.

"His mother was at the house that night. I don't even know who the call came from. I don't really remember," Yuovene recalled.[2]

"Your husband has been shot," said the voice on the other end of the line.

"Come again?" Yuovene asked.

"Wesley has been shot. In Gary," his uncle replied.

"I remember getting the call saying he had been shot, and just [being in] disbelief," she said.

After Yuovene made a call to pass along what had happened and to let some of the other women know she couldn't host the Bible study, she and Annie set off immediately for Los Angeles International Airport, where they would catch a direct flight to Chicago.

After calling Yuovene, Lyman's uncle called the Water Tower Hyatt, the Angels' hotel in downtown Chicago, where he got in contact with Freddie Frederico, the Angels' trainer. After speaking with Turner for a few minutes and learning about the shooting, Frederico reached Buzzie Bavasi in Anaheim, who told him that they would begin the process of notifying the players, starting with one of Lyman's best friends on the club, Don Baylor. Baylor had joined fellow Angels veterans Nolan Ryan and Joe Rudi for an evening on the town following the tough afternoon loss to the White Sox.

"After the game I joined Rudi and Ryan at Eli's for some music and dinner," Baylor recalled.[3]

Returning to his room, Baylor was suddenly besieged by phone calls. One was from Bavasi. "When we got back to the hotel, our phones were ringing off the hook. Turns out it was Buzzie calling, saying Lyman had been shot," Baylor recalled. "The news spread like wildfire, and within a few minutes, everybody knew."

"The room phone rings. It was our trainer, Freddie," Kenny Landreaux recalled for *The Lyman Bostock Story*.

"Landreaux, listen. I've got some bad news," Frederico said.

"What do you mean? What happened?" asked the bewildered ballplayer.

"Lyman is in the hospital. He got shot in the head," the Angels trainer responded.

* * *

After an evening on the town, Angels pitcher Ken Brett was returning to the Water Tower Hyatt around midnight, more than an hour after the shooting in Gary. Walking through the lobby, he tapped the elevator button and awaited its arrival. When the doors opened, out stepped Don Baylor, a horrified look on his face.

"There was Don Baylor, looking like he had seen a ghost," Brett would say later to Mike Penner of the *Los Angeles Times*.

Baylor gave Brett the grim news. "Lyman's been shot. It doesn't look good."

"Freddie Frederico was going to drive [Baylor] to the hospital. Everybody else went up to Freddie's room and waited to hear something," said Brett. In the end, however, Baylor was not able to go the hospital.

Ten minutes later, another update from Gary reached the Angels trainer. They heard the dreadful news that had become quickly clear to the doctors in the intensive care unit. Lyman's injuries weren't survivable.

"Lyman hasn't got a chance," Frederico told the players. "All they can do is make him comfortable before he dies."[4]

As the Angels players started to collect in Frederico's room, some thrashed about in anger, vowing to avenge Lyman's shooting. "Let's go get the guy who did this!" exclaimed Ron Jackson. "Let's find him!"[5]

Baylor and others wanted to go to Gary to see Lyman. They wished to do something—anything—that might salvage the desperate situation.

"We asked Buzzie where Lyman was," Baylor said. "We wanted to go see him. But Buzzie said we couldn't go there because he had over a hundred pellets in his head, and they didn't expect him to live."[6]

"I tried to make it out to the hospital and say something to him, and ask him if there was anything he wanted," added Kenny Landreaux to Steve Dilbeck of the *San Bernardino Sun-Telegram*. "If he just would have seen more and nodded his head it would have made it a lot easier for me."

None of the players wound up heading to Gary that night, for there was very little they could do for Lyman at that point. Devastated and helpless, the players stammered around the hotel. Many were in tears as they awaited final word on their teammate's fate. "We were stunned, and sat out in the hallway just staring at the walls," Baylor remembered for the book *Once They Were Angels*. "Hotel guests walked around us, on us, and over us, but we didn't even notice. We just sat out in the hallway and cried. We couldn't believe it. It was the worst night I ever had in baseball. No one really slept that night."

After initially being ready to walk the streets of Gary to hunt down Lyman's attacker, Ron Jackson had broken down, overcome with emotion. Carney Lansford and Rance Mulliniks had just turned off the light in their hotel room when Kenny Landreaux and Danny Goodwin barged in.

"That night, Rance Mulliniks and I were rooming together at the hotel. Kenny Landreaux and Danny Goodwin came in—we had just turned off our TV, just ready to fall asleep. I think our eyes had just closed," Lansford said to Mike Damergis for "Remembering Lyman Bostock." "We heard those guys walking in. They were in the room right next to us. They said something about, 'We just heard them say something about they don't think he was going to make it.' But we didn't pay any attention because we didn't know what was going on."

Moments after Landreaux and Goodwin entered their room, the phone rang. It was Mulliniks's wife. "Probably about thirty seconds later our phone rang, and it was Rance Mulliniks's wife in Southern California saying that Lyman had been shot, and they didn't think he was going to make it."

It was naturally an anxious time for both Yuovene and Lyman's mother as they raced toward the LAX airport, running red lights, speeding through the streets of Los Angeles. They tried to think positive thoughts. That Lyman would pull through. That he hadn't been struck in any vital organs. That it wasn't as bad as they might have thought. Finally, after what must have seemed like weeks, Yuovene screeched into the airport.

Angels manager Jim Fregosi had grabbed a meal and a few drinks not too far from the hotel that night. When he initially returned to the Water Tower Hyatt, there didn't seem to be anything terribly amiss. "It all seemed like a perfectly calm Saturday evening," Fregosi would say a few hours later to Dave Nightingale with the *Chicago Tribune*. "I went out for dinner and came back to our team hotel about 11:30 pm to look for messages. There weren't any. A jeweler friend and I went out for a couple drinks at that time. And I got back to the hotel around 1:30 am."

Within minutes after Fregosi left for his brief trip out, word started getting around. Upon his return to the hotel, Fregosi saw two of his players in the lobby. It was unusual to see players milling around the hotel lobby that late at night. It was a circumstance that initially frustrated the rookie manager.

"The first people I saw in the lobby were Kenny Landreaux and Danny Goodwin," he said.

Fregosi, annoyed at a pair of rookies who were up so late, demanded an explanation. "Hey, it's kind of late for you guys to be up, isn't it?" the manager bellowed.

Fregosi then noticed that both players had tears streaming down their faces. "It was only then that I noticed both of them were bawling their heads off," he said. "I was about to ask where they were headed at that hour when I noticed they were in tears—that they were crying like babies."[7]

"Lyman's been shot," Landreaux said solemnly.

Fregosi immediately joined his players in sorrow.

"Jimmy got real emotional about it," recalled Ken Brett to Penner of the *Los Angeles Times*. "Lyman was one of his guys. He'd been with him through all the ups and downs."

Around the same moment Fregosi walked in on Landreaux and Goodwin sobbing in the lobby of the Water Tower Hyatt, the end was approaching for Lyman over in Gary. He had held on for more than two hours since the shotgun blast, but his breathing continued to slow, drawing thinner and lighter, his heart monitor beeping with less and less regularity, until they discontinued altogether. Between one thirty and two o'clock Central time, in the early morning of September 24, 1978, Lyman Wesley Bostock Jr. was pronounced dead at St. Mary's Mercy Hospital.

"Finally after a while his breathing stopped, and shortly after his heart monitor flatlined," Paul Hutchins recalled. "He was dead."

A nurse came to Lyman's bedside and began to remove the medical devices that had been attached to him shortly after his arrival at the hospital. It was only at this point that the nurse realized that Paul had been left directly beside Lyman, watching him slowly die that early Sunday morning in the intensive care ward.

"The nurse went to him and unhooked his monitor and IVs," Hutchins remembered. "She then noticed I was watching and pulled the curtain around him so I couldn't see him.

"After she came out, she asked me if I was all right, and I told her I had never seen a man die before."

In Los Angeles, Yuovene and Annie were waiting to catch a plane at their gate when Yuovene was paged for a phone call. It was her husband's uncle with the unimaginable.

"Lyman's dead. He didn't make it," the caller explained.

Upon being told that her baby boy had been killed, Lyman's beloved mother fainted, falling onto the floor of the airport terminal as Yuovene stood by in shock.

"As soon as Annie Pearl learned her only son was gone, she passed out and collapsed to the floor," wrote Jeff Pearlman in his ESPN article, "Fifth and Jackson." "The two women soon boarded a United flight and were isolated in first class."

"I was just trying to be strong for her," Yuovene told Pearlman. "But inside I was thinking, 'What am I going to do?' To this day, I don't understand why they told us he died right before we boarded the plane. It could have waited."

As the plane raced through the Western evening sky, Annie repeated over and over, "My baby. My baby," pressing her hands to her heart.

* * *

Back in Anaheim, a large group of festive partygoers had convened at the Big A that Saturday afternoon and evening for what turned into an epic day of music and fun. With the Angels in Chicago, the club's home ballpark had been turned into a concert venue for the weekend. More than fifty-five thousand paying customers streamed through Anaheim Stadium for Summerfest, a daylong music festival featuring Boston as the headliner, along with Ozzy Osbourne and Black Sabbath, Journey, Richie Lecea, Sammy Hagar, and a young local group called Van Halen. It was a sweltering day in Southern California, with thermometers hitting and passing the hundred-degree mark. As the concertgoers left Anaheim Stadium following Boston's performance, however, their rush from an entertaining day of music was quickly diminished as they turned on their radios and heard the horrific news coming out of the Chicago area.

At the KTLA Channel 5 television studio in downtown Los Angeles, Dick Enberg was in a quandary. Enberg had become one of the top sports personalities in Southern California over the previous decade. He had called and reported on some of the more memorable sporting events in Los Angeles since the mid-1960s, and was one of the voices of the California Angels. Enberg had witnessed firsthand UCLA's dominance of college basketball in the 1960s and early 1970s under John Wooden. He had been in the Astrodome that legendary Saturday night in 1968 when Elvin Hayes and the Houston Cougars stunned Lew Alcindor and the Bruins in front of a record crowd at what was billed as "The Game of the Century."

Enberg would go on to call Super Bowls, World Series, and Final Four games for NBC, and in time he would become the voice of the San Diego Padres. In the summer of 2015, Enberg would receive the ultimate honor for a baseball commentator—the Ford C. Frick Award for excellence in baseball broadcasting and recognition at the National Baseball Hall of Fame in Cooperstown, New York. But nothing in Enberg's experiences, past, present, or future, prepared him for appearing live on the air a little before midnight Pacific time the evening of September 23, 1978, to tell the people of Southern California that Lyman Bostock was dead.

"His shocking death came while the Angels were in Chicago to play the White Sox," Enberg recalled. "There was no Internet at that time, so news did not travel so instantly as today. The murder happened on a Saturday night in Gary.[8]

"We televised on Channel 5, KTLA, the weekend Angels games, and it was my duty to come on the air and announce what had happened, a daunting task."

Enberg had a unique tie to Bostock, having spent time with the San Fernando Valley State baseball program himself in the early 1960s as an assistant coach. "Lyman came to SFVSC after I had left as an assistant baseball coach and assistant professor," Enberg said. "[Bob] Hiegert had taken the head coaching job from Stan Charnofsky, with whom I coached in the early 1960s. [Lyman] was in the wrong place at the wrong time. A wonderful, talented young man taken from us."

"It was horrific," Enberg added in the 2013 MLB Network special, *The Lyman Bostock Story*. "I mean, who expects to go on the air having to announce that one of your ballplayers, someone that everyone cares about, is dead suddenly? We are not trained to handle a tragedy like that, are we? You think in all of baseball history how many times has that happened? Where a ballplayer plays one day and the next day he's expected to appear, but he's gone?"

Painful and stunning as it was, Enberg had a job to do that night. And he did it.

"We begin today's broadcast with terrible news," the veteran commentator told his viewers. "Lyman Bostock was murdered in Gary, Indiana."

* * *

Up in Northridge, Lyman's college coach, Bob Hiegert, had finally arrived home after a busy day. Hiegert had attended a Cal State Northridge football game that Saturday night, returning home between eleven and midnight. "I was the athletic director at Cal State Northridge. I was the baseball coach and athletic director," Hiegert remembered. "We'd had a home football game that night. When I got home—it was about eleven or eleven thirty—*Saturday Night Live* was on."[9]

In those early days, *Saturday Night Live* was breaking new ground with its in-your-face humor. The "Not Ready for Prime Time Players" were shocking and mesmerizing their huge audiences on NBC with zany antics, over-the-top jokes, and physical comedy that hadn't been seen on network television before. "When they were first starting *Saturday Night Live*, their comedy, they were just off the wall," Hiegert said.

So when Hiegert saw a scroll at the bottom of the television saying that California Angels outfielder Lyman Bostock had been the victim of a shooting, his initial response was that it was a joke in very poor taste. "My wife was in bed and I was just relaxing for a few minutes, lying down," he remembered. "I saw at the bottom of this *Saturday Night Live* thing saying Lyman Bostock had been shot. I thought that was kind of a sick thing to do."

The scroll at the bottom of the screen kept running. Through the various sketches. Through commercials. The dreadful message continued rolling across the screen until, finally, the message declared that Lyman Bostock had been pronounced dead.

"Sure enough, it said Lyman Bostock was pronounced dead and had been killed in a shooting," he recalled. "I made a bunch of phone calls, and it was true. That's how I found about it. I allowed it to sink in and everything, but it took a while."

Down the road, the timing of Lyman's death was creating a dilemma early that morning in the offices of the *Los Angeles Times*. Although the breaking news of the night's tragic events reached California a little after 9:00 p.m. Pacific time through phone calls from Gary and Chicago, the official word of Lyman's death didn't come until just before midnight on the West Coast. After confirming with the Gary Police Department that Lyman was indeed dead, the newspaper had only enough time before going to print that early morning to place a small blurb on the front page of its Sunday edition. Not much more was known at that moment than what the paper reported:

> California Angel outfielder Lyman Bostock, 27, was shot and killed late Saturday night in Gary, Ind., a police spokesman said. Bostock was shot while riding in a car and died later at St. Mary's Hospital in Gary. The Angels are currently playing with Chicago White Sox, and Bostock was in Gary visiting a cousin. Bostock was signed by the Angels last winter to a five-year, $2.25 million contract after playing out his option with the Minnesota Twins. Bostock was born in Birmingham, Alabama, but grew up in Los Angeles, attending Manual Arts High School and Cal. St. Northridge University.

14

SAYING GOODBYE
(SEPTEMBER 24–28, 1978)

When he shall die, take him and cut him out in little stars, and he will make the face of heaven so fine that all the world will be in love with night, and pay no worship to the garish sun.—William Shakespeare, *Romeo and Juliet*

Don Baylor woke up that Sunday morning with a splitting headache. "The next morning, my head was killing me, so I walked down to Walgreen's to get some Excedrin," he would later say.[1]

Like most all of the rest of his teammates, Baylor had gotten little to no sleep the previous night. The Angels players' heads tossed and turned all early morning with visions of their fallen teammate, their priceless season together, and everything that had been taken away in the blink of an eye.

It was an equally sleepless night for many back in Southern California, as members of the Angels organization, the players' wives, and the club's legions of fans started to come to grips with what had happened in Gary. Angels outfielder Rick Miller, who had arrived in California the same time as Lyman and competed with him for the center fielder job, received a phone call in the middle of the night from his terrified wife. "My wife called at 3:30 and said she was scared, she couldn't sleep. I couldn't either," Miller recalled to Ross Newhan of the *Los Angeles Times*. "You try to find a way to put it out of your head, but it's impossible. You search for words and can't find them."

There was a game that would have to be played that Sunday, regardless of the events that had taken place just twelve hours earlier. As professionals, Baylor, Miller, and the rest of the Angels got themselves together and prepared to head over to the ballpark to play the White Sox one last time that season.

"We had just lost a teammate. But, damn it, we still had to play a ball game. So off we went," Baylor said.[2]

By the time the Angels arrived at White Sox Park that morning, the flags atop the roof were already at half-mast. Upon entering the visitor's locker room, Baylor encountered a photographer snapping images of an empty locker. Lyman's locker was much the way he had left it the day before—largely bare, his cleats in front of a small metal folding chair. A steel nameplate—BOSTOCK 10—was still hanging at the top. The uniform he'd thrown in a bundle after making the last out the previous day had been laundered. His gray road Angels jersey was now hanging along the right side of the locker, his pants beside the jersey to the left.

"When I got there [to the locker room], there was some damn photographer and he was taking a picture of Lyman's empty locker," Baylor said. "I threw him the hell out."

Within minutes, Lyman's belongings were bagged up and removed from sight. One television crew wanted to film the empty locker, but manager Jim Fregosi nixed that plan. "Someone asked to take a shot of the empty locker," he said. "I didn't think that proper."[3]

For Fregosi, it had been a sleepless night filled with phone calls from numerous people, from Angels officials to reporters to friends. They asked all kinds of questions, some of which stunned Fregosi. "The phone in my room started ringing and it never stopped. And as the night wore on, it became more and more incredible. I couldn't believe the ghoulish questions that people asked me," Fregosi replied to Dave Nightingale of the *Chicago Tribune*.

Chicago's Channel 7 was the first television camera crew to arrive at White Sox Park that Sunday morning, and Fregosi, hopping into a T-shirt and some shorts, walked outside the locker room to greet them. "I lost a friend—a good friend. He was a super kid, just a super kid. I first got to know him when he came up with the Twins in 1975 and I was still hanging around the American League," Fregosi told the reporters.

"I can't believe it. I just can't believe it. And I can't believe the tragedies that keep following this team," the Angels manager added, recalling the deaths of Mike Miley, Bruce Heinbechner, Dick Wantz, and Minnie Rojas.

"As far as I'm concerned, I lost a very close personal friend," Fregosi continued in an Associated Press article. "He was the type of kid who was a great guy to have on a ball club. He had ability, but that's not what we're really talking about here. It was his ability as a man. He had feelings. He cared. I know myself I'm going to miss him very much.

"Right now, the team has to be secondary. A man has lost his life. A good friend is gone. Lyman Bostock had a super feeling for the game. He was close to everyone. I'll hold a meeting, but there's not much I can say. Everyone knows what kind of guy he was."[4]

"He cared about things. He cared about this team. And I liked him," Fregosi explained.

The Angels manager was asked whether or not any thought had been given to canceling the last game of the set with Chicago and flying back to California without playing. "We haven't even discussed it," Fregosi said of canceling the game. "This is our business. They're all professionals."[5]

Fregosi was taken slightly aback when someone asked him whom Lyman was close to on the Angels squad. Nightingale wrote that Fregosi responded with annoyance: "Who was he close to on this team? He was close to everybody. He was just a wonderful guy, a concerned guy."

Another reporter asked Fregosi what effect Lyman's death would have on his ballclub. "Somebody asked me, 'What effect will this have on your team?' I said to them, 'A man just lost his life. How can you ask me a question like that?'" Fregosi replied.

After the camera crew asked to film Lyman's empty locker, Fregosi had finally had enough. Fregosi told the security guard outside the California locker room to keep them out, exclaiming, "That's it. No cameras in the clubhouse."

Fregosi shut the door to the locker room and addressed the team—many of whom were red-eyed from crying and lack of sleep. "Batting practice is cancelled," Fregosi told his club, choking back more tears. He reminded the Angels that a Sunday prayer service, which they might find beneficial, would be held later that morning.

"I didn't have much to say to the players," Fregosi said later in the Associated Press article on the murder. "I told them all I knew about it.

There's not really too much you can say. Everybody on the club knew what a good guy he was. He was a lot of fun to be around."

On "This Week in Baseball" Fregosi reflected, "There was a lot of tears—there was a lot of emotion. This young man was loved. He was deeply cared about.

"As manager of a ballclub, you lose a player. But as a man, you lose a friend."

"I've been in this game fifty-four years and it's probably the most difficult day I've ever spent," Fregosi added in 2013 for MLB Network's *The Lyman Bostock Story*, a few months prior to his own death at the age of seventy-one. "To be surrounded by that type of atmosphere, it is something I would never want to go through again."

Later in the morning, the security official came back to Fregosi's office and asked if one of the women from local television could come in.

"The clubhouse guard came in and said, 'Is it okay for the lady from television to come in?'

"'No,' was Fregosi's stern response. 'I don't want her here. No cameras.'"[6]

Though the cameras weren't allowed in, the beat reporters were admitted into the California dressing room. But they found it quite difficult to do their jobs that particular morning, with the players at a total loss for words.

"The Angels approached the day cautiously, with uncertainty," said *Chicago Tribune* columnist David Israel. "When they filed into their clubhouse in Comiskey Park Sunday morning at 11:13, they were absolutely silent. No one said a word. Their entrance was not accompanied by the music that usually plays loudly in dressing rooms. The only sounds you heard were the rustling of hangers or the occasional pop of a fist into a glove. The Angels were fatigued and unnerved. Most of them had spent the night sleeplessly as word filtered in after midnight that Bostock had been murdered."

"The clubhouse was silent as each player sat in front of his locker, occupied in private thoughts," wrote *Los Angeles Times* staff writer Ross Newhan. "Men with notebooks were hesitant to ask their questions, forming instead a huddle of their own, inquiring of one another if they could remember an athletic clubhouse so devoid of noise."

Eventually, the reporters trickled around toward some of the Angels veterans, most of whom simply weren't in the mood to talk about that day's game, or their fallen teammate.

"Please, not now," sighed Joe Rudi.

Don Baylor simply put up a hand, gesturing that he had nothing to say.

"What a waste," replied Angels coach John McNamara, his eyes filled with tears.[7]

Nolan Ryan, that day's starting pitcher for the Angels, attempted to capture the solemn environment with carefully chosen words. "We're all in too much of a state of shock to get any kind of grip on our emotions," said Ryan to Newhan. "What can I say? I'm sure everyone on the club would rather not have to go out and play."

Ron Fairly had played only briefly with Lyman, but he spoke with Newhan of how the young outfielder had put him at ease as a teammate. "I had my locker next to his in Anaheim, and he was the type of guy who always walked into the clubhouse with a smile and a nice word," Fairly remembered. "He was a good man who always made you feel comfortable around him. But really, whatever I say won't be good enough. Words are pretty hollow right now. It's hard to talk when you feel as if you were just hit below the belt."

Angels hitting coach Bob Skinner, whom Lyman had called his "big baby sitter" as Skinner helped him work through his spring slump, was wiping tears away from his eyes as he talked with some of the writers. "I've met a lot of people in this business and Lyman was one of the best. I don't think there was anyone closer to him. He laid his whole soul out at different times and he really had only one goal in life and that was to make the Angels a winner. I'm certain he would have done it."[8]

"Our clubhouse was just like a morgue," Baylor would say several years later. "We had no batting practice, or anything. Losing Lyman was a hard one. He was a great player. But losing a friend and a teammate, that was the worst of it. It was a brutal day—an absolutely brutal day.

"It was the end of the season and we were [still mathematically in the American League West race], but after that happened, the guys just wanted to get the season over with."[9]

Television announcer Bruce Roberts came up to Baylor in the Angels training room. Baylor was sitting with an ashen look on his face, saying nothing. Approaching the Angels slugger, Roberts said he understood that he and Lyman had been close friends. Baylor nodded his head in affirmation. Roberts told Baylor that while he'd like to get his thoughts about Lyman on camera, he would respect him if he wasn't ready to talk about it then. Without responding directly to the commentator's inquiry, silently, solemnly, Baylor began to weep.

* * *

Sunday morning chapel services were typically held in a tiny room adjacent to the visitor's clubhouse, where those who wished to worship would be able to do so in a quiet atmosphere without taking away from the normally loud and festive pregame atmosphere in the primary locker room.

This particular Sunday morning, the chapel service was held in the Angels clubhouse. Every single member of the organization that was at the ballpark would sit in for the brief Scripture reading and reflection. Mal Schaus, an executive with First National Bank and official with the Fellowship of Christian Athletes, presided over the brief ceremony. Standing in the middle of a silent room, Schaus referred to the New Testament, where, in the Epistle to the Romans, the apostle Paul explained how salvation could come to all men through recognition and understanding of God's word. "Who shall separate us from the love of Christ? Shall tribulation, or distress, or persecution, or famine or nakedness, or peril, or sword?" Schaus read from Romans 8:35.

He continued reading: "As it is written: 'For thy sake we are killed all the day long; we are accounted as sheep for the slaughter.' Nay, in all these things we are more than conquerors through him that loved us. For I am persuaded, that neither death, nor life, nor angels, nor principalities, nor power, nor things present, nor things to come, nor height, nor depth, nor any other creature, shall be able to separate us from the love of God that is in Jesus Christ our Lord."

"It was the hardest thing I've ever done," Schaus said following the service. "I read from Romans Chapter VIII, verses 35–39, and made some comments. It [Bostock's death] was senseless and meaningless."[10]

"I don't know if Lyman was a religious man," added teammate Danny Goodwin. "Everybody has his own religion, whether you show it or keep it within yourself. He helped everybody by the way he played every day and cheered for everyone. He was the reason the Angels came back as far as they did this year."[11]

It was the last weekend home game of the season for the White Sox. While the club would play two more contests in Comiskey on Monday and Tuesday, they would finish the regular season with a four-game set in Anaheim against the Angels. Given that it was the last Sunday home game, the White Sox organization had planned a few extras for that afternoon's spectators. A pregame wedding had been scheduled at home plate. Max Patkin was on hand to perform some of the same skits and comedic stunts that Lyman had enjoyed six years earlier, during his first summer in the minor leagues, when he'd first seen the Clown Prince perform. However, nobody was in the mood to laugh and joke around before that Sunday's ballgame. Patkin took the day off out of respect to Lyman—the first time since World War II that the Clown Prince missed a performance.

"Max Patkin, the baseball clown, was supposed to perform that day," recalled Baylor. "He came in and told me, 'My fee is $5,000, but I don't want to go on.' He refused to do it out of respect for Lyman."[12]

* * *

The lamentations for Lyman and his sudden, tragic death didn't come solely from the visitor's locker room at Comiskey Park that Sunday morning. Chicago rookie infielder Joe Gates, a Gary native, had made his major league debut with the White Sox just twelve days before, on September 12. Gates knew Lyman's uncles and cousins well, and indicated that his parents had planned to ride with the Turner brothers to that day's game on the South Side.

"I live just a few blocks from Lyman's kinfolk in Gary—the kinfolk he always comes over to visit when he's in town," said Gates to the *Chicago Tribune*'s Dave Nightingale. "Matter of fact, his uncle was coming over with my folks to watch today's game. Guess that's all changed now."

As Lyman's last team in the big leagues prepared to play on without him that Sunday, his first team in the big leagues, the Minnesota Twins, were taking on the Royals again at Metropolitan Stadium. Minnesota's loss to Kansas City the night before had crippled the Angels' playoff hopes even further. The Royals needed to win only two out of their last seven games to ensure a third straight appearance in the American League Championship Series. For the Twins, it was a largely meaningless late September game—a chance to provide some youngsters valuable playing time while giving veterans a chance to pad their stats. But baseball talk was pushed to the side that morning in the Minnesota locker room as the players caught wind of what had happened the night before in Gary.

Dan Ford couldn't contain himself—the outfielder sat in a chair at his locker and cried his eyes out upon hearing the news. The man who at one time had been a competitor in Minnesota's talented outfield rotation had become something much more to Ford. "It makes you think of life a little bit," Ford would say later to Earl Gustkey of the *Los Angeles Times*. "You can be here today and happy, and gone tomorrow. You wonder, 'Why?' I don't know."

Others in the Twins locker room stood in hushed silence—a pall coming over a normally vibrant and upbeat pregame scene.

"I think I wouldn't be alone in admitting that I was thinking about Lyman and his wife," added shortstop Roy Smalley to *Minneapolis Tribune* columnist Gary Libman. "It's a terrible thing."

"He was such a close personal friend. It's like I'm looking in a mirror, and not seeing my reflection by Lyman's. One minute it's there. Then it's not. It's hard to fathom," said another former Twins teammate, Craig Kusick, to Gutskey.

"I'm shocked. I'm angry. I'm sick. People don't realize the strong feeling of admiration and respect that develop on a ballclub. I thought the world of that man," added Twins manager Gene Mauch, who had wanted nothing more than the chance to renew his relationship with Lyman in California.[13]

"I know his wife real well, and all of us share in her grief," added Rod Carew. "[He was] liked by everybody on the club."[14]

Over on the Kansas City side, Lyman's nemesis Al Hrabosky learned about his death though strange, twisted circumstances. Following the Royals-Angels brawl in Kansas City earlier in the month, Hrabosky "went to visit a friend at a nightclub and was introduced to another man Hrabosky described as a bouncer/hitman type," wrote Mike DiGiovanna in the *Los Angeles Times* in 1992. "He said he was at the game and got so mad during the fight that he wanted to come out and help me. Then, he said, 'As a matter of fact, if you want, he [Bostock] is dead.'

"'I told him to forget about it, that he was blowing it all out of proportion,' Hrabosky said.

"As Hrabosky rode the elevator in a Minnesota hotel, he overheard people saying Bostock had been killed," DiGiovanna continued. "When Hrabosky got to the park that day, [Royals manager Whitey] Herzog told

Hrabosky there were a couple of detectives that wanted to talk to him. Hrabosky's jaw dropped. It was a joke.

"'That was some sick humor,' Hrabosky said. 'But the bottom line is we were in Yankee Stadium for the playoffs, and I got a telegram that said, "Wishing you were here, Lyman Bostock," a month after his death. There are some weird people out there.'"

Ford nailed a solo home run off Kansas City's Steve Mingori that Sunday afternoon in the bottom of the sixth inning, breaking a 3–3 tie and helping lead the Twins to a 6–4 triumph that delayed the Royals' eventual conquest of the Western Division title by at least one more day.

"I can't really say that I played the game for Lyman or that I dedicated the home run to him," Ford said afterward of his fallen teammate. "I guess it was a thought beforehand, though. When the game began he was on my mind."[15]

Ford admitted that throughout that afternoon's contest, he couldn't help but look out at the big scoreboard beyond the fence in right-center field in Metropolitan Stadium to see what was happening on Chicago's South Side. "Every time I looked at the scoreboard and saw the Angels' score it came to mind," he said.

In Milwaukee, the Brewers were taking on the Oakland A's that afternoon. Oakland was staring a ninety-loss season in the face. The Brewers were still technically in the hunt in the American League East—trailing the Yankees by 4.5 games and the Red Sox by 3.5 games with a week to go. But like the Angels, the Brewers were in need of a miracle that wouldn't come. For Brewers' fans, it was one last chance for see the home squad in action before they embarked on a six-game West Coast road trip to finish out the regular season. One of Milwaukee's top players, however, couldn't bring himself to play that day.

Upon hearing of Lyman's death, Larry Hisle was overwhelmed. He was sobbing nearly uncontrollably as he entered the Milwaukee locker room that morning, but at first planned to take the field as a tribute to his fallen former teammate. Hisle was briefly seen in the locker room that morning, red-eyed and unable to speak without losing composure.

"How could such a thing happen? I don't know what to say," Hisle said through tears. "He was the best friend I had in this game."[16]

Though Hisle got into his Brewers uniform and entered the dugout planning to play that Sunday afternoon's contest with Oakland, it wound up being simply too much for him to take the field that day. He asked the club's management if he could sit that day's game out, and they obliged.

"Larry feels terrible. He and Bostock were like brothers," said Brewers manager George Bamberger. "We gave him permission to do what he wanted to do. I was in the Brewer bullpen working with the pitchers when [Brewers trainer] Curt [Rayer] called and said, 'Larry doesn't feel he can make it.'"[17]

"I feel for Larry," added Brewers rookie and future Hall of Famer Paul Molitor, a resident of St. Paul. "I never got to know Bostock very well, but Larry introduced me to him in spring training, and I know just from my first year in the big leagues that Lyman was one of the most respected persons in baseball."

The Brewers would hold a brief moment of silence that afternoon in County Stadium before going on to claim a 5–2 victory over Oakland. Later that day, a reporter called Hisle's home. His wife, Sheila, answered and told the journalist that Larry had a headache and was resting.

Back in Anaheim, Gene Autry, Buzzie Bavasi, and other members of the Angels organization expressed dismay and astonishment at that weekend's events in Gary. "I hate to even think about this, but I keep wondering why it couldn't have been, somebody not as nice as Lyman," said an Angels secretary to Associated Press columnist John Nadel. "He was always so pleasant, so easy to deal with."

"I talked to him a lot of times and saw him practically every game. I always went down to the clubhouse to visit with him and all the team," said Autry. "He was a very, very fine fellow. We were very happy with him."[18]

"All of us are in a state of shock. You read about things like this and never realize the impact until it touches home. What a waste. What a fine young man," added Bavasi. "I mean, here was the man who was the mainstay of our club now and in the future. He was the kind of young man you build a club around. I've had a lot of joy and heartache in this business, but never anything like this."[19]

Naturally, one of the first questions presented to Bavasi was what the Angels would do to overcome Lyman's loss. It was not an easy question to answer. The Angels had invested heavily in Lyman, assuming he'd be a star in the outfield for years to come—perhaps for the next decade or more.

"We have to change our thinking completely. We had come up to the last week of the season still in the race, still thinking we were only one player away, agreeing that our only real need was for a left-handed power hitter," Bavasi indicated. "We thought we might be able to do it without trading any of our front-line pitching, without breaking up what we feel is the best young pitching staff in baseball.

"Now, with the new void in the outfield, I don't see how we can help but give up some of the pitching. Certainly one pitcher, maybe even two."

Bavasi suggested that the Angels might once again dip into the free agent pool to find Lyman's long-term replacement. Or, they'd have to trade from a prone position, with clubs knowing they were desperate for an outfielder.

"While we've been saying that we weren't going into the free agent market again, now I would think that if someone comes along with who we feel can help us, we'll have to reconsider," the Angels executive replied. "We're getting a lot of sympathetic calls from baseball people and I'm very appreciative of that. But when it comes time to talk trade, these same people are going to know they have us over the barrel and they'll try to stick it to us. It's the way this game is. I don't blame them. It's tough to fill holes when the other people know you have to fill them."

* * *

As hard as it was, a game had to be played that Sunday. A lineup had to be selected. So Jim Fregosi sat down, wiped his eyes a few more times, and dutifully wrote in his choices. He replaced Lyman in the Angels starting lineup that afternoon with Lyman's old semipro teammate from Los Angeles—the young man who had one day dreamed of playing in the major leagues in the same outfield.

Kenny Landreaux had gotten a chance to live out his big league dream alongside Lyman for one magical, fun-filled summer. Now he was summoned into Fregosi's makeshift office in the bowels of Comiskey Park and was asked to take his friend's place. "The skip called me into his office and said just do the best you can," Landreaux would say later to Steve Dilbeck of the *San Bernardino Sun-Telegram*. "I don't know how I played. All I can say is why? It's really hard for me to go out there and play [but] I talked to Lyman a lot. I know he would have wanted me in the starting lineup."

While Landreaux replaced Lyman in the California outfield, Fregosi elected to hit Lansford in Lyman's third spot. "Lo and behold, we get to the park the next day and Fregosi hits me third," Lansford said. "And I just immediately think, 'How am I going to do this? I can't replace this guy. This is Lyman Bostock. Are you kidding me?'"[20]

Perhaps the last of the White Sox and the Angels personnel in Cosmiskey Park to find out about what had happened to Lyman was Chicago's starting pitcher, Francisco Barrios. As he prepared to begin final warm-ups for the day's start, Barrios was made aware of the stunning news from the night before.

"What? That's terrible," said Barrios later. Just the week before, Barrios's own cousin died in a car crash back in his native Mexico. "I can't explain it," he said to the *Chicago Tribune*'s Richard Dozer. "But it just wasn't the same pitching out there today. So many things on my mind."

As game time approached, the Angels players began to file out of the dressing room and collect in the visitor's dugout, temporarily putting aside their pain to do their job. But the day would bring constant reminders of what had been lost. A few minutes before the first pitch, the White Sox announced a moment of silence in remembrance of Lyman. As the crowd moved solemnly to its feet, the Angels players, coaches, and team personnel stood at the edge of the visitor's dugout. Their heads bowed, their right hands pressing their hats into their chests, the Angels thought of Lyman. They thought of the good times. They thought of the man himself. They thought about Yuovene. Some stared out into the expanses of Comiskey Park's lush green field. They looked out at the scoreboard—that giant exploding scoreboard that had been the source of so much excitement over the decades—and saw no number 10 in the Angels line-up that afternoon. They looked out in right field, where a different player would be taking Lyman's place. Finally, it was game time.

Rick Miller led off for California and smoked a double to center field. After Lyman's replacement Landreaux grounded out to second, Carney Lansford stepped up. For much of the 1978 season, Lansford had benefited from hitting in the number two spot in front of Lyman, but today he would receive what some might call divine intervention, hitting where Lyman usually hit, in the third position.

"It was Francisco Barrios, he was pitching that day. My first time up for whatever reason, God blessed me and I hit a home run," Lansford recalled in *Remembering Lyman Bostock*. "And I just remember trotting to first base and kind of just pointing to the sky. And I was just like, 'This is for you Lyman.' And I just kind of broke down. I couldn't deal with that whole thing."

Perhaps it wasn't all too surprising that Jim Fregosi was out of the game by the third inning—ejected for his complaints about a call at second base. The outburst was fairly atypical of Fregosi, as he unleashed his pain and anger on second-base umpire Lou DiMuro in a heated exchange before getting the boot. "It was a very tough day in every way," the California skipper said later.[21]

The two runs produced by Lansford's homer were all the Angels mustered off Barrios until the top of the sixth, when Don Baylor led off with a deep shot that cleared the left-field fence for a solo homer. "I felt I had to do something for him, so I homered," Baylor recalled. "No batting practice, no warmups, I just swung and it went out. To this day I don't know how I got around the bases, my legs just felt so heavy. When I got back to the bench, our equipment man, Mickey Shishido, came up to me. 'That was for Lyman, wasn't it? You hit that one for Lyman.'"[22]

Baylor's home run ignited a California rally, as the Angels scraped together a collection of six hits to score five runs and put the game away in an eventual 7–3 victory. But there was no joy in the Angels clubhouse afterward, as the players collected their belongings and readied for the trip back to the West Coast.

For one Angels teammate, the opportunity to have a keepsake of Lyman's was too much to pass up as the California players grabbed their equipment from the dugout for the trip home. Rick Miller, who had shared center-field duties with Lyman at times and had played in the same lineups other times, pulled out one of the murdered outfielder's brown-stained bats. Knowing that nobody was likely to stake a claim for it right then and there, Miller took it for himself. It's been a treasured possession of the retired ballplayer for nearly four decades.

"I took it so I could keep it," Miller said to Jeff Pearlman for his article, "Fifth and Jackson." "Somebody might think I should sell it on eBay—well, there's no chance in hell. That bat is still with me, and it's gonna stay with me until I pass. Then my son will have the honor of getting it—the honor of owning something that belonged to Lyman Bostock."

* * *

As the Angels were doing battle with the White Sox in Chicago, Lyman's body was being prepared back at St. Mary's Mercy Hospital to be flown back to California. Throughout the morning hours, Lyman's body remained in the intensive care area on the first floor, where Paul Hutchins had one of the more traumatic experiences of his young life for the second time in the span of a month. Annie and Yuovene had flown on a red-eye flight from California and arrived in Chicago a few hours after Lyman's passing. They were brought over by police escort to the Gary hospital that Sunday to see Lyman before he was prepared for burial.

"Early afternoon the next day, his family arrived," Hutchins recalled. "Before they came to see him, the nurse went in to clean him up. She came out and her arms were full of blood soaked sheets. She then called down and said he was ready.

"His wife was a beautiful young woman. I believe the older woman was his mother. There were also a few gentlemen with them. I could hear the policeman tell what they thought had happened and that they caught a suspect."[23]

An indelible image was seared into Yuovene's mind as she stared at her dead husband's body. "The worst ever was just seeing his lifeless body lying there and thinking, 'What a waste.' It didn't get any worse than that," she remembered in *The Lyman Bostock Story*.

On Monday, around the same time that Leonard Smith was being charged with first-degree murder in a courtroom in Crown Point, Indiana, Lyman's body returned to his beloved Southern California. Yuovene and Annie accompanied Lyman's casket on the journey, and the two women would now make preparations for the young man's funeral, which would be held three days later in Vermont Square. Needless to say, it had been a whirlwind forty-eight hours for the two women. They were exhausted, mentally drained, devastated.

Bavasi called Yuovene to inform her that the Angels would honor Lyman's full contract. In addition, she would receive $100,000 in life insurance from the Major League Baseball Players Association. Although Lyman was not vested in the association as a full four-year member, having only missed by a week, the organization ensured that Yuovene would also receive widow's benefits of $300 a month for the rest of her life.

The tributes poured in from around the major leagues.

On "This Week in Baseball," aired three days after the tragedy in Gary, the great Mel Allen paid his respects. "All events on the diamond were thrown into the background by the tragedy that struck the California

Angels," Allen said. "Star outfielder Lyman Bostock, fatally and without reason, shot at the age of 27. A player of exceptional talents. A .311 career batting average. And his best years still ahead.

"As a much sought-after free agent, Bostock chose California. It was his home. Lyman made headlines when an early-season slump prompted him to give his first month's salary to charity. One of those items of good news—hard for many to believe. But nothing so hard to believe as the bad news, for all players. Especially teammates past and present."

"So the flag flies at half-mast for a man known to friends for his lively chatter and constant good humor," Allen continued. "And to fans for his stylish and enthusiastic play on the field. To friend and fan alike, indeed a very sad week."

"He wanted to be the best, and we always used to get a kick out of him saying he wanted to outhit Rod Carew. So I don't know. He might go up there and be playing with Ty Cobb and some of these guys right now, and maybe he'll become a better hitter upstairs," said Rod Carew on that same episode of "This Week in Baseball."

Remembrances were pouring into the *Los Angeles Times*, as locals expressed their thoughts and grief over the unexpected loss of a true community hero. "I can't believe that the man who wanted to donate his April salary to charity because he didn't feel he deserved it is gone," wrote Bill Walker of Glendale. "It can't be true that Lyman Bostock, the No. 10 who crashed into walls to save home runs, dove into the power alleys, glove extended, to flag down extra-base hits, rattled clutch hits all over the American League for the Angels is no longer with us."[24]

"I am thankful that Lyman Bostock chose to play for the California Angels and that I was fortunate enough to see him play," penned Patricia Lutgen of Riverside. "He was an extraordinary man who carried himself with as much dignity off the field as on."

"I have watched many sports events, controversies, and tragedies, but I have never been moved to write as I have by the death of Lyman Bostock," added Mike Terry of Los Angeles. "I have only two things to say. The loss of Lyman Bostock the player is incalculable. The loss of the human being is simply unfair."

By the early fall of 1978, Richard Nixon was four years removed from the White House. The only man in history to resign the presidency of the United States, Nixon had gone home to California after flying out of Washington, D.C., settling in at his seaside estate in San Clemente. Nixon had always been a baseball fan, relishing his opportunities as commander in chief to throw out first balls on Opening Day and other ceremonial events such as All-Star Games and World Series showdowns. Now largely out of public life—with the exception of some speaking engagements and his famous one-on-one interview with David Frost—Nixon enjoyed sitting back at "La Casa Pacifica" and watching the occasional Angels game on television. Like everyone else, the former president couldn't believe the stunning news from Gary, and in response he made a monetary donation to Lyman's church.

"I read with shock and sadness of Lyman Bostock's tragic death," Nixon wrote to Gene Autry. "He was a fine man, on and off the field. I am enclosing my check which I would appreciate your forwarding to the Teen Challengers of the Vermont Square Methodist Church in Southwest Los Angeles."[25]

In early November, the *Gary Post-Tribune* newspaper, in conjunction with the People Action Coalition and Trust, a local nonprofit organization, established their own memorial fund for the fallen ballplayer.

The baseball games had to go on, of course. Following their Sunday afternoon win over the White Sox, the Angels flew home, minus one teammate who had made the journey to the Midwest with them, for the final week of the regular season.

After a day off on Monday, during which the players reconnected with their families and tried to make some sense of the recent disaster, the Angels tried to cling to life in the Western Division race on Tuesday, September 26, two days after Lyman's death. Kenny Landreaux homered in the eighth inning, and Carney Lansford came through with a tenth-inning walk-off single for a victory. But the Angels' 5–4 triumph over the Brewers proved to be all for naught, as Kansas City clinched the American League West with a 4–1 victory at home over the Mariners. As he rounded Anaheim Stadium's bases, Landreaux couldn't help but think about his dead friend—the fun-loving guy he used to warm up with down the road at Ross Snyder Park when they were both young men eager to make it in baseball.

"When I hit that home run, that's when I thought about him the most. I wish he would have been there to see it," Landreaux said after the game.[26]

As the Angels claimed a relatively meaningless 4–1 win over the Brewers on Wednesday, September 27, Lyman's former Twins teammate

Larry Hisle was given the night off. The Milwaukee slugger was assisting Yuovene and Annie with the arrangements for Lyman's funeral, which would be held the next day back in Lyman's neighborhood.

* * *

The young reporter awaited anxiously, taking in his surroundings and jotting down the occasional note. It was a sweltering early fall afternoon in inner-city Los Angeles, and there was no respite from the sweaty, sticky conditions. The reporter, a two-year veteran of the *Los Angeles Times*, should have been anywhere else than where he was. On such a late September afternoon, he should have been doing any number of other things. Researching that week's NFL matchups, perhaps. Previewing the Dodgers' upcoming National League Championship Series rematch with the Philadelphia Phillies. Assessing whether Kareem Abdul-Jabbar and the Lakers had any shot of competing with the Seattle Supersonics for supremacy in the NBA's Western Conference. Debating whether or not Southern Cal could challenge for a national championship on the gridiron that fall.

At just twenty-six years of age, Skip Bayless was already an award-winning reporter, having earned accolades the year before for his coverage of Seattle Slew's run to horse racing's Triple Crown. The *Los Angeles Times* had lured him away from the *Miami Herald* two years earlier, and soon after, the *Dallas Morning News* would convince Bayless to head to Texas. Later he would become a household name around the country for his commentary on ESPN.

He should have been anywhere else that particular day—Thursday, September 28, 1978.

But the young reporter was in a crowded church in Vermont Square in South Los Angeles, awaiting the most somber gathering of the year in Southern California. He would be responsible for an article describing the surreal and emotional happening that was Lyman Bostock's funeral. Vermont Square Methodist Church was filled to the brim, as a congregation estimated to be between eight hundred and a thousand mourners jammed into the sanctuary, filling every space in the pews and leaving the aisles congested as the organist played "Send in the Clowns," symbolic of Lyman's upbeat personality.

Every major league team had sent flowers. The floral arrangements stretched across the front of the church—surrounding the altar and much of the available space around Lyman's open coffin with colorful bouquets. Angels pitcher Frank Tanana, as well as many other California players and spectators, walked up to Lyman's open casket, peering inside. The view was too much for many of those in attendance, who wailed in anguish at the sight of Lyman lying dead inside.

Tanana solemnly blessed his former teammate, lowering his head in a brief moment of prayer and reflection. As he turned back to sit in a nearby pew, tears filled the All-Star hurler's eyes. In later years, Tanana would cite Lyman's death, as well as an arm injury during his days with the Angels, as motivating factors for seeking a relationship with Jesus Christ.

"Both events had a profound effect on my life," Tanana later said to John Weyler of the *Los Angeles Times*. "I believed in eternal life. I wanted to go to heaven, and the death of Lyman made me think, 'Hey Frank, tomorrow it could be you.' It led me to Christ and changed my life."

There was nowhere to sit, no room to stand, and little space to move around by the time the church's doors were closed so the proceedings could begin. There were almost as many outside the church as inside. An estimated crowd of five hundred to eight hundred people stood solemnly outside the packed church, unable to see the proceedings but feeling obligated to pay their final respects to a hometown kid who hadn't forgotten where he'd come from.

They came by car. They came by foot. They came by bus. They came by bicycle. They surrounded the small community church and enveloped the block—and adjacent Budlong Avenue—in a sea of humanity. Although Angels owner Gene Autry didn't attend because of his own personal feelings about funerals, most of the rest of the organization did. The Angels players and wives were bussed to the church's front steps.

As the strains of "Onward Christian Soldiers" played on the organ, Annie and Yuovene were ushered into the sanctuary. Dressed elegantly in all white, Yuovene was serene, demonstrating remarkable poise. She would later say she was in a daze, but she showed little emotion throughout the ceremony. Annie, wearing a lovely purple dress, tried to hold her composure together in the midst of such a sorrowful gathering. Lyman Bostock Sr., Lyman's four half-brothers, and numerous other relatives filled much of the front right side of the church.

It would later be reported that temperatures reached 105 degrees inside the church, as mourners waved the memorial bulletins as fans in front of their sweating faces.

John Robertson, the man who sang the national anthem at Angels home games in Anaheim Stadium, began the formal proceedings with a heart-tugging lyrical rendition of the Lord's Prayer. Dr. Milton H. Davis, minister of the Church of the Master in Los Angeles, had been in the Virgin Islands when Lyman was killed. He hurriedly rushed home to take part in the funeral ceremony, and was the first to speak.

"Even in that part of our country, his name was a household name," Davis told the congregation. "As I passed through Puerto Rico on my way home, I noticed the people of that island, the home of Roberto Clemente. Lyman's death was the talk of the town."

"We live in a time of uncertainty when such a senseless act can wipe out such a great life as that of Lyman Bostock," Davis concluded.[27]

Pitcher Ken Brett spoke on behalf of the Angels players, who had provided a large floral arrangement—red roses formulating a background, with white roses spelling out Lyman's number 10. Jim Fregosi was initially going to speak, but, overcome with emotion, the young Angels manager couldn't follow through with it.

"At the funeral, Jimmy was supposed to do the eulogy, but he came up to me and said, 'I just can't do it.' As the players' rep, he asked me to do it. So I did," said Brett to *Los Angeles Times* columnist Mike Penner.

Brett recalled Lyman's endearing, fun-loving nature, which had made him a valued friend and respected teammate in two American League clubhouses. "We called him Mr. Jibber Jabber, because he enlightened every clubhouse scene, chasing tension, drawing laughter in the darkest hour of defeat. When winning wasn't in the plan, Lyman knew the sun would come up the next morning," Brett remembered, choking back tears. "He enlivened our clubhouse and took us out of the darkness of defeat. But he was a winner. He enjoyed life so much because he had so little in the beginning."

"When he found the road to success, his first thoughts were to help the people who had helped him. There remains for us only one consolation—that we are all better persons for having known Lyman and having had him touch our lives. We've been deprived of a great player. A great friend. And an unmatched spirit has left the Angel clubhouse," Brett concluded.

A solo singer, Chester Prescott, rose and walked to the front of the congregation. He began singing a variation of a hit song recorded by Dion in the late summer of 1968, shortly after the murders of Martin Luther King Jr. and Robert F. Kennedy. Prescott added an extra lyric—a moment that brought on a wave of weeping and widespread expressions of grief throughout the standing-room-only congregation.

> Has anybody here, seen my old friend Lyman?
> Can you tell me where he's gone?
> I thought I saw him walking, over the hill with Abraham, and Martin, and John.

The Angels team chaplain, John Werhas, didn't attempt to answer the most confusing and tragic question of all—why? Werhas himself had been a professional ballplayer, having spent time with the Los Angeles Dodgers and Los Angeles Angels for parts of four seasons in the mid-1960s, before he received a call to serve God. "Humanly speaking, there is no answer," Werhas said. "I hope we all again will get to see Lyman's smiling face. He not only lives in our hearts and minds, but he lives in Heaven with our Lord and Savior."

Referring to the New Testament, Werhas evoked the example of Martha, whom Jesus comforted prior to the raising of her brother, Lazarus, from the dead. "I am the resurrection and the life," Werhas stated, reciting Jesus' words in John 11:25. "He who believes in me shall live, even though he dies. Do you believe this?"

Werhas explained Martha's response: "She answered like Lyman Bostock would have. 'Yes, Lord, I believe that you are the Christ and the Messiah.'"

Finally, Reverend John C. Bain—the man who had been Lyman's pastor and spiritual advisor from his early teenage days—took the pulpit. Bain celebrated Lyman's life, reminding his listeners that this man was much more than a big contract and a professional ballplayer.

"A star has fallen," Bain said. "A promising career has been shattered."[28]

"Don't get lost dreaming about two million dollar contracts," Bain added, his voice permeating throughout the room. "That was just icing on a cake which had already been baked."

He credited Annie for her tremendous job raising Lyman and the Los Angeles public schools for instilling elements critical to his development. "The ingredients were already there. Those ingredients were deep religious conviction taught in the home, the discipline and guidance he received in public school, and his desire to be somebody," said Bain. "Lyman was compassionate, fair, honest, a strong competitor, and generally full of fun."

Bain's booming voice brought replies of "That's right!" and "Amen!" from the hundreds in the congregation. As the funeral concluded, several Angels players, designated as honorary pallbearers, hoisted Lyman's light-colored casket, walking it through the front entrance of the church and out into an awaiting hearse. The family slowly moved outside, with Yuovene and Annie leading the way. Family members filled several limousines as a large procession of cars, well over a mile in length, formed behind them. The destination was Inglewood Park Cemetery, Lyman's final resting place.

"As cameramen jockeyed for position on the sanctuary steps, the family filled five gray limousines at the head of the procession. Policemen

On Thursday, September 28, 1978, four days following his death, Lyman was laid to rest in his native Los Angeles. His funeral, held at Vermont Square Methodist Church, was attended by several hundred mourners. Lyman was buried at Inglewood Park Cemetery, located approximately five miles from his boyhood home along South Hoover Street in Vermont Square. (Bettman/Corbis.)

stopped traffic at every light on the approximately five-mile drive to the cemetery," wrote Bayless.

As the procession snaked its way down the Harbor Freeway for the short drive to the cemetery, nearby drivers slowed and pulled to the side, paying their own final respects. Arriving at Lot 342, Grave D, at Inglewood Park Cemetery, one last prayer was extended at the gravesite, and it was all over. Don Baylor approached the casket, sliding his hand along the smooth exterior. "Goodbye Lyman," he said before pulling away and walking off, sobbing.

As she walked away from the grave of her only child, Annie Bostock reminded everyone within earshot exactly who had been lost. "He was my son," Annie said stoically.[29]

"Yes, he was your son," responded some of the guests and family members nearby.

"He was my son," she repeated time and time again.

"Yes, he was your son."

15

THE TRIALS OF LEONARD SMITH (1979)

> Drop, drop—in our sleep, upon the heart sorrow falls, memory's pain, and to us, though against our very will, even in our own despite, comes wisdom by the awful grace of God.—Aeschylus, Greek philosopher, *Agamemnon*[1]

After firing a single shotgun blast into the back seat of Tom Turner's Buick Electra at the corner of Fifth and Jackson in downtown Gary, Leonard Smith sped off toward his residence—a three-story, stand-alone row house at 1151 Jackson Street owned by his mother. Squealing away from the scene of the crime, Leonard turned right on Madison Street and sped south, racing past Bowman Square Park on his right toward Eleventh Avenue, where he hung a right before turning quickly left onto Jackson Street for the short remaining distance to his home.

Multiple witnesses around the intersection of Fifth and Jackson had heard the shotgun blast, and Leonard's estranged wife Barbara had noticed him immediately after the shooting. Barbara was treated at the hospital in fair condition, having taken some pellets to the face but not from close enough range to penetrate her skull. She confirmed to the police that Leonard had done the shooting.

"Barbara Smith recognized the driver as Leonard Smith, her estranged husband," said Gary police sergeant Charles Highsmith. "At Fifth and Jackson Streets, the suspect pulled alongside and fired point blank into the car."[2]

Around the time an ambulance was racing Lyman over to St. Mary's Mercy Hospital, Leonard was hiding the murder weapon and trying to lay low inside his residence. No one will ever know if Leonard was able to sleep that fateful night. Surely he must have been wondering if he had seriously hurt or even killed anyone, and whether or not the police would come. A little less than seven hours after the shooting—around five thirty early Sunday morning—Leonard got his answer. Gary patrolman Randy Grout located Leonard's car outside his house. Taking a peek inside Leonard's Ford, the officer found information revealing his address. Grout quickly realized that they were indeed at Leonard's residence and that he was likely inside.

Within minutes, a barrage of Gary police offers surrounded the triple-decker apartment at 1151 Jackson Street, calling inside to let the murder suspect know he was surrounded and had nowhere to go. In response, Leonard surrendered without incident. "The officers telephoned in, and he came out peacefully," said police corporal Thomas Harbrecht.

Although they didn't immediately find the .410 bore shotgun that had taken Lyman's life, the police were convinced that they had their man. Detectives stated rather quickly that Leonard was likely attempting to shoot his wife, Barbara. But because Lyman was most directly in the path of Leonard's shotgun blast, he was the one who was mortally wounded.

"Lyman was a victim of circumstances. [Smith's] intended victim was his wife, not Lyman," said Gary police corporal Charles Hicks. "Lyman was in the wrong place at the wrong time."[3]

Gary police officials also quickly determined that Barbara Smith and Lyman had not been seeing each other inappropriately. Lyman had gone into one of Gary's worst neighborhoods to see an old friend—nothing more, nothing less—and it had cost him his life.

"It'll probably come out like he was having some kind of affair with the woman," said Gary police sergeant Bob Scheerer. "But it wasn't like that at all. They had been together for a total of about 20 blocks before the shooting. It's just a shame."[4]

"I doubt very much he knew what hit him," Scheerer added. "It's just a tragedy. He didn't even know Mrs. Smith."[5]

Lyman's agent also sought to dispel any false rumors of infidelity. "He was not out flirting with women," said Abdul-Jalil Al-Hakim. "The women were his uncle's godchildren. They were like brothers and sisters. He had been out signing autographs for kids in the Gary ghetto and minutes later he's shot in the head."[6]

"I wouldn't have gone out if I'd known," Barbara Smith said in the hours immediately after the shooting. "I would have never jeopardized someone else's life."[7]

When he arrived at the police station that early Sunday morning, Leonard Smith had little to say, though one phrase repeatedly crossed his lips. "It's all about that bitch," he sneered.

The next day, a preliminary hearing was held in Lake County Criminal Court in nearby Crown Point, where Leonard was ordered to be held without bond for the murder of Lyman Bostock.

"In Gary Saturday night, a creep with a gun killed a hero," wrote Bill Gleason of the *Chicago Sun-Times* in that Monday morning's paper. "Lyman Bostock, bright, confident, fun-loving, charitable, extroverted, is not coming back among us. Agonizing over the 'how' of his slaying will not enable us to see him again swinging, running, sliding, throwing. He is gone. He has joined the company of so many others who have been blown away in the ghettos of our nation. That's the expression. The word 'murder' rarely is used. He or she was 'blown away.'"

Leonard didn't appear at the preliminary hearing, which was held just minutes after Lake County prosecutor Jack Crawford formally filed one count of first-degree murder against the thirty-one-year-old former steelworker. Following the preliminary hearing, deputy prosecuting attorney David Nicholls told journalists that his office planned to present evidence to a Lake County grand jury "at the earliest possible time."

On Friday, September 29, the day after Lyman's funeral back in Los Angeles and less than a week after the shooting, Leonard pled innocent to the crime, requesting a jury trial. No immediate date was set for the trial, and Leonard was taken back to Lake County Jail, where he was being held with no bond.

The November 2, 1978, edition of the *Gary Post-Tribune* explained: "If Smith is judged insane, psychologists would be asked to determine if Smith is mentally incompetent or a danger to himself or others. [The judge] then would have to decide whether to begin Smith's commitment to a state mental hospital or free the Gary man because he has recovered from his insanity."

* * *

It took nearly ten months before the state of Indiana was ready to present its case, but by midsummer the prosecution was ready to move forward. With senior judge James Kimbrough presiding, Leonard Smith's trial for the murder of Lyman Bostock finally began in Lake County Superior Court in Crown Point, Indiana in July 1979. Smith had been in custody at the Lake County Jail in Gary since his initial arrest, just a few hours after he had fired his .410 bore double-barrel shotgun into the backseat of Tom Turner's car.

Nick Thiros, a well-respected attorney in northwest Indiana, had been hired by Smith's mother, Mildred Scurlock, to defend her son. Thiros had the task of convincing a jury that Smith hadn't acted in a premeditated fashion specifically to kill Lyman, as the first-degree murder charge required, and that he had shot him in a crazed state of mind that met Indiana's legal definition of insanity at the time. Because there were witnesses that could place Leonard at the scene of the shooting and his estranged wife claimed she saw him moments after pulling the trigger, insanity was Leonard Smith's only realistic hope of avoiding a lifetime in prison.

"It's not a defense of 'Who done it?' As we know. Everybody knew that Leonard did it. The only option that I recognized at the time was to file a defense of insanity," Thiros said three decades later.[8]

For the prosecution, led by Jack Crawford, as well as for Lyman's family and those who knew and loved him, the case seemed cut-and-dried. Leonard Smith had shot and killed Lyman Bostock. He had done it in premeditated fashion, following the group through the streets of Gary before seizing the opportunity to commit his crime. Leonard did it. End of story. Case closed.

The accused murderer had been deemed by court-appointed psychiatrists as competent to stand trial, and he faced up to sixty years in prison for the homicide.

"This should have been an open-and-shut case," Crawford said for ESPN's *Outside the Lines*. "That's what it should have been, and that's how we as prosecutors looked at it. The state psychiatrist said that Leonard Smith was completely sane the night he killed Lyman Bostock. That he didn't have a mental disease or defect. And certainly he understood the difference between right and wrong."

"I didn't believe that he was insane. And never have and I never will, and I still today don't believe that he was insane," added Tom Turner.

Jury selection was completed on July 9, and the next day testimony began from the two individuals who had been riding in the front seat of the car at the time of Lyman's murder—Lyman's uncle, Tom Turner, and

Turner's goddaughter, Joan Hawkins. Hawkins testified that she saw a man pick up a "long, dark object" just moments before the blast that took Bostock's life. Turner repeated Barbara Smith's exclamation in the seconds immediately following the shotgun blast that killed his nephew.

"Tom, I seen him. I seen him. Go get him. That's my stupid old husband."

After the prosecution rested its case, Thiros went on the defensive, placing blame on Smith's wife, Barbara, for flaunting her numerous dalliances with men in the months following her separation from Leonard and leading up to the night of the shooting. "She ultimately destroyed this man and his ability to conform to the law," said Thiros.[9]

Testifying on his own behalf, Leonard told the court that he suspected that the unidentified man in the backseat of Tom Turner's Buick was having an affair with his wife. In his own words, Smith said that his wife's dating other men made him "jealous and despondent over the welfare of my daughters."

The accused murderer told the prosecutor and jurors of his desire to reconcile with Barbara the day of the shooting. And while he could recall trailing behind his wife in his car through the streets of Gary after she got into Tom Turner's Buick with the other man, he couldn't remember the shooting, nor what he did immediately after the shooting. Leonard said that the last thing he clearly remembered was looking into the car at what he thought was Lyman kissing his wife or whispering in her ear.

Two court-appointed medical experts—Dr. Lee Periolat and Dr. Frank Hogle—testified July 12 that Smith was sane and in full control of his actions that night in Gary. But both conceded that the Smiths' stormy marriage had drained him emotionally. Hogle testified that Smith didn't remember shooting Bostock, but added that Leonard cried when he mentioned not being able to remember the incident. "Perhaps crying was an indication that he did remember," said Hogle.[10]

Leonard's mother, Mildred Scurlock, also testified on July 12, indicating that she had spoken to him on the day of the shooting. According to Scurlock, Smith told her, "I've tried to keep the family together. I just don't know what to do."

In his closing statement, Crawford stressed that the jurors should look closely at the evidence, as it all pointed to Leonard Smith being Lyman Bostock's killer. While no eyewitnesses aside from Barbara Smith had stepped up to say that they had seen Leonard shoot into the Buick, there was plenty of proof he had done it. Crawford also challenged the defense's strategy of pinning the blame on Barbara Smith as the instigator of her husband's so-called insanity. In the prosecution's view, if Smith had been so distraught over his wife's infidelities and was out to kill her instead of Lyman Bostock, why didn't he shoot her at Joan Hawkins's house before they set out for the fateful drive into the dilapidated downtown district of Gary?

"When he saw his wife and Bostock get into a car, that wasn't a provocation," said Crawford. "That was his opportunity to kill Barbara Smith. He had that shotgun on his lap, ready."

Instead, Smith lurked quietly on the scene—effectively stalking his soon-to-be ex-wife as she jumped into the car with a good-looking, sharply dressed young man that Leonard had never laid eyes on before. Was this dashing young man the reason why she was leaving him?

The prosecution contended that when Leonard finally met up with the group and approached the backseat of the Buick at the corner of Fifth and Jackson, he knew exactly what he was doing and what he was trying to accomplish. "[Smith was] next to the car, he knew where he was aiming, and he pulled the trigger with intent to kill," added deputy prosecutor James Olzewski.

Thiros cast all blame on Barbara Smith. "Barbara Smith played with Leonard Smith like a yo-yo," Thiros said. "Barbara Smith is responsible for this entire incident. She put Leonard Smith in the state of mind he was in."[11]

After three days of testimony, the case went to the jury on the evening of Thursday, July 12. For approximately ten hours, the jury of nine men and three women weighed the evidence, but they couldn't reach any clear consensus. Judge Kimbrough was given no choice but to declare a mistrial.

* * *

The same day the mistrial was declared—Friday, July 15—the prosecution announced that they would immediately begin efforts to seek a new trial. By the following week, a new trial date had been set.

"We are naturally quite disappointed [at the hung jury in the first trial], and are looking forward to a successful completion of the case at the next trial setting," said Crawford.[12]

Leonard Smith's second trial for the murder of Lyman Bostock began with jury selection on Monday, November 12, and prosecutor Crawford and defense attorney Thiros agreed on three initial jurors that day. Within a couple days the jury—consisting of ten women and two men—was finalized, and testimony began on November 14.

With one major exception, the defense took nearly the same approach in the second trial as they did in the first, casting doubt on Leonard Smith's sanity based on the infidelities of his wife and the rocky marriage they'd lived. But this time around, Leonard Smith wouldn't testify. Barbara Smith was called to the stand the first day of the second trial, where she engaged in an extensive review of her stormy ten-year relationship and four-year marriage to Leonard. While she admitted seeing other men during her many separations over the years from her husband, Barbara denied cheating on Leonard while she was living with him. She cited Leonard's abusive nature as one of the compelling motivations for her impending divorce.

Three psychiatrists testified in the second trial—two on behalf of the prosecution, and one for the defense. The defense's expert spoke on Friday, November 16—the final day of the trial. Frank Brogno, a psychologist from Merrillville, Indiana, had been one of Thiros's professors during his days as an undergraduate at Indiana University. The defense counsel knew the charming witness could cast doubt in the jurors' minds regarding Leonard's sanity. Brogno, using nonclinical terms, told the jurors that Leonard was insane when he pulled the trigger. The defense's expert witness cast Leonard as a schizophrenic individual who was incapable of controlling or understanding his actions on the night of Lyman's murder.

In his closing thoughts, the prosecutor appealed to the common sense of the jurors. How could Leonard Smith have been insane, Jack Crawford argued, if he had the presence of mind to drive to where Barbara Smith was staying, stalk her as she drove the streets of Gary, and then shoot and kill Lyman Bostock?

In his closing statement, Thiros cast the tragedy as the final explosion in a combustible marriage that had seen numerous estrangements and separations. Leonard Smith, in Thiros's eyes, couldn't be held responsible for Lyman Bostock's murder because he had acted in an uncontrollable rage that met Indiana's criteria at the time for insanity.

From there, the case was handed over to the jury.

As the proceedings were dismissed, Leonard was led out—his life now in the hands of twelve arbiters. After deliberating for five hours, the jury let the judge know that they had reached a verdict in the case. The court officials were summoned back to the courtroom, where shortly thereafter the verdict was read. Not guilty by reason of insanity.

The prosecution, some of Lyman's family members—many of whom were in the courtroom for the reading of the verdict—and much of the general public were mortified at the verdict. How in the world could Leonard Smith be found not guilty by reason of insanity, given the circumstances?

It was an extremely difficult ruling to swallow for people who knew and loved Lyman. It was especially difficult for Crawford, who believed that the courtroom strategy of Leonard Smith's lawyer wiggled him out of a certain murder conviction.

"He got away with murder. Leonard Smith got away with murder. He did it legally, through the system as it existed. But that's the bottom line," Crawford would say later for *Outside the Lines*.

"Well, the jury said no," added Thiros.

The defeated prosecution asserted that if Smith were set free, he would likely make another attempt on his wife's life, putting others in danger as well. Although they had effectively lost the case, the prosecution implored the judge to quickly set a commitment meeting, which he did, three days after the ruling, on Monday, November 19.

At the meeting, Smith was committed to Logansport State Hospital for 180 days of psychiatric evaluation. The hospital would evaluate Leonard, keep track of his movements and mental makeup, and then make a determination as to whether he should permanently stay committed or be released from custody.

As Smith headed off to Logansport, those who had been devastated by Lyman's death—and those equally devastated by the judgment rendered by the Lake County jurors—attempted to put the tragedy in the past and move on with their lives. But it wouldn't be long before another outrage in the case opened the wound all over again.

* * *

Bright and early on the morning of Friday, June 20, 1980, Leonard Smith was released from Logansport State Hospital. Showing no emotion, Leonard hopped into the passenger-side backseat of his mother's car—the same spot Lyman Bostock had been sitting in his uncle's car the night he was gunned down by Smith—and was driven away from the hospital for a return trip to Gary.

Under the existing law at that time in the state of Indiana, Smith could only be committed for a period of 180 days because of his acquittal by reason of insanity. The hospital's only two options were to commit Smith permanently or to consider him mentally sane and release him. But because the hospital didn't consider Smith insane in its 180-day review, they had no choice but to turn him loose that Friday morning.

"We did not find Mr. Smith mentally ill, and by law we may not keep as a patient someone who is not mentally ill," said Logansport State Hospital official Ann Hansen.[13]

In all, Leonard Smith was incarcerated less than twenty-two months for murdering Lyman Bostock.

"We're opposed to it and very disturbed," said Crawford. "Through the insanity loophole he's going to wiggle out and be a free man. We've been disgusted by the jury verdict all along. A verdict like this is a legal tragedy for the family of Bostock and Smith's wife, who will have to live in fear that he'll come back to finish what he started."[14]

Changes to the criminal insanity loophole were already being considered, but attention from Lyman's case forced legislators into swift action. On September 1, 1980, a new law went into effect, stipulating that offenders could be found "guilty but mentally ill" instead of simply "not guilty by reason of insanity." Under the new statute, a person found mentally incompetent would be committed for a predetermined period of time, as Leonard Smith was. But if a perpetrator was later deemed competent, as Leonard was, under a "guilty but mentally ill" conviction, they would immediately be sent to prison instead of being released onto the streets.

"One good thing that happened was, there was such a public outrage over the killer's release that the laws in Indiana now say you can be 'guilty but insane.' After you're deemed fit to leave the mental hospital, you'll be sent to jail to serve your whole sentence," said Hutchins.[15]

The law made a lot of sense. But, tragically, it came too late for Lyman Bostock's killer, who was allowed to go free and return to his home in Gary after less than two years of confinement for what many considered to be cold-blooded murder.

"Lyman was instrumental in having the rules and the laws change in Indiana, so I guess in some ways Lyman still lives. But to me, that's too great a cost," said his agent, Abdul-Jalil Al-Hakim.[16]

16

MOVING ON (1979–1980S)

> He left a great many loving friends who miss and think of him often. But when they think of him, it's not how he died that they remember. But how he lived. How he did live!—Jack Warden as coach George Halas, *Brian's Song*

In hindsight, America moved on very quickly from the shock and outrage of Lyman Bostock's death. While those close to him would mourn his passing for years, the baseball world had no choice but to continue on, and it did. Divisional winners had to be decided that last week of the regular season, and it just so happened that two of baseball's most storied rivals, the New York Yankees and Boston Red Sox, were going down the wire in a race for the ages in the American League East. Just days after the baseball world learned that Lyman Bostock was no more, its collective attention shifted rapidly to the day-to-day drama of Boston and New York's race to the finish line.

On Monday, October 2, just eight days after Lyman was pronounced dead and four days after he was buried, the Yankees took down the Red Sox at Fenway Park in a one-game playoff on their way to a second straight World Series title. If he had chosen to sign with the Yankees instead of the Angels, Lyman probably would have been out on the field at Fenway celebrating with Graig Nettles, Goose Gossage, Reggie Jackson, and the rest of the New York stars that early October Monday afternoon. But if Leonard Smith hadn't committed his heinous act, Lyman would have been in position to have his own celebration with his brothers in Anaheim the following year.

As the Red Sox–Yankees clash turned baseball's attention away from Lyman's death, the world's focus was shifted away on the day he was buried, September 28. It was on that day that John Paul I, the last Italian-born pope, died—just thirty-three days after a papal conclave elected him leader of the Catholic Church. Just hours after America's front pages and television broadcasts were splashed with news about Lyman Bostock, he was replaced by the late pope. As more and more time went on, Lyman drifted into the annals of history.

It was difficult for Lyman's uncle, Edward Turner, to watch baseball games during the spring and summer of 1979. Though the seasonal ritual of warm weather brought back the annual struggle for supremacy across the two major leagues, it would never be the same for the retired U.S. Steel employee. No longer would his vibrant young nephew call him to set up the arrangements for an upcoming visit to Gary when his team was in town to play the White Sox.

"Usually we'd look at the schedule and see Lyman is coming in and we'd be looking forward to it. When he came to town, he knew I would be at the airport," his uncle said less than a year after Lyman's death.[1]

Edward hadn't been in the car with Lyman that night, but he still couldn't get out of his head the horror that his younger brother Tom and the two women in the car experienced as Lyman's life was extinguished at the hands of Leonard Smith. "Any time I watch a ball game, it's kind of sad to think about it. I think about that kid every day. I see all the other ballplayers and I wonder why of all the ballplayers it had to be him. It's not that I want it to happen to anybody else. I just wonder why it had to be him."

Despite the magnitude of their loss and no longer having a relative to see play, the Turner brothers nonetheless drove west across the border to Illinois and into Chicago's South Side when the Angels returned in 1979 to play the White Sox at Comiskey Park.

Once again, Jim Fregosi's squad was in the middle of a pennant race, and they simply couldn't resist being there when Lyman's former team took the field. "The leadoff man is Rick Miller," Turner said. "Lyman probably would bat second, and Carew third. That would cross my mind—this is the spot where Lyman probably would be batting if he lived."

"I love baseball, but watching it is still hard, especially in the month of September," added Tom Turner, the uncle who was in the car driving

Lyman through the streets of Gary the night he was murdered. "When I watched the Angels, I expected him to be out there."[2]

Bob Hiegert kept thinking about the last day he'd spent with Lyman on the field at Anaheim Stadium, just four days before his fateful encounter with Leonard Smith. "I still haven't gotten over that. It was just a whole series of bad, bad stuff," said Hiegert.[3]

Neither could Dick Enberg, who called the Cal State Northridge coach to get the ball rolling on fulfilling one of Lyman's great ambitions—to give back to the program that gave him his shot in baseball.

"Enberg called me. He was with the Angels, and he called me," Hiegert replied.

"We need to do something," said Enberg.

"Absolutely we do," Hiegert replied.

"I'll talk to the Angels," Enberg said, to which Hiegert replied, "We'll get our alumni steps squared away."

And with that, efforts began to organize the first annual Lyman Bostock Memorial games to benefit the scholarship fund in the former Matador outfielder's name.

"Yuovene's wishes were in lieu of flowers, that they would go to a scholarship fund in his name—the Lyman Bostock Memorial Scholarship Fund. So we set that up," said Hiegert. "I talked to Yuovene, and after the funeral we got it all set up—the Lyman Bostock Memorial Scholarship Fund. She was very receptive to it at the time. That was a nice thing that happened out of it all."

The first annual Lyman Bostock Memorial baseball game took place on Cal State Northridge's campus on Sunday, February 4, 1979—less than five months after Lyman's passing. Jim Fregosi agreed to manage a group of major league stars, including numerous Angels and a couple Boston Red Sox players such as Fred Lynn and Rick Burleson, against the Northridge varsity baseball squad.

"We had a Lyman Bostock Memorial baseball game that we held for four or five years after. The California Angels agreed to come out and to play us, the college, with major league All-Stars, to support the fund," recalled Hiegert. "The Angels were very, very supportive. The Angels supplied major league players, and we had the game that February."

"The love for him by the professional baseball players was really apparent," Hiegert continued. "I mean, that was the thing that really separates him from some of the other guys. He had the same effect on a major league team that he had with college players.

"This weird thing happened to him way too early. But there's so much support coming out of it. It's incredible."

Don Baylor played an especially important role in compelling teammates, as well as players on other teams, to participate for the good of Lyman's scholarship fund at Northridge. "He was really a good friend of Lyman's when he was with the Angels," said Hiegert of Baylor. "He was really instrumental in helping get the Lyman Bostock game off the ground."

Yuovene was invited, as was Lyman's mother, Annie. Both women made their way to Northridge and were recognized before the game. While Annie Bostock was honored by all the attention brought to her late son, the whole thing was unsettling for Yuovene, who was being forced to relive the greatest pain and horror of her life.

"We brought [Yuovene] back along with Annie Bostock, Lyman's mother, to the first Lyman Bostock Memorial," recalled Hiegert. "She was very, very accommodating, but she was very uncomfortable. She did not want to relive that. It was a very sad time for her. His mother was very appreciative of the thing."

Coming off the success of the first year's contest, there were two Lyman Bostock Memorial games played in 1980—one at Northridge and one in Los Angeles on the campus of Loyola Marymount. Angels minor league talent and future big leaguer Tom Brunansky homered for the Lyman Bostock All-Stars against Cal State Northridge, though the makeshift club lost, 10–8, to the college players. Loyola defeated the All-Stars, 2–1, in the second contest.

In the 1981 edition of the Lyman Bostock Memorial game, one of Lyman's old buddies from the minor leagues, Al Cowens, was in the on-deck circle awaiting a turn at the plate when a foul tip caromed off his bat and into his face. The top and bottom rims of Cowen's glasses sliced into his head, requiring a total of thirteen stitches in his cheek and eyebrow area, and forcing him to miss the start of the season with the Detroit Tigers. The incident at the 1981 game with Cowens contributed to major league baseball discouraging its players from playing in the Lyman Bostock Memorial, where they faced off against college kids using aluminum bats.

"Major league baseball came down prohibiting major league players playing against college kids, because we use aluminum bats," said Hiegert. "We had to discontinue that."

In 1982, the Milwaukee Brewers came to Northridge to play the Matadors in the fourth annual Lyman Bostock Memorial game, which turned out to be one of the last benefit contests memorializing the former outfielder. By 1985, the game was called off. Without the draw of big leaguers playing in the contest, it was becoming more difficult to draw enough spectators to justify hosting the game. There was another effort to find players in the winter of 1986, but it proved unsuccessful. Like Lyman himself, the Lyman Bostock Memorial game faded into history.

"I do not intend to have Lyman's name attached to anything that does not represent the first-class manner and high standards with which Lyman conducted himself," said Terry Craven, who replaced Bob Hiegert as head baseball coach at Cal State Northridge.[4]

Yuovene and Annie returned to Northridge for the second game in 1980, but that was the last time Yuovene could bring herself to attend. It was just too difficult in those years for her to be reminded of what had happened. "They came the first and the second games. And then the third game, Yuovene said, 'I can't do this anymore. It's too hard reliving it.' I respected that a lot," said Hiegert. "I felt very sorry for her afterwards, as did a lot of Angel players."

In the months and even first couple of years after Lyman's death, she would go to his grave at Inglewood Park Cemetery. She would just sit with him, sometimes talking, a lot of times not.

"I couldn't even say that he was murdered. The words would not come off. He just 'died.'" she would say thirty-five years later in *The Lyman Bostock Story*. "Just admitting that he was murdered was very traumatic."

For a number of years, she held a grudge against Lyman's family in Gary, believing that if they had just let him stay in Chicago with the rest of the Angels, he would still be alive. "I was mad at Lyman's family for a long time," Yuovene told Jeff Pearlman for "Fifth and Jackson." "I felt that if they'd just let him go to Chicago and play ball and not bother him, he wouldn't have been with them. People were always pulling on him, and he was never able to say no. He should have never been put in that position in the first place."

It would take the passage of time, as well as years of psychological counseling, for Yuovene to come fully to terms with Lyman's death.

Eventually, she would stop going to Lyman's grave and would move on with her life. She got remarried and had a daughter that she lovingly raised in Los Angeles. She finished up her bachelor's degree at Cal State Northridge, then went back to her alma mater to earn a master's degree in child development and family studies. She would later become a program manager for Crystal Stairs in Los Angeles. She would also be appointed to the board of directors of the California Child Care Resource & Referral Network.

"Once I was able to work through my own personal pain and get clarity on that, it really was about Lyman and just his legacy," she said.[5]

* * *

On February 3, 1979, the Angels sent one of Lyman's longtime friends, Kenny Landreaux, to Minnesota as part of a trade that brought Rod Carew to Anaheim. Despite Lyman's absence, the 1979 Angels got off to a fast start, winning twelve of their first fifteen ball games. With Carew joining the mix, the Angels were a run-scoring juggernaut. And with Nolan Ryan and Frank Tanana still anchoring the pitching staff, the Angels could beat anybody they played on any given day. Though they slid some in late April and early May, dropping nine of thirteen contests, the Angels caught fire in late spring, winning six straight from May 15 to May 20 and reeling off twenty-three wins in thirty-six games between May 15 and June 20, building a five-game lead in the American League West. While the race stayed close between California and Kansas City throughout the summer and into the fall, the Angels finally prevailed, clinching the Western Division on Tuesday, September 25, with a 4–1 triumph over the Royals. It was exactly one year and one day since the Angels had lost Lyman Bostock.

"I've seen a lot of bad days my life," said Gene Autry. "This makes up for all the bad times."[6]

"Jim Fregosi did a great job and all the players were tremendous. But I think I'm most happy for the fans. They have been very loyal. We had a lot of trouble last year, including the death of Lyman Bostock," Autry continued. "It's a pity he can't be here."

Though the Angels would eventually fall to the Baltimore Orioles in a hard-fought American League Championship Series, the club's first-ever divisional title was a sign of good days to come. The Angels would claim the Western Division crown again in 1982 and 1986, though they fell short of finally reaching the World Series.

Fans, journalists, and even the California players themselves would be left to ponder how good the Angels could have been in 1979 and into the early 1980s if Lyman Bostock had been in the team's stable of stars. "We won the division the next year, and you add Bostock to that lineup we had in '79, and oh my, it would've been staggering," said Brian Downing.[7]

In the ensuing years, Don Baylor couldn't make his way through the bowels of Comiskey Park without having thoughts of his fallen friend. "Even after all these years, every time I go back to Chicago, I think about him," Baylor would say. "Losing Lyman was a hard one. He was a great player. But losing a friend and a teammate, that was the worst of it."[8]

Baylor would play another decade in the big leagues after 1978, finally reaching the World Series again in 1986 with the Boston Red Sox and then winning it the following year with the Minnesota Twins. Baylor played his entire career in the American League, making trips frequently to Comiskey Park in the years after Lyman's death.

The oldest ballpark in the major leagues at the time of its final game in 1990, the venerable yard at 324 West Thirty-Fifth Street hosted American League baseball for eighty years. But there was no sadder day in the history of Comiskey than the day the White Sox and Angels had to play a ballgame just a few hours after Lyman Bostock was murdered.

"Every time I walk into Comiskey Park, I think of Lyman most of all," said Baylor in his autobiography, *Nothing but the Truth: A Baseball Life*. "Looking back, I wish I had said that one last thing to him before he walked out of that clubhouse forever."

* * *

Paul Hutchins eventually healed up and was able to leave St. Mary's Mercy Hospital in the winter after Lyman was killed. Hutchins too was left with lifelong scars—not only from his brush with death along the rails but from seeing a vibrant young life pass away before his very eyes. "I found the whole experience quite disturbing," Hutchins recalled. "I checked into Lyman Bostock and discovered he was one of those kind of guys that should have lived a whole lot longer. He was involved in private charity work, and seemed to devote a lot of time to kids, especially baseball fans.

"I had heard about how he wanted to give his salary back because he didn't think he earned it. He was a real class act. A true baseball hero. On top of being a great ballplayer whose potential we will never know. I guess God needed him on his team."[9]

In the coming months, there would be even more bad news, both on and off the field. In April 1979, another star ballplayer, former Negro Leagues and Cleveland Indians standout Luke Easter was shot and killed during a botched robbery when he was transporting payroll checks to a bank in Euclid, Ohio. And only a few weeks later, Lyman's old pal with the Twins, Larry Hisle, was playing right field for the Milwaukee Brewers in Baltimore's Memorial Stadium when he felt a weird stinging pain after he released the ball on a throw back into the infield. In a freak injury, Hisle had torn his rotator cuff, and he would never again be the same player. He would play in only twenty-six games in 1978, as he debated whether to have shoulder surgery. From there, Hisle appeared in just fifty-three more games in the major leagues, hitting twelve homers with thirty-two RBIs.

On August 2, 1979, the baseball world was stunned once again when New York Yankees star catcher and captain Thurman Munson died while practicing takeoffs and landings in his personal airplane at the Akron-Canton Regional Airport in Ohio. For the second time in less than a year, the sport was swept up in widespread emotion over the loss of one of the game's greats. In the span of less than a year, two of the brightest stars of the American League had been suddenly and violently taken away.

Shortly thereafter, pitcher Matt Keough lost his spot in the Oakland A's starting rotation after dropping his eighteenth consecutive decision. But Keough had perspective after seeing the recent tragedies befalling two American League stars in the preceding months. "When I look at the thing that happened to Thurman Munson and remember that Lyman Bostock was killed last year, I realize that baseball is an important part of a player's life. But not all his life."[10]

17

LYMAN BOSTOCK'S LEGACY

> Tho' much is taken, much abides. And tho' we are not now that strength which in old days moved earth and heaven, that which we are, we are. One equal temper of heroic hearts, made weak by time and fate, but strong in will to strive, to seek, to find, and not to yield.—
> Alfred Lord Tennyson, *Ulysses*

Nearly forty years have gone by since Lyman Wesley Bostock Jr. was laid to rest on a warm early fall afternoon in Los Angeles. He's been gone more than a decade longer than he lived. The flat, rectangular gravestone can be easily missed among the many celebrity plots at Inglewood Park Cemetery unless one knows where to look. It carries a simple, understated message.

Lyman Wesley Bostock Jr.
Beloved Husband, Son
November 22, 1950–September 24, 1978

On the left-hand side of the stone marker, a batter—a left-handed batter—is taking a mighty swing and makes contact. On the right-hand side lies the California Angels' well-known "A" logo of Lyman's era, with the halo above it.

An entire generation of fans across America have grown up loving the game of baseball—and are now raising children of their own who love the sport—since Lyman was shot and killed by Leonard Smith on a late September Saturday night in Gary, Indiana. Though his story was well-known to those covering and following major league baseball in the late

1970s, the tragedy within the tragedy is that Lyman Bostock isn't remembered by more people in modern times. He is worth remembering for who he was as a person as much as for his abilities on the field. It sounds cliché, but he was an even greater person than he was a player.

Though his exploits on the field would largely pass from the public's consciousness, Lyman's tremendous generosity during his spring 1978 slump wouldn't be forgotten as easily. When Bo Jackson spurned the Tampa Bay Buccaneers and their $7 million offer as the number one overall selection in the 1986 NFL Draft to play baseball with the Kansas City Royals that summer, columnist Gregg Patton of the *San Bernardino County Sun* recalled Bostock's offer to give back his April 1978 salary.

"Today, Bo Jackson is my hero," Patton said in his column of June 22, 1986. "This may be the first time we've been able to say something nice about an athlete and money since the late Lyman Bostock offered to return paychecks to the Angels until he started hitting better."

As far as doing his part in the community and serving as a role model to youths, Lyman Bostock walked the walk, even if he didn't talk the talk. Though he liked to talk about a wide variety of subjects, he wasn't comfortable being singled out or recognized for things he did from the goodness of his heart. This was why he requested the donations from his salary be kept private. For Lyman, it wasn't about the accolades. It was about the act itself.

Unlike so many prima donna athletes of past and present, Lyman was approachable. Fans were warmed by his friendly nature and generous spirit. You won't find any stories of Lyman being rude to a kid or denying someone's autograph request. He took time for his fans, especially young fans. He knew they were the future of the sport he loved so dearly, and he didn't want a single one of them leaving his presence with a negative experience.

He was beloved by most all who came in contact with him because he didn't portray himself as anything more than who he was. He was friendly, enjoyed conversation about a variety of topics, and made people feel good when they talked to him. He was sincere with reporters, but didn't tell them everything. However, those who knew him best had no doubt about Lyman's priorities and his commitment to giving back to the people who helped him make it.

If Lyman hadn't crossed Leonard Smith's path, there's a very good chance he'd still be alive. Lyman was in peak athletic condition at the time of his death. Both of his biological parents lived well into their eighties. Lyman Sr.'s mother, Lilly, also enjoyed a long life, passing away in 1980 at the age of ninety, living to be more than sixty years older than her grandson.

* * *

Would Lyman Bostock have been able to keep up the impressive batting prowess of his first four big league seasons over a much longer career with the Angels? That's one of the more tantalizing questions about Lyman. If he would have been able to build a career around the numbers he posted in 1976, 1977, and the second half of the 1978 season, he truly could have emerged as one of the greatest players of his entire generation.

"He wanted to be one of the great players in the game. He wanted to lead the league in hitting more than me. I think he had a chance to do great things and be a Hall of Famer," said Carew.[1]

"I hate to talk in would've and could've, but he definitely would have gone down as one of this franchise's greatest players," added former Angels teammate Brian Downing.[2]

Lyman didn't play long enough in the major leagues to be universally considered among the game's all-time greats. He only played four full seasons and appeared in just over five hundred big league games—not exactly a long career. He didn't appear in any All-Star Games or playoff games at the major league level. He played only one season in a major media market. Yet the things he accomplished over his short career leave tantalizing "what if" questions that will never be answered.

Lyman's .311 lifetime average would have placed him among the top one hundred hitters in baseball history had he accumulated the necessary 3,000 at bats to qualify. Lyman died with 2,204 official major league at bats. The .311 mark Lyman put up with Minnesota and California from 1975 to 1978 is the exact same lifetime batting average Jackie Robinson posted in his illustrious career with the Brooklyn Dodgers, ahead of numerous Hall of Famers including Luke Appling, Richie Ashburn, Hack Wilson, Paul Molitor, Hank Aaron, and George Brett.

Had Lyman lived, he would have been in a position not only to go down as one of the all-time great California Angels but also to live a long and productive life as an ambassador of baseball. Maybe Lyman would have gone into management, as his old pal Don Baylor and other teammates did. Perhaps he would have become a hitting coach or found some other role in professional baseball, such as the one providing community outreach that his old pal Larry Hisle found working in the Milwaukee Brewers organization. Or maybe he would have spent a happy retirement in Southern California, taking care of his mother and enjoying the children that he and his wife never had a chance to have.

"I still think about him a lot, because he was such a great guy. He was such a great guy in the clubhouse," said Carney Lansford, who would go on to win a batting title with the Boston Red Sox in 1981. "I still miss him tremendously. The things that we used to talk about, just what a great player he was. I thought he was an underrated outfielder as well as such a great hitter."[3]

Annie Bostock would remain in Los Angeles, living out her days reasonably comfortably thanks to the payout from Lyman's contract by the Angels and Yuovene's generosity, who knew Lyman's wish that his mother be taken care of. Though her heart was broken by Lyman's death, Annie would live for nearly thirty more years, eventually relaxing after retiring from her hospital job. She died in January 2005, barely a month after she celebrated her eighty-seventh birthday.

Nearly a half century after he last played in the Negro Leagues, Lyman Bostock Sr. finally received something from Major League Baseball, which had rejected him and most of his contemporaries during their careers. In 1997, MLB approved a plan to provide pensions to approximately ninety living former pro ballplayers. Many had played long careers in the Negro Leagues, mostly prior to 1947, when Jackie Robinson had integrated the game and the players' pension program began.

Approximately eight years later, on a hot late June day in 2005, Lyman Bostock Sr. took his final breath. He outlived his father by more than sixty years, his mother by twenty-five years, and his oldest son and namesake by three months shy of twenty-seven years. He left behind two other sons, as well as numerous friends. While Bostock Sr. was denied the chance to play major league baseball because of the color of his skin, his son was ultimately cheated out of his life and career by a man of his own race. A man who clearly didn't think about the ramifications of his actions. A man who took a life and essentially got away with it. A man who lived alone for most of the rest of his sad life.

* * *

Leonard Smith went back to Gary after his release from Logansport Hospital, and he never again ran afoul of the law. He worked odd jobs, ran a used car lot for a while, went back to school for a time. All the while, he never left the Jackson Street triple-decker apartment that he had run back to after committing his act of cruelty and hatred.

Leonard may not have rotted away in an Indiana prison cell for his misdeeds. He may not have been forced to live with criminals, to adapt to a prison routine, to adjust to a lifetime of incarceration. But with little money and few prospects outside of his hometown, Leonard would find himself trapped in a psychological prison of his own making. How often did his thoughts go back to that night? Did he secretly wish he had made a different choice? Or was he able to suppress it, allowing the years and the memories to fade into the distance? No man can say the thoughts that ran through Leonard's mind, but it's hard to imagine that he was able to get the shooting completely out of his head. He lived a reclusive existence, rarely coming out of his residence in his later years. Leonard Smith passed away on December 17, 2010, at the age of sixty-four, outliving the man he killed by thirty-two years and two months.

"Whatever happens to people's lives, they have to live with themselves. And sometimes that's tougher than any kind of punishment you can ever do out through a court system," said Jim Fregosi for ESPN's *Outside the Lines*.

* * *

Driving into Gary, Indiana, today, it doesn't take long to see that years of neglect and urban flight have taken their toll on this once-proud beacon of American industrial growth. Gary, in so many ways, is a war zone, a casualty of the precipitous decline of America's steel production throughout the last half century. A little over fifty years ago, Gary bustled with over 175,000 residents. It was a crown jewel in what would later become known as the Rust Belt. Many Gary residents of the 1950s and early 1960s considered the town an ideal place to raise a family. The streets were lined with pleasant homes, filled with families supported well by the abundant good-paying jobs that were a staple of the booming American steel industry.

Modern-day Gary is a jigsaw puzzle of middle- and lower-class homes, interspersed with long-abandoned buildings of all kinds. The steel mills huddled around Lake Michigan's southern shoreline still billow plumes of white and grayish-white smoke hundreds of feet into the sky each day, while the casino industry has brought much-needed employment and revenue to the area. But there has been enough necrosis of the soul within Gary's city limits over the last five decades to create a dreadful pall over much of the area. Gary of the early twenty-first century is a cemetery of brick, stone, and concrete. Rows of empty, abandoned townhouses, patches of neglected single-family homes, and an array of gutted public and private buildings of all kinds—including warehouses, strip malls, hospitals, churches, and theaters—tell the story of modern-day Gary.

Gary's population has dipped below 80,000 in recent years—less than half its peak population in the early 1960s. With town officials unable to come up with the necessary funds to raze many of the city's abandoned public buildings, they endure in various stages of decay as white elephants—relics of the city's former glory. Some are boarded up; jagged glass hangs loosely from broken windows in others. Many have become breeding grounds for crimes ranging from burglary to crack smoking. Vandals, addicts, the curious, and teenagers looking for kicks or something to do have stripped most anything of tangible value. Some have graffiti and gang-related imagery spray-painted on them, as various groups mark turf that might have in earlier times hosted happy, healthy, and loving families. Or might have hosted families like Leonard Smith's—broken, angry, violent.

At the intersection of Fifth and Jackson, there is no longer a stoplight. Nor is one needed. Turning right down Jackson Street, one finds a bumpy, unlined asphalt track leading to a row of townhouses. Most of them seem to be occupied, but a handful in the vicinity appear to be abandoned and neglected. There is no longer a Bi-LO store at the intersection. The grocery store that Tom Turner raced into to call an ambulance for his mortally wounded nephew has long since left the corner. A liquor store lies directly in front of the intersection along Fifth Street, heading east toward Monroe Street. Just a few feet farther down the road lies a Family Dollar store, its front windows and doors secured with large wrought iron bars.

Back in the spring of 1978—just weeks before the start of what turned out to be his final season—Lyman had spoken about how liquor stores spread throughout the nation's ghettos were holding back his people. He was trying to work with liquor store owners in some of the worst communities in Los Angeles to donate to his Teen Challengers project.

"I talk to liquor store owners and managers of supermarkets trying to get them to donate money," Lyman said to *Sporting News*. "Liquor stores

The intersection of Fifth and Jackson Streets in Gary, Indiana, where on September 23, 1978, a car carrying Lyman Bostock, his uncle Thomas Turner, Joan Hawkins, and Barbara Smith had a fateful encounter with Leonard Smith, Barbara's estranged husband. (Photo by Adam Powell.)

are responsible for the alcohol problem. They should donate money to help people dry out. It would help the supermarkets to get people off drugs. They go into stores to steal to support their habit. There are little kids sticking needles in their arms."

A vacant lot, filled with chunks of concrete and sporadic patches of grass and weeds, rests to the immediate south of Fifth and Jackson. A building once stood there, but it was torn down a couple years back. Across the street from the intersection sits a three-story yellow brick building. The building, with a small placard at the top stating "Building No. 5," appears completely boarded up along the first floor. An electric marquee has been pulled out, leaving an ambiguous empty metal frame. It might have once held a sign welcoming patrons to a pub or another business, but now there's no way for passersby to know what the building held inside. There is absolutely nothing in this tiny corner of northwest Indiana to identify that a vibrant, talented, young life—one of the bright-

The intersection of Fifth and Jackson no longer has a stoplight, nor does it have any symbol or acknowledgment of the horrific and random events that took place there. (Photo by Adam Powell.)

est stars in baseball—was cruelly and senselessly ended by a man he never met, and probably never saw.

St. Mary's Mercy Hospital was once renowned in the Midwestern medical community as one of the top medical facilities in the region. Its biggest claim to fame was as the site where the members of the Jackson family, including Michael Jackson, were born. Today, the hospital is one of the more glaring and tragic victims of Gary's urban decay. Moving along the outer perimeter of the brick hospital building, a photographer comes across a cornerstone dated 1927. This particular cornerstone represents one of the major renovations of the hospital that enlarged it to more than three hundred beds, making it at the time one of the largest hospitals in the entire Midwest. This part of the building—a five-story all-brick rectangular edifice that upon its completion was one of the finest hospitals in the entire state of Indiana—now lies in a state of ruin.

As the photographer attempts to document the cornerstone, the camera struggles to focus, almost as if the camera itself is ashamed to shoot the building in its present state. The hospital fell into financial trouble in the

After being shot in downtown Gary, Lyman Bostock was rushed to nearby St. Mary's Mercy Hospital, where he passed away in the early morning hours of September 24, 1978. In the two decades since its closing in the mid-1990s, the abandoned hospital has been subjected to neglect, vandalism, and exposure to the elements. (Photo by Adam Powell.)

1960s and was sold and resold multiple times over the next three decades before shutting its doors for good around Thanksgiving 1995, ending nearly a century of medical service to the people of Gary and leaving hundreds of the region's best and brightest unemployed. Most of the exterior windows of the hospital have been busted out, allowing the elements—along with two decades' worth of visitors of all kinds—to ransack the halls and the rooms, like rats eating their way through a garbage bag. There's talk around Gary that feral cats have begun to take over the interior.

Numerous individuals have snuck their way into the old hospital over the years, and some have even documented their experiences online. From scavengers to souvenir hunters, from enterprising photographers to ghost chasers, St. Mary's Mercy Hospital still fascinates a wide range of individuals more than twenty years after treating its last patient and delivering its last baby. Looking in from the outside, one can still see sinks, mirrors, and clocks adorning the walls. Medical equipment still sits in some of the patient rooms and offices. Outside, shrubs and small trees grow everywhere that isn't concrete, taller and taller as time passes.

One side doorway—ironically labeled the "New Life Center" by a small placard still hanging above the door—has been boarded up with several sheets of plywood. The emergency room entrance, where the unresponsive body of Lyman Bostock was wheeled in, has also been boarded shut, forcing potential intruders to find other locations to sneak into the building.

Gary's police department currently uses a newer section of the hospital that was completed in the mid-1970s. As the photographer walks around the perimeter of the decaying hospital, an armed Gary police officer, wearing a bulletproof vest and camouflage military-style pants, approaches. "What are you doing?" the officer asks incredulously.

"Just taking some pictures of the old hospital for a project," says the photographer.

Seemingly satisfied with the response, the officer continues on his way into the police building without comment. Moving farther down the side of the complex, one can look up and identify a pair of crosses on either side of the former main entrance—giving the building an air of dignity and deity despite its decay. The powers that be in Gary don't have the resources to raze the building, so it will continue to sit, reminding anyone who passes of the way things once were in Gary and just how far the area has fallen.

* * *

There aren't too many happy endings in the Lyman Bostock story, but one silver lining was the institution of the Lyman Bostock Memorial Scholarship on the campus of Cal State Northridge, which to this day provides scholarships for Matadors baseball players with financial need.

Another was the institution of stiffer laws in the state of Indiana for those who commit violent crimes. No longer was there a loophole that would let cold-blooded killers like Leonard Smith walk the streets a couple of years after claiming temporary insanity.

But those are very small consolations when considering what was lost. For Lyman Bostock, it wasn't enough simply to be a great ballplayer, even if that was probably the man's greatest single obsession. Few people in history willed themselves into greatness in major league baseball quite the same way Lyman had.

"In all the years that I've managed, I don't know of a player who was any more desirous of being a complete baseball player than Lyman Bostock," Gene Mauch said of his star outfielder in 1976, the day after he hit for the cycle against the Chicago White Sox. "He is bound and determined to be the best ballplayer there is."[4]

But Lyman wanted just as much to be respected by his teammates for the way he carried himself on and off the field. He genuinely cared about his relationships with his teammates. It was important for him that his teammates trusted and revered him. And to a man, they did.

"When I finish my career I want them to say, 'He was one of the best hitters who ever played baseball, but he was a team player,'" Lyman had once said.[5]

"Everyone knows what kind of hitter Lyman was," said Angels reliever Dave LaRoche. "But he helped us off the field, too. We all admired him. We didn't have much time to get to know him, but we all admired him."[6]

The question of why Lyman was killed looms large in this story. After all, it was one of the more senseless and tragic acts to ever befall anyone anywhere in history. An entirely innocent man caught in the crossfire of other people's troubles. "How many millions of people will always want to know why?" said Paul Hutchins, the man who witnessed Lyman's final moments on earth.[7]

At the end of the day, the question simply can't be answered. It never will be answered. There's no possible way to ever understand it. Nobody can rationally explain how such a beautifully gifted and well-spoken man could be living his young, adventurous life in one instant and then be gone in the blink of an eye. It's too easy to blame guns or insanity or any number of things for why Leonard Smith did what he did, but what can probably be agreed by anyone who understands the circumstances of September 23, 1978, is that it was an act of jealousy.

Leonard was jealous of his wife for leaving him on her terms—having gotten the upper hand. He was jealous of the freedom that allowed her to defy him in such a way. He was jealous that she was moving on with her life. Instead of moving on himself—instead of finding a way to put aside his pride and leave his wife to live a new life without him—Leonard chose to fire a gun spontaneously into a parked car.

No, the why will never be fully answered.

The secrets of the past died with Leonard. As the years went by and he lived in the daily shackles of self-imposed seclusion, perhaps Leonard himself couldn't explain why he pulled the trigger that night. Maybe that's why he couldn't face those that raised the subject, the journalists who made admirable efforts in Leonard's final years to get his story.

In the end, the real concern as one looks back on the life and times of Lyman Bostock isn't why. What the man accomplished deserves significantly more recognition than it's gotten over the years. His legacy deserves serious examination by true students of baseball. Nothing will ever bring Lyman Bostock back, but he deserves to be remembered as a great player, a great teammate, and a decent human being.

"It happened because it was meant to be. And it was just the way it was meant to be," said Bob Hiegert.[8]

In his famous poem, "Stopping by Woods on a Snowy Evening," Robert Frost pondered his mortality, challenging it to keep its distance: "The woods are lovely, dark, and deep, but I have promises to keep, and miles to go before I sleep," Frost wrote.

In the end, Lyman Bostock had made it out of the woods, lovely, dark, and deep. He had gotten himself back on track as one of the outstanding ballplayers in the American League by the early fall of 1978. There were promises he intended to keep, but sleep came way too soon for him to keep those promises. So others kept them for him, preserving his memory and legacy for years to come through his scholarship fund.

Lyman Bostock will never grow old. He will always be the young, effervescent superstar. The high-spirited guy with the silly laugh and the big, friendly smile on his face. He may not have had time to become a Hall of Famer, but he will always be remembered as an elite ballplayer, having died during his peak. Age never had a chance to catch up to Lyman. At the same time, how much would anyone give to reverse the past—to stop what happened from happening? To give Lyman a chance to live the long, happy life he deserved?

Nothing can change the past, of course. But in Lyman Bostock's case, that's not entirely a bad thing. His is a glorious past of baseball excellence, as well as a solid track record of helping others in his community with his time as well as his money. And in the final analysis, when one looks at Lyman's entire life, the sum of what he did on and off the baseball field vastly outweigh the extraordinary circumstances of his death.

NOTES

1. CALIFORNIA DREAMING (1950–1968)

1. Greeley, *New York Tribune*, July 13, 1865.
2. Rinaldi and Barr, "Tragedy of Lyman Bostock."
3. Dilbeck, "Time is right for California's Bostock," D(1).
4. Jacobson, "Twin outfielder Lyman chip off old Bostock."
5. Galvin, "Bostock was to visit Melbourne uncle."
6. Connaughton, "Lyman Bostock."
7. Ringolsby, "Bostock dips into Autry's saddlebags for $3.2 million."
8. "Angels give Bostock $3 million contract."
9. Fowler, "Bostock bat brings out grins on Twins."
10. Fowler, "Bostock bat brings out grins on Twins."
11. Author's interview with Bob Hiegert.
12. Pearlman, "Fifth and Jackson."
13. "Angels mourn a good man."
14. Briere, "Bostock says he's always been a winner."
15. Nigro, "Twins' Bostock, at .330, still faces anonymity."
16. Gustkey, "Bostock gave something back to his community," C(1).
17. Author's interview with Bob Hiegert.
18. Gustkey, "Bostock gave something back to his community," C(1).
19. Jacobson, "Twin outfielder Lyman chip off old Bostock."
20. Nigro, "Twins' Bostock, at .330, still faces anonymity."
21. Gustkey, "Bostock gave something back to his community," C(1).

2. COMING OF AGE IN TIMES OF CONFUSION (1968–1970)

1. King, "I've Been to the Mountaintop."
2. Author's interview with Bob Hiegert.
3. Nigro, "Twins' Bostock, at .330, still faces anonymity."
4. Pearlman, "Fifth and Jackson."
5. Ritter and Wertz, "Valley state demonstrators hold building for four hours."
6. "Students with knives hold officials prisoner."
7. "Teachers tell of takeover by blacks at Calif. college."
8. "College president rejects agreement."
9. Ritter and Wertz, "Valley State demonstrators hold building for four hours."
10. "3 Students in takeover supported."
11. "San Fernando State faculty tells of actions by militant students."
12. Pearlman, "Fifth and Jackson."

3. NEW DECISIONS, NEW OPPORTUNITIES (1971–1972)

1. Harry Edwards quote found on www.goodreads.com/quotes/161952-we-must-teach-our-children-to-dream-with-their-eyes.
2. Author's interview with Bob Hiegert.
3. Gustkey, "Bostock gave something back to his community," 5.
4. Nadel, "Bostock funeral slated Thursday."
5. Nigro, "Twins' Bostock, at .330, still faces anonymity."
6. "Carew has team rival."
7. Mazzeo, "Bostock takes Angel riches."

4. THE PATH TO THE BIG LEAGUES (1972–1974)

1. Arthur Ashe quote found on www.brainyquote.com/quotes/authors/a/arthur_ashe.html.
2. Author's interview with Bob Hiegert.
3. Gault, "First game is toughest."
4. Hartman, "Griffith: Charlotte isn't baseball town."
5. Dilbeck, "Landreaux sets aside grief to help Angels win."
6. Jacobson, "Twin outfielder Lyman chip off old Bostock."
7. Briere, "Bostock says he's always been a winner," 2(C).

8. "Griffith won't move despite gate slump."
9. Richman, "Nothing phony about Bostock."
10. Kellogg, "Haines surprised, pleased in Tucson."
11. "Carew has team rival."
12. Kallestad, "Twins looking for help."

5. A ROOKIE'S JOURNEY (1975)

1. Ted Williams quote found at www.brainyquote.com/quotes/authors/t/ted_williams.html.
2. Richman, "Nothing phony about Bostock."
3. Richman, "Nothing phony about Bostock."
4. Briere, "Twins may keep rookie catcher, send Roof to bullpen as coach."
5. Associated Press, March 31, 1975.
6. "Bostock's death leaves his friends sad, bewildered."
7. Libman, "Ex-mates mourn 'Mr. Logic's' death."
8. Briere, "Bostock says he's always been a winner," 2(C).
9. Kallestad, "Injured Twins rookie ready to play."
10. Briere, "Twins get moral victory, lose 7–3."
11. Briere, "Quilici: We were in no position to stand around on damp field."
12. Kallestad, "Injured Twins rookie ready to play."
13. Anderson, "Why Bostock spurned Yanks, Mets."
14. Libman, "Rain halts Twins game."
15. "Bostock quits griping, sparks Twins victory."
16. "Twins' Bostock breaks up games instead of bones."
17. "Carew has team rival."
18. Fowler, "Twin Bostock aims for five-star rank."
19. "Twins clip Royals."
20. Bostock quits griping, sparks Twins victory."
21. "Twins clip Royals."
22. Libman, "Baseball."

6. THE GREAT BREAKOUT (1976)

1. Lou Brock quote found at www.brainyquote.com/quotes/authors/l/lou_brock.html.
2. Nigro, "Twins' Bostock, at .330, still faces anonymity."
3. "Lowly Montreal Expos clean out their house."

4. Kallestad, "Mauch plans to open camp with a clean slate."
5. Fowler, "Twin Bostock aims for five-star rank."
6. Greene, "Hunter has rude awakening."
7. Kallestad, "Twins outslug Brewers."
8. Libman, "Baseball."
9. "Twins' Bostock sparkles in club's 5–3 victory."
10. "Bert Blyleven is the key player in a six-man trade."
11. Cullum, "Bostock goes all out."
12. "Aging Oliva rises to occasion."
13. "Carew has team rival."
14. Kallestad, "Indians hold off Twins 7–6 at Met."
15. Jacobson, "Twin outfielder Lyman chip off old Bostock."
16. Jacobson, "Twin outfielder Lyman chip off old Bostock."
17. Fowler, "Twin Bostock aims for five-star rank."
18. Author's interview with Bob Hiegert.
19. Hawkins, "Tiger rivals beg to see the bird."
20. Briere, "Bostock, Twins clobber Chicago 17–2."
21. Libman, "Rain halts Twins game," C(1).
22. Libman, "Baseball."
23. Hartman, "Bostock almost quit."
24. Libman, "Rain halts Twins game."
25. "Lyman Bostock hits for the team."
26. "Twins' Bostock breaks up games instead of bones."
27. "Twins' Bostock breaks up games instead of bones."
28. Barnard, "Bostock has perfect night in Twins 3–1 win."
29. "Carew has team rival."
30. "Twins."
31. "Bostock bottles Texas, 3–1."
32. "Twins' Bostock breaks up games instead of bones."
33. "Bostock powers Twins to win."
34. "Tanana twirls Angels to 4–1 win over Twins."

7. SOMETHING TO PROVE (1977)

1. Rod Carew quote found at www.brainyquote.com/quotes/authors/r/rod_carew.html.
2. Fowler, "All fans alike, Oliva learns—they want winner."
3. Kallestad, "Down to the wire."
4. "Bostock wants to sign pact."
5. "Bostock wants contract before season opens."

6. Ringolsby, "Bostock a troubled star in Minnesota."
7. "Bostock, Twins stage meeting."
8. Ostler, "Bostock wants to play like million dollars."
9. "Bostock will play out option."
10. "Bostock moving on?"
11. "Bostock rejects Twins offer."
12. "Bostock, Carew work over KC."
13. Libman, "Ex-mates mourn Mr. Logic's death."
14. "Carew has team rival."
15. "Twins bury Rangers, 11–4."
16. Barnard, "Twins smother Twins Friday."
17. "Twins to lose star outfielder."
18. "View from both sides of the combat zone."
19. "Bostock makes record 13th catch a souvenir for lucky bleacher fan."
20. Kallestad, "Twins, Johnson 'walked' into win over Yankees."
21. "Twins seem to feast on Red Sox pitching."
22. "Gene burns as Sox win."
23. "Twins stand to lose a lot."
24. "New player agent blossoms."
25. Weir, "The man who turns hits into millions."
26. "New player agent blossoms."
27. "Pennant buying is still impossible."
28. Ringolsby, "Bostock a troubled star in Minnesota."
29. Kallestad, "Down to the wire."
30. "Rod boosts mark to .395 in 12–2 rout."
31. McKenzie, "Rod Carew Profile."
32. "Sorenson cools Twins, Carew up to .411."

8. SETTLING INTO STARDOM (1977)

1. Curt Flood quote found at www.brainyquote.com/quotes/quotes/c/curt-flood298796.html.
2. "Twins aren't identical."
3. Ringolsby, "Bostock a troubled star in Minnesota."
4. Ostler, "Bostock wants to play like a million dollars."
5. "Bostock a cancer—Griffith."
6. Kelley, *Voices from the Negro Leagues*, 65.
7. "Brett beats Twins for first Angels win."
8. Kallestad, "Goltz escaping the shadows to become Twins mound star."
9. Greene, "Bostock rips every strike Kaycee offers."

10. "Twin hurlers check Kansas City hitters."
11. Greene, "Bostock rips every strike Kaycee offers."
12. "Twin hurlers check Kansas City hitters."
13. "Carew four-for-five in Twins win."
14. Linkugel and Pappas, *They Tasted Glory*, 221.
15. Vincent, "A trip to remember—Tigers, Sally Rand, and 15,000 miles."
16. Penner, "Remembering Lyman Bostock," 1.
17. "Bostock knocks in three runs to spark Twins win."
18. Boswell, "Praise pours in—too late for Bostock."
19. "Twins have cash to sign players."
20. "Sweet swinging Carew heading for sixth title."

9. A LIFE-CHANGING NEGOTIATION
(1977 OFF-SEASON)

1. Autry, "1979: Family."
2. Anderson, "Why Bostock spurned Yanks, Mets."
3. "Twins stars prove very popular."
4. Linkugel and Pappas, *They Tasted Glory*, 221.
5. "Kuhn sounds warning."
6. "Baseball's re-entry draft draws mixed feelings."
7. LaHammer, "Griffith planning to continue talks."
8. LaHammer, "Twins covet Hisle, Bostock."
9. "Bostock, Hisle, Torrez tops on free agent shopping list."
10. "Bostock top target in free agent draft."
11. Ringolsby, "Bostock a troubled star in Minnesota."
12. "Angels pluck prize Bostock."
13. "Free baseball agents seeking glory money."
14. Mazzeo, "Bostock newest Angel millionaire."
15. "Twins owner holding firm on Mauch compensation."
16. Weir, "The man who turns hits into millions."
17. Weir, "The man who turns hits into millions."
18. Dilbeck, "Time is right for California's Bostock," D(1).
19. Libman, "Bostock humble despite star's salary."
20. Schrader, "Peanuts for the media, dollar bills for Bostock," C(1).
21. "Angels sign Lyman Bostock."
22. "Angels sign Lyman Bostock."
23. Ringolsby, "Bostock dips into Autry's saddlebags for $3.2 million."
24. Schrader, "Peanuts for the media, dollar bills for Bostock," C(2).
25. Ostler, "Bostock wants to play like a million dollars."

26. Chass, "Baseball owners spent more on free agents."
27. Ringolsby, "Bostock dips into Autry's saddlebags for $3.2 million."
28. Schrader, "Peanuts for the media, dollar bills for Bostock," C(2).

10. THE BIG SLUMP (1978)

1. Miller, "Lyman's pie in the sky proves to be Angel food."
2. Miller, "Lyman's pie in the sky proves to be Angel food."
3. Ringolsby, "Bostock dips into Autry's saddlebags for $3.2 million."
4. "Angels to wear black armbands; charges filed."
5. Ostler, "Bostock wants to play like a million dollars."
6. "Bostock's slump finally over."
7. Author's interview with Bob Hiegert.
8. Dilbeck, "Time is right for California's Bostock," D(2).
9. Miller, "Lyman's pie in the sky proves to be Angel food."
10. "Carew viewed by Autry as link to A.L. pennant."
11. Dilbeck, "Time is right for California's Bostock," D(2).
12. Author's interview with Dick Enberg.
13. Swift, "Remembering the great Lyman Bostock."
14. Ostler, "Brett stymies Twins, Carew in 5-hitter, 3–0."
15. "Bostock rebounds from slump."
16. Boswell, "Praise pours in—too late for Bostock."
17. Libman, "Ex-mates mourn 'Mr. Logic's' death."
18. "Bostock offers to refuse April salary from Angels."
19. Bragg, "Free agent $$ or a winner? Trammell hedges, leans."
20. "Bostock rebounds from slump."
21. Linkugel and Pappas, *They Tasted Glory*, 222.
22. Richman, "Bostock's offer legitimate, but Autry won't withold pay."
23. Damergis, "Remembering Lyman Bostock."
24. "Bostock insists: Salary to charity."
25. "Bostock makes good on promise."
26. Kelley, *Voices from the Negro Leagues*, 66.
27. "Tigers club slump-ridden Angels, 10–2."
28. "Tigers top millionaire Angels."
29. "Angel notes."
30. Saylor, "Sports people."
31. "New blood pumps White Sox."

11. REDEMPTION AND HAPPINESS (1978)

1. Nolan Ryan quote found at www.brainyquote.com/quotes/authors/n/nolan_ryan.html.
2. "Gene Autry says no to future free agents."
3. "Fregosi replaces Angels' Garcia."
4. Dilbeck, "Fregosi Motivated to Motivate."
5. "Bostock's slump finally over."
6. "Bostock's slump finally over."
7. "Once ready to donate his salary, Bostock rediscovers batting stroke."
8. "Bostock leads Angels over Yanks."
9. "Fregosi makes losing debut."
10. Richman, "Bostock's offer legitimate, but Autry won't withhold pay."
11. "Once ready to donate his salary, Bostock rediscovers batting stroke."
12. "Bostock's slump finally over."
13. "Bat does talking for Angels' Bostock."
14. Dilbeck, "Bostock Earns Keep in Angel Win."
15. Libman, "Baseball."
16. "Twins defeat Rangers 3–1."
17. "Bostock's slump finally over."
18. "AL West lead close."
19. Hill, "Reports on big brothers of Orange County."
20. "Bat does talking for Angels' Bostock."
21. "Bat does talking for Angels' Bostock."
22. Dilbeck, "Angels split twin bill."
23. "Bostock, Rudi earn their pay as Angels."
24. "Once ready to donate his salary, Bostock rediscovers batting stroke."
25. "Angel notes."
26. "Once ready to donate his salary, Bostock rediscovers batting stroke."
27. "Fergie 3-hits Angels, 1–0."
28. "Count 'em: 1, 2, 3, 4, 5, 6, 7, 8, 9, 10, 11, 12, 13."
29. "Digest."
30. Dilbeck, "California has a brawl beating Royals 4–3," D(5).
31. Libman, "Ex-mates mourn 'Mr. Logic's' death."
32. Author's interview with Bob Hiegert.
33. Author's interview with Dick Enberg.
34. Penner, "Remembering Lyman Bostock."

12. ANOTHER DAY IN COMISKEY AND GARY (SEPTEMBER 23, 1978)

1. "Baseball dazed at death of Angels' star Bostock."
2. Gutman, *Baseball Babylon*.
3. Goldman, *Once They Were Angels*, 135.
4. Allen and Armour, *Pitching, Defense, and Three-Run Homers*, 137.
5. Damergis, "Remembering Lyman Bostock."
6. Pearlman, "Fifth and Jackson."
7. Costas, *Lyman Bostock Story*.
8. "Bostock innocent victim of senseless shooting."
9. Ulman, "Bostock 'happy' before last game."
10. "Memory of Bostock lingers—eight months later, Turner mourns death."
11. "Baseball dazed at death of Angels' star Bostock."
12. Pearlman, "Fifth and Jackson."
13. Rinaldi and Barr, "Tragedy of Lyman Bostock."
14. Pearlman, "Fifth and Jackson."

13. PASSING INTO LEGEND

1. Author's interview with Paul Hutchins.
2. Costas, *Lyman Bostock Story*.
3. Goldman, *Once They Were Angels*, 135.
4. Penner, "Remembering Lyman Bostock."
5. Pearlman, "Fifth and Jackson."
6. Goldman, *Once They Were Angels*, 135.
7. Newhan, "Angel tears, kind words for Lyman," 1.
8. Author's interview with Dick Enberg.
9. Author's interview with Bob Hiegert.

14. SAYING GOODBYE (SEPTEMBER 24–28, 1978)

1. Goldman, *Once They Were Angels*, 135.
2. Goldman, *Once They Were Angels*, 135.
3. "Players shocked over Bostock's murder."
4. Newhan, "Angel tears, kind words for Lyman."
5. "Players shocked over Bostock's murder."

6. "Players shocked over Bostock's murder."
7. Gleason, "Bostock's death a waste."
8. Newhan, "Angel tears, kind words for Lyman."
9. Goldman, *Once They Were Angels*, 135.
10. Linkugel and Pappas, *They Tasted Glory*, 223.
11. "Players shocked over Bostock's murder."
12. Goldman, *Once They Were Angels*, 135.
13. Gutman, *Baseball Babylon*, 65.
14. Linkugel and Pappas, *They Tasted Glory*, 224.
15. "Ford's homer stalls Royals."
16. Linkugel and Pappas, *They Tasted Glory*, 224.
17. "Hisle, Bostock like brothers."
18. Linkugel and Pappas, *They Tasted Glory*, 224.
19. Newhan, "Bostock: Angels wanted a person."
20. Damergis, "Remembering Lyman Bostock."
21. "Tough day for Angels."
22. Goldman, *Once They Were Angels*, 135.
23. Hutchins, "A chilling account of Lyman Bostock's death."
24. "Letters—Bostock's death."
25. "Bostock to be buried today."
26. Dilbeck, "Landreaux sets aside grief to help Angels win."
27. "Lyman Bostock buried."
28. "Lyman Bostock buried."
29. Bayless, "Bostock funeral—800 pay their final respects."

15. THE TRIALS OF LEONARD SMITH (1979)

1. Aeschylus, *Agamemnon*, cited at www.bartleby.com/73/1995.html.
2. Green and Secter, "Bostock just 'in the wrong place.'"
3. Ulman, "Bostock 'happy' before last game."
4. "Suspect charged in Bostock case."
5. Ulman, "Bostock 'happy' before last game."
6. "Angels Bostock shot, killed while visiting in Gary."
7. "Innocent victim Bostock dead."
8. Rinaldi and Barr, "The Tragedy of Lyman Bostock."
9. "Bostock case goes to jury."
10. "Bostock case goes to jury."
11. "3 with Bostock didn't see gun, trial told."
12. "Deadlocked jury creates mistrial in Bostock case."
13. Rinaldi and Barr, "The Tragedy of Lyman Bostock."

14. "Baseball star's killer leaves state hospital."
15. Hutchins, "A chilling account of Lyman Bostock's death."
16. Costas, *The Lyman Bostock Story*.

16. MOVING ON (1979–1980S)

1. "Memory of Bostock lingers—eight months later, Turner mourns death."
2. Johnson, "You don't want to believe it happened."
3. Author's interview with Bob Hiegert.
4. "Bostock memorial called off as pro baseball begs off."
5. Costas, *The Lyman Bostock Story*.
6. "Autry's long agony ends."
7. Penner, "Remembering Lyman Bostock."
8. Goldman, *Once They Were Angels*, 135.
9. Hutchins, "A chilling account of Lyman Bostock's death."
10. "Keough suffers 18th loss in row."

17. LYMAN BOSTOCK'S LEGACY

1. Rinaldi and Barr, "The Tragedy of Lyman Bostock."
2. Penner, "Remembering Lyman Bostock."
3. Damergis, "Remembering Lyman Bostock."
4. Cullum, "Bostock goes all out."
5. "Carew has team rival."
6. Newhan, "Angel tears, kind words for Lyman."
7. Author's interview with Paul Hutchins.
8. Author's interview with Bob Hiegert.

BIBLIOGRAPHY

"3 students in takeover supported." *Valley News*, November 29, 1968, 27.
"3 with Bostock didn't see gun, trial told." *Indianapolis Star*, July 11, 1979, 6.
Aeschylus, *Agamemnon*. In *Three Greek Plays*, translated by Edith Hamilton. New York: W. W. Norton, 1937. Cited on www.bartleby.com/73/1995.html .
"Aging Oliva rises to occasion." Associated Press, June 29, 1976.
Allen, Malcolm, and Mark Armour. *Pitching, Defense, and Three-Run Homers: The 1970 Baltimore Orioles*. Lincoln, Neb.: University of Nebraska Press, 2012.
"AL West lead closes." Associated Press, July 2, 1978.
Anderson, Dave. "Why Bostock spurned Yanks, Mets." *New York Times*, March 7, 1978, 28.
"Angel notes." *San Bernardino Sun-Telegram*, May 4, 1978, D(2).
"Angels Bostock shot, killed while visiting in Gary." Associated Press, September 25, 1978.
"Angels give Bostock $3 million contract." United Press International, November 22, 1977.
"Angels mourn a good man." Associated Press, September 25, 1978.
"Angels pluck prize Bostock." Associated Press, November 22, 1977.
"Angels sign Lyman Bostock." United Press International, November 22, 1977.
"Angels to wear black armbands; charges filed." Associated Press, September 26, 1978.
Autry, Gene. "1979: Family." *Baseball's Seasons* (Season 1, Episode 8), MLB Network (MLB Productions), November 18, 2009.
"Autry's long agony ends." United Press International, September 25, 1978.
Barnard, William. "Twins smother Twins Friday." Associated Press, April 24, 1977.
Barnard, William R. "Bostock has perfect night in Twins 3–1 win." Associated Press, September 9, 1976.
"Baseball dazed at death of Angels' star Bostock." Associated Press, September 25, 1978.
"Baseball star's killer leaves state hospital." United Press International, June 20, 1980.
"Baseball's re-entry draft draws mixed feelings." Associated Press, November 2, 1977.
"Bat does talking for Angels' Bostock." Associated Press, August 3, 1978.
Bayless, Skip. "Bostock funeral—800 pay their final respects." *Los Angeles Times*, September 29, 1978, 3(8).
"Bert Blyleven is the key player in a six-man trade." Associated Press, June 2, 1976.
"Bostock a cancer—Griffith." Associated Press, July 14, 1977.
"Bostock bottles Texas, 3–1." *Irving Daily News*, September 9, 1976, 18.
"Bostock, Carew work over KC." Associated Press, April 19, 1977.
"Bostock case goes to jury." Associated Press, July 13, 1979.
"Bostock, Hisle, Torrez tops on free agent shopping list." Associated Press, November 5, 1977.
"Bostock innocent victim of senseless shooting." Associated Press, September 25, 1978.
"Bostock insists: Salary to charity." United Press International, May 1, 1978.

"Bostock knocks in three runs to spark Twins win." Associated Press, August 22, 1977.
"Bostock leads Angels over Yanks." Associated Press, June 12, 1978.
"Bostock makes good on promise." United Press International, May 1, 1978.
"Bostock makes record 13th catch a souvenir for lucky bleacher fan." *Minneapolis Tribune*, May 27, 1977, 3(C).
"Bostock memorial called off as pro baseball begs off." *Los Angeles Times*, February 9, 1985. http://articles.latimes.com/1985-02-09/sports/sp-4165_1_bostock-memorial.
"Bostock moving on?," Associated Press, April 9, 1977.
"Bostock offers to refuse April salary from Angels." Associated Press, April 20, 1978.
"Bostock powers Twins to win." Associated Press, September 22, 1976.
"Bostock quits griping, sparks Twins victory." Associated Press, July 29, 1975.
"Bostock rebounds from slump." Associated Press, August 22, 1978.
"Bostock rejects Twins offer." Associated Press, April 9, 1977.
"Bostock, Rudi earn their pay as Angels." United Press International, August 16, 1978.
"Bostock to be buried today." Associated Press, September 28, 1978.
"Bostock top target in free agent draft." Associated Press, November 5, 1977.
"Bostock, Twins stage meeting." Associated Press, March 28, 1977.
"Bostock wants contract before season opens." Associated Press, March 26, 1977.
"Bostock wants to sign pact." Associated Press, March 26, 1977.
"Bostock will play out option," United Press International, April 9, 1977.
"Bostock's death leaves his friends sad, bewildered." Associated Press, September 25, 1978.
"Bostock's slump finally over," Associated Press, June 13, 1978.
Boswell, Thomas. "Praise pours in—too late for Bostock." *Washington Post*, September 26, 1978, E(1).
Bragg, Brian. "Free agent $$ or a winner? Trammell hedges, leans." *Detroit Free Press*, January 25, 1980, 4(D).
"Brett beats Twins for first Angels win." Associated Press, July 23, 1977.
Briere, Tom. "Bostock says he's always been a winner." *Minneapolis Tribune*, April 8, 1975, C(1).
———. "Bostock, Twins clobber Chicago 17–2." *Minneapolis Tribune*, July 25, 1976, 1(C).
———. "Quilici: We were in no position to stand around on damp field." *Minneapolis Tribune*, April 28, 1975, 2(C).
———. "Twins get moral victory, lose 7–3." *Minneapolis Tribune*, April 16, 1975, 3(C).
———. "Twins may keep rookie catcher, send Roof to bullpen as coach." *Minneapolis Tribune*, March 21, 1975, 6(C).
Caray, Harry. Twins vs. White Sox. WSNS-TV Channel 44, September 21, 1976. http://mediaburn.org/video/sox-reel-3.
"Carew four-for-five in Twins win." Associated Press, August 8, 1977.
"Carew has team rival." United Press International, August 13, 1976.
"Carew viewed by Autry as link to A.L. pennant." United Press International, February 5, 1979.
Chass, Murray. "Baseball owners spent more on free agents." *New York Times News Service*, January 31, 1978.
"College president rejects agreement." Associated Press, November 5, 1968.
Connaughton, Tim. "Lyman Bostock." Society for American Baseball Research. http://sabr.org/bioproj/person/9bb77e84.
Costas, Bob, narrator. *The Lyman Bostock Story*. Documentary film, 22 minutes. Produced by MLB Network, 2013.
"Count 'em: 1, 2, 3, 4, 5, 6, 7, 8, 9, 10, 11, 12, 13." Associated Press, September 16, 1978.
Cullum, Dick. "Bostock coming." *Minneapolis Tribune*, August 28, 1975, 3(D).
———. "Bostock goes all out." *Minneapolis Tribune*, July 26, 1976, C(2).
———. "Oakland sweeps two from Twins." *Minneapolis Tribune*, April 21, 1975, 1(C).
Damergis, Mike. "Remembering Lyman Bostock." YouTube video, 3:59. September 21, 2013. https://www.youtube.com/watch?v=MPueMaRUB90.
"Deadlocked jury creates mistrial in Bostock case." Associated Press, July 14, 1979.
"Digest." *St. Louis Post Dispatch*, September 18, 1978, 2(B).

BIBLIOGRAPHY

DiGiovanna, Mike. "Mad man is now a mild man: Colorful reliever Hrabosky becomes Cardinal color analyst." *Los Angeles Times*, July 15, 1992. http://articles.latimes.com/1992-07-15/sports/sp-3976_1_color-analyst.
Dilbeck, Steve. "Angels fire Garcia, bring back Fregosi." *San Bernardino Sun-Telegram*, June 2, 1978, D(1).
———. "Angels split twin bill." *San Bernardino Sun-Telegram*, August 6, 1978, D(1).
———. "Bostock earns keep in Angel win." *San Bernardino Sun-Telegram*, August 3, 1978, D(1).
———. "California fans not angelic." *San Bernardino Sun-Telegram*, May 30, 1978, B(8).
———. "California gas a brawl beating Royals 4–3." *San Bernardino Sun-Telegram*, September 17, 1978, D(1), D(5).
———. "Fregosi motivated to motivate." *San Bernardino Sun-Telegram*, June 3, 1978, C(2).
———. "Landreaux sets aside grief to help Angels win." *San Bernardino Sun-Telegram*, September 27, 1978, D(1).
———. "Time is right for California's Bostock." *San Bernardino (California) Sun-Telegram*, March 22, 1978, D(1–2).
Dozer, Richard. "Angels' win still a loss." *Chicago Tribune*, September 25, 1978, 5(4).
Durso, Joseph. "44 players are drafted—Yankees and Mets have 13 in common." *New York Times*, November 5, 1977, 15–18.
"Fergie 3-hits Angels, 1–0." Associated Press, September 12, 1978.
"Ford's homer stalls Royals." Associated Press, September 25, 1978.
Fowler, Bob. "All fans alike, Oliva learns—they want winner." *Sporting News*, February 26, 1977, 46.
———. "Bostock bat brings out grins on Twins." *Sporting News*, April 5, 1975, 40.
———. "Twin Bostock aims for five-star rank." *Sporting News*, July 3, 1976, 13.
Fox, Doug. "This day in 1978, Van Halen supposedly parachutes into Anaheim stadium & Eddie meets Sammy Hagar!" *Van Halen News Desk*. September 23, 2014. http://www.vhnd.com/2014/09/23/van-halen-parachutes-into-anaheim-stadium-eddie-meets-sammy-hagar/.
"Free baseball agents seeking glory money." Associated Press, November 16, 1977.
"Fregosi makes losing debut." Associated Press, June 3, 1978.
"Fregosi moves into game of musical chairs." Associated Press, June 3, 1978.
"Fregosi replaces Angels' Garcia." Associated Press, June 2, 1978.
Galvin, Terry. "Bostock was to visit Melbourne uncle." *Florida Today*, September 27, 1978, 2(B).
Gault, Earl. "First game is toughest." *Spartanburg Herald-Journal*, June 20, 1972.
"Gene Autry says no to future free agents." United Press International, June 21, 1978.
"Gene burns as Sox win." Associated Press, June 7, 1977.
Gleason, Bill. "Bostock's death a waste." *Chicago Sun-Times*, September 26, 1978.
———. "Why? Bostock becomes victim of a gun-toting nation." *Chicago Sun-Times*, September 25, 1978.
Goldman, Robert. *Once They Were Angels*. Champaign, Ill.: Sports Publishing, 2006.
Green, Larry, and Bob Secter. "Bostock just 'in the wrong place.'" *Los Angeles Times*, September 25, 1978, C(2).
Greene, Bob. "Bostock rips every strike Kaycee offers." Associated Press, August 2, 1977.
———. "Hunter has rude awakening." Associated Press, April 19, 1976.
"Griffith won't move despite gate slump." Associated Press, June 2, 1974.
Gustkey, Earl. "Bostock gave something back to his community." *Los Angeles Times*, September 26, 1978, C(1, 6).
Gutman, Dan. *Baseball Babylon: From the Black Sox to Pete Rose, the Real Stories behind the Scandals that Rocked the Game*. New York: Penguin, 1992.
Hartman, Sid. "Bostock almost quit." *Minneapolis Tribune*, July 30, 1976, 2(C).
———. "Griffith: Charlotte isn't baseball town." *Minneapolis Tribune*, June 12, 1998, C(3).
———. "Old timers hit." *Minneapolis Tribune*, July 17, 1976, 2(B).
Hawkins, Jim. "Bostock means it—April salary will go to charity." *Detroit Free Press*, May 2, 1978, 5(D).

———. "Tiger rivals beg to see the bird." *Detroit Free-Press*, July 21, 1976, D(1).
"'He was the best,' Calif. Angels exec. mourns Bostock." *Jet Magazine*, October 19, 1978, 52.
Hewitt, Brian. "Bostock earned respect of fans, teammates." *Chicago Sun-Times*, September 26, 1978. https://www.washingtonpost.com/archive/sports/1978/09/26/bostock-earned-respect-of-fans-teammates/2233c580-d803-46e6-bdc1-72ca740a2da0/ .
Hill, Bob. "Reports on big brothers of Orange County." *Tustin News*, July 6, 1978, 2(1).
"Hisle, Bostock like brothers." *Milwaukee Journal Sentinel*, September 25, 1978.
Hutchins, Paul. "A chilling account of Lyman Bostock's death." http://www.angelfire.com/journal2/davismi/eyewitness.html.
"Innocent victim Bostock dead." Associated Press, September 25, 1978.
Israel, David. "A young and gifted man dies on a Saturday night." *Chicago Tribune*, September 25, 1978, 5(1).
Jacobson, Steve. "Twin outfielder Lyman chip off old Bostock." *Pittsburgh Press* (via Newsday Wire Services), July 31, 1977, D(4).
Johnson, K. C. "You don't want to believe it happened," *Chicago Tribune*, June 23, 2002. http:/ /articles.chicagotribune.com/2002—06-23/sports/0206230416_1_lyman-bostock-gary-comiskey-park .
Kallestad, Brent. "Down to the wire." Associated Press, March 24, 1977.
———. "Down to the wire." Associated Press, August 18, 1977.
———. "Goltz escaping the shadows to become Twins mound star." Associated Press, July 26, 1977.
———. "Indians hold off Twins 7–6 at Met." Associated Press, July 17, 1976.
———. "Injured Twins rookie ready to play." Associated Press, May 4, 1975.
———. "Mauch plans to open camp with a clean slate." Associated Press, January 29, 1976.
———. "Twins, Johnson 'walked' into win over Yankees." Associated Press, June 2, 1977.
———. "Twins looking for help." Associated Press, October 5, 1974.
———. "Twins outslug Brewers." Associated Press, May 2, 1976.
Kelley, Brent. *Voices from the Negro Leagues: Conversations with 52 Baseball Standouts of the Period 1924–1960*. Jefferson, N.C.: McFarland, 1998.
Kellogg, Dave. "Haines surprised, pleased in Tucson." *Tucson Daily Citizen*, July 18, 1974, 39.
Kennedy, Ray. "Money: The monster threatening sports." *Sports Illustrated*, July 17, 1978, 29.
"Keough suffers 18th loss in row." Associated Press, August 9, 1979.
King, Martin Luther, Jr. "I've Been to the Mountaintop." Speech given April 3, 1968, at the Mason Temple in Memphis, Tennessee. Video excerpt posted as "Martin Luther King's Last Speech: 'I've Been To The Mountaintop," Youtube.com, 2:37, by NewsPoliticsInfo, April 4, 2010. https://www.youtube.com/watch?v=Oehry1JC9Rk.
"Kuhn sounds warning." Associated Press, November 18, 1977.
LaHammer, Gene. "Griffith planning to continue talks." Associated Press, October 6, 1977.
———. "Twins covet Hisle, Bostock." Associated Press, November 2, 1977.
Leavitt, Michael. "Dinner with Jose & 1978 Summerfest memories." Michael Leavitt & Co Inspections, August 22, 2012. http://www.thehomeinspector.com/Family/Leavitt-Times_2012_8-22.html.
"Letters—Bostock's death." *Los Angeles Times*, September 30, 1978.
Libman, Gary. "Baseball." *Minneapolis Tribune*, August 1, 1976, 11(C).
———. "Bostock humble despite star's salary." Associated Press, September 26, 1978.
———. "Ex-mates mourn 'Mr. Logic's' death." *Minneapolis Tribune*, September 25, 1978, 1(C).
———. "Oldtimers share frustration of age in annual game." *Minneapolis Tribune*, July 18, 1976, 4(C).
———. "Rain halts Twins game." *Minneapolis Tribune*, July 28, 1976, 5(C).
Linkugel, Wil A., and Edward J. Pappas. *They Tasted Glory: Among the Missing at the Baseball Hall of Fame*. Jefferson, N.C.: McFarland, 1998.
"Lowly Montreal Expos clean out their house." Canadian Press, October 2, 1975.
Lyle, Sparky, and Peter Golenback. *The Bronx Zoo*. Chicago: Triumph, 2005.
"Lyman Bostock buried." United Press International, September 30, 1978.
"Lyman Bostock finishes third in PCL in batting." *Valley News*, October 1, 1974, 27(A).

"Lyman Bostock hits for the team." Associated Press, July 29, 1976.
"Matadors, Fullerton to battle." *Valley News*, April 30, 1971, 31.
Mazzeo, Frank. "Bostock newest Angel millionaire." *Valley News*, November 22, 1977, 5(2).
———. "Bostock rises, dollars don't." *Valley News*, March 31, 1977, 2 (section 4).
———. "Bostock takes Angel riches." *Valley News*, November 22, 1977, 2(5).
McDonald, Mark. "Young Twins eye big bucks." *Abilene Reporter News*, August 31, 1977, C(1).
McKenzie, George. "Rod Carew Profile." KMSP-TV (Minneapolis ABC Affiliate), July 1977. Video posted as "Rod Carew Profile - 1977," Youtube.com, 4:00, by redvetinc, September 20, 2008. https://www.youtube.com/watch?v=wYvd0egKpj4.
"Memory of Bostock lingers—eight months later, Turner mourns death." Associated Press, May 27, 1979.
Merry, Don. "Angels make Bostock top salaried player." *Los Angeles Times*, November 22, 1977, 3(1).
Miller, Dick. "Lyman's pie in the sky proves to be Angel food." *Sporting News*, March 15, 1978, 3.
"MLB network to air 'The Lyman Bostock Story' this Sunday, September 22." MLB.com, Press Release, September 18, 2013. http://m.mlb.com/news2/article/60975420/mlb-network-to-air-the-lyman-bostock-story-this-sunday-september-22.
Morlan, Cliff. "Cliff Morlan's Sports Review," *Bemidji Pioneer*, September 28, 1977, 6.
Murray, Jim. "Cheerful, chatty, and level swing." *Los Angeles Times* (syndicated), September 28, 1978.
Nadel, John. "Bostock funeral slated Thursday." Associated Press, September 26, 1978.
"New blood pumps White Sox." Associated Press, May 31, 1978.
Newhan, Ross. "Angel tears, kind words for Lyman." *Los Angeles Times*, September 25, 1978, 12.
———. "Bostock: Angels wanted a person." *Los Angeles Times*, September 26, 1978, 3(5).
"New player agent blossoms." Associated Press, June 11, 1977.
Nightingale, Dave. "Slaying of Bostock overwhelms Angels." *Chicago Tribune*, September 25, 1978, 5(1).
Nigro, Ken. "Twins' Bostock, at .330, still faces anonymity." *Baltimore Sun*, August 11, 1976, C(5).
Olderman, Murray. "Just ask." Newspaper Enterprise Association (syndicate), *Corsicana Daily Sun*, July 31, 1977, 2(B).
"Once ready to donate his salary, Bostock rediscovers batting stroke." Associated Press, August 23, 1978.
Ostler, Scott. "Bostock wants to play like million dollars." *Los Angeles Times*, March 1, 1978, 8.
———. "Brett stymies Twins, Carew in 5-hitter, 3–0." *Los Angeles Times*, April 11, 1978, 3(1).
———. "The highest Angels." *Los Angeles Times*, July 13, 1978.
Painter, Jill. "Lyman Bostock left indelible imprint at Cal State Northridge." *Los Angeles Daily News*, September 23, 2008.
Pearlman, Jeff. "Fifth and Jackson." ESPN.com, September 23, 2008. http://espn.go.com/espn/eticket/story?page=bostock.
"Pennant buying is still impossible." United Press International, July 24, 1977.
Penner, Mike. "Remembering Lyman Bostock." *Los Angeles Times*, September 23, 1988, 14.
"Players shocked over Bostock's murder." Associated Press, September 25, 1978.
Reusse, Patrick. "Lyman Bostock blazed trail to Anaheim." *Minneapolis Tribune*, April 2, 2008. http://www.startribune.com/lyman-bostock-blazed-trail-to-anaheim/17247959/.
"Rice destined for greatness despite personality problem." *Los Angeles Times*, August 12, 1978.
Richman, Milton. "Bostock's offer legitimate, but Autry won't withhold pay." United Press International, April 21, 1978.
———. "Nothing phony about Bostock." United Press International, September 26, 1978.

Rinaldi, Tom, and John Barr. "The Tragedy of Lyman Bostock." *Outside the Lines*. ESPN, September 21, 2008. Video posted as "Lyman Bostock Story Part 1," Youtube.com, 6:37, by Abdul Jalil, December 28, 2008. https://www.youtube.com/watch?v=HMKx2Uc4084.
Ringolsby, Tracy. "Bostock a troubled star in Minnesota." *Long Beach (California) Independent*, July 10, 1977, S(4).
———. "Bostock dips into Autry's saddlebags for $3.2 million." *Long Beach (California) Independent*, November 22, 1977, C(1).
Ritter, Brad, and Paul Wertz. "Valley State demonstrators hold building for four hours." *Valley News*, November 5, 1968, 1.
Roberts, Rich. "Twins' Carew has it all except privacy, pennant." *Los Angeles Times*, April 11, 1978, 3(1).
"Rod boosts mark to .395 in 12–2 rout." Associated Press, June 24, 1977.
Russo, Neal. "Cub payoff in victory is tumbling catch." *St. Louis Post Dispatch*, August 2, 1978, 1(D).
"San Fernando State faculty tells of actions by militant students." Associated Press, November 8, 1968.
Saylor, Jack. "Sports people." *Detroit Free Press*, May 28, 1978, 2(E).
Schrader, Loel. "Peanuts for the media, dollar bills for Bostock." *Long Beach Independent-Press-Telegram*, November 22, 1977, C(1–2).
Singer, Tom. "Bostock a tragic figure in history of draft," MLB.com, May 15, 2007. http://m.mlb.com/news/article/1965878/.
Smith, Claire. "Owners finally coming around to Griffith's way of doing things." *Hartford Courant*, October 26, 1987, C(6).
"Sorenson cools Twins, Carew up to .411." United Press International, June 30, 1977.
Soucheray, Joe. "This snow job requires a lot of uncovering." *Minneapolis Tribune*, March 19, 1975, 1(C).
"Students with knives hold officials prisoner." Associated Press, November 6, 1968.
"Suspect charged in Bostock case." United Press International, September 26, 1978.
"Sweet swinging Carew heading for sixth title." Associated Press, September 29, 1977.
Swift, Robert. "Remembering the great Lyman Bostock." Eye on Gaming, Forum, December 19, 2005. http://forums.eog.com/showthread.php/338799-Remembering-the-great-Lyman-Bostock.
"Tanana twirls Angels to 4–1 win over Twins." Associated Press, September 27, 1976.
"Teachers tell of takeover by blacks at Calif. college." United Press International, November 8, 1968.
"Tigers club slump-ridden Angels, 10–2." *San Bernardino Sun-Telegram*, May 3, 1978, D(1).
"Tigers top millionaire Angels." Associated Press, May 4, 1978.
"Tough day for Angels." United Press International, September 25, 1978.
"Twin hurlers check Kansas City hitters." Associated Press, August 2, 1977.
"Twins." *Minneapolis Tribune*, August 20, 1976, C(3).
"Twins aren't identical." *Detroit Free Press*, July 15, 1977, D(2).
"Twins' Bostock breaks up games instead of bones." Associated Press, August 3, 1976.
"Twins' Bostock sparkles in club's 5–3 victory." Associated Press, May 23, 1976.
"Twins bury Rangers, 11–4." Associated Press, April 22, 1977.
"Twins clip Royals." United Press International, July 29, 1975.
"Twins defeat Rangers 3–1." United Press International, September 9, 1976.
"Twins have cash to sign players." Associated Press, September 26, 1977.
"Twins owner holding firm on Mauch compensation." *Los Angeles Times*, November 16, 1977.
"Twins seem to feast on Red Sox pitching." Associated Press, June 4, 1977.
"Twins stand to lose a lot." Associated Press, June 21, 1977.
"Twins stars prove very popular." Associated Press, November 5, 1977.
"Twins to lose star outfielder." Associated Press, April 28, 1977.
Ulman, Howard. "Bostock 'happy' before last game." Associated Press, September 25, 1978.
"View from both sides of the combat zone." Associated Press, April 29, 1977.
Vincent, Charlie. "A trip to remember—Tigers, Sally Rand, and 15,000 miles." *Detroit Free Press*, August 11, 1977, D(1).

Weir, Tom. "The man who turns hits into millions." *Oakland Tribune*, February 9, 1978, 49.

Weisberg, Sam. "Dracut's brotherly love." *Lowell Sun*, October 26, 1977, 18.

Weyler, John. "On the road again: Frank Tanana still has value after all these years, but probably not to the Mets, who see a trade to a contender in his future." *Los Angeles Times*, July 23, 1993. Available at http://articles.latimes.com/1993-07-23/sports/sp-16077_1_frank-tanana/2.

Wilner, Barry. "Oakland coach has relationship with stormy Finley." Associated Press, June 24, 1978.

INDEX

Aaron, Hank (baseball player), 11, 136, 289
Aaron, Wilmer, 11
Abilene Reporter News, 152
Abbott, Glenn (baseball player), 76
Abdul-Jabbar, Kareem (basketball player), 244, 263
Adams, Glenn (baseball player), 135, 138
Adams, John (president of the United States), 231
Adams, John Quincy (president of the United States), 231
Aeschylus (Greek philosopher), 269
African-Americans, 6, 7, 8, 12, 22, 24, 46, 133, 227; migration from rural South to northeastern and western cities, 6, 227; unrest among urban residents and high school/college students, 12, 21, 22, 37
Agamemnon, 269
Akron-Canton Regional Airport (Ohio), 286
Al-Hakim, Abdul-Jalil (Lyman Bostock's agent), 116, 117, 118, 132, 133, 164, 165, 168, 170, 172, 173, 174, 175, 176, 177, 178, 270, 277
Alabama, 4, 5, 6, 101
Albuquerque, New Mexico, 64, 65, 67
Alcindor, Lew. *See* Kareem Abdul-Jabbar
Ali, Muhammad (professional boxer), 72
Allen, Dick (baseball player), 120

Allen, Mel (baseball announcer), 126, 129, 135, 136, 137, 148, 153, 260, 261
Allison, Bob (baseball player), 99
Americans. *See* United States of America
American League, 1, 10, 48, 59, 62, 71, 74, 80, 81, 85, 89, 91, 92, 93, 95, 97, 98, 99, 104, 106, 108, 109, 110, 111, 112, 113, 114, 115, 119, 124, 126, 127, 128, 138, 139, 140, 141, 142, 144, 147, 148, 151, 152, 153, 154, 156, 157, 159, 162, 165, 166, 169, 175, 177, 205, 206, 211, 212, 219, 224, 226, 238, 248, 261, 265, 285, 286, 298; batting championship and race, 91, 95, 97, 104, 105, 106, 109, 110, 112, 113, 114, 115, 124, 131, 134, 139, 144, 147, 152, 153, 154, 156, 157, 221; Championship Series, 112, 113, 159, 224, 226, 253, 284; Cy Young Award, 127, 128, 206; Eastern Division, 81, 127, 128, 165, 255, 279; Most Valuable Player, 85; Rookie of the Year, 85; Western Division, 48, 81, 82, 84, 93, 94, 96, 98, 110, 114, 120, 126, 128, 129, 130, 134, 137, 139, 147, 148, 152, 153, 154, 165, 169, 222, 223, 224, 226, 251, 255, 262, 284
Anaheim, California, 9, 83, 93, 171, 239, 243, 251, 253, 256, 279, 284
Anaheim Angels. *See* California Angels
Anaheim Stadium, "The Big A" (Anaheim, California), 144, 172, 173, 243, 244,

319

262, 265, 281
Anderson, Dave, 101, 132, 160, 173, 176
Anderson, South Carolina, 54
Appling, Luke (baseball player), 289
Arizona, 6, 36
Arizona State University, 17, 36
Arlington National Cemetery, 19
Arlington, Texas, 80, 122
Arlington Stadium (Arlington, Texas), 73, 90
Arnett, Glenn, 24
Ashburn, Richie (baseball player), 289
Ashe, Arthur (professional tennis player), 53
Asheville, North Carolina, 60
Asian-Americans, 7
Associated Press, 68, 119, 130, 140, 147, 148, 164, 249, 256
Astrodome (Houston, Texas), 244
Atlanta, Georgia, 149
Atlanta Braves (professional baseball club), 72, 133, 164
Autry, Gene (actor, California Angels owner), 159, 167, 168, 169, 170, 171, 172, 174, 175, 184, 192, 193, 194, 195, 199, 200, 202, 256, 262, 264, 284

Bailor, Bob (baseball player), 144
Bain, John C. (Los Angeles minister), 266, 267
Bair, Doug (baseball player), 145
Baltimore, Maryland, 83, 106, 126, 127, 149, 286
Baltimore Orioles (professional baseball team), 11, 81, 106, 107, 127, 128, 149, 150, 152, 164, 165, 225, 284
Baltimore Sun (newspaper), 100, 106
Bamberger, George (baseball manager), 256
Bannister, Alan (baseball player), 103
Barker, Len (baseball player), 117
Barrios, Francisco (baseball player), 258, 259
Baton Rouge, Louisiana, 170
Battey, Earl (baseball player), 99
Bavasi, Emil Joseph (Buzzie) (professional baseball executive), 168, 169, 171, 172, 173, 174, 178, 239, 240, 241, 256, 257, 260

Bayless, Skip (sportswriter/television personality), 263, 267
Baylor, Don (baseball player), 183, 217, 222, 223, 225, 239, 240, 241, 247, 248, 251, 252, 253, 259, 268, 282, 285, 289
The Bingo Long Traveling All-Stars & Motor Kings (1976 movie), 99
Belanger, Mark (baseball player), 127
Bemidji Pioneer (newspaper), 155
Beniquez, Juan (baseball player), 122
Birmingham, Alabama, 1, 4, 5, 227, 246
Birmingham Barons (professional minor league baseball team), 62
Birmingham Black Barons (professional baseball team), 1, 101, 143
Birmingham News (newspaper), 61
Black Power movement, 13, 21
Black Sabbath (band), 243
Blair, Paul (baseball player), 11
Blomgren, Paul M., 24, 25
Bloomington, Minnesota, 97, 99, 128, 134, 135, 139, 144, 153, 155
Blue, Vida (baseball player), 96
Blyleven, Bert (baseball player), 49, 83, 90, 94, 95, 105, 122, 134
Bochte, Bruce (baseball player), 66
Borgmann, Glenn (baseball player), 127
Bosman, Dick (baseball player), 96
Bostock, Annie Pearl (Lyman Bostock Jr.'s mother), 4, 5, 6, 7, 8, 9, 12, 15, 16, 17, 48, 49, 51, 82, 168, 173, 178, 227, 239, 241, 243, 260, 263, 264, 266, 267, 268, 282, 283, 289, 290; assistance in son's professional signing, 48, 49, 51; move to Los Angeles, 6; relationship with Lyman Bostock Sr., 5
Bostock, Lilly (Lyman Bostock Jr.'s grandmother), 289
Bostock, Lyman Wesley, Jr. (baseball player), 3, 4, 5, 6, 7, 8, 9, 10, 11, 12, 14, 15, 16, 17, 18, 19, 20, 21, 22, 23, 25, 26, 27, 28, 29, 30, 33, 34, 35, 36, 37, 38, 39, 40, 41, 42, 43, 44, 45, 46, 47, 48, 49, 50, 51, 53, 54, 55, 56, 57, 58, 59, 60, 126, 127, 128, 129, 130, 131, 132, 133, 134, 135, 137, 138, 139, 140, 141, 142, 143, 144, 145, 146, 147, 148, 149, 150, 151, 152, 153, 154, 155, 156, 157, 159, 160, 161, 163, 164, 165, 166,

INDEX 321

167, 168, 169, 170, 171, 172, 173, 174, 175, 176, 177, 178, 179, 180, 181, 182, 183, 184, 185, 186, 187, 188, 189, 190, 191, 192, 193, 194, 195, 196, 197, 198, 199, 200, 201, 202, 203, 204, 205, 206, 207, 208, 209, 210, 211, 212, 213, 214, 215, 216, 217, 218, 219, 220, 221, 222, 223, 224, 225, 226, 227, 228, 229, 230, 231, 232, 233, 236, 237, 238; attempt to return April, 1978 salary to California Angels, 261, 285, 288; baseball influences and childhood favorite players, 10, 11; baseball roots in Los Angeles, 7, 8, 10, 57, 58; base running abilities, 35, 60, 93, 115; batting ability and approach, 10, 35, 36, 37, 81, 82, 85, 97, 104, 105, 106, 107, 109, 116, 144, 145, 146, 147, 151, 157, 289; changes in Indiana criminal law, 277; childhood in California, 8, 9, 11; collegiate career at San Fernando Valley State College, 26, 27, 28, 29, 30, 33, 34, 35, 36, 37, 38, 39, 40, 41, 42, 43, 44, 45, 46, 47, 49; contract negotiations with Minnesota Twins (1977), 115, 116, 117, 118, 119, 122, 123, 130, 132, 142, 148, 159, 160, 161, 163, 172, 173; dismissal from San Fernando Valley State College baseball team, 28, 29; first spring training with Minnesota Twins/making major league club, 70, 71, 72, 77, 78; free agency, 4, 116, 133, 144, 161, 163, 164, 165, 166, 167, 168, 170, 171, 172, 173; funeral, 263, 264, 265, 266, 267, 268, 271; hitting for the cycle (1976), 102, 103; injury in first spring training, 1975, 72; injury in minor leagues with Orlando Twins, 1973, 59; injury in rookie season with Minnesota Twins, 1975, 76, 77, 78, 79, 86; interactions with children, 46, 47, 69, 285, 288; lack of recognition in early big league career, 97, 282, 283; Lyman Bostock Memorial Scholarship Fund, 281, 282, 296, 298; minor league career with Charlotte Twins (1972), 54, 55, 56, 68; minor league career with Orlando Twins (1973), 59, 60, 61, 68; minor league career with Tacoma Twins (1974–1975), 62, 63, 64, 65, 66, 67, 68, 79; murder in Gary, Indiana (Sept. 23, 1978), 269, 270, 271, 272, 273, 274, 275, 276, 292; opinions of opposing coaches and managers, 45, 145, 150; outfield skills and development, 8, 35, 37, 44, 54, 56, 75, 85, 142; personality, 9, 11, 15, 17, 40, 41, 48, 107, 120, 121, 122, 148, 171, 266, 288; physical attributes, 17, 40; relationship with his father, 3, 4, 9, 15, 99, 100, 101; relationship with fans, 149; relationship with his teammates, 15, 30, 34, 41, 72, 107, 108, 120, 121, 141, 143, 171, 265, 297; relationship with the press, 121, 148, 156; return to San Fernando Valley State baseball team, 29, 30, 33; rookie major league season with Minnesota Twins (1975), 72, 73, 74, 75, 76, 77, 78, 80, 81, 82, 83, 84, 85, 86; selection by Minnesota Twins in 1972 MLB draft, 48, 49; similarities in playing ability to his father, 3, 58; signing with the Minnesota Twins out of college, 50, 51; signing with the California Angels (1977), 171, 172, 173, 174, 176, 177; shooting at the hands of Leonard Smith, 232, 233; tying major league record for outfield assists in a game (1977), 124, 125; visits to Gary, Indiana during youth, 39; winter league baseball in South America, 69, 70, 87, 115; work with the Teen Challengers, 262, 292

Bostock, Lyman Wesley, Sr. (Negro League baseball player), 1, 3, 4, 5, 58, 90, 99, 100, 101, 123, 141, 143, 195, 196, 264, 289, 290; negotiations for more money in Negro Leagues, 143; relationship with Annie Bostock, 5, 101; relationship with his son, 3, 4, 9, 99, 100, 101, 195; similarities in playing ability to his son, 3, 58

Boston, Massachusetts, 124, 126
Boston (band), 243, 244
Boston Braves, 125
Boston Red Sox (American League baseball club), 10, 62, 69, 71, 81, 83, 95, 96, 102, 116, 124, 125, 126, 129,

139, 147, 151, 165, 167, 255, 279, 280, 281, 285, 290
Boyd, Arnold, 26
Braun, Steve (baseball player), 71, 75, 90, 112
Brett, George (baseball player), 97, 104, 105, 109, 110, 112, 113, 114, 153, 154, 156, 289
Brett, Ken (baseball player), 240, 242, 265
Brewer, Chet (baseball player, semipro manager), 58
Brian's Song, 279
Briere, Tom (sportswriter), 75
Briggs, John (baseball player), 80
Brock, Lou (baseball player), 87
Brogno (Indiana psychologist), 275
Bronx, New York, 82, 151, 159, 166, 175
Brophy, George (baseball executive), 57
Brooklyn, New York, 10, 168
Brooklyn Dodgers (professional baseball club), 58, 168, 289
Brunansky, Tom (baseball player), 282
Brye, Steve (baseball player), 71, 75, 104
Burgmeier, Tom (baseball player), 155
Burleson, Rick (baseball player), 281

California, 5, 6, 7, 9, 10, 58, 73, 87, 101, 144, 149, 159, 165, 167, 168, 169, 174, 175, 180, 181, 184, 191, 203, 208, 215, 225, 246, 247, 249, 254, 260, 261
California Child Care Resource and Referral Network, 284
California Angels (American league baseball club), 10, 74, 75, 82, 83, 93, 94, 111, 112, 134, 139, 140, 144, 145, 159, 164, 167, 168, 169, 170, 171, 172, 173, 174, 175, 176, 177, 178, 179, 181, 182, 183, 184, 185, 186, 187, 188, 189, 190, 191, 192, 193, 194, 195, 197, 198, 199, 200, 201, 203, 204, 205, 206, 207, 208, 209, 210, 211, 212, 213, 214, 215, 216, 217, 218, 219, 220, 221, 222, 223, 224, 225, 226, 236, 238, 239, 240, 242, 243, 244, 245, 246, 247, 248, 249, 250, 251, 252, 253, 254, 255, 256, 257, 258, 259, 260, 261, 262, 264, 265, 266, 267, 279, 280, 281, 282, 283, 284, 285, 288, 289, 290, 297; *Heaven Can Wait* (team's 25th-anniversary film), 225
California Collegiate Athletic Association (CCAA), 29, 36, 37
California State University, Northridge, 17, 18, 19, 20, 21, 23, 25, 26, 27, 28, 29, 30, 33, 34, 35, 36, 37, 38, 39, 40, 41, 42, 43, 44, 45, 46, 47, 48, 49, 51, 53, 54, 55, 58, 61, 75, 87, 221, 223, 230, 244, 245, 246, 281, 282, 283, 284, 296; baseball program, 17, 18, 21, 26, 27, 28, 29, 30, 33, 35, 36, 37, 38, 39, 40, 41, 42, 43, 44, 45, 46, 47, 48, 49, 53, 58, 59, 244, 281, 282, 283, 296; Black Studies program/Black Student Union, 21, 22, 23, 24, 25, 26, 28, 29; campus unrest in late 1960s, 21, 22, 37; faculty, 26; Northridge Hall, 20, 25; Students for a Democratic Society, 22, 24; Students for Education, Action, and Change, 24
California State University, Irvine (UC-Irvine), 38, 42
California State University, Pomona (Cal Poly), 41
California State University, Riverside (UC-Riverside), 36, 41; Zelzah Avenue, 20
Campanella, Roy (baseball player), 168
Campaneris, Bert (baseball player), 76
Campbell, Bill, 70, 90, 116
Campbell, Jim (baseball executive), 102
Canada, 3, 5, 88, 124, 165
Canfield, Bob (Lyman Bostock's college baseball teammate), 43
Canseco, Jose (baseball player), 61
Caray, Harry (baseball announcer), 110, 111
Cardinals. *See* St. Louis Cardinals
Carew, Rod (baseball player), 60, 62, 80, 81, 82, 83, 89, 93, 94, 98, 106, 107, 109, 110, 111, 112, 113, 115, 119, 120, 122, 124, 127, 128, 129, 130, 134, 135, 136, 137, 138, 139, 140, 144, 145, 146, 147, 148, 149, 150, 156, 157, 160, 161, 186, 188, 189, 212, 254, 261, 280, 284, 289
Carter, Gary (baseball player), 89
Carter, Jimmy (president of the United States), 178
Carty, Rico (baseball player), 136

Catholic Church, 280
Census. *See* United States Census
Chambliss, Chris (baseball player), 113
Chance, Dean (baseball player), 62
Channel 7 (Chicago television station), 248
Chapman University (California), 42
Chappas, Harry (baseball player), 223
Charlotte, North Carolina, 54, 57
Charlotte Hornets (minor league baseball franchise), 59
Charlotte Twins (minor league baseball franchise), 54, 55, 56, 57
Charnofsky, Stan (college baseball coach), 244
Chass, Murray (sportswriter), 170
Cheney Stadium (Tacoma, Washington), 63, 66
Cherry, Jeff (Lyman Bostock's college baseball teammate), 45
Chicago, Illinois (Windy City), 6, 39, 40, 94, 101, 102, 103, 109, 110, 111, 139, 143, 165, 183, 196, 218, 219, 222, 225, 226, 227, 229, 236, 239, 243, 244, 246, 248, 253, 255, 259, 260, 280, 283, 285; South Side, 94, 103, 139, 183, 222, 226, 236, 253, 255, 280; Water Tower Hyatt, 229, 239, 240, 242
Chicago American Giants (Negro League baseball club), 196
Chicago Cubs (National League baseball club), 49, 188
Chicago Sun-Times, 208, 271
Chicago Tribune, 182, 194, 242, 248, 250, 253, 258
Chicago White Sox, 62, 93, 102, 103, 104, 109, 110, 111, 124, 129, 130, 135, 139, 147, 148, 153, 155, 156, 159, 164, 165, 183, 187, 199, 221, 222, 223, 224, 225, 226, 228, 229, 230, 236, 237, 239, 244, 246, 249, 252, 253, 258, 259, 262, 280, 281, 285, 297
Christmas, 6
Cincinnati Reds (professional baseball club), 126, 162, 166
Clark, Al (baseball umpire), 150
Clark, Earl (baseball player), 125
Clemente, Roberto (baseball player), 26, 265
Cleveland, Ohio, 109

Cleveland Indians (professional baseball club), 49, 80, 95, 98, 101, 119, 139, 146, 147, 286
Cleveland, Reggie (baseball player), 102
Click, Bill, 149
Click, Carl, 149
Click, John, 149
Cobb, Ty (baseball player), 261
Colburn, Jim (baseball player), 146, 154
College Division World Series, 29, 37, 38, 42, 43, 44, 45, 47, 54
Comiskey Park (Chicago, Illinois), 1, 93, 103, 110, 111, 153, 165, 221, 222, 248, 250, 252, 253, 257, 258, 280, 285
Cooperstown, New York, 244
Corbett, Brad (professional baseball owner), 94, 166, 174
County Stadium (Milwaukee, Wisconsin), 84, 139, 256
Cowens, Al (baseball player), 282
Craven, Terry (college baseball coach), 283
Crawford, Jack (Indiana attorney), 271, 272, 273, 274, 275, 276, 277
Crown Point, Indiana, 260, 271, 272; Lake County Criminal Court, 271; Lake County Superior Court, 272
Cubbage, Mike (baseball player), 94, 95, 103, 121, 122
Cullum, Dick (sportswriter), 76, 84, 85

Dade, Paul (baseball player), 139
Dallas, Texas, 165
Dallas Morning News (newspaper), 263
Dalton, Harry (baseball executive), 168
Damergis, Mike, 241
Dangerfield, Levi, 25
Daniels, Christine (sportswriter), 240, 242, 265
Darwin, Bobby (baseball player), 73, 79, 80
Davenport, Jim (baseball player), 100
Davis, Dr. Milton H. (Los Angeles minister), 265
DeCinces, Doug (baseball player), 20, 150
Denahy, Robert F. (Los Angeles high school principal), 12, 13, 14
Democratic National Convention, 9
Denny's (restaurant), 37

Dent, Bucky (baseball player), 128
Detroit, Michigan, 6, 102, 109
Detroit Tigers, 62, 71, 95, 97, 101, 102, 146, 157, 282
DiGiovanna, Mike (sportswriter), 254
Dilbeck, Steve (sportswriter), 160, 241, 257
Dillard, Steve (baseball player), 124
DiMuro, Lou (major league umpire), 259
Dion (singer), 266
Dodger Stadium, 149
Downing, Brian (baseball player), 223, 285, 289
Dozer, Richard (sportswriter), 258
Drysdale, Don (baseball player), 20, 26, 168
Durso, Joseph (sportswriter), 164, 165

Easter, Luke (baseball player), 286
Eastwick, Rawly (baseball player), 164
Ebbets Field (Brooklyn, New York ballpark), 10, 74, 168
Eckersley, Dennis (baseball player), 95, 98, 99, 147
Edwards, Harry (American sociologist), 33
Eisenhower, Dwight (American Army general, president of the United States), 227
Ellis, Dock (baseball player), 169
Ellsbury, Jacoby (baseball player), 126
Enberg, Dick (sportscaster), 221, 244, 245, 281
Ermer, Cal (baseball manager), 61, 62, 71, 79
ESPN, 20, 263, 272; *Outside the Lines*, 272, 291
Euclid, Ohio, 286
Evans, Dwight (baseball player), 125
Exhibition Stadium (Toronto, Ontario), 124, 149

Fairly, Ron (baseball player), 223, 251
Fellowship of Christian Athletes, 252
Fenway Park (Boston, Massachusetts), 43, 62, 124, 125, 126, 151, 171, 279
Ferrer, Sergio (baseball player), 65
Fidrych, Mark "The Bird" (baseball player), 101, 102
Field of Dreams (movie), 61

Fifth and Jackson (2008 ESPN.com article), 20, 243, 259, 283
Figueroa, Ed (baseball player), 128
Fingers, Rollie (baseball player), 96
Finley, Charles O. (professional baseball owner), 96, 162, 166
Fisk, Carlton (baseball player), 124, 134, 139
Flanagan, Mike (baseball player), 127
Flood, Curt (baseball player), 139
Flores, Jesse Sandoval (Mexican pitcher, professional baseball scout), 49, 50, 51
Flores, Jesse Sandoval, Jr. (professional baseball scout), 49, 50, 51, 71
Florida, 4, 59, 69, 71, 116
Florida Southern College, 43, 44, 45, 46, 47
Flynn, Doug (baseball player), 69, 70, 166
Ford C. Frick Award, 244
Ford, Dan (baseball player), 76, 81, 90, 112, 115, 119, 121, 124, 127, 129, 138, 254, 255
Forster, Terry (baseball player), 164
Fowler, Bob (sportswriter), 82
Fox, Howard (professional baseball executive), 117, 118, 119
Frazer, Fred T. (Los Angeles high school principal), 14
Frazier, Clyde (basketball player), 173
Frederico, Freddie (California Angels trainer), 239, 240
Freed, Donald (college professor), 26
Fregosi, Jim (baseball player, manager), 10, 199, 200, 201, 202, 205, 206, 207, 208, 210, 212, 214, 242, 248, 249, 250, 257, 259, 265, 280, 281, 284, 291
Frick, Ford (baseball executive), 168
Frick, Fred, 168
Friedman, Marty (Lyman Bostock's college teammate), 35, 39, 44, 46, 47
Frost, Robert (American poet), 298; *Stopping by Woods on a Snowy Evening*, 298

Gabel, Martin (television narrator), 6
Gamble, Oscar (baseball player), 159, 164, 177
Garner, Phil (baseball player), 76
Garrett, Adrian, 70

INDEX

Gary, Indiana, 4, 5, 6, 39, 93, 111, 221, 224, 225, 226, 227, 228, 229, 230, 231, 232, 233, 235, 236, 237, 239, 240, 241, 242, 244, 246, 247, 253, 254, 256, 260, 262, 269, 270, 271, 272, 273, 274, 275, 276, 277, 280, 281, 283, 287, 290, 291, 292, 293, 294, 295, 296; Bi-LO grocery store, 232, 233, 292; Bowman Square Park, 269; casino industry, 291; Family Dollar store, 292; Fifth Street, 231, 232, 292; Grant Street, 232; intersection of Fifth and Jackson Streets, 232, 236, 269, 274, 292, 293, 294; Jackson Street, 231, 269, 270, 291, 292; Lake County Jail, 271, 272; Lincoln-Johnson Park, 232; Madison Street, 269; McKinley Street, 232; Methodist Hospital, 5; Monroe Street, 292; People's Action Coalition and Trust, 262; Police Department, 246, 269, 270, 271, 296; Roosevelt Street, 232; Roosevelt Park, 4; St. Mary's Mercy Hospital, 233, 236, 237, 239, 242, 259, 269, 285, 294, 295, 296; Sixth Street, 236; steel mills, 5, 227, 228, 235, 291; Tyler Street, 236; urban decay, 291, 292, 293, 294, 295

Gary Post-Tribune, 262, 271

Garr, Ralph (baseball player), 103

Gastonia, North Carolina, 54

Gastonia Pirates, 55, 57

Gates, Joe (baseball player), 253

Gehrig, Lou (baseball player), 92

The Gene Autry Show, 167

Gideon, Bill (baseball player), 94

Gleason, Bill (newspaper journalist), 271

Glendale, California, 261

Goltz, Dave (baseball player), 112, 119, 129, 146, 154, 155, 156

Goodwin, Danny (baseball player), 223, 241, 242, 252

Gorinski, Bob (baseball player), 128

Gossage, Rich (Goose), 93, 159, 164, 167, 174, 177, 279

Graham, Archibald "Moonlight", 61

Grant, Bud (professional football coach), 74

Grant, M. Donald (baseball executive), 170

Great War. *See* World War I

Greene, Bob (sportswriter), 147

Greenville, South Carolina, 54

Greenwood, South Carolina, 54, 56

Greenwood Braves, 55, 56

Greyhound (Bus Line), 5, 6, 9, 73

Grich, Bobby (baseball player), 168, 222, 223

Griffith, Calvin (baseball owner), 59, 62, 64, 65, 68, 71, 72, 77, 88, 89, 94, 102, 115, 116, 117, 118, 119, 120, 122, 123, 132, 133, 134, 140, 142, 143, 148, 152, 155, 159, 160, 161, 162, 163, 171, 173, 179

Griffith, Clark (baseball player, owner), 61

Griffith Park (Charlotte, North Carolina), 54, 56, 57

Griffith Stadium (Washington, D.C.), 61

Grimsley, Ross (baseball player), 164

Grout, Randy (Gary, Indiana, police officer), 270

Guadalajara, Mexico, 49

Guerrero, Mario (baseball player), 134

Guidry, Ron (baseball player), 128

Gustkey, Earl (sportswriter), 254

Haas, Moose (baseball player), 156

Hagar, Sammy (musician), 243

Halas, George (football coach), 279

Hall of Fame (Cooperstown, New York), viii, 20, 75, 90, 92, 95, 99, 101, 122, 144, 166, 201, 212, 244, 256, 289, 298

Hansen, Ann (Logansport State Hospital official), 277

Harbrecht, Thomas (Gary, Indiana police corporal), 270

Hartford Courant, 173

Harrah, Toby (baseball player), 90, 121

Hartman, Sid (sportswriter), 79, 99

Hartzell, Paul (baseball player), 140

Hassler, Andy (baseball player), 130, 153

Hawaii, 63

Hawaii Islanders (professional minor league baseball club), 63, 79

Hawkins, Joan, 39, 230, 231, 233, 270, 273, 274, 293

Hayes, Elvin (basketball player), 244

Hayes, Tom (Negro Leagues baseball owner), 143

Heathrow Airport, London, 19

Heaven Can't Wait (California Angels 25th-anniversary documentary), 167
Heinbechner, Bruce (baseball player), 169, 249
Hemingway, Ernest (American author), 235
Henderson, Ken (baseball player), 122
Herzog, Whitey (baseball manager), 112, 113, 254, 255
Hicks, Charles (Gary, Indiana, police corporal), 229, 270
Hiegert, Robert (college baseball coach, athletic director), 8, 9, 15, 17, 18, 21, 22, 23, 25, 27, 28, 29, 30, 33, 34, 35, 36, 37, 38, 39, 40, 41, 42, 43, 44, 45, 46, 47, 48, 49, 50, 51, 53, 58, 59, 60, 61, 72, 101, 133, 221, 244, 245, 246, 281, 282, 283, 298
Highsmith, Charles (Gary, Indiana, police officer), 269
Hisle, Larry, 73, 79, 80, 89, 94, 97, 107, 112, 116, 117, 119, 120, 121, 127, 129, 133, 134, 135, 137, 142, 144, 146, 152, 155, 156, 159, 160, 161, 163, 164, 165, 174, 177, 218, 255, 256, 263, 286, 290
Hisle, Sheila, 256
Hispanics, 7, 46, 49
Hogle, Frank (medical expert witness), 273
Holland, George, 24
Holtzman, Ken (baseball player), 76
Honolulu, Hawaii, 62, 63
Hopson, Butch (baseball player), 125, 151
Horton, Willie (baseball player), 122
Houk, Ralph (baseball manager), 101
Houston, Texas, 149
Houston Astros (professional baseball club), 88, 117
Houston Colt .45s. *See* Houston Astros
Hrabosky, Al (baseball player), 254, 255
Hughes Stadium (Sacramento, California), 63
Huggins, Miller (baseball manager), 92
Humphrey, Hubert H. (Minnesota senator), 21, 148
Hunter, Jim "Catfish" (baseball player), 90, 92, 151, 166
Hutchins, Paul (eyewitness to Lyman Bostock's death), 235, 236, 237, 238, 239, 243, 260, 277, 285, 297

Illinois, 47, 48, 280
Indiana, 235, 271, 272, 275, 277, 291, 294, 296
Indiana University, 275
Isreal, David (sportswriter), 250

Jackson, Andrew (president of the United States), 231
Jackson, Bo (baseball/football player), 61, 288
Jackson, Michael (entertainer), 294
Jackson, Reggie (baseball player), 61, 159, 166, 167, 170, 171, 176, 279
Jackson, Ron (baseball player), 223, 225, 226, 240
Jarry Park (Montreal, Quebec), 89
Jefferson, Jesse (baseball player), 103
Jenkins, Ferguson (baseball player), 73
John Paul I (Pope, 1978), 280
John, Elton (musician), 178
Johnson, David (baseball player), 151, 152
Johnson, Lamar (baseball player), 222
Johnson, Tom (baseball player), 145
Jones, James Earl (actor), 99
Jones, Shelton, 26
Joplin, Janis (musician), 19
Journey (band), 243

Kaat, Jim (baseball player), 62
Kallestad, Brent (sportswriter), 68, 119, 120, 140, 148
Kansas City, Missouri, 120, 121, 147, 159, 213, 214, 215, 217, 254
Kansas City Monarchs (professional baseball team), 58
Kansas City Royals, 83, 84, 85, 93, 94, 96, 97, 106, 109, 110, 112, 113, 114, 120, 129, 130, 146, 147, 148, 151, 152, 153, 154, 157, 159, 164, 166, 170, 183, 206, 207, 210, 211, 213, 214, 215, 216, 217, 219, 220, 222, 223, 224, 226, 253, 254, 255, 262, 284, 288
Kapstein, Jerry (agent), 133
Kelley, Brent (author), 143
Kelly, Pat (baseball player), 127
Kelly, Tom (baseball player, manager), 77
Kennedy, John Fitzgerald (American politician, president of the United States), 9, 19, 266

INDEX

Kennedy, Ray (sportswriter), 177
Kennedy, Robert Francis (American politician, attorney general, senator), 19, 266
Kent State University, 25
Keough, Matt (baseball player), 286
Key Largo, Florida, 169
Killebrew, Harmon (baseball player), 26, 62, 64, 85, 99
Kimbrough, James (Lake County, Indiana, judge), 271, 274, 276
King, Martin Luther, Jr. (civil rights activist), 19, 266
Kingman, Dave (baseball player), 119, 159
KMSP-TV (Minneapolis ABC affiliate), 136
Knapp, Chris (baseball player), 103
Koosman, Jerry (baseball player), 117, 130, 132
Koufax, Sandy (baseball player), 168
Krimel, Donald, Dr., 24, 25
KTLA (Los Angeles television station), 244
Kuiper, Duane, 70
Kuhn, Bowie (commissioner of baseball), 96, 162
Kusick, Craig (baseball player), 65, 254

LaGrow, Lerrin (baseball player), 130, 135, 223
Lahoud, Joe (baseball player), 75
Lake County, Indiana, 271, 276
Lake Michigan, 291
Lakeland, Florida, 71
The Land of Make Believe (Chuck Mangione/Esther Satterfield song), 221
Landreaux, Kenny (baseball player), 57, 58, 225, 226, 240, 241, 242, 257, 258, 262, 284
Lane, Frank (Angels scout), 168
Langford, Rick (baseball player), 145
Lanphier Park (Springfield, Illinois), 42, 43, 44, 46
Lansford, Carney (baseball player), 222, 223, 225, 226, 241, 257, 258, 259, 262, 290
LaRoche, Dave (baseball player), 98, 297
LaRussa, Tony (baseball manager), 99
Latin America, 49

Lecea, Richie (musician), 243
Lee, Bill (baseball player), 151
Lee, Roy (college baseball coach), 44, 45
LeFlore, Ron (baseball player), 97, 102
Legion Stadium (Greenwood, South Carolina), 56
Lemon, Bob (baseball manager), 130
Lemon, Chet (baseball player), 222, 223
Leonard, Dennis (baseball player), 96, 120
Libman, Gary (sportswriter), 100, 121, 254
Lincoln, Abraham (president of the United States), 266
Lindblad, Paul (baseball player), 122
Littell, Mark (baseball player), 97
Logansport State Hospital (Indiana), 276, 277, 290
Long Beach Independent Press-Telegram (newspaper), 3, 141, 163, 172
LoPriesti, Bob, 38, 39, 43
The Lord's Prayer, 265
Los Angeles, California, 4, 6, 7, 8, 9, 10, 12, 15, 16, 17, 20, 21, 36, 37, 39, 49, 50, 57, 58, 59, 61, 71, 77, 117, 167, 168, 170, 171, 172, 225, 227, 239, 241, 243, 244, 246, 257, 261, 263, 266, 267, 271, 282, 284, 287, 290, 292; Ambassador Hotel, 19; board of education, 13, 14; Budlong Avenue, 264; Chatsworth High School, 14; Chavez Ravine, 10; Compton, 20, 57; County Jail, 37; Crystal Stairs, Inc. (child care development agency), 284; civil unrest in 1960s, 12; Dodger Stadium, 10; Dominquez High School, 57; Dorsey High School, 14, 20; Disneyland, 9; Fremont High School, 14; Harbor Freeway, 7, 268; Harvard Playground, 49; Helms Athletic Board, 20; Hoover Street, 7, 10; Inglewood Park Cemetery, 267, 268, 283, 287; Los Angeles High School, 14; Los Angeles International Airport, 239, 241; Los Angeles Memorial Coliseum, 7, 10; Los Angeles Memorial Sports Arena, 7; Los Angeles Police Department, 25; Los Angeles Rams (professional football team), 74; Maclay Junior High School, 14; Monroe High School, 20; Ross Snyder Park, 57, 262; San Bernardino

High School, 20; Superior Court, 14; Vermont Avenue, 13; Vermont Square, 7, 8, 10, 11, 48, 49, 260, 263; Vermont Square Methodist Church, 262, 263, 265, 267; Watts, 7, 12; Wrigley Field, 10

Los Angeles Angels of Anaheim. *See* California Angels

Los Angeles Dodgers (National League baseball club), 10, 20, 65, 117, 126, 149, 159, 168, 172, 263, 266

Los Angeles Lakers (professional basketball team), 263

Los Angeles Daily News (newspaper), 38

Los Angeles Times (newspaper), 19, 20, 26, 118, 177, 222, 240, 242, 246, 247, 250, 254, 261, 263, 264, 265

Louisiana, 170

Louisiana State University (LSU), 170

Lowell Sun, 167

Loyola Marymount University, 282

Luchesi, Frank (baseball manager), 117

Lugar (gun model), 70

Lyle, Sparky (baseball player), 83, 128

The Lyman Bostock Story (MLB Network documentary), 230, 240, 245, 250, 260, 283

Lynn, Fred (baseball player), 36, 85, 125, 281

Maggard, Dave (baseball player), 132

The Making of the President, 1964 (1966 documentary), 6, 7

Major League Baseball, 4, 16, 22, 26, 114, 118, 159, 166, 283; acceptance of African American players, 3; All-Star Game, 95, 97, 137, 139, 141, 144, 176, 289; amateur draft, 16, 48, 71, 170; MLB Network, 245, 250

Major League Baseball Players Association, 26, 95, 260; reentry draft (1976–1977), 159, 162, 163, 164, 165, 168, 170, 171; reserve clause 22, 161

Maloney, George (professional umpire), 81

Man-Dak League (Canadian professional baseball league), 99

Mangione, Chuck (musician), 221

Manual Arts High School (Los Angeles, California), 11, 12, 13, 14, 15, 16, 17, 18, 20, 21, 25, 26, 27, 30, 39, 49, 57, 71, 230, 246; faculty, 13, 14, 25, 39; fall 1967 riots, 12, 13, 14; junior varsity baseball, 11; junior varsity basketball, 14; *The Artisan* (school yearbook), 13, 14; varsity basketball, 14; varsity baseball, 11, 14, 15, 20, 49

Manuel, Charlie (baseball player, manager), 66

Manush, Heinie (baseball player), 156

Marcus Aurelius (Roman emperor), 221

Martin, Billy (baseball manager), 128, 151, 171

Martinez, Dennis (baseball player), 151

Martinez, Tippy (baseball player), 150

Matthews, Gary (baseball player), 20

Mauch, Gene (baseball player/manager), 88, 89, 90, 92, 93, 95, 96, 97, 98, 100, 102, 104, 105, 107, 109, 112, 113, 126, 135, 136, 138, 142, 144, 146, 147, 151, 153, 161, 185, 186, 254, 297

May, Rudy (baseball player), 127

Mayberry, John (baseball player), 130, 153

Mays, Willie (baseball player), 8, 26, 101, 136

Mazzeo, Frank (sportswriter), 34, 173

McCarthy, Eugene (American politician), 19

McDonald, Mark (sportswriter), 152

McGregor, Scott (baseball player), 150

McKenzie, George (sportscaster), 136

McNally, Dave (baseball player), 161

McNamara, John (professional baseball coach/manager), 251

McRae, Hal (baseball player), 97, 109, 110, 112, 113

Meditations (writings of Roman emperor Marcus Aurelius), 221

Medich, Doc (baseball player), 174

Mee, Tom (Twins spokesman), 155

Memorial Stadium (Baltimore, Maryland), 106, 126, 286

Meoli, Rudy (baseball player), 66

Merry, Don (sportswriter), 177

Messersmith, Andy (baseball player), 161

Metropolitan Sports Area Commission, 123

Metropolitan Stadium (Bloomington, Minnesota), 59, 64, 71, 72, 74, 85, 89,

94, 95, 97, 98, 99, 100, 101, 102, 104, 105, 111, 112, 119, 123, 128, 135, 137, 140, 145, 149, 150, 154, 155, 223, 253, 255

Mexican Americans. *See* Hispanics

Mexico, 58, 115, 258; Los Mochis, 115

Mazatlan, 115

Miami Herald (newspaper), 263

Mickey Mouse, 173

Miley, Mike (baseball player), 169, 170, 249

Miller, Dick (sportswriter), 171, 176

Miller, Dyar (baseball player), 223

Miller, Marvin (labor leader), 26

Miller, Rick (baseball player), 223, 247, 248, 258, 259, 280

Millhouse, Dorothy (Los Angeles school teacher), 25, 26

Milwaukee, Wisconsin, 139, 156, 174, 255

Milwaukee Brewers (professional baseball club), 62, 80, 84, 92, 93, 109, 138, 139, 151, 154, 156, 164, 165, 168, 174, 255, 256, 262, 263, 283, 286, 290

Mincher, Don (baseball player), 99

Mingori, Steve (baseball player), 130, 255

Minor Leagues, 53, 62; Single A, 50, 54, 59; Double A, 11, 53, 56, 59, 61; Triple A, 53, 59, 61, 64, 79

Minneapolis, Minnesota, 55, 64, 77, 79, 94, 98, 119, 121, 136, 141, 142, 161

Minneapolis Tribune (newspaper), 72, 75, 76, 79, 84, 99, 100, 121, 154, 174, 175, 254

Minnesota, 4, 48, 71, 79, 83, 85, 87, 89, 95, 96, 119, 120, 125, 129, 136, 137, 148, 160, 161, 164, 166, 171, 172, 173, 174, 180, 183, 184, 186, 198, 200, 204, 206, 218, 222, 254

Minnesota Twins (professional baseball club), 48, 49, 50, 51, 53, 57, 59, 60, 61, 62, 63, 64, 65, 67, 68, 69, 70, 71, 72, 73, 74, 75, 76, 77, 78, 79, 80, 81, 82, 83, 84, 85, 86, 87, 88, 89, 90, 92, 93, 94, 95, 96, 97, 98, 99, 100, 101, 102, 103, 104, 105, 106, 107, 108, 109, 110, 111, 112, 113, 114, 115, 116, 117, 118, 119, 120, 121, 122, 123, 124, 125, 126, 127, 128, 129, 130, 132, 133, 134, 135, 137, 138, 139, 140, 141, 142, 143, 144, 145, 146, 147, 148, 149, 150, 151, 152, 153, 154, 155, 156, 159, 160, 161, 163, 172, 173, 179, 182, 184, 185, 186, 188, 189, 194, 205, 210, 217, 218, 219, 220, 222, 246, 248, 253, 254, 255, 262, 284, 285, 286, 289

Minnesota Vikings, 72, 74

Mississippi, 170

Missouri, 29

Molitor, Paul (baseball player), 256, 289

Money, Don (baseball player), 138

Monroe, Larry (baseball player), 111

Montreal, Quebec, 89

Montreal Expos (Canadian professional baseball club), 71, 88, 89

Moore, Junior (baseball player), 133

Morlan, Cliff (sportswriter), 155, 156

Moses, Robert, 168

A Movable Feast (Ernest Hemingway novel), 235

Mulliniks, Rance (baseball player), 241

Munson, Thurman (baseball player), 92, 129, 286

Murray, Jim (sportswriter), 222

Murtaugh, Danny (professional baseball manager), 55

Musial, Stan (baseball player), 136

Nadel, John (sportswriter), 256

Namath, Joe (football player), 173

National Basketball Association (NBA), 263

National Broadcasting Corporation (NBC), 45, 94, 244; "Game of the Week", 94; *Saturday Night Live* (television show), 245

National Collegiate Athletic Association (NCAA), 29, 33, 38, 44

National Football League, 74, 263; NFL Draft, 288; NFL Films, 126; National Football Conference, 74; National League, 1, 88, 89, 98, 163, 166, 168; Championship Series, 263; Eastern Division, 89, 166; Western Division, 126, 166

Negro Leagues (professional baseball league), 1, 3, 4, 8, 15, 58, 99, 100, 101, 143, 286, 290

Nelson, Dave (baseball player), 73

New Jersey, 168
New Testament, 252, 266; Book of John, 266; Epistle to the Romans, 252; Jesus Christ, 252, 266; Lazarus, 266; Martha, 266; Paul (apostle), 252
Nettles, Graig, 129, 279
New Mexico, 6
New York City, New York, 6, 47, 82, 90, 109, 144, 149, 151, 159, 165, 166, 168, 171, 176; Plaza Hotel, 149, 159, 162, 163
New York Mets (professional baseball club), 88, 117, 119, 130, 132, 164, 166, 170
New York Times (newspaper), 101, 132, 160, 164, 165, 170, 176
New York Yankees (professional baseball club), 81, 82, 83, 88, 90, 92, 95, 96, 106, 112, 113, 126, 128, 129, 151, 152, 157, 159, 164, 165, 166, 167, 170, 171, 172, 173, 174, 175, 176, 177, 226, 255, 279, 280, 286
Newhan, Ross (sportswriter), 247, 250, 251
Nicholls, David (Indiana attorney), 271
Nicholls State University, 29
Nightingale, Dave (sportswriter), 242, 248, 249, 253
Nigro, Ken (sportswriter), 100, 106
Nixon, Richard Milhouse (president of the United States), 21, 261, 262
North Carolina, 54, 57, 90
Northridge, California, xi, 18, 20, 25, 29, 37, 39, 48, 51, 55, 58, 61, 87, 245, 282, 283

O'Malley, Walter (baseball executive), 168
Oakland, California, 76, 77, 87, 96, 118, 132, 133, 144, 165
Oakland Coliseum, 76, 144
Oakland Athletics (professional baseball club), 76, 81, 82, 83, 85, 86, 96, 99, 104, 106, 109, 119, 120, 145, 157, 162, 164, 165, 166, 225, 255, 256, 286
Odom, Johnny Lee "Blue Moon", 103
Ohio, 286
Olderman, Murray (syndicated columnist), 143, 144

Oliva, Tony (baseball player), 62, 73, 97, 99, 100, 115, 146, 161
Olzewski, James (Indiana attorney), 274
Once They Were Angels (book), 241
Onward Christian Soldiers (song), 264
Orlando, Florida, 57, 59, 70, 71, 116
Orlando Twins (minor league professional baseball club), 59, 60
Orta, Jorge (baseball player), 103
Osbourne, Ozzy (musician), 243
Ostler, Scott (sportswriter), 118
Otis, Amos (baseball player), 153

Pacific Coast League (professional baseball league), 49, 61, 62, 63, 64, 65, 66, 67, 68, 79; All Star Game (1974), 66; Eastern Division, 66; Western Division, 65, 66, 67
Pacific 8 Conference (Pac-8), 17, 36
Paige, Satchel (baseball player), 1
Painter, Jill (sportswriter), 38
Palm Springs, California, 169, 237
Palmer, Jim (baseball player), 127
Parker, Dave (baseball player), 144
Parsons, Bill (baseball player), 66
Patek, Fred (baseball player), 84
Patkin, Max (Clown Prince of Baseball), 56, 253
Patton, Gregg (sportswriter), 288
Paul, Gabe (baseball executive), 171
Pearl Harbor, 1
Pearlman, Jeff (sportswriter), 20, 226, 243, 259, 283
Penner, Mike. *See* Christine Daniels
Periolat, Lee, Dr. (medical expert witness), 273
Perry, Gaylord (baseball player), 80, 90, 121, 122
Philadelphia, Pennsylvania, 6, 88, 97
Philadelphia Athletics (professional baseball club), 49, 61
Philadelphia Phillies (professional baseball club), 20, 66, 88, 263
Phoenix, Arizona, 62
Phoenix Giants (professional minor league baseball club), 64
Picciolo, Rob (baseball player), 120
Piniella, Lou (baseball player), 129, 167

INDEX

Pittsburgh Pirates, 55, 95, 144, 159, 164, 166, 169, 170
Pittsburgh Rookies (Los Angeles semipro baseball team), 57
Pomona, California, 41
Portage, Indiana, 235
Porter, Darrell (baseball player), 109, 153
Prescott, Chester, 266
Pryor, Greg (baseball player), 223
Pryor, Richard (actor), 99
Puerto Rico, 65, 265

Quilici, Frank (professional baseball manager), 55, 71, 75, 76, 81, 84

Rand, Sally, 149
Randall, Bobby (baseball player), 112
Rau, Doug (baseball player), 117
Ray, James Earl (murderer of Martin Luther King Jr.), 19
Renko, Steve (baseball player), 89
Reusse, Patrick (sportswriter), 174
Rice, Jim (baseball player), 125, 147
Richman, Milton (sportswriter), 168
Rickey, Branch (baseball executive), 168
Ringolsby, Tracy (sportswriter), 3, 141, 142, 163
Rivers, Mickey (baseball player), 167
Riverside, California, 261
Roberts, Bruce (television announcer), 251, 252
Robertson, John (Angels singer), 265
Robinson, Brooks (baseball player), 26
Robinson, Frank (baseball player), 98, 99
Robinson, Jackie (baseball player), 1, 58, 289, 290
Rojas, Minnie (baseball player), 169, 249
Romeo and Juliet (Shakespeare play), 247
Roof, Phil (baseball player), 98
Roosevelt, Theodore (president of the United States), 227
Rose, Pete (baseball player), 26
Royals Stadium (Kansas City, Missouri), 93, 120, 121, 154, 214, 215, 217
Rudi, Joe (baseball player), 96, 134, 168, 223, 239, 240, 251
Rudolph, Ken (baseball player), 150
Ruiz, Chico (baseball player), 169

Ruth, George Herman "Babe" (baseball player), 92
Ryan, Nolan (baseball player), 75, 94, 112, 144, 239, 240, 251, 284

Sacramento, California, 63, 65
Sacramento Solons (professional minor league baseball club), 63, 65
Sadowski, Bob (baseball player, manager), 56
St. Louis Cardinals (professional baseball club), 16, 17, 87, 88
St. Louis Cardinals (professional football team), 74
St. Paul, Minnesota, 99, 256
Salt Lake City, Utah, 65
San Bernardino County Sun (newspaper), 160, 241, 257, 288
San Clemente, California, 261; La Casa Pacifica (Richard Nixon's residence), 262
San Diego, California, 40, 49, 166, 169
San Diego Padres (professional baseball club), 132, 164, 166, 169, 177, 244
San Diego State University, 40
San Fernando Valley State College. *See* California State University, Northridge
San Francisco, California, 133
San Francisco Giants (National League baseball club), 164, 166
Satterfield, Esther (musician), 221
Schaus, Mel (banking executive), 252
Scheerer, Bob (Gary, Indiana, police sergeant), 270
Schrader, Loel (sportswriter), 172
Schueler, Ron (baseball player), 151, 155
Scott, Fred (Los Angeles high school baseball coach), 14, 15, 17
Scott, George (baseball player), 109, 124, 125
Scurlock Mildred (Leonard Smith's mother), 228, 272, 273, 276
Seattle, Washington, 119, 149, 165
Seattle Slew (racehorse), 263
Seattle Mariners (professional baseball club), 119, 123, 140, 146, 154, 162, 165, 262
Seattle Supersonics (professional basketball team), 263

Seaver, Tom (baseball player), 166
Seitz, Peter (arbitrator), 161
Send in the Clowns (song), 263
Shakespeare, William (English playwright), 247
Shishido, Mickey (California Angels equipment manager), 259
shotgun (.410 bore, weapon used in Lyman Bostock's murder), 270, 272, 273
Singer, Bill (baseball player), 94
Singleton, Ken (baseball player), 152, 153, 154
Sisler, George (baseball player), 136
Skinner, Bob (baseball coach/manager), 251
Smalley, Roy (baseball player), 94, 95, 103, 121, 122, 127, 128, 130, 140, 146, 151, 186, 189, 254
Smith, Barbara (Leonard Smith's wife), 228, 229, 230, 231, 232, 233, 269, 270, 271, 273, 274, 275, 277, 293, 297
Smith, Claire (sportswriter), 173
Smith, Conrad Arnholt (baseball owner), 169
Smith, Jay (college pitcher), 47
Smith, Leonard (killer of Lyman Bostock), 228, 229, 231, 232, 233, 237, 238, 260, 269, 270, 271, 272, 273, 274, 275, 276, 277, 279, 280, 281, 287, 288, 292, 293, 296, 297, 298; actions after shooting of Lyman Bostock, 269, 270, 290, 291; commitment to Logansport State Hospital, 276, 277; first criminal trial (July 1979), 271, 272, 273, 274; release from Logansport State Hospital, 276, 277; second criminal trial (November 1979), 274, 275, 276; shooting of Lyman Bostock, 232, 233
Soderholm, Eric (baseball player), 72, 222
Sorenson, Lary (baseball player), 138
Soucheray, Joe (sportswriter), 72
South America, 69, 70, 115
South Carolina, 54
Southern Illinois University Edwardsville, 43, 44, 45
Southern League (professional minor league baseball league), 59, 60, 61, 62
Southern League Eastern Division, 60
Southwest Missouri State University, 29

Spartanburg, South Carolina, 54, 55
Spartanburg Phillies, 54, 55
Spencer, Harold, 24
Splittorff, Paul (baseball player), 153
Springfield, Illinois, 42, 45
Springfield, Missouri, 29, 42
Spokane, Washington, 66
Spokane Indians (professional minor league baseball club), 65, 66, 77, 79
Sporting News, 7, 62, 82, 115, 171, 176, 292
Sports Illustrated, 177
Squires, Mike (baseball player), 223
Staub, Rusty (baseball player), 102
Steinbrenner, George (professional baseball owner), 92, 166, 167, 171, 172, 173
Summerfest (1978 concert), 243
Sundberg, Jim (baseball player), 73
Super Bowl, 74

Tacoma, Washington, 59, 62, 63, 65, 66, 79, 80, 82, 84
Tacoma News-Tribune, 63; $5,000 hole at Cheney Stadium, 63
Tacoma Twins, 59, 61, 62, 63, 64, 65, 66, 67, 68, 71, 77, 79, 80, 119
T-Twins Boosters, 63
Tallis, Cedric (baseball executive), 171
Tampa Bay Buccaneers (professional football team), 288
Tanana, Frank (baseball player), 264, 284
Tangerine Bowl (Orlando, Florida), 59
Tempe, Arizona, 36
Tennyson, Alfred Lord (British poet), 287
Terrell, Jerry (baseball player), 128, 150, 155
Texas (Lone Star State), 6, 73, 75, 80, 94, 109, 121, 263
Texas Rangers (professional baseball club), 73, 80, 90, 94, 95, 104, 105, 109, 111, 117, 121, 122, 134, 148, 152, 157, 164, 165, 166, 174
Thiros, Nick (Indiana defense attorney), 272, 273, 274, 275
This Week in Baseball (television show), 126, 129, 135, 137, 148, 153, 250, 260, 261
Thomas, Derrel (baseball player), 20

INDEX

Thompson, Danny (baseball player), 94, 95
Thormodsgard, Paul (baseball player), 153
Tiant, Luis (baseball player), 102
Tiger Stadium (Detroit, Michigan), 109
Tigres de Aragua (Venezuelan baseball club), 69, 71
Tinker Field (Orlando, Florida), 59, 71, 116
Torburg, Jeff (baseball manager), 147
Toronto, Ontario, 123, 124, 149
Toronto Blue Jays (Canadian professional baseball club), 117, 119, 124, 144, 149, 154, 162, 164, 165
Torres, Rusty (baseball player), 223
Torrez, Mike (baseball player), 164
Tucson, Arizona, 62, 66
Turner, Edward (Lyman Bostock's uncle), 110, 221, 225, 226, 229, 230, 253, 280
Turner, Herman (Lyman Bostock's uncle), 5
Turner, Lillie (Lyman Bostock's aunt), 229
Turner, Thomas (Lyman Bostock's uncle), 5, 9, 110, 224, 225, 226, 229, 230, 231, 232, 233, 237, 239, 253, 269, 272, 273, 280, 292, 293
Twin Cities (Minneapolis/St. Paul, Minnesota), 74, 85, 112, 123, 148

Ulysses, 287
United Press International, 168
United States of America, 5, 12, 22, 26, 49, 87, 88, 97, 126, 137, 141, 168, 178, 227, 287, 291
United States Census, 6
U.S. Steel, 227, 235, 280
University of California, Berkeley, 21, 132
University of California, Los Angeles (UCLA), 36, 244
University of Houston, 244
University of Puget Sound (Washington), 38, 42
University of San Diego, 38
University of Southern California (USC), 17, 36, 85, 263

Valley News (newspaper), 21, 26, 34, 37, 68, 173
Vancouver, Washington, 149
Van Halen (band), 243

Venezuela, 69, 70, 87, 166
Venezuelan League, 69, 71, 87, 166
Versalles, Zoilo, 100
Veteran's Stadium (Philadelphia, Pennsylvania), 97
Vietnam War, 12
Virgin Islands, 265

Warden, Jack (actor), 279
Walker, Tom (baseball player), 71
Wall, Stan (baseball player), 65
Wallace, George (American politician), 21
Wallace, Randy. *See* Abdul-Jalil Al-Hakim
Wantz, Dick (baseball player), 169, 249
Warner, Harry (baseball manager), 59
Washington, D.C., 19, 83, 261
Washington Senators (professional baseball club), 59, 61
Weaver, Earl (baseball manager), 127, 149, 150
Weisberg, Sam (sportswriter), 167
Werhas, John (California Angels team chaplain), 266
Wescott, Tom (Minnesota Twins batboy), 78
West Palm Beach, Florida, 72
Western Carolinas League, 54, 57
Weyler, John (sportswriter), 264
Whistler, Yuovene Brooks Bostock (Lyman Bostock's wife), 20, 21, 23, 26, 28, 34, 58, 61, 77, 173, 174, 178, 229, 230, 239, 241, 242, 243, 258, 260, 263, 264, 267, 281, 282, 283, 284, 290
White House, 9
White Sox Park. *See* Comiskey Park
Wilfong, Rob (professional baseball player), 55
Williams, Billy Dee (actor), 99
Williams, Ted (baseball player), 69, 136, 156
Willis, Bob (professional baseball executive), 60
Willoughby, Jim (baseball player), 223
Wills, Maury (baseball player), 115
Wilson, Hack (baseball player), 289
Winfield, Dave (baseball player), 132, 166
Winnipeg, Manitoba, 123
Wood, Wilbur (baseball player), 135
Wooden, John (basketball coach), 244

World Series, 66, 88, 95, 126, 130, 159, 163, 166, 171, 176, 226, 279, 284, 285
World War I, 1
World War II, 1, 3, 62, 143, 168, 227, 235, 253; Italian Campaign, 168
Wortham, Rich (baseball player), 222, 223
Wynegar, Butch (baseball player), 92, 98, 107, 122, 128, 140, 144, 146, 149

Yankee Stadium (New York, New York), 62, 81, 82, 90, 92, 113, 137, 144, 159
Yastrzemski, Carl (baseball player), 10, 11, 26, 125, 137, 139

Zahn, Geoff (baseball player), 140
Zimmer, Don (baseball manager), 151
Zisk, Richie (baseball player), 137, 159, 174, 177

ABOUT THE AUTHOR

Adam Powell is a native of Sneads Ferry, North Carolina, and a 2001 graduate of the University of North Carolina at Chapel Hill. He currently lives in Mebane, North Carolina, with his wife Julie, his son Colt, and his daughter Jenna. Powell has been in the sportswriting business for fifteen years as an author, freelance writer, and publisher.

Lyman Bostock: The Inspiring Life and Tragic Death of a Ballplayer is Powell's fourth published book. His first book, a comprehensive history of the first fifty years of Atlantic Coast Conference football titled *Border Wars*, was published by Rowman & Littlefield in 2004. His second and third books—pictorial histories of UNC basketball and football—were published by Arcadia Publishing in 2005 and 2006.

Powell has been a contributor to the *ACC Sports Journal* and ACCSports.com since 2004, and served as editor in 2014 and 2015. In addition, Powell also currently works as a full-time reporter for his hometown newspaper, the *Mebane Enterprise*, writing about local government, education, business, and sports.

Powell worked in the Rivals.com network as full-time publisher of the team websites for North Carolina (TarHeelIllustrated.com) from 2006 to 2014 and Wake Forest (DeaconsIllustrated.com) in 2011 and 2012. He has also written for the *Chapel Hill News* (Chapel Hill, N.C.), *Sanford Herald* (Sanford, N.C.), and *South Boston News & Record* (South Boston, Va.) newspapers, as well as *Cavalier Corner* and *Carolina Blue* magazines. Powell is a licensed real estate broker in the state of North Carolina and a member of the National Association of Realtors.